The Why, Who
and How of the Editorial Page

Kenneth Rystrom
University of Redlands

The Why, Who and How of the Editorial Page

Random House New York

For Anne, Margaret and Victoria

First Edition
987654321
Copyright © 1983 by Random House, Inc.

All rights reserved under International and Pan-American Copyright Conventions. No part of this book may be reproduced in any form or by any means, electronic or mechanical, including photocopying, without permission in writing from the publisher. All inquiries should be addressed to Random House, Inc., 201 East 50th Street, New York, N.Y. 10022. Published in the United States by Random House, Inc., and simultaneously in Canada by Random House of Canada Limited, Toronto.

Library of Congress Cataloging in Publication Data

Rystrom, Kenneth, 1932–
  The why, who and how of the editorial page.

  Bibliography: p.
  Includes index.
  1. Editorials. I. Title.
PN4778.R95 1983   070.4′1   82-15107
ISBN 0-394-32985-6

Manufactured in the United States of America

Text and Cover Design by Nancy Bumpus

Contents

Preface

The purposes of this book are twofold. One is to help students and other would-be editorial writers learn to write editorials and perform other tasks associated with the editorial page. The other purpose is to help them understand what it is like to be an editorial writer today and how the role of the editorial writer has changed in the past and is changing now.

The idea for the book came from a suggestion by officers of the National Conference of Editorial Writers that I give some thought to a textbook that would bridge two gaps—one between the theory and the practice of editorial writing and one between students who would be getting their first taste of editorial writing and professional journalists who might want to become editorial writers or, if writers already, better editorial writers. As the name of the book, *The Why, Who and How of the Editorial Page,* may imply, I have leaned toward the practical side in talking about editorial writing and the editorial writer. As the name also implies, the book consists of three main sections.

The opening section, ''The Why of the Editorial Page,'' looks at various images that have been associated with editorial writers, briefly traces the changing role of the editorial writer in the United States and suggests some of the directions in which the editorial page may be headed today.

The second section, ''The Who of the Editorial Page,'' contains material not generally found in previous books on the editorial page. It is concerned with how men and women become editorial writers, how they can prepare themselves to become writers, or better writers, and how the editorial writer fits into the newspaper organization and into the wider community. Included here are separate chapters on relations with publishers, the news staff, the editorial page staff and the community. The chapter on relations with the community discusses the opportunities and possible conflicts of interest that editorial writers face in participating in public affairs. To a large extent, in all these relationships, the role of the editorial writer is changing today. In many instances, at least, editorial writers are beginning to play a larger role in setting editorial policy. They also are beginning to receive more personal and professional recognition, on their newspapers and in their communities.

The third and largest section of the book, ''The How of the Editorial Page,'' is concerned with actually writing editorials and producing an editorial page. Emphasis is placed not only on how writers and editors do their jobs but also on how they can do their jobs better, whether in writing editorials, handling letters to the editor and syndicated features, bringing diverse opinions to the page or packaging the page in an attractive manner.

The text discussion is illustrated with numerous examples of the experiences and written products of editorial writers and editors. These include many thoughts, some of them contradictory, from writers and editors about how editorials should be written and editorial pages produced. In identifying these and other sources, I have referred to the newspapers or other affiliations with which writers were associated at the time they made the statements I have cited. Consequently a writer, editor or professor may be identified differently from one part of the book to another.

From the reading of this book, it should be clear to readers that most of these editorial people like their jobs and think that they hold some of the most stimulating and personally rewarding positions in the media today. As I recount some of my own experiences and state my opinions in this book, I hope readers will catch my enthusiasm for editorial page work, whether it involves writing editorials or handling syndicated columns and letters to the editor. My delight in that work never flagged during 20 years in the daily newspaper business, 17 of which were spent associated with editorial pages, on both fairly large and medium-sized papers.

As the book grew from a concept to its final form, I accumulated five years of experience in teaching editorial writing. During this time I used early drafts of the manuscript as a text. Some of the changes that were made as the book progressed reflected suggestions from students about what they thought should go into or come out of the book. So the text at this point has had some measure of field-testing, albeit at the hands of an instructor who was somewhat favorably inclined toward it from the beginning.

Much of the material about other writers and editors has come from *The Masthead*, which has been the quarterly publication of the National Conference of Editorial Writers since the late 1940s. To the officers and members of NCEW, I am grateful for their permission to draw freely on *The Masthead* material. I am especially grateful to several recent presidents of NCEW. They are in no way responsible for what appears in this volume, but they offered suggestions and encouragement and helped me interest Random House, Inc., in publishing the book. My thanks also go to the reviewers whose many substantive contributions helped me to refine and improve the content of the text. They are R. Thomas Berner, The Pennsylvania State University; Kenneth Edwards, University of Alabama; Robert C. Kochersberger, Jr., State University of New York, College at Cortland; William McKeen, Western Kentucky University; and Robert M. Ours, West Virginia University.

Also contributing to this book, in a more general manner, have been the love of writing that I learned first from a fine teacher, my mother, Zella Rae Borland Rystrom; the love of reporting that I learned from my managing editor on the *Columbian,* Erwin Rieger; the love of editorial writing that I learned from my editor on the *Des Moines Register and Tribune,* Lauren Soth; and the inspiration to pursue first a career in journalism and then one in teaching from Professor Nathaniel B. Blumberg. To Professor Blumberg also goes credit for helping me to envision the format and contents of this book and for offering suggestions as various drafts emerged. To my departmental secretary, Eleanor Otte, goes my appreciation for her persistent, meticulous and patient efforts in getting the manuscript into presentable form. To my wife, Billie, goes the credit for first, and repeatedly, telling me to quote fewer other people and to tell more of what I myself had to say. I have received that advice often since then, including from Mary Shuford and Martha Leff of Random House, with whom, after my initial shock over the rewriting they had in mind, it has been a pleasure to work. I have attempted to follow this advice to make the book more of a firsthand account. Still a great deal of credit goes to the many writers and editors whose names remain in the book, since without their ideas, opinions and writings this text would not have been possible at all.

Kenneth Rystrom

Redlands, California
January 1983

Introduction

Many people don't understand editorials. Some say editorials are written by a capitalist, conservative publisher to perpetuate his publishing empire. Others consider editorials to be the irrational drivel of a batch of witless hirelings. The misinformation about editorials is monumental.
—*William C. Heine*
London *(Ontario)* Free Press[1]

Something like one of every 50,000 persons in the United States is an editorial writer on a daily newspaper. Consequently, chances are slim that any particular newspaper reader has even a passing acquaintance with an editorial writer. So what kind of image does the editorial writer project when readers' knowledge is limited to what they read on the editorial page?

To some readers, editorial writers seem to be only mouthpieces for publishers. Others see editorial writers dwelling in "ivory towers," far above the practicalities of everyday life. Some see them as powerful opinion leaders, imposing their judgments on readers. To others, they appear as anonymous, ineffective writers hiding behind the editorial "we." Still others may have heard the newspaper legend that editorial writers are worn-out reporters on the verge of retirement.

All of these images carry some measure of truth. Editorial writers on American newspapers have been all of these. But these conceptions do not provide a full description of what editorial writers have been in the past or of what they are today. Certainly they do not describe editorial writers on the best editorial pages.

Some editorial writers have been, and probably always will be, publishers' mouthpieces—"mindless robots with a knack for parroting other people's ideas," as Kenneth McArdle of the *Chicago Daily News* put it.[2] But publishers, busy with other phases of the newspaper business, can't be expert enough on most editorial topics to hold their own in discussions with knowledgeable editorial writers. Editorial writers, more than ever before, are being hired because of their education and experience; they are being given more opportunities to do their own thinking. Owners of most newspaper groups proclaim loudly that the editorial policy of each of their newspapers is strictly independent. Publishers are presumed to be especially receptive to the interests of local advertisers, but publishers with an eye on circulation won't put their faith in the views of a single segment of the community, even if that segment provides most of the revenue for their newspapers. Instead of worrying about what their publishers may think, most editorial writers today are concerned about making sense of complicated issues.

Of course editorial writers can be given too much credit. The promotion department of my newspaper, the Vancouver (Wash.) *Columbian,* once ran a full-page ad, half of it devoted to depicting me in a reflective pose. "Jolting the Conscience of Clark County" proclaimed a headline an inch high. Editorial writers sometimes are viewed as living wonderful lives in their ivory towers, free to consider the grand ideas of the universe or the smallest bit of trivia, free from the everyday cares of the common person. That enviable writer, and a personal firsthand view of him, appeared in a 1954 *Masthead* article entitled "What a Wonderful World He Must Live In." The author was Minnie Mae Murray, wife of Don Murray, who won the 1958 Pulitzer Prize for his editorial writing in the *Boston Herald.* Ms. Murray wrote:

Most people read editorials—I live them.

My husband is an editorial writer on a large daily. He is observant, romantic, and imaginative—and sometimes embarrassing.

There was the time we moved from a city apartment to a tiny rented house in the suburbs. Two days later a little mood piece appeared at the bottom of the editorial page. It was called "Moving Day."

It fairly reeked with nostalgia about leaving the old and greeting the new, discovering forgotten treasures while packing, and meeting the ghosts of former owners. It was both sad and gay. It was a little masterpiece. But I remember the pretty little dust kittens, the quaint moving man who chewed—and spat—tobacco, and the soft light of one candle—we'd forgotten to notify the light company. . . .

One Saturday morning I baked bread.

On Monday there was a small item which lauded the all-but-forgotten arts of domesticity. His description made it look so easy. No kneading. No mixing. Just "Presto," and there it was. I wondered what I'd done with the day. . . .

"What a wonderful world he must live in," people say, as they read of a winter morning when Jack Frost had painted castles in Spain on the window pane, when the snow cuddled the rock wall like a soft-white comforter, and when the elms were etched with ice. Sounds great, doesn't it?

But you ought to see him get up in the morning. See beauty? He can't even find his slippers. And the soft, white billows of snow are burned off the drive by his language when he departs to dig out the car. . . .

Nothing escapes his rose-colored eyes.

The Thanksgiving turkey, the Christmas baking, the family celebration (no mention of family feuds), and even a disgracefully dirty mitten found after the first thaw—all end up on the editorial page.

Faithfully, I read them all. And I, like other readers, wonder in what exotic world the writer lives. . . .

I'd like to go there someday. To that land where fog is always mysterious and never damp, where gardens bloom without weeding, where winds always whisper and don't blast, where coal stoves are better than gas.

Instead, I stay home and have neighbors who bring in clippings of my husband's editorials, and say, "Isn't that beautiful? You must live a lovely life."

Phooey! Wait till he changes his first diaper. Let him write an editorial about that![3]

When my second daughter went off to kindergarten, I wrote a nostalgic piece about a little girl who was always losing her shoes. I may have gotten more response from readers on that editorial than on any other I wrote in 17 years of editorial writing. Several women told me that they had kept the piece, and one showed me that she carried it with her in her purse. Sometimes these mood pieces come easily for the writer. Sometimes they must be squeezed out word by word. In any case, after a successful feat at the typewriter, the writer returns home and finds that the little girl, indeed, has lost her shoes again.

The ivory tower also offers another view than the rose-colored one. From that tower it is easy to see what the city council ought to do when faced with a multimillion-dollar sewer project. The interests of long-range planning seem clear to an editorial writer. But, when it comes time for the council to decide, it hears from taxpayers who say they can't afford the assessments and from developers who say the sewers are in the wrong place. It is easy to tell the president to keep the United States out of Central America or the governor to take firmer leadership against the Mediterranean fruit fly. But putting these ideas to paper is a lot easier than carrying them out.

Yet the ivory tower role is an important one for editorial writers. Communities, states and nations need to hear from idealists as well as from pragmatists.

Rather than impractical idealists, editorial writers are sometimes perceived as powerful opinion leaders in their communities and in the larger world. Newspapers may be accused of trying to run the town, and editorial writers accused of trying to tell the community what it ought to think. Candidates endorsed by newspapers generally win more often than they lose. Policies that newspaper editorials support often are approved by voters or governing bodies. No doubt the support of a newspaper can make a difference in public policy, especially if editorial arguments reflect facts, logic and reality. But in some communities elected leaders are very careful to avoid the appearance of doing what the local papers tell them to do. It is usually easy for them to ignore advice from editorial writers who don't know what they are talking about.

Sometimes editorial writers simply are not taken seriously. Writing anonymously, they are not perceived to be real people. Through their ponderous prose, they turn would-be readers away from the editorial page. Some readers think that editorial writers timidly hide behind the editorial "we," the unsigned opinion. When writers are perceived in this manner, they have only themselves to blame. They may not have a choice in writing anonymously; newspaper policy may dictate unsigned editorials. But, if they can't write spirited copy, they ought not to be editorial writers, no matter how wise they may be about the affairs of the world.

An article written by a porter for the Milwaukee Railroad satirized ponderous editorial writing. C. F. Kyle wrote in a 1950 *Masthead* that "most editorials are merely an endless stream of poorly selected words grouped into dull, hard-to-digest phrases spreading out into life-less sentences that finally impart a zombie-like quality to the completed paragraph, making the whole thing about as interesting to read as a thesis on the celebration of wood ticks." He urged writers to write in a more down-to-earth manner, "so as to give the reader the feeling that the writer is *talking* to him, and in his own, everyday language."[4]

Although many newspaper editorials remain unsigned, editorial writers are becoming less anonymous, in their communities as well as among fellow editorial writers. Many are writing signed articles and some are signing their names or initials to editorials. Some of their faces appear on the editorial page or op-ed page (page opposite the editorial page). A few are writing signed articles that dissent from the official policies of their papers. Increasingly editorial policy is being set by a board, instead of by the publisher or a single editor.

As editorial writers are coming out of their closets, they are coming out better prepared to write editorials. Hovering over many newsrooms used to be the cliche that the editorial writer was an old reporter whose legs had given out, that the editorial page was, as press critic Ben H. Bagdikian put it, "a substitute for a pension plan . . . a company-paid nursing home for geriatric cases."[5] Young journalists gave little thought to preparing themselves for a career in editorial writing, since, if they thought of it at all, they perceived it as something a long way in the future.

Now publishers and editors are starting to seek younger men and women to become editorial writers. Some are finding that digging out stories at the courthouse and writing objective news stories may not be the most suitable background for editorial writers. Editorial writing requires the evaluation as well as the presentation of facts. It also requires knowledge, not just about one or two beats, but about every possible subject that might merit comment. Thus, today's editorial writers are better educated and informed than those of the past. Many have advanced degrees. Many get out of the office to attend short courses on college campuses, editorial writers' workshops, meetings of local organizations, state legislative sessions and national political conventions.

Editorial writers are earning more respect from their publishers. They are also earning more money and gaining more freedom than most other newspaper staff members. In fact many editorial writers are even daring, on occasion, to talk back to publishers (although not all of them keep their jobs after doing so).

Even if editorial writers are better informed and better paid, some skeptics contend that the American editorial itself serves little purpose these days. The editorial page, critics acknowledge, may have served a purpose when reporters and editors thought that news columns could be objective and that opinion could be set aside in the editorial columns. It might have served, they say, when most public decisions were made by an elite leadership and when the publisher and the editor spoke to and belonged to that leadership. The editorial page might have had more influence when the credibility of newspapers, and many other American institutions, was higher. More specifically, critics argue, Americans now are relying more on television than on newspapers for news and opinions. They argue that the editorials tend to talk only to the intellectual and political elites and that most citizens no longer look to the elites for leadership. Further, they contend, editorials are not persuasive because they convince only those persons who already agree with them. Finally, editorials are no longer needed because interpretive reporting has removed the dividing line between news and opinion.

Compared to the front page, sports, comics and the local news, editorial pages draw relatively low readership. Until a few years ago this low readership was accepted and explained in terms of what was called the "two-step theory" of communications, according to which opinions trickled down from an opinion-setting elite to the masses of society. If the opinion leaders followed the editorial page, and it was assumed that they did, editors could make their mark indirectly on the larger electorate. However, research indicates that people formulate their opinions in a more complex manner, drawing on many sources; those they look to for guidance are not always those who traditionally have been identified as leaders. Instead of looking to the socially, economically and politically prominent, American voters were found to look more to persons they knew at work, in their neighborhoods or organizations and in their families. Any effect that an editorial may have, according to recent theorists, tends to stop with the first level of persuasion, that is, with the readers themselves.

The idea that an elite readership is not a conduit to the masses should not bother today's editorial writer, however. The type of writers who get onto the streets and into people's lives shouldn't have trouble talking to readers of all sorts, shouldn't have to worry about having lofty thoughts translated for the common person. If editorial writers make sense and aren't just preaching at their readers, or talking over their heads, they should stand a good chance of building a strong, if not a universal, readership.

Two principal answers can be given to the charge that editorials are persuasive because readers tend to expose themselves only to what they find comfortable reading. First, more editors than ever before are trying to bring opinions of all kinds onto their pages and to create a community forum in which everyone can feel that he or she is being listened to. Second, editors can engage in the type of editorial writing that does not antagonize readers by telling them what to think but that helps them understand what to think about and then lets them think on their own.

One of the tasks of an editorial page, especially when there is only one paper in town, is to get readers to think about issues from more than one point of view, to encourage within the readers' own minds a debate over the issues. The assumption is that modern readers, generally more sophisticated than those of earlier days, are not going to be convinced by merely being told what to think and how to act. Only by helping readers through a thinking process can an editorial writer hope to affect community opinion.

Philip L. Geyelin, editorial page editor of the *Washington Post,* contended that readers don't want to be told what to think or what to do as much as they want to know what matters. "They want to know, not what *we* think, but what *they* ought to be thinking about," he said. It is not necessary to tell today's reader where you are. "If you tell the readers how you got there, step by step, and well enough, . . . they will know. . . . What's more, it's barely possible that even those newspaper readers who don't like where you are—and who don't agree with where you wound up—may still want to go along for the ride."[6]

Some critics think that, with interpretive journalism and in-depth reporting, all the analysis that readers want is provided in the news columns. What need is there for an editorial page or an editorial writer? Some critics go so far as to argue that newspaper owners have no right to use their monopoly to force opinions on the public. There are some editorial pages that might as well be turned over to interpretive reporting—or to Ann Landers or a gossip column.

While the passage from in-depth reporting to analytical writing to interpretive reporting to opinion writing may be gradual and imperceptible in some instances, there is a difference between explaining events and expressing an opinion about them. Editors of *The Masthead* asked a sampling of editorial writers if they saw interpretive reporting as a threat to their jobs. Nearly all saw plenty of room for interpretive reporting in the news columns. Most thought the integrity of the news columns could be maintained if articles that went beyond the recounting of facts were labeled analysis or interpretive article. Most seemed to think that analysis in the news columns is acceptable if it does not express a specific position on an issue or advocate specific action.

Individual editors will differ over what is interpretation and what is opinion. Some are more willing than others to let a reporter display a point of view in the news columns. Of course it is fashionable to point out that there is no such thing as truly objective journalism. But that realization should not keep editors from indicating as clearly as possible to readers when they are trying to present information and when they are trying to express an opinion. To a large extent, the integrity—the believability—of the news product depends upon making this distinction clear. The most generally acceptable way to do this on American newspapers is to move opinion wherever possible to the opinion or editorial page and carefully label it as such.

We might find it easier to answer the question of why editorial pages seem to be surviving—and reviving—if we look briefly at how editorial pages have changed in the approximately two centuries of their existence. In that time editorial pages have undergone several transformations, staying alive by responding to changing circumstances. In the end, we will find that those editorial pages of today that have not headed for the museum are being transformed into pages quite different from those of the past.

1
SECTION

The Why of the Editorial Page

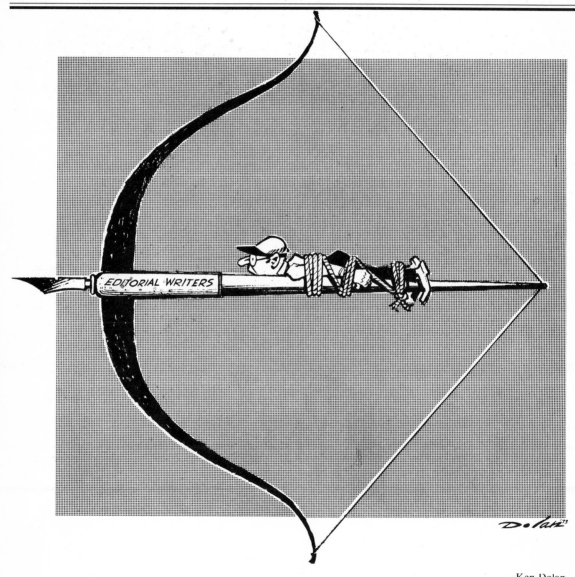

—Ken Dolan
Flint (Mich.) *Journal* for *The Masthead*

The Editorial Page That Used to Be

[Horace Greeley] has done more than any other man to bring slaveholders to bay, and place the Northern fingers on the throat of the slavery institution. . . . His influence is now immense.
—E. L. Godkin, 19th-century editor[1]

. . . editorials neither make nor mar a daily paper, . . . they do not much influence the public mind, nor change many votes.
—James Parton, 19th-century biographer[2] *(following the death of Greeley)*

Editorial writing is not what it used to be.

Now, you may assume that I am comparing today's editorial writers with Horace Greeley or James Gordon Bennett or Charles Dana. And I am. No editorial writer today is blessed with the name recognition or devoted readership of these giants of the days of "personal journalism." But I also have a much more recent comparison in mind. Many of today's editorial writers are different from editorial writers of only a few years ago. They are better prepared for their jobs and better known in their communities than those "anonymous wretches" that one participant described as assembling at the first national meeting of editorial writers in 1947.

Editors no longer thunder in the manner of a Greeley, whose editorials could send a screaming mob to New York's city hall or provoke an ill-prepared Union Army into fighting the Battle of Bull Run. Editors of the first half of the 19th century often spoke with the editorial "I," and when they used "we," they meant "I." Editorials didn't have to be signed; readers knew who wrote the editorials in the papers they read.

Readers usually agreed with editorials in the papers they subscribed to. The large number of newspapers in most cities represented a wide variety of political opinions, and people read the papers they found most compatible with their own views. Consequently, editors could be as dogmatic and vitriolic in their editorials as they wished to be and know that their readers would not only agree with what they said but enjoy every nasty word against mutual opponents. Editors could find comfort in the fact that, even if they did not know any more about an issue than their own political party's line, they were more knowledgeable than the vast majority of their readers. During the days of the "penny press" (when some papers actually did cost only one penny), many readers were immigrants—new to the country and new to the language—and most of them, as well as readers born in America, were aware only of what they read in their papers.

Those were great days for editors who were sure of what they wanted to say and said it boldly. But, in addition to spreading their views, they spread a great deal of misinformation and fear among their readers. You have only to recall how the circulation war between Joseph Pulitzer and William Randolph Hearst whipped up a frenzy that helped ignite the Spanish-American War.

No editor of today has that kind of power over the emotions of readers. Today's journalists may lament the passing of the great days of personal journalism, but they can't lament the shenanigans, the (sometimes self-) deception and outright lying, those great editors engaged in. The days of the "great editorialists" have been gone for a century—or at least since the turn of the century.

Compared to Horace Greeley, today's editorial writers are not well known to their readers. They rarely sign their names to what they write. Their editorials are the anonymous opinions of "the newspaper." Since today's readers have virtually no choice of a local daily newspaper, modern editorial writers know that those who read what they write hold as many varieties of opinion as exist in the community. This diverse readership is one reason that editorial writers no longer roar like Greeley. If writers take a strong stand on a controversial issue, they know they will please those who agree with them but displease those who disagree (if these people read the editorials at all). Today's writers suspect that, if they come on too strong in their editorials, they will antagonize the readers they think they have the best chance to influence, those in the middle who have not made up their minds. Expression of a strong editorial opinion also may suggest to readers that the paper is using its news columns to advance that same opinion.

Writers know that a lot of their readers are as well educated as they. Readers may not see another daily newspaper, but they have many other channels of communication through which to learn what is happening in their communities and the world. Today's public has a far better chance of finding out whether editorial writers know what they are talking about than did readers of a century ago. If an editorial hands out the party line, those who are unfamiliar with the issue at hand may be swayed for the moment. But, if the editorial has told only half the story, and the readers come across the other half at a later time, they are likely to sway right back again—and will thereafter be warier when the newspaper tries to tell them something.

These are some of the ways in which editorial writing is different now from the way it was in the days of Greeley, Bennett and Dana. How, then, does today's editorial writing differ from that of more recent times?

Personal journalism began to die out in the 1870s. Newspapers became corporately, instead of individually, owned. Publishers became more important than editors. Editorial-writing staffs, at least on larger papers, grew in size. If editorials did not specifically represent the handed-down views of the publisher, they were at least the product of a group rather than the thoughts of an independent editorial writer. When the group of "anonymous wretches" assembled in Washington, D.C., in 1947, the 26 editorial writers, all men, had not previously met one another. The majority had never heard of most of the others. Only a few of the persons whose work appeared on editorial pages then were very well known. Beginning in the early 1930s editorial page columnists such as Walter Lippmann, David Lawrence, Raymond Clapper and Arthur Krock had gained many readers through interpreting national and international events. Their bylines were displayed prominently, generally on the right side of the editorial page. But the opinions on the left side of the editorial page, those of "the newspaper," almost invariably were left unsigned. These writers were not well known, and they were not well paid. If they disagreed with what they were told to write, they could try to find another job. Participants at the Washington meeting speculated that they were among the last newspaper groups to form a national organization because their publishers didn't want them to get any ideas about gaining an independent voice.

Since then, editorial writers on many newspapers have carved out for themselves more secure and more prominent positions in relations with their publishers and with their communities. They have adapted to, and helped to change, the conditions in which they work.

Change and adaptation, in fact, have been at work in the evolution of the American editorial page ever since the introduction of the first newspapers on the continent. The changes began long before Greeley and Bennett and Dana appeared on the journalistic scene. The strong editor of personal journalism comes in the third of five general phases through which American newspapers, and editorial pages, have passed since Colonial days. The five phases can be described as follows:

1.   During the Colonial era and the period immediately after the Revolutionary War, little effort was made to separate opinion from news. Both appeared intertwined in the columns of the press. Newspapers openly proclaimed that they were partisan voices.

2.   With the writing of the new Constitution, in 1787, came political parties and the partisan press. Editorials began to appear as distinct forms. Each newspaper was committed to a political party.

3. With the populist ("penny") press that emerged in the 1830s came the strong editor, who initially was concerned with sensationalized news and not with editorials but who, as readers became more literate and sophisticated, began to produce highly personalized editorial pages—and better news products as well. Ties to political parties began to weaken.

4. Following the Civil War, and more so following the turn of the century, anonymous corporate editorial staffs began to replace the famous editors. Writing became more bland. Newspapers, while claiming increasing independence, generally remained committed to conservative editorial policies.

5. In recent years, beginning in the politically active 1960s, a younger, more aggressive and more pragmatic editorial writer has started to emerge. This type of writer tends to be nonpartisan but committed to a general editorial philosophy.

In each of these phases, newspapers and their editorials served different purposes, according to the readers' changing needs. Those papers—and editorials—that succeeded in changing with the times survived; those that did not perished.

The remainder of this chapter will briefly describe the first four phases. The last phase will be discussed in the following chapter and throughout this book.

NEWS MIXED WITH OPINION

During the Colonial period, the first newspapers were heavily influenced by British tradition. The British press was licensed and printers published under the authority of the crown. Licenses could be suspended if the printer published anything that displeased the authorities. The publisher of the first newspaper on American soil, Benjamin Harris, quickly learned what would happen if opinions displeased the Colonial governor in Boston. In his *Publick Occurrences, Both Foreign and Domestick,* published on Sept. 25, 1690, he said that the English had postponed attacking the French because their Indian allies had failed to provide promised canoes. If that were not a clear enough criticism of Colonial policy, Harris proceeded in his news columns to call the Indians "miserable savages, in whom we have too much confided." The governor shut the newspaper down, and it died after one issue.

For a large part of the Colonial period, American readers were more interested in what was happening on the European continent than what was happening in the Colonies. Events in the Colonies did not seem very important except as they related to events in Europe. Consequently the Colonialists primarily looked for news from abroad in their early newspapers.

The first generally recognized American newspaper, the *Boston News-Letter,* started in 1704—14 years after Harris' first attempt—was a printed version of what had been a written newsletter circulated by Boston postmaster John Campbell. Not much concerned with politics, Campbell avoided Harris' troubles by publishing with the permission of the government. But he did not hesitate to offer opinions, unpolitical though they were. At the conclusion of a news item about a woman's suicide, he said he hoped that the recounting "may not be offensive, but rather a Warning to all others to watch against the Wiles of our Grand Adversary." The reporting of the whipping of a prisoner who had sold tar mixed with dirt was "here Inserted to be a caveat to others, of doing the like, least a worse thing befal (sic) them."

With the *News-Letter* already in existence, the father of James, and Benjamin, Franklin thought James was making a mistake in starting the *New England Courant* in 1721. The continent could not support more than one newspaper, he felt. Franklin not only dared to publish; he dared to publish without the required license. The *Courant,* carrying little news and few advertisements, contained mostly commentary and essays. One of Franklin's targets was a group that advocated smallpox inoculations. He also attacked civil and religious leaders and questioned some of the religious opinions of the day. Franklin so enraged the Rev. Increase Mather that Mather called the *Courant* the work of the devil. If the government did not do something about the paper, he proclaimed from his pulpit, "I am afraid some *Awful Judgment* will come upon this land, and that the *Wrath of God will arise, and there will be no Remedy.*" However, what finally provoked the Colonial Council to charge Franklin with contempt was an allegation that the government had not done enough to protect Boston from pirates. Franklin was thrown into jail and ordered not to publish again. Subsequent issues were listed as being published by his younger brother Benjamin.

Benjamin Franklin began publishing his own *Pennsylvania Gazette* in 1729. He was not averse to inserting opinions into what he wrote, but, being a skilled writer and diplomat, he was able to avoid the trouble that James had encountered. One device that Benjamin Franklin used to help arouse the Colonies was the printing of a snake divided into eight parts representing New England and seven other Colonies, accompanied by the motto "Join or die." It was run with an account of the killing and scalping of frontier Colonists in Virginia and Pennsylvania by the French and Indians.

British tradition also insisted that, in matters of libel, the only task of the jury was to determine whether the alleged words had been published. A comment mixed with news in John Peter Zenger's *New York Weekly Journal* began the first step toward putting an end to that tradition on American soil. Zenger "reported" in a story on election results that voters had been harassed about their qualifications for voting, and in another story that Gov. William Cosby had allowed the French to spy on Colonial naval defenses. In 1734, a year after his first issue had appeared, Zenger was charged with "raising sedition." An elegant appeal by Andrew Hamilton, then an 80-year-old Philadelphia lawyer, convinced the jury that it should ignore English common law, which would have limited the jury to finding Zenger innocent only if the alleged libel had not been published. The favorable decision for Zenger did not immediately change Colonial law, but it encouraged other editors to speak out and finally became accepted law before the end of the century.

The Stamp Act of 1765, through which the British levied a heavy tax on newspapers, produced a variety of editorial protests. Franklin suspended the *Gazette* for three weeks, during which time he printed as substitutes large handbills headed "Remarkable Occurrences" and "Stamped paper not to be had." The day after the act took effect, William Bradford III's *Pennsylvania Journal and Weekly Advertiser* ran a black border, usually indicating mourning, in the shape of a tombstone.

As the Revolution approached, Colonial papers began to mix more and more editorial comment into the news columns. The papers generally split into three camps: Tory, Whig and Radical. The Tories championed the status quo, continued Colonial relations with Britain. In 1772, one of the most prominent Tories, James Rivington, began publishing *Rivington's New York Gazetteer or the Connecticut, New Jersey, Hudson's River and Quebec Weekly Advertiser*. Rivington tried giving space to all sides of the political issues—an unusual practice at the time. But, to quote Rivington himself, "the moment he ventured to publish sentiments which were opposed to the dangerous views and desires of certain demagogues, he found himself held up as an enemy of his country." In 1775 a party of armed men on horseback broke into his print shop, destroyed his press, carried away his type and melted it into bullets.

The Colonial Whigs represented a rising business class that at first was more interested in protecting itself from economic harassment by the British than in effecting political and social change. One of the most widely published Whigs was John Dickinson, who argued for the preservation of property and for self-taxation in several articles entitled "Letters From a Farmer in Pennsylvania." First published in the *Pennsylvania Chronicle* and the *Boston Gazette* in 1767, they were widely reprinted through the Colonies.

One of the most successful publishers of the Revolutionary and post-Revolutionary periods was Isaiah Thomas (who, incidentally, published *The History of Printing in America* in 1810). In 1770 he founded his *Massachusetts Spy,* advertising it as "A Weekly Political and Commercial Paper—Open to All Parties, but *influenced* by None." Thomas tried to open the *Spy* to both Whigs and Tories and to put their respective positions before the public. But he found he could not maintain this stance. The Tories stopped taking his paper, and Thomas concluded that the *Spy* would have to have "a fixed character." Since he was in principle opposed to the British economic measures, he made it a Whig paper. As issues became even sharper, Thomas and other Whigs joined the Radicals.

One of the first avowed Radical publications was the *Boston Gazette and Country Journal*. As early as 1764 publishers Benjamin Eades and John Gill were writing and providing space for anti-British essays. Thomas thought that no other paper or publisher played a greater role in bringing about the independence of the United States.[3]

Samuel Adams, who wrote for the *Gazette,* reasoned that in the cause of liberty events and facts could be twisted and interpreted to help arouse the Colonists against the British. One example, with a slight difference, was the "Journal of Occurrences," in which anonymous authors working for Adams compiled the verbal and physical assaults of British soldiers in Boston. In 1768, the "Occurrences" began appearing in John Holt's *New York Journal,* a Radical paper. They were widely reprinted. Although historians have since concluded that some of the "facts" were not quite true, the authors made a point of distinguishing between facts and comments by printing their opinions in italics. This attempt at differentiation between fact and opinion in news columns represented a step toward the use of the editorial as distinct from the news article.

Another Radical opinion writer who helped ignite the Revolution was Tom Paine, more pamphleteer than newspaper writer. His *Common Sense,* which appeared in early 1776, pleaded the cause of independence, with an eye to persuading the Whigs who were still on the fence. During the war he published a series called "The Crisis." The papers presented no new facts or arguments but, in the fashion of editorial writers of more than one later era, put ideas into words that could be understood by the less literate.

THE PARTISAN PRESS

The framers of the Constitution in 1787 thought they had achieved sufficient compromises between large and small states and between the central government and the states to eliminate the divisiveness that had characterized the late Colonial period. James Madison expressed the hope in "The Federalist," also known as "The Federalist Papers," that under the new government there would be no need for factions. One of the reasons for nominating George Washington, the leader of the Continental Army and symbol of Colonial resistance, as the first president was to rally all Americans around the new government.

The "Federalist Papers" themselves, written by Alexander Hamilton, James Madison and John Jay to support ratification of the Constitution, were first published in a newspaper, the *New York Independence Journal.* They were a mixture of fact, argument and opinion. In spite of the hopes for political unity under Washington, disagreements over how strong the federal government should be began to appear. Hamilton, as secretary of the Treasury, pushed for an active national administration. Since he favored the business community, he wanted firm financial support for the government and, specifically, he wanted a national bank. Thomas Jefferson and others wanted a weaker federal government. The Jeffersonians tended to be favorably disposed toward the French Revolution. Those around Hamilton generally allied themselves with Great Britain. Factions (later called "parties") eventually formed around these two leaders, the Hamiltonians becoming known as Federalists, the Jeffersonians as Democratic-Republicans.

To foster public support for the Washington administration, in which he was a dominant influence, Hamilton provided the inspiration for founding the first partisan newspaper under the new Constitution, the *Gazette of the United States*. It appeared in New York in 1789 under the editorship of John Fenno.

Other Federalist papers followed. *Porcupine's Gazette and Daily Advertiser*, founded by William Cobbett in Philadelphia in 1797, was known for its vitriolic attacks on the opposition. Cobbett's attacks on the French became such a scandal that President John Adams, a Federalist himself, considered ordering Cobbett to leave the country under provisions of the Alien Act. Noah Webster, of dictionary fame, edited a Federalist paper called the *American Minerva*, founded in 1793. After initially placing editorials under his "New York" (local news) heading, by 1796 he was placing them under the heading of "The Minerva" (the nickname of the paper). This heading was the forerunner of what we now call the masthead, a box on the editorial page that carries the name of the paper, the identification of key editorial and business persons and other information about the paper. Webster's innovations represented additional steps toward differentiating editorials from news.

Once the Federalist press began extolling the virtues of the Washington administration, it was not long before plans were laid to present another point of view. James Madison, even though he had contributed to the "Federalist Papers," found himself urging Jefferson, as secretary of state, to provide government subsidies to Philip Freneau, who had written Patriot poetry in the Revolution, to start an anti-Federalist newspaper. The resulting *National Gazette* was published only from 1791 to 1793, but in that time Freneau's virulent attacks on the Federalists inspired other anti-Federalists to speak up. The anti-Federalists opposed increasing the powers of the central government. They opposed increased taxes. They did not want a national bank. Generally they spoke for agricultural interests, the less affluent, the smaller states and Americans who sympathized with the French Revolution.

For most of American history, American citizens have considered George Washington to be beyond reproach. But some of the anti-Federalist writers did not. One of the most outspoken was Benjamin Franklin Bache, grandson of Benjamin Franklin, who founded the *Philadelphia General Advertiser*, which was more widely known as the *Aurora*, in 1790. When he wrote that the nation had been "debouched" by Washington, Federalists wrecked his office and beat him. Of Bache, *Porcupine's Gazette* stated: "This atrocious wretch (worthy descendant of old Ben) knows that all men of any understanding put him down as an abandoned liar, as a tool and a hireling. . . . He is an ill-looking devil. His eyes never get above your knees." One day on the street, Fenno, of the *Gazette of the United States*, hit Bache in the face. Bache struck Fenno over the head with his cane. This started a long tradition of street encounters between rival nineteenth-century editors. The *Aurora* was the first, in 1800, to make its second page specifically an editorial page. It also used the editorial "we." Other editors began to follow both practices.

Several historians have called this the Dark Age of Journalism because of the scurrility of the press. But others have seen this emotional outpouring, especially among the anti-Federalists, as a venting of stored-up anger against the British and against anything that resembled the imposition of the strong government that the British attempted to impose on the Colonies. Because of their antipathy toward Britain and sympathy for the French Revolution, the anti-Federalists attacked the administration's inclination to support the British and oppose France. This opposition helped account for the passage of the Alien and Sedition Acts of 1798, which forbade "any false, scandalous and malicious writing . . . against the government of the United States, or either house of the Congress . . . or the same President . . . or to excite against them the hatred of the good people of the United States. . . ." These acts were aimed at the anti-Federalists and were used solely against them. They did not mention the vice president, who at the time was Thomas Jefferson, an anti-Federalist. The administration of the law was so unfair—so obviously against anti-Federalist editors—that the apparent injustice contributed to the defeat of John Adams and to the election of Jefferson. Jefferson pardoned the imprisoned editors, and the laws were allowed to expire.

With the election of Jefferson, the press became less vicious but remained strictly partisan. Now it was the Federalists' turn to establish a press in opposition to the government. In 1801, the year Jefferson took office, Hamilton founded the *New York Post,* with William Coleman as editor. Hamilton wrote many of the editorials. The *Post* pushed Federalist policies—such as a strong merchant marine and navy and an internal revenue system—and defended the Alien and Sedition Acts. Mostly it saw its purpose as ridiculing the Jefferson administration.

Coleman acknowledged that the Louisiana Purchase, one of Jefferson's accomplishments, was "an important acquisition" but suggested that its principal value might be to trade for the Floridas, "obviously of far greater value to us than all the immense, undefined region west of the river." When Jefferson reported to Congress that up the Missouri River was a mountain of rock salt, the *Post* said:

Methinks such a great, huge mountain of solid, shining salt must make a dreadful glare in a clear sunshiny day, especially just after a rain. . . . We think it would have been no more fair in the traveler who informed Mr. Jefferson of this territory of solid salt, to have added that some leagues to the westward of it there was an immense lake of molasses, and that between this lake and the mountain of salt, there was an extensive vale of hasty pudding, stretching as far as the eye could reach. . . .

Coleman kept up the Federalist fight against Jefferson and later against James Madison, but by 1816, when James Monroe was elected president overwhelmingly during the "Era of Good Will," the Federalist Party had dwindled nearly to obscurity. According to the formerly Federalist *Post,* the Republican-Democrats, soon to be known as the Democrats, had taken over the Federalist principles. The *Post* continued as a voice for the commercial community but began espousing Democratic principles.

Beginning with Jefferson, every president through John Buchanan, elected in 1856, had an official newspaper in Washington, The principal purpose of the administration paper was to serve as a mouthpiece for the president. The party faithful read the official organ to find out the official line of the party in power. Even though the *National Intelligencer* became the official paper of the Jefferson administration, editors Joseph Gales Jr. and William W. Seaton built a reputation for separating their editorial positions from their news reporting and for providing nonpartisan coverage of Congress.

The most effective use of an official newspaper was made by President Andrew Jackson, who became president in 1829. He first made his influence felt with the party faithful through the *United States Telegraph,* founded in 1825 by Duff Green. When Green switched allegiance to Jackson's rival, John C. Calhoun, Jackson brought Francis P. Blair to Washington to establish a new administration organ, the *Washington Globe.* Blair, who had been on the *Argus of Western America,* the official Democratic Party paper published in Frankfort, Ky., came to have great influence on Jackson and came to be one of Jackson's "kitchen cabinet." Another *Argus* editor, Amos Kendall, became Jackson's principal writer.

The Jackson charm also worked to bring editors under "Old Hickory's" spell, allowing Jackson to gain influence over a substantial number of other newspapers throughout the country. He appointed many editors to government positions; local postmasterships were among the most popular.

One of the papers that shifted its editorial policy to support Jackson was the *Post.* William Cullen Bryant, who became editor the same year Jackson took office, supported low tariffs and opposed the national bank, positions also held by Jackson. Bryant was one of the first editors to speak out for the right of free speech for abolitionists and the right of labor to organize. Although he loyally supported the Democrats, his editorials—unlike those of the earliest party press—were not marked by excessively partisan, shrill tones. The *Post,* also unlike most other party papers, was seeking to expand its readership beyond a few thousand politically aware readers and merchants. Bryant, who could write to satisfy the best of literary critics with his poetry, used such techniques as beginning an editorial with a humorous saying or an appropriate story to try to win subscribers from among a new and growing working class.

The *Post* succeeded in making the transition from the era of the party press to that of the populist press. Most of the other party papers did not. One reason was that the vast majority of presidents between Jackson and Abraham Lincoln were weak leaders, incapable of inspiring strong journalistic voices. A more important reason was that, unlike the *Post,* the party papers attempted to remain party papers when the new, growing readership in the country was not much interested in politics. Much of it was barely literate. Partisan politics became extremely confusing during this time: The Whig Party split apart, then died; the new Republican Party came out of almost nowhere; and the Democratic Party divided along North–South lines.

By the time Lincoln became president, designation of an administration paper had become little more than a formality, and Lincoln didn't even bother to seek an official voice. By then most of the readership was concentrated in the populist press, or at least what had evolved into the populist press. It was this press, not the party press, that became important for politicians.

THE POPULIST PRESS

The first papers that reflected the nation's interest in something besides party politics were the mercantile dailies, which became prominent in the business community in the 1820s. But like the party papers, they found only a few thousand readers sufficiently interested in their offerings to read them regularly. They offered little editorial comment.

Ignored by both party and mercantile press was a rapidly growing potential readership, resulting partly from immigration, partly from increasing literacy. These readers may not have been especially interested in party politics, but they were interested in what was going on in their communities. Out of this development grew an opportunity to publish papers that would sell to the masses.

Day, Bennett, Greeley and Raymond

The first of the populist papers were called the "penny press" because some of them actually cost only a penny. The others cost two or three cents. In the first years much of the content was crime news and gossip. Courts and the police record were favorite sources for stories, many of them full of sex, blood and drunkenness. The readers loved these new papers, and circulation soared into the tens of thousands.

Editorial pages were slow in working their way into these papers. The first of the penny press papers was the *New York Sun,* founded in 1833 by Benjamin H. Day. He allied himself with no political party and employed no regular editorial writer. The few editorials that appeared dealt briefly with the latest sensations, municipal affairs, and morals and manners. One example: "SUDDEN DEATH— Ann McDonough, of Washington Street, attempted to drink a pint of rum on a wager, on Wednesday afternoon last. Before it was half swallowed Ann was a corpse. Served her right." Another example: "DUEL—We understand that a duel was fought at Hoboken on Friday morning last between a gentleman of Canada and a French gentleman of this city, in which the latter was wounded. The parties should be arrested." The *Sun* had only this to say when the 1843 New York Legislature adjourned: "The Legislature of this State closed its arduous duties yesterday. It has increased the number of our banks and fixed a heavy load of debt upon posterity.''

The *New York Herald,* founded in 1835 by James Gordon Bennett, offered even more sensationalism than the *Sun*. In the early years, Bennett offered little serious editorial comment, but he loved to flaunt his ego and wit before his readers; they loved his swagger and flippancy. He was the first of the editors noted for ''personal journalism.'' Concerning the *Herald,* he wrote: ''Nothing can prevent its success but God Almighty, and he happens to be on my side.'' Although he liked to attack speculators, pickpockets and competing editors for their ''crimes and immoralities,'' his editorials contained more bombast and personal references than solid opinion. Bennett's famous competitor, Horace Greeley, while perhaps not the most objective of critics, accurately characterized Bennett as ''cynical, inconsistent, reckless, easily influenced by others' opinions, and by his own prejudices.''

Bennett's biting editorial language and sensational news practices earned him occasional physical abuse. Several times he was horsewhipped in the streets. Usually he took advantage of these attacks to parade his fearlessness before his readers. After James Watson, editor of the *Courier and Enquirer,* had pushed Bennett down some stone steps, Bennett reported that he had suffered only a scratch and three torn buttons, but that Watson's ''loss is a rent from top to bottom of a very beautiful black coat, which cost the ruffian $40, and a blow in the face, which may have knocked down his throat some of his infernal teeth for anything I know.'' He concluded self-righteously: ''As for intimidating me, or changing my course, the thing cannot be done. . . . I tell the honest truth in my paper, and leave the consequences to God.''

Bennett's ego was never more evident than in an editorial announcing his engagement. The heading was: ''To The Readers of the Herald—Declaration of Love—Caught at Last—Going to Be Married—New Movement in Civilization.'' The editorial said in part:

I am going to be married in a few days. The weather is so beautiful; times are getting so good; the prospects of political and moral reform so auspicious, that I cannot resist the divine instinct of honest nature any longer; so I am going to be married to one of the most splendid women in intellect, in heart, in soul, in property, in person, in manner, that I have yet seen in the course of my interesting pilgrimage through human life.

. . . I cannot stop in my career. I must fulfill that awful destiny which the Almighty Father has written against my name, in the broad letters of life, against the wall of heaven. I must give the world a pattern of happy wedded life, with all the charities that spring from a nuptial love.

In later years, as readers became more sophisticated and Bennett less flippant, the *Herald* developed a serious and thoughtful editorial page. But it is to Horace Greeley that credit traditionally has gone for making the editorial page a significant and respectable portion of the daily newspaper. Greeley might also have been credited with establishing the first penny press. He published his first issue on a snowy day in January 1833, but readers could not get out to buy the paper, and he did not sell enough copies to be able to put out a second issue. His second effort came in 1841 with the founding of the *New York Tribune.*

Tribune editorials, written in a variety of styles but almost always with literary merit, commented on a broad range of topics, generally following a consistent editorial policy. Several writers contributed to the thinking behind the editorials and to the writing of the editorials, but it was customary for readers to think of the *Tribune*'s editorial page, if not the *Tribune* itself, as a one-man show. Subscribers read the paper to see what Greeley thought, and they assumed that every word was his. The *New York Weekly Tribune,* in particular, with circulation across the country, was read with devotion.

With Day's and Bennett's papers appealing mostly to Democratic voters, Greeley's *Tribune* was the first of the populist press with a Whig editorial outlook. But Greeley's philosophy was far more radical than that of most Whigs. He favored high tariffs, as did the Whig Party, but not just to protect business; he wanted the creation of an American economy that would benefit merchants, workers and farmers as well. His interest in socialist and utopian ideas reflected the belief that all classes working together in an ideal community could produce wealth and harmony for all. He not only preached this belief in his editorial columns but he traveled the country lecturing to audiences on his ideas.

Greeley strongly believed in Western expansion and supported the march of farmers and merchants westward. But he did not support the methods he saw being used in annexing Texas. The only New York editor to oppose the Mexican-American War, Greeley wrote this editorial after the Senate had voted to annex Texas:

> The mischief is done and we are now involved in war! We have adopted a war ready made, and taken upon ourselves its prosecution to the end. We are to furnish the bodies to fill trenches and the cash to defray the enormous expense. Mexico, despoiled of one of her fairest provinces by our rapacity and hypocrisy, has no choice but to resist, however ineffectively, the consummation of our flagitious designs.

Greeley was an early advocate of the abolition of slavery. E. L. Godkin, editor of the *New York Evening Post,* concluded that by the early 1860s Greeley had "done more than any other man to bring slaveholders to bay, and place the Northern fingers on the throat of the institution." Godkin perceived that Greeley had "waged one of the most unequal battles in which any journalist ever engaged with a courage and tenacity worthy of the cause, and by dint of biting sarcasm, vigorous invective, powerful arguments, and a great deal of vituperation and personality."[4]

But, for all that, Godkin accused Greeley of treating his opponents with contempt, of being half-educated "and very imperfectly educated at that." According to Godkin, Greeley had "no grasp of mind, no great political insight"; his brain was "crammed with half truths and odds and ends of ideas which a man inevitably accumulates who scrapes knowledge together by fits and starts on his way through life." Greeley was saved, Godkin said, by his unflagging enthusiasm, an unshakable faith in principles and a writing style virtually unsurpassed in vigor, terseness, clearness and simplicity. But he was known also for his coarse and abusive language. As Godkin wrote: "He calls names and gives the lie, in his leading articles, with a heartiness and vehemence which in cities seem very shocking, but which out in the country, along the lakes, and in the forests and prairies of the Northwest, where most of his influence lies, are simply proofs of more than ordinary earnestness."

Illustrating both Greeley's penchant for name calling and his devotion to the anti-slavery cause was an editorial entitled "Stephen A. Douglas as the Volunteer Executioner," published on Feb. 22, 1854. Greeley depicted a scene in which "a poor, miserable, half-witted and degraded Wretch, who consorted with the negroes," was about to be lynched by a mob. As the execution was about to take place, there was hesitation. He wrote then:

A moment more and there would have gone up in the crowd a cry, "Let him go," "Let him go;" but at this moment a person unknown to the crowd was seen to move toward the cart. Springing upon it and rudely seizing the dangling rope, he turned round to the astonished spectators and said: "If none of you will act as hangman, I will. Damn the Abolitionists!" In another instant the fatal cord was adjusted, the cart driven off, and there was suspended between heaven and earth the trembling—the dead—form of an innocent man.

Now who was this hangman? Who was this fierce defender of the peculiar institution? Was he a Southern man? No. Was he a citizen identified with the South? No. It was on the contrary a Northern man, from a free State—in fact, one who had been but two days in the place. It seemed as if, suspecting his own principles, revolting in his heart at slavery and afraid that in the excitement of the hour he might next be arraigned, he took this fearful and terrible office of executioner in order to place himself, as he supposed, on "high Southern ground". . . . And here is to be seen reflected the true picture of Mr. Douglas's turpitude. Southern men may have in the madness of the hour conceived such iniquity as is embodied in the Nebraska bill. They may have prepared the halter for the neck of the Missouri Compromise—but the last fatal act would never have been undertaken had not the Senator from Illinois volunteered to act as executioner, had been willing to mount the scaffold, and call down the infamy of murdering liberty upon his own head.

Greeley wanted desperately to be elected to high political office. He did win one term in Congress, but his self-righteous attitude toward his colleagues made him unpopular. For a time he was one of the three Whig leaders in New York state, but invariably, just as he thought he was about to be nominated for a position on the Whig ticket, his political allies would outmaneuver him, promising him a chance next time. When the Whigs disintegrated, divided in part over the issue of slavery, he became one of the leaders in the formation of the Republican Party. Finally, when he was old and the nomination was not worth much, some of Greeley's fellow editors and others nominated him for president on a coalition Democratic-liberal Republican ticket in 1872. But he was overwhelmingly defeated by Ulysses S. Grant. Greeley died a few weeks later.

Another editor of the populist press era who was interested in holding public office was Henry J. Raymond, who with George Jones founded the *New York Times*. Raymond, like Greeley, helped form the Republican Party when the Whig Party disintegrated. But he was more successful than Greeley in winning office and in fact was nominated and elected lieutenant governor of New York at a time when Greeley hoped to be nominated.

Raymond's goal in establishing the *Times* was to publish a paper that was more objective in its news columns and less emotional in its editorials than were the *Tribune,* the *Herald* and other populist papers. In this he succeeded. The *Times* was less flamboyant and more respectable than its competitors. It was also less exciting to read. Raymond's inability to make up his mind about whether he was more editor or more politician also affected the vitality of the *Times*. If he had not been lured into politics, he would have been a better editor, in Godkin's view "the most successful journalist that has ever been seen." But, to quote Godkin, Raymond had a tendency to hold doubts about his political convictions and lacked the "temper which was necessary to victory" in the political realm; and a "sense of the necessities and limitations of his position as a politician" kept him from being the journalist he could have been.

Other Voices

Not all of the strong editorial voices were confined to New York. In Chicago the *Tribune,* which had been founded in 1847, achieved a formidable reputation after Joseph Medill assumed control in 1855. This paper took a strong anti-slavery stand, promoted the new Republican Party and pushed fellow Illinoisan Lincoln for the presidency. In the Northeast, the *Springfield* (Mass.) *Republican,* founded by Samuel Bowles II in 1824, earned respect for conservative, enlightened, well-written editorials. In 1884, the *Republican* displayed its political independence by switching its support to a Democrat, Grover Cleveland, in the race for president. (Dana, whose *Sun* was neutral in that election, called papers that deserted the Republican Party mugwumps.)

One of the strong voices after the Civil War was that of Colonel Henry Watterson of the *Louisville Courier-Journal*. Watterson had edited a Southern paper during the Civil War but thought that secession was wrong. For half a century he preached conciliation between North and South—and both sides listened to him.

In 1868, when Kentucky was being criticized for having elected anti-Reconstruction Democrats to office, Watterson reminded the North that Kentucky had not seceded during the war: "Kentucky's head was with the Union and her heart was with the South; for it is in the nature of a generous and manly people to sympathize with the weak in its struggle with the strong.'' Watterson said that the laws were better enforced and there was less crime in Kentucky than in Indiana and Ohio. While Tennessee and Missouri were poor and overrun by despots who ignored the liberties and private rights of the people, Kentucky had no limitations on voting. The people of Massachusetts tended to vote Republican but people in Kentucky tended to vote Democratic. He concluded:

> We are perfectly honest, and think we have a right, as free citizens of a free republic, to decide for ourselves. For so doing and so thinking we are denounced as traitors to our country and a despotism is sought to be placed over us by those who claim that we ought to be forced to vote for Republican candidates and Republican measures, and who declare that if we do not, we are guilty of rebellion and should be punished therefor.

Abolition and the Civil War

The Civil War and events leading up to it provided editors of the time plenty of opportunities to express their strong and diverse viewpoints. We have already noted Greeley's conversion to the cause of abolition. The popularizing of the abolition movement began with the publication of the *Liberator,* founded by William Lloyd Garrison in 1831. At first Garrison was ignored and almost forced into bankruptcy. Even those who sympathized with his views found his blunt, coarse language offensive; in some cases it proved counterproductive. The *Liberator* might have failed in its first year if a black preacher named Nat Turner had not led a slave revolt in Virginia that resulted in the deaths of 57 whites. Although Garrison had no subscribers in the South at the time, his writings were perceived to have induced Turner to riot. Southern editors, who wished to place blame on abolitionist interference from the North, began reprinting Garrison's writings as examples of inflammatory material. Garrison was immediately thrust into the editorial leadership of the abolitionist movement.

Illustrative of Garrison's work was his response when President Millard Fillmore called for new, tougher legislation after abolitionists had defied the Fugitive Slave Act by rescuing a slave from a U.S. deputy marshal in Boston. Garrison wrote:

> Nobody injured, nobody wronged, but simply a chattel transformed into a man, and conducted to a spot where he can glorify God in his body and spirit, which are his!
>
> And yet, how all the fiends in the pit are writhing and yelling! Not tormented before their time, but just at the right time. Truly, 'devils with devils damned firm concord hold!' The President of the United States is out with his Proclamation of Terror, conveying it to us in tones of thunder and on the wings of the lightning; even as though in the old Bay State chaos had come again, and millions of foreign mymidons (sic) were invading our shores! A poor, hunted, entrapped fugitive slave is dexterously removed from the courtroom, and the whole land is shaken! . . . Henry Clay—with one foot in the grave, and just

ready to have both body and soul cast into hell—as if eager to make his damnation doubly sure, rises in the United States Senate and proposes an inquiry into the expediency of passing yet another law, by which everyone who shall dare peep or mutter against the execution of the Fugitive Slave Bill shall have his life crushed out!

Abolitionist editors who spoke out strongly risked their property and their lives. Garrison barely escaped an angry mob in Boston in 1835 by jumping out a window and voluntarily spending the night in jail. Threats discouraged abolitionist editor James G. Birney from attempting to organize an abolition movement in Kentucky: when he founded the *Philanthropist* in Cincinnati in the mid-1830s, a mob attacked his office. The abolitionist editor who became the most honored was Elijah Lovejoy. Anti-abolitionists twice destroyed the offices of his *St. Louis Observer,* which had been forced to move from St. Louis to Alton, Ill. When he re-established his paper for a third time, in 1837, a mob destroyed the office and killed him.

One of the editors whom Garrison helped to launch was Frederick Douglass, the best known of the black abolitionist editors. Douglass toured the Western states and Europe with Garrison, then went his own way in 1847 to found the *North Star.* He continued to promote the black cause in a series of publications until 1875. By then both he and Garrison were widely honored, at least among blacks and Northerners.

The *Post,* under the editorship of Bryant, defended the right of the unpopular abolitionists to meet and demonstrate as early as 1833 and spoke sympathetically of John Brown at the time of his raid into Virginia in 1859 to free slaves and incite insurrection. While Southerners were arguing for the extension of slavery, the *Post* foresaw a growing threat of uprising among the blacks: "But while they speak the tocsin sounds, the blacks are in arms, their houses are in flames, their wives and children driven into exile and killed, and a furious servile war stretches its horror over years. That is the blessed institution you ask us to foster and spread and worship, and for the sake of which you even spout your impotent threats against the grand edifice of the Union!"

Raymond's *Times* characteristically took a more moderate stance, opposing abolition until after the Civil War had begun even though it had strongly supported the election of Lincoln in 1860. Bennett's *Herald* also remained against abolition until after the war began, but it did not favor the election of Lincoln and in fact demonstrated strong sympathy for the South both before and during much of the war. Following the firing on Fort Sumter, the *Herald* contended that "the tempest which now threatens so menacingly" could be entirely dispelled if the Northern states would only call constituent assemblies to ratify constitutional amendments proposed by the South. The amendments would recognize property rights of all citizens everywhere, provide full liberty to carry slaves into common territory, and assume toleration of opinion respecting slavery as a social institution in the states in which it existed.

At the opposite end of the political and geographical spectrum in the pre-Civil

War period were the Southern "fire-eaters." Robert Barnwell Rhett, of the *Charleston* (S.C.) *Mercury,* was ignored in 1832 when he first began writing that the South should secede; in later years, however, he and others not only gained credence but helped convince their fellow Southerners that the North would let the South go.

When the war began, Northern papers supported Union policies; but the *Times* was the only major paper, and only one of three or four of the seventeen New York dailies, to consistently support Lincoln throughout the war. On the day after the bombardment of Fort Sumter, the *Times* editorialized:

... For the first time in the history of the United States, an organized attempt is made to destroy, by force of arms, the government which the American people have formed for themselves—and to overthrow the glorious Constitution which has made us the envy of the world. The history of the world does not show so causeless an outrage. ... One thing is certain. Now that the rebels have opened the war, the people will expect the government to defend itself with vigor and determination. There is no room for half-way measures now. ... *The South has chosen war, and it must have all the war it wants.* ...

By 1864, however, Raymond feared that Lincoln stood no chance for re-election, barring some bold stroke, but he kept his doubts out of his newspaper columns.

The *Herald,* reflecting its sympathy for the South, chided the Union's misfortune whenever it could find cause and became increasingly bitter against Lincoln. A month after Lincoln took office, the *Herald* referred to the "vicious, imbecile, demoralized Administration." Because the *Herald* was the most widely read American paper in Europe, readers on that continent got many of their impressions of the war from the pro-South *Herald.* After initially promoting Ulysses S. Grant for the Republican nomination for president in 1864, the *Herald* gradually softened its opposition to Lincoln. A rumor indicated that Lincoln had offered Bennett the ambassadorship to Paris. Whether or not he actually had made such an offer, Bennett wrote a note to Lincoln declining the appointment.

Greeley ran hot and cold on both Lincoln and the war in spite of his alleged strong abolitionist beliefs. Shortly after Fort Sumter, he argued for letting the South secede if that was what the Southern people really wanted. But a few weeks after that, the *Tribune* urged immediate action to bring the seceding states back into the Union. As the summer of 1861 approached, the *Tribune* ran a war slogan atop its editorial page every day for a week:

The Nation's War-Cry

Forward to Richmond! Forward to Richmond! The Rebel Congress must not be allowed to meet there on the 20th of July! BY THAT DATE THE PLACE MUST BE HELD BY THE NATIONAL ARMY!

The *Tribune* editorials contributed to the pressures that pushed the Union army into battle prematurely at the First Battle of Bull Run. Casualties were heavy, and the troops retreated in disarray to Washington. The editorials had been written by Fitz-Henry Warren, the *Tribune*'s Washington correspondent, while Greeley was away and Charles A. Dana was in charge of the paper. However, if the slogan ran for a week, Greeley must have known what was being said. In any case, he accepted responsibility for the articles in print and, convinced of the power that he and the *Tribune* had, accepted responsibility "as a scapegoat for all the military blunders of the last month." He suffered so much personal remorse that he became physically ill and could not leave his bed.

During the war when things were going well, Greeley was optimistic and tended to speak well of Lincoln. When they were not, he became despondent and blamed Lincoln. In 1864 Greeley suddenly switched to supporting Lincoln after pressing for a substitute presidential nominee. In his case a rumor circulated of a possible postmastership in the second Lincoln administration.

The *Post* strongly supported the war and the administration's measures to wage it, but Bryant became increasingly impatient with Lincoln when the president delayed until 1863 the issuance of the Emancipation Proclamation freeing the slaves. Bryant was also disgusted with newspapers that professed to support the Union but took every possible opportunity to criticize it and taunt it. In fact he published a sarcastic editorial entitled "Recipe for a Democratic Paper," which historian Allen Nevins summarized in this fashion:

(1) Magnify all rebel successes and minimize all Federal victories; if the South loses 18,000 men say 8,000, and if the North loses 11,000 say 21,000.

(2) Calumniate all energetic generals like Sherman, Grant and Rosecrans; call worthless leaders like Halleck and Pope and master generals of the age.

(3) Whenever the Union suffers a reverse, declare that the nation is weary of this slow war; and ask how long this fratricidal conflict will be allowed to continue.

(4) Expatiate upon the bankruptcies, high prices, stock jobbers, gouging profiteers and "shoddy men."

(5) Abuse Lincoln and the Cabinet in two ways: say they are weak, timid, vacillating, and incompetent; and that they are tyrannous, harsh, and despotic.

(6) Protest vehemently against "nigger" brigadiers, and the atrocity of arming the slaves against their masters.

(7) Don't advise open resistance to the draft. But clamor against it in detail; suggest doubts of its constitutionality; denounce the $300 clause; say that it makes an odious distinction between rich and poor; and refer learnedly to the military aristocracies of France and Prussia.[5]

Even more anti-Union than the "Democratic Papers" were the Copperhead papers, which spoke for Northern Democrats who openly sympathized with the South. The most prominent of the Copperheads was Clement Laird Vallandigham, who became co-owner of an anti-abolitionist magazine, the *Dayton* (Ohio) *Empire,* in 1847. When the governor of Ohio prepared to answer Lincoln's call for troops after Fort Sumter, the *Empire* declared: "Governor Dennison has pledged the blood and treasure of Ohio to back up a Republican administration in its contemplated attack upon the people of the South. . . . What right has he to make such a pledge? Does he promise to head the troops which he intends to send down South to butcher men, women and children of that section?''

One effect of the Civil War was to put a premium on news. Readers wanted to know how the war was going more than they wanted to know some editor's opinion concerning that war. Newspapers that could not afford correspondents of their own pooled their resources and formed cooperative news reporting services. Since these services provided news to papers of widely differing editorial viewpoints, they had to be careful to report in as objective a manner as possible to keep from offending the editors. Reliance on the telegraph for transmission provided further incentive to keep stories factual and short. The line between news and editorials became more marked. The press became more impersonal. Shortly after the war, the great populist editors died, Raymond in 1869 at the age of only 49, both Bennett and Greeley in 1872.

"The prestige of the editorial page is done," wrote James Parton, who might not have been the most objective observer, since he had written a highly laudatory biography of Greeley. With the great voices gone, editorials no longer "much influence the public mind, nor change many votes, and . . . the power and success of a newspaper depend wholly and absolutely upon its success in getting, and its skill in exhibiting the news."[6]

Dana and Godkin

American newspapers were approaching the threshold of corporate journalism, the fourth phase in the development of the editorial page. But, even as most editors were lapsing into corporate anonymity, a few continued to make their voices heard. Two of these were Charles A. Dana of the *New York Sun* and E. L. Godkin of the *Nation* and later of the *New York Evening Post*.

Dana had quit the *Tribune* in 1862 after disagreement over Greeley's criticism of the war effort. He joined the *Sun* after serving as assistant secretary of war in the Lincoln administration. With the deaths of the great editors, Dana was "left alone to tell the tale of old-time journalism in New York," wrote Colonel Henry Watterson, the young editor of the *Louisville* (Ky.) *Courier-Journal*. Watterson said Dana was as "blithe and nimble" as the young editors in the country, and was "no less a writer and scholar than an editor."

During the early days of Dana's editorship, he took editorial swings at the corruption of the Tweed regime in New York and waged campaigns for reforms in government. But as the years went by the *Sun* became more cynical toward reform. Turning a good phrase and enticing readership through humorous, clever writing assumed greater importance. Edward P. Mitchell, later editor of the *Sun* himself, recalled that, before he joined Dana's staff as an editorial writer, he had been told, "Dana's a good teacher for condensation and for saying what you want to say, but as to what he generally wants to say!—''

Dana's sarcasm could be so strong that readers would take him at his literal word. When a public campaign to raise money to erect a statue of Tweed seemed to lag, Dana wrote:

Has Boss Tweed any friends? If so, they are a mean set; it is now more than a year since an appeal was made to them to come forward and put up the ancillary qualities to erect a statue to Mr. Tweed in the centre of Tweed Plaza; but as yet only four citizens have sent in their subscriptions. . . . the hundreds or rather thousands of small-potato politicians whom he has made rich and powerful stand aloof, and do not offer a picayune. . . . we have not decided whether it shall represent the favorite son of New York afoot or a-horseback. In fact, we rather incline to have a nautical statue, exhibiting Boss Tweed as a bold mariner, amid the foretop-gallant buttock shrouds of his steam yacht. But that is a matter for future consideration. The first thing is to get the money; and if those who claim to be Mr. Tweed's friends don't raise it we shall begin the rumor that the Honorable P. Brains Sweeney has turned against him, and has forbidden everyone to give anything toward the erection of the projected statue.

The yacht mentioned in the editorial was one of the luxurious perquisites enjoyed by Tweed but no doubt financed by the public purse. P. Brains Sweeney was Tweed's lieutenant, Peter B. Sweeny.

Edwin Lawrence (E. L.) Godkin came to the United States to cover the Civil War for English papers. He stayed after the war to found the *Nation* magazine, devoted to discussing political and economic issues. One of his interests was in a more equal distribution of the economic and social benefits of prosperity. Philosopher William James described Godkin as "the towering influence in all thought concerning public affairs" during the 1880s and 1890s. James said Godkin influenced many writers who never bothered to quote him and "determined the whole current of discussion" during that era.

Godkin's style was complex and carefully written, but, when he so desired, lively, humorous and ironic. Concerning the appointment of Elihu B. Washburne as President Grant's secretary of state, Godkin cited the "general, and apparently well-founded belief" that Washburne's "installation in the State Department would be the commencement of his intimate acquaintance with the precedents and principles of international law."

In describing an anarchists' picnic, at which there was a riot, Godkin wrote: "The meeting was a great success in the way of promoting practical anarchy, the rioting being protracted to a late hour in the afternoon. Anarchy, like charity, should always begin at home."

Godkin's successor, Edwin P. Mitchell, credited Godkin with being the first in New York to use daily conferences of his editorial writers. Mitchell recounted that every writer was encouraged to propose his own topic and to comment freely on topics proposed by other writers. But Godkin had no mercy on unsound and commonplace ideas. "If the junior editor had nothing worth while to say, Godkin would cut across his flounderings with 'O, there's nothing in that,' or 'We said that the other day,' or 'O everybody sees that.' " But, when a writer came up with a new idea, "Mr. Godkin's eye would kindle with interest, he would lean forward alertly, and catching up the theme, he would perhaps begin to enlarge it by ideas of his own, search its depths with penetrating inquiries, and reveal such possibilities in it that the original speaker had the feeling of having stumbled over a concealed diamond." Sometimes, Mitchell recalled, Godkin became so enthusiastic about the idea that he would decide to write on the subject himself.[7]

Pulitzer and Hearst

Before focusing on the trend toward corporate journalism that began after the Civil War, let us note two newspaper giants who stood out as exceptions against the background of general lethargy in New York journalism. With the purchase of the *New York World* in 1883, Joseph Pulitzer brought to the East Coast the sensational, aggressive style of news reporting that he had developed with the *St. Louis Post-Dispatch*—and a strong commitment to the editorial page. The other giant was of course William Randolph Hearst.

In St. Louis, Pulitzer had campaigned editorially for the middle class at the expense of the wealthy. In New York, he took on the cause of the more numerous poor, including workers and the millions of new immigrants. The irresponsible rich, he said, had "the odor of codfish and not the mustiness of age." The *World*'s editorial opinion was that "such an aristocracy ought to have no place in the republic." Pulitzer printed the following list of governmental goals for social justice that the *World* would pursue:

1. Tax Luxuries.
2. Tax Inheritance.
3. Tax Large Incomes.
4. Tax Monopolies.
5. Tax the Privileged Corporations.
6. A Tariff for Revenue.
7. Reform the Civil Service.
8. Punish Corrupt Officers.
9. Punish Vote Buying.
10. Punish Employers who Coerce their Employees in Elections.

At the end of the list, Pulitzer tacked this notice: "This is a popular platform of 10 lines. We recommend it to the politicians in place of long-winded resolutions."

The *World* generally supported Democrats, but it reluctantly backed William McKinley for president in 1896 because Pulitzer thought that the Democratic candidate, William Jennings Bryan, was ignorant on important issues and that the mining and coining of more silver (the "free silver" issue) would not solve the problems of economic depression. But, even though he praised McKinley's election, Pulitzer took the occasion to say that some of the problems that Bryan and the Populists had been talking about were real:

There is no doubt that in this Republic, based as it is upon simplicity and ideas of equality before the law, there are growing inequalities of privilege and increasingly offensive encroachments and vulgarities of the rich.

The trust combinations are fostered by tariffs that protect them from foreign competition. They grow every year more arrogant, more despotic, and more oppressive in their exactions. Yet the laws against them are not only not enforced, but no honest effort is made to enforce them. . . .

In the same way the people have seen bargains made in secret between the Treasury authorities and a Wall Street syndicate for the sale of millions of bonds for 15 cents on the dollar less than their open market value. . . .

They have seen State legislatures of both parties dominated by corporations so that no measure of relief from wrong doing by corporations could become law. . . .

In brief, money is too largely usurping power and influence of manhood. . . .

The New York press was further enlivened when Hearst ventured off his home base in San Francisco in 1895 to out-sensationalize Pulitzer with his newly acquired *New York Journal.* Hearst too undertook the cause of the have-nots, but his editorial approach was a more simplistic, emotional, entertaining appeal to readers. On the first birthday of the new *Journal,* Hearst editorialized:

What is the explanation of the *Journal*'s amazing and wholly unmatched progress? . . . When the paper was purchased by its present proprietor, a year ago today, the work contemplated was at once begun. . . . The *Journal* realized what is frequently forgotten in journalism, that if news is wanted it often has to be sent for. . . .

No other journal in the United States includes in its staff a tenth of the number of writers of reputation and talent. It is the *Journal*'s policy to engage brains as well as to get the news, for the public is even more fond of entertainment than it is of information. . . .

To entice readers, some of whom were not very literate, Hearst used large type for editorials, used large headlines to call attention to the editorials, spread editorials over several columns and sometimes published them on page one. Editorial cartoons added further interest to the page.

Arthur Brisbane, one of many editors and reporters hired away from Pulitzer, became a master at expressing Hearst's views and promoting his causes in clear, direct language that no reader could misunderstand. The *Journal* addressed such topics as "The Existence of God," "What Will 999 Years Mean to the Human Race?" "Crime Is Dying Out," "Have the Animals Souls?" and "Woman Sustains, Guides and Controls the World." Brisbane editorials often had a simple moralistic tone. An example is "Those Who Laugh at a Drunken Man," written during the prohibition movement following World War I:

How often have you seen a drunken man stagger along the street!

His clothes are soiled from falling. His face is bruised. His eyes are dull. Sometimes he curses the boys that tease him. Sometimes he tries to smile in a drunken effort to placate pitiless, childish cruelty.

His body, worn out, can stand no more, and he mumbles that he is going home.

The children persecute him, throw things at him, laugh at him, running ahead of him.

Grown men and women, too, often laugh with the children, nudge each other, and actually find humor in the sight of a human being sunk below the lowest animal.

The sight of a drunken man going home should make every other man sad and sympathetic. . . .

That reeling drunkard is going home.

He is going home to children who are afraid of him, to a wife whose life he has made miserable.

He is going home, taking with him the worst curse in the world—to suffer bitter remorse himself after having inflicted suffering on those whom he should protect. . . .

. . . we cannot call ourselves civilized while our imaginations and sympathies are so dull that the reeling drunkard is thought an amusing spectacle.

The trouble with Spain over Cuba in the late 1890s was ready-made for Hearst in his efforts to overtake Pulitzer. Hearst had a new underdog to champion—the Cuban rebels. Sensationalizing news and editorial comment about Spain and Cuba sold papers, and Hearst's circulation soon caught up with Pulitzer's. Pulitzer responded in kind. The battle between the two to see who could find, or invent, the most grisly revelations about Spanish atrocities helped create the political climate in which President McKinley finally concluded he had little choice but to seek a declaration of war against Spain. Following the sinking of the U.S.S. *Maine* in the Havana harbor in 1898, the *Journal* pretended to withhold judgment concerning the cause of the explosion and to urge caution. But it concluded that, no matter how the investigation turned out, there was no reason not to proceed with freeing Cuba. The editorial stated:

To five hundred thousand Cubans starved or otherwise murdered have been added an American battleship and three hundred American sailors lost as the direct result of the dilatory policy of our government toward Spain. If we had stopped the war in Cuba [between Spain and the rebels] when duty and policy alike urged us to do so the Maine would have been afloat today, and three hundred homes, now desolate, would have been unscathed.

It was an accident, they say. Perhaps it was, but accident or not, it would never have happened if there had been peace in Cuba, as there would have been had we done our duty. . . .

The investigation into the injuries of the Maine may take a week, but the independence of Cuba can be recognized today. . . . The American fleet can move on Havana today and plant the flag of the Cuban Republic on Morro and Cabanas. It is still strong enough for that in the absence of further "accidents." And if we take such action as that, it is extremely unlikely that any further accidents will appear.

Both Hearst and Pulitzer had political ambitions. Pulitzer satisfied his ambition with one term in Congress and some service in the Missouri legislature. But it took Hearst a long time to learn that he was not destined for high office. Narrow defeats in races for mayor of New York City and governor of the state did nothing to lessen his efforts to become president. Hearst was a serious contender for the Democratic nomination in 1904 but he deluded himself into thinking he was a possible nominee in the three subsequent presidential elections. Few took him seriously as a candidate in those years.

Hearst's editorial urgings toward war, in the case of the Spanish-American War, were not repeated in the periods leading up to World War I and World War II. The Hearst papers took a pacifist and anti-British position, in both news and editorials, in 1914 through 1917. Hearst dismissed critics who charged him with being pro-German. When the United States entered the war in April 1917, the Hearst papers scrambled to support the cause. In World War II, Hearst followed a similar pattern of expressing opposition to entering the war, then switching to strong support, but in that instance a change of policy on the war did not indicate an end to Hearst's growing bitterness toward President Franklin D. Roosevelt. Part of his resentment resulted from a growing conservatism on social issues; part resulted because Roosevelt was not paying as much attention to Hearst as he had in the early days of his administration.

THE CORPORATE EDITORIAL PAGE

We have already noted that a shift in emphasis from opinion to news became evident following the Civil War. The metamorphosis from prominent editors to anonymous editorial writers came gradually. Dana continued for some years to run the editorial page on the *Sun* as he wished, as did Godkin on the *Post*. Most readers of Hearst's papers knew that Brisbane wrote the editorials that they read, and many knew that Irvin S. Cobb, Pulitzer's handpicked editorial writer and eventual successor, wrote the editorials on the *World* until Cobb's death in 1923. But few names today remain associated with other papers in the last decades of the 19th century and the first decades of the 20th century.

Illustrative of the change occurring in American newspapers was the experience of the *New York Times*. The *Times* had one brief moment of glory following the Civil War before lapsing into journalistic grayness. One of the underlings of W. M. Tweed, boss of New York's Tammany Hall, had been going from newspaper to newspaper trying to interest editors in publishing records that showed the corruption that existed in city government. Finally, after several editors refused, the *Times,* under the late Henry L. Raymond's partner, George Jones, published the revelations. It listed column after column of fraudulent bills, totalling millions of dollars, that had been paid to Tweed's friends and supporters. The stolen money, the *Times* said editorially, went "to meet the expense of the Ring in the matter of fast horses, conservatories, handsome horses and newspaper editors." After news stories had reported that $360,751.61 had been paid to an obscure carpenter named C. S. Miller for one month's work and $2,870,464.06 had gone to plastering work done by Andrew J. Garvey, a *Times* editorial said: "As C. S. Miller is the luckiest of carpenters, so Andrew J. Garvey is clearly the Prince of Plasterers. His good fortune surpasses anything in the Arabian Nights." (Thomas Nast, with his famous cartoons in *Harper's Weekly,* also helped rouse the public to oust Boss Tweed and send him to jail.)

That was about the last that was heard from the *Times*. "The mistake of the *Times* was in lapsing into the dulness (sic) of respectable conservatism after its Ring fight," Dana wrote in the *Sun* in 1875. "It should have kept on and made a crusade against fraud of all sorts." By the mid-1890s, the *Times* had fallen onto hard financial times. A new owner, Adolph S. Ochs, took over the paper in 1896. Primarily interested in presenting a good news product, Ochs was satisfied with a bland, anonymous editorial page. In recounting the history of the *Times,* Harrison E. Salisbury noted that "there were those who felt he would have been happier had there been no editorial page."[8] The page was plain and dignified: small headlines, regular type sizes, one-column measure, no political cartoons. One of the few *Times* editorial themes in the early 20th century was a defense of industrial entrepreneurs against the encroachment of legislation and the attacks of critics.

Newspapers in general during this period were closely allied with the growing business and industrial community. The papers themselves began to grow more prosperous and to become capitalistic enterprises. They became more dependent on advertising for revenue and on increasing circulation to justify higher advertising rates. The business side of journalism overshadowed the editorial side.

The Social Reformers

By the beginning of the 20th century most of the literary effort directed toward social reform was confined to magazines and books. One reason these publications took on the role that might have been performed by newspaper editorial writers and investigative reporters was that they were able, unlike newspapers, to reach a nationwide audience for recruiting readers and building up a mass circulation. At the local level readers interested in hearing about the evils of society were a minority in the years before World War I, when the prevalent attitude in America and Western Europe was that the world was moving forward toward social and economic progress.

The most prominent platforms for the social reform writers, dubbed "muckrakers" by President Theodore Roosevelt, were *McClure's,* Hearst's *Cosmopolitan, Collier's* and Edward W. Bok's *Ladies' Home Journal.* The articles that appeared in these magazines, by such writers as Lincoln Steffens, Ida M. Tarbell and Ray Stannard Baker, were part investigative reporting and part editorializing.

One of Steffens's best known efforts was a series of six articles in *McClure's* on corruption in American cities. His findings later appeared in modified form in a book, *The Shame of the Cities.* One of the assumptions of the reformers of an earlier day, including E. L. Godkin on the *New York Evening Post,* was that municipal corruption arose out of the conditions of the poor, the illiterate and the immigrant classes, which in their ignorance were easily manipulated by the bosses. Steffens tried to show that corruption came from the top of the economic and social order, from the business community and the educated: "... don't try to reform politics with the banker, lawyer, and drygood merchant, for these are business men."[9]

Upton Sinclair, another muckraker, wrote in *The Brass Check,* an expose of American journalism, that "American corruption was the buying up of legislatures and assemblies to keep them from doing the people's will and protecting the people's interests."[10] Sinclair set out to show how the press, even the so-called reform press, had sold out to business. He contended that Charles Dana, on the *New York Sun,* while once "something of a radical," had "turned like a fierce wolf upon his young ideals" and now "had one fixed opinion, which was that everything new in the world should be mocked at and denounced."[11] Sinclair recognized Godkin as "a scholar and a lover of righteousness" but wrong in viewing corruption as stemming from the pandering of venal politicians to an ignorant mob. Concerning the typical municipal reformer supported by Godkin, Sinclair wrote: "The candidate was swept into office in a tornado of excitement, and did what all 'Evening Post' candidates did and always do—that is, nothing."[12]

A Few Noted Editors

Several 20th-century editors have stood out. Walter Lippmann, as much a political philosopher as editorial writer and columnist, earned a reputation as a wise analyst in writing, successively, for the *Nation* magazine, the *New York World* and the *New York Herald Tribune*. His column was widely syndicated. Lippmann did, however, have his detractors. He himself acknowledged that he had made a mistake in opposing the League of Nations following World War I. He had criticized it not because of too much internationalism but because of too little, claiming that President Woodrow Wilson had agreed to too many compromises. Later he changed his mind. Lippmann was also criticized for an ambivalent attitude toward the politically powerful; in seeking their confidence and favor, he created an apparent conflict of interest. He earned back some of his critics' respect, however, when he broke sharply with President Lyndon Johnson's policies supporting the Vietnam War.

William Allen White became perhaps the most famous small-town newspaper editor during the first decades of the 20th century. He had written articles exposing social evils for a time for *McClure's,* but he earned his nationwide reputation initially with an editorial entitled "What's the Matter With Kansas?" Written in a satirical tone, the editorial argued that the populists, who were complaining that the state was headed for bankruptcy and an exodus of population, were wrong. White's editorials were widely quoted for their down-to-earth, yet idealistic, approach to national and regional issues. In the days before World

War II, White served as chairman of the Committee to Defend America by Aiding the Allies, one of whose purposes was to encourage newspapers to support the Allied cause.

Hearst was one publisher who was not convinced by White's efforts. Others included what Henry Luce's *Time* magazine called "the Three Furies of Isolationism"—the three grandchildren of Joseph Medill: Robert McCormick, who had taken over Medill's *Chicago Tribune*; Joseph Medill Patterson, who had founded the *New York Daily News* in the 1920s, and Eleanor Medill "Cissy" Patterson, who became publisher of the *Washington Times-Herald* when the McCormick-Patterson interest purchased that newspaper. In an editorial in the *News,* Joseph Patterson contended that the United States had been pushed into World War I, and that "some of the same forces" were pushing the country into World War II. In two editorials entitled "Family Portrait," he said that the Pattersons had descended from a Scotch-Irish ancestor "whose great ambition was to get as far away from England and English aristocratic ideas as they could possibly get. . . . It is also natural for us, with our midwestern background, to think first of America in times like these, and to hate to see Americans kidded and cajoled into impossible crusades to remake the world. . . ."

In establishing the paper in New York, Patterson had set out to remake the world of journalism. A tabloid, the *New York Daily News* championed the cause of the poor and the latest immigrants, and offered them sensational, easy-to-understand news and lots of pictures. But the editorial page, with its casual, simplified, often flippant style, seemed incidental. Soon the *News* had surpassed Hearst's papers in circulation.

At the *New York Post,* a simplification of style was also occurring: Godkin's scholarly editorials had given way to short comments on the news and headlines that summarized the editorials that followed them.

20th Century Conservatism

During the first decades of the 20th century most of the press was extremely conservative in its politics. The *New York Sun,* which had had a liberal bent under Dana, warned against the perils of American entrance into the League of Nations supergovernment. Hearst expressed anger with France for not using "some of her German indemnity to pay her honest debts to America, especially because if it had not been for America she would now be paying indemnity instead of receiving it." Many newspapers joined in the "witch hunt" for "subversives" in the 1920s.

During the 1920s Americans were routinely electing Republicans as presidents, and most American newspapers were routinely endorsing them. New doubts about the power of the editorial page appeared in the 1930s when readers saw that the press was attacking and opposing the election and re-election of Franklin D. Roosevelt, a candidate whom the voting public continued to support. Editorials may have been the place readers previously had looked for interpretations of current events and general enlightenment. But, with Roosevelt's New Deal and the Depression, the United States faced an economic and social, if not political, revolution. The country required greater quantities and kinds of information and insights. Most of the nation's anonymous editorial writers were unwilling or unable to provide what readers wanted. Many of their editorial pens were stuck with automatic reactions to proposals for change. One result was the sudden growth in popularity of bylined columnists, hired by newspapers and syndicated services to explain to readers what was going on, primarily in Washington, D.C. The columns, generally interpretive in nature, were usually published on the editorial page. They were more lively and informative than most of the unsigned editorials that represented the views of the corporate newspaper.

By the 1950s, most newspapers had shed the formal labels that tied them to one party or the other (usually the Republican), but they did continue by wide margins to endorse Republicans for president and, to a lesser degree, Republicans for lower-level offices. In 1952 President Harry Truman leveled the charge of "one-party press" at the newspapers in the race between Dwight D. Eisenhower and Adlai Stevenson. A subsequent study found that the editorial pages of the nation had backed Eisenhower by a margin of almost five to one and that partiality had been evident in the news columns in only 6 of 35 newspapers studied.[13]

In that same era only a few editorial voices were raised early against "McCarthyism," the emotional and largely unsubstantiated campaign against "communists" and "un-American activities" that took its name from Sen. Joseph McCarthy, a Republican from Wisconsin. Alan Barth of the *Washington Post* was one of those few voices, but the voice that came through strongest of all was that of Edward R. Murrow. Murrow put together a documented television program on CBS that showed McCarthy for the demagogue that he was. The broadcast helped move public opinion toward eventual support of censure of McCarthy by his Senate colleagues.

One looks in vain for many examples of strong editorial leadership in the 1950s and 1960s. If the Eisenhower administration was content to let social issues lie dormant, so was most of the press. If editorial writers responded to John F. Kennedy's challenge of a "New Frontier" in the early 1960s, it may have been more because of their fascination with the personality and glamour of the new administration than because of concern for civil and social injustices. On the eve of his assassination in 1963, President Kennedy's programs were in deep political trouble, and he himself was faced with much antagonism among political leaders and voters. The assassination shocked editorial writers, as it did most Americans. One result was that voters, and editors, rallied around Lyndon Johnson, the new president, and in 1964 overwhelmingly elected him to the presidency. For the first time in the 20th century more newspapers supported a Democrat than a Republican for president.

The euphoria over the Johnson administration did not last long. The high hopes of the "Great Society" proved overly optimistic, partly because funds that might have gone to fight poverty and racial inequality were sent to fight a war in Vietnam. Editorial writers in general, like administration officials, failed to realize that the country was not willing or able to wage full-scale battles on both foreign and domestic fronts, or, in the phrase of the day, to supply both "guns and butter." Only a few editors recognized that the country was unwilling or unable to accomplish what it set out to do in Vietnam. Among the early skeptics over the war were Robert Lasch of the *St. Louis Post-Dispatch* and Lauren Soth of the *Des Moines* (Iowa) *Register and Tribune*. A later skeptic was the *Washington Post,* which continued its support of the war until Russell Wiggins was replaced as editorial page editor by Philip Geyelin. Editorial endorsements returned to supporting Republicans in the 1968 election when Richard Nixon barely defeated Hubert Humphrey for president. Even though much of the press, and the public, had grown weary of the Vietnam War and become convinced by that time that it could not be won, the war dragged on, at a somewhat reduced level, for Nixon's entire first term. The press eagerly endorsed Nixon for a second term in 1972, even though many of the revelations later to be known as "Watergate" had been published during the campaign. The documented details of Watergate eventually emerged, and Nixon resigned from the presidency—nearly two years after the break-in at the Watergate complex. A few newspapers, notably the *Washington Post,* deserved credit for the early revelations and for keeping public attention centered on the affair. But the Watergate story was essentially a news story, not an editorial page accomplishment.

HISTORICAL SUMMARY

In the nearly three centuries in which editors on the North American continent have been commenting on public issues, the function of opinion has taken on different roles. For the first century or so, editorial comment was sparse and generally intermixed with (often highly personalized) accounts of news. Then, as tension mounted between the Colonies and Great Britain, editors began to feel called to a cause. As the Revolutionary War approached, journals tended increasingly to be filled with opinion.

In the first decades following the ratification of the Constitution in 1787, newspapers, including editorial pages, served as mouthpieces for political parties. The function of editorials, which began appearing during this era on a designated page, was to argue the party line as forcefully as possible for the party faithful. The stronger and more emotional the tone of the editorial, the more likely it was to please the reader.

Beginning in the 1830s, the new populist press began appealing to a much broader and less political group of readers. At first these penny papers offered mostly crime, sex and gossip. Unsophisticated readers were not interested in editorial comment. But as readers became more literate and editors more concerned about issues, the populist press became more serious. In the two decades before the Civil War the major issues facing the nation got a thorough, if highly emotional and personalized, airing in the editorial columns. Editors did not hesitate to put into print their concerns about the conduct of the Civil War.

The Civil War brought new interest in news, and the day of the great personalized editorialist began to wane. A few voices still spoke out; writers such as Charles Dana, E. L. Godkin, William Randolph Hearst and Joseph Pulitzer raised a ruckus in the late 19th and early 20th centuries. But the trend was clear. Editorial writers were retreating into anonymity on conservative newspapers owned by corporations. One looks in vain for more than a few examples of strong, enlightened editorial leadership on national and international issues during much of the period dominated by the corporate press.

Only recently, and only in some instances, have readers had reason to look to editorial pages for insightful examinations of the real issues of the day—and to expect to find anything except predictable responses to issues. These instances, although limited in number, hold the promise of a new era for editorial pages in America. The signs of that new era, and the possibilities open to the practice of editorial writing in the future, are the subject of the next chapter.

QUESTIONS AND EXERCISES

1. Why do you think that little distinction was made between news and opinion in the columns of most of the Colonial press?

2. What contributed to the decline and eventual demise of the partisan press of the first years of the Republic under the Constitution?

3. Why do you think that Benjamin Day and James Gordon Bennett were not interested in editorial comment during the early days of the populist press?

4. What contributed to making Horace Greeley the most famous editor of the mid-19th century? Was the esteem in which he was held fully merited?

5. From examples in the chapter (plus other samples if available) contrast the writing styles of Horace Greeley and William Cullen Bryant. What does the difference suggest concerning readers of their papers?

6. Why has Charles Dana been better known than E. L. Godkin?

7. Based on material in this chapter and information from other sources, do you think that the *New York Journal* and the *New York World* were primarily responsible for the political atmosphere that allowed the Spanish-American War to occur?

8. Why did most of the writing exposing social problems in the early 20th century appear in magazines rather than in the daily press?

9. What factors contributed to the trend toward anonymity of editors in the corporate newspaper era?

10. Why have recent decades produced no Horace Greeleys, Henry J. Raymonds, William Randolph Hearsts, Joseph Pulitzers or William Allen Whites?

Shoe

Dear Editor:
    In my last letter to you I told you to "stick it in your kazoo." I apologize for that remark.

It was uncalled for, snide, and totally disrespectful to you and your fine newspaper. Please allow me to rewrite that ill-conceived letter:

Dear Editor:
    While wrapping some catfish the other night, I noticed an item on your editorial page.

—Jeff MacNelly
Reprinted by permission of Jefferson
Communications, Inc., Reston, Virginia

The Editorial Page
That Should, and Could, Be

CHAPTER
2

Nothing but a newspaper can drop the same thought into a thousand minds at the same moment. A newspaper is an adviser that does not require to be sought, but that comes of its own accord and talks to you briefly every day of the common weal, without distracting you from your private affairs.
—Alexis de Tocqueville[1]

The first step toward understanding the role that the American editorial page can play today is to understand the nature of the readership of the page. In general, readers today are better educated than readers of the past. They are also probably more sophisticated, although many may not be as interested in public issues as were the faithful followers of editorials in the more partisan papers of the past. Most of today's readers do not read editorials as consistently as readers did when they could subscribe to, and relish reading, a newspaper with which they agreed politically. In most communities today's readers have little or no choice of a daily paper; they take the one that is available or none at all. In fact, a growing percentage of families today does not subscribe to a daily paper. Those who do subscribe represent not the narrow range of the faithful, as in the past, but a diverse political, philosophic, economic and social range. Unlike newspaper readers of the past, most of today's subscribers are exposed to many other sources of information and opinion from media—television, radio, magazines—and from social, civic, labor and business organizations.

All of these interrelated characteristics of the modern editorial page audience suggest major implications for editorial page editors and writers who want to do the most effective job of informing and persuading their readers. The purpose of this chapter is to examine those implications and to see how editors deal with them in an age of a more diversified, more disinterested audience. My major point will be that there is still room for strong editorial leadership—for editorial crusades—but the best chances for editorial writers to achieve credibility and to be persuasive lie in being informed, reasonable, articulate and sensitive to the feelings and opinions of others.

A FEW BUGLE CALLS

In 1977 editors of *The Masthead* asked several editorial writers for their views about editorial campaigning by newspapers. As we will note later, several took the occasion to disclaim their faith in the effectiveness of outspoken campaigning. But others cited specific instances in which they thought strong editorials had made a difference in the outcome of public issues.

George P. Crist Jr. thought a long, persistent effort by his paper, the *Bay City* (Mich.) *Times,* to stimulate more public awareness of the problems of nuclear power had had an effect.[2] Brian Dickinson of the *Providence* (R.I.) *Journal and Evening Bulletin* said his paper had taken "every possible opportunity to rail against" a court system in which the legislature elected state judges. He thought support of the paper had helped contribute to the legislature's eventual tightening of the selective process.[3] Tom Kirwan of the *Fresno* (Calif.) *Bee* thought his paper's editorials had helped build public understanding of the newspaper's position when they defended the "Fresno Bee Four," staff members who were jailed when they refused to reveal a source for stories about a sealed grand jury transcript.[4]

Some editors, such as Harry S. Ashmore of the *Arkansas Gazette* of Little Rock and Paul Greenberg of the *Pine Bluff* (Ark.) *Gazette,* won Pulitzer Prizes for wise, though not necessarily popular, counseling of their communities in desegregation crises. John S. Knight's *Charlotte* (N.C.) *Observer* helped the community endure the trauma of school busing with its editorial counseling. In these instances involving racial crises, a calm, rational voice coming from a community's major mass medium helped establish an atmosphere in which others were encouraged to act moderately.

Some publishers allowed their newspapers to take a stand on the controversial issues surrounding the Vietnam War and Watergate. A number of editors risked public (and their publishers') wrath by speaking out against the Vietnam War in the middle and late 1960s. As noted in the previous chapter, one of these editors was Robert Lasch of the *St. Louis Post-Dispatch.* The paper I was working for at the beginning of the war, the *Des Moines* (Iowa) *Register and Tribune,* also spoke out early. The *New York Times* and the *Washington Post,* despite the federal government's opposition, fought to print the Pentagon Papers, which revealed how the United States had been drawn into the Vietnam War. The

Chicago Tribune, traditionally a very conservative paper, created a stir when it became one of the first major newspapers to call for the resignation of President Nixon during the Watergate affair.

In most instances in which a newspaper's goals are achieved, it is difficult, if not impossible, to determine precisely to what extent, if any, an editorial campaign contributed to the outcome. The newspaper is usually only one participant in the process. This was true in regard to the hardest fought campaign waged by the *Columbian,* of Vancouver, Wash., while I was on that paper. The Port of Portland had proposed to expand the runways and parking area of the Portland International Airport by dumping a square mile of fill into the Columbia River. The river separates Portland from Vancouver as well as Oregon from Washington, and the *Columbian's* but not the Portland papers' circulation area. The Portland papers and, at the beginning, the major public figures in Portland firmly supported the expansion plan. Opinion seemed divided on the Washington side of the river. Some Washington citizens were concerned that altering the course of the river would have detrimental effects, especially on the Washington bank. But others were concerned that, if the airport were not expanded at its present location, convenient to Vancouver, the port would relocate it on the other side of Portland.

Before the *Columbian* had declared an editorial position on the proposal, two local citizens, both of whom owned property on the river across from the airport, came to me with research they had done into the hydrological and legal aspects of changing the channel of a river. They convinced me that building a runway into the river would increase airplane noise in Vancouver and possibly threaten the stability of the Washington bank. They were trying to raise enough money to retain a prominent environmentalist as an attorney to press their case in court and they wanted the *Columbian's* support. We gave it. In the next two to three years opponents of the airport plan won not a single court decision, and lost several, at both the federal district and court of appeals levels. The project did not get under way, however, because the port had agreed not to begin until the last legal hurdle had been cleared.

Our paper was able to make no discernible impact on opinion across the river, but in a succession of editorials we made a strenuous effort to shore up community support for the opponents as they tried to carry their battles to the courts and later to Congress. Without the *Columbian's* legitimizing of their efforts, they would have had a much more difficult time raising money. Without the *Columbian's* firm stand, the board of directors of the Vancouver Chamber of Commerce, greatly concerned about the moving of the airport, might have backed the expansion.

Delay proved the undoing of the project. A new projection of future usage of the airport showed that original estimates had been far too high. The years of delay coincided almost exactly with the rise of the environmental movement of the late 1960s and early 1970s. More voices expressed concern over the environmental impact of the plan. Finally, a new mayor, Neil Goldschmidt, was elected in Portland and he began questioning the dimensions of the expansion. Soon the port simply abandoned its original plan and came up with one that could be accommodated on existing land.

If I were deserving of a feather for my editorial bonnet, it probably would be for the *Columbian*'s efforts in this cause. One reason for this lengthy discussion of the airport proposal is that I would be hard pressed to think of another instance in which we waged a similar editorial campaign. In other editorials we worked for home rule, fairer taxes, more money for schools and land-use controls, with goals that were usually pursued not as part of a concerted campaign but as general comment on daily news topics. I would be even harder pressed to come up with evidence of the newspaper's impact on these broader issues, and yet I am certain that the *Columbian*'s persistent support for these causes did produce results with readers over an extended period of time. I could also cite any number of other instances in which our editorials seemed to have no impact at all, immediate or long term. For example, we didn't seem to sell residents of adjacent suburbs on the idea of annexing to the city or residents of the county on doing much about modernizing county government.

Some of the editors who responded to *The Masthead*'s inquiry about editorial campaigns offered examples of frustrating experiences with intended recipients of persuasion. Ed Williams of the *Charlotte Observer* recalled that his paper had been pushing "a couple of things for as long as the oldest editorial writer here, roused gently from his slumbers, can remember": a less regressive sales tax system and a liberalizing of the sale of alcohol. He noted, ironically, that that very year "we were rewarded . . . by a legislative attempt to give manufacturers yet one more tax break." On the matter of liquor, in an equally ironic tone, he said that, "thanks, no doubt, to our rational, persuasive editorials," Charlotte residents "can now walk into a bar and buy a mixed drink—if they are willing to drive 25 miles" to South Carolina.[6] Bob Reid, editorial editor for the Lindsay-Schaub Newspapers of Decatur, Ill., while suggesting that "maybe we just aren't dynamite enough writers," concluded that in his community there probably wasn't much worth accomplishing that could be attained in one or two hard-hitting editorials. "Sometimes it takes a decade or more to get even fairly minor change," he wrote. "So patience and lack of patience, as well as a high tolerance level for the same subject written in many different ways, are important qualifications for a crusading editorial writer."[7]

A number of vivid ways have been used to warn editorial writers against expecting too much from editorial campaigns. Bernard Kilgore, publisher of the *Wall Street Journal*, said he thought it was all right for newspapers to regard themselves as thunderers and for editorial writers to picture themselves "with a bolt of lightning in each hand about to smash down on something." But he urged writers to be "very careful about demolishing a subject with one swoop, because good subjects for the editorial pages are very hard to come by."[8] His point was that most editorial topics require analysis and study over a period of time, not a single definitive pronouncement Donald Tyerman, former editor of the *Economist* of London, reminded editorial writers at an NCEW meeting that they are neither Moses nor God. He warned against the Tablets of Stone theory—"that you can hand down the truth or, indeed, that you have it to hand down." Nor did he believe that editorial writers can effect a conversion such as occurred to Saul of Tarsus on the road to Damascus.[9]

At another NCEW meeting Philip Geyelin of the *Washington Post* recalled that James Cain, who served with Walter Lippmann on the *New York World* and wrote *The Postman Always Rings Twice,* had argued that a newspaper ought to fight for its beliefs as hard as it could. He turned to music for an illustration, noting that a piano has eight octaves, a violin three, a cornet two, but a bugle has only four notes. "Now if what you've got to blow is a bugle there isn't much sense in camping yourself down in front of piano music," Cain said. To which Lippmann replied, "You may be right, but goddamit, I'm not going to spend my life writing bugle calls."[10] A bugle call may be appreciated by readers once in a while, and it may mobilize them in a worthy cause, but readers can quickly tire of answering bugle calls. Editorial writers may not have an eight-octave persuasive tool at their disposal, but they ought to be able to play a lot more complex tunes than Reveille and Charge!

A MORE COMPLEX MELODY

That readers look to the editorial page for more than bugle calls is demonstrated by a number of surveys. One survey showed that the highest percentage of regular readers of the editorial page were those who followed the page either to feel they were participating in current events or to strengthen their arguments on issues. Others read the editorial page to help make decisions on issues, to use in discussion with friends, to determine what is important, to keep up with the latest events, to agree with editorial stands, or to help form opinions. Thus the major reasons readers offered for approaching the editorial page were to gain information for discussions and arguments. Seeking guidance in forming opinions ranked at the bottom of the list.[11]

I am not one to recommend that editors slavishly fashion their journalistic products to reflect readership surveys. The decision that editors face—whether to give readers what they want or what the editors think they should have—must still be made. The wisest choice is usually a compromise between the two. The best situation is, however, when the interests of editorial readers and editorial writers coincide. The aim of the writer should be toward the mind, as Lenoir Chambers of the *Richmond* (Va.) *News Leader* advised editorial writers. "Indeed, it had better be," he said, "for everybody is better educated now, and the editorial writer has a harder job to stay out in front." If writers don't know what they are talking about, he said, readers soon spot them for phonies.[12]

Readers do not look to editorials for a rehash of the news columns, and they want something more than unsubstantiated opinion. "Unless an editorial can add something to what appears in the news columns—something besides mere opinion—it has no business in the paper,'' James J. Kilpatrick emphasized in a *Masthead* article.[13] He had in mind the use of historical background, comparisons of parallel situations, related material, fresh facts from other publications and research sources, interpretive analysis and the setting straight of misinformation.

It is easy to dash off an editorial that merely expresses opinion, and it is easy to rewrite the news, but it is often hard work to find something to say about a subject that has not appeared in the news columns or gone through the minds of readers. Here is where time, previously acquired knowledge, ingenuity and an abundance of resources pay off. When editors of *The Masthead* asked editorial writers for one suggestion each for improving editorial pages, Al Southwick of the *Worcester* (Mass.) *Telegram* said he thought that 99 percent of all editorials could benefit from just one-half hour more of research. "That one extra fact, that one additional insight" is what makes the difference between a routine editorial and "something that causes readers to sit up and take notice," he said.[14]

In another symposium in *The Masthead,* syndicated columnist Neal R. Pierce said he advised editorial writers to do their homework. It was clear that writers on the best editorial pages "have studied issues in depth, so that the commentary offered is neither knee-jerk nor shoot-from-the-hip, but rather based on extensive knowledge." Pierce's weekly column, which usually relates to local or state government, provides a good example of what he was talking about. His column and one written by Lauren Soth on food and agriculture may be the most information-packed syndicated editorial columns in newspapers today. Pierce acknowledged that most editorial writers do not have the luxury, as he does, of writing only one piece a week. To produce a column, he said, he may conduct half a dozen interviews, read scores of background papers and spend hours writing and rewriting to make maximum use of space. He thought more hurried editorial writers could achieve similar results by keeping comprehensive files on subjects likely to be written about. He warned that newspaper libraries are likely to be a "weak reed to lean on"; writers need their own files. His second suggestion was that newspapers should make certain that their editorial writers have time to get out of the office in order to talk personally with a range of public officials and other experts. "An editorial writer who treats local government issues, for instance," he said, "is at a tremendous disadvantage if he or she can't find the time to interview, on a periodic basis, the mayor or county executive, major department heads, the political 'outs,' and other savants on the local scene." One of his favorite techniques was to ask an official or an expert to "name—in his or her own words—the priority subjects that will be coming up in the following months." He said subjects came up that he had never dreamed of.[15] In Chapter 4, "Preparation of an Editorial Writer," we will examine more extensively what editorial writers can do to keep themselves informed and acquire information and sources needed for daily comment on public affairs.

Even though editorial writers may be as pressed for time as reporters, their writing needs to give the impression that they are not—that they had all the time necessary to research and to write their stories. Speaking to editorial writers,

Professor Thomas Williams of the University of Southern Illinois at Carbondale wrote: "We need to break down that amorphous block of events, slow down the flow of information with explanation and relate these events to the readers." He noted that print journalism does the best job of presenting information in depth and in step-by-step analysis. "And the editorial page equals dignity and the page to turn to when you want a little more than just the story."[16]

Not only must editorial writers slow down the news that streams through the news columns, but they should also be constantly seeking topics for comment that never find their way into the news columns. To improve the editorial page, Herb Knowlton of the *Toledo* (Ohio) *Blade* suggested: "Look beyond the news columns for ideas once in a while. Most editorial pages are tied too closely to current news items." His suggestion for sources included publicity handouts, government releases, popular culture and literature.[17] The editorial writer who reads widely—the mail, news magazines, specialty magazines, current fiction and non-fiction, the classics—is certain to come across many ideas worth sharing with readers who are looking for more than the same old commentaries. We will talk more specifically about those sources in Chapter 4.

Robert Bartley of the *Wall Street Journal*, in his suggestion for a better editorial page, referred to the search by editorial writers for new material as engaging in "fresh reporting" and "operating off their own agenda." "Their reporting needs to be guided not by yesterday's events, but by some kind of intellectual framework that tells them what might be worth learning about the issues of the day," he wrote. "If they have this kind of curiosity, and go to work developing their own news sources, they are going to find a lot of news readers otherwise would never see."[18]

A VARIETY OF TUNES

The diverse composition of today's editorial page audience presents another challenge to editorial page editors. Not only must they recognize, when they write their own editorials, that readers out there hold a variety of opinions, but they also need to create opportunities for those viewpoints to be presented. Because of time limits and the fleeting nature of messages on film and tape the broadcast media are not able to carry varied viewpoints in depth. That responsibility must fall to the print media. When you are the only newspaper in town, that responsibility falls on you. Providing opportunities for and encouraging readers to write letters to the editor represents a start in this direction. How a strong letters forum can be built will be discussed in Chapter 14, "Letters to the Editor." But providing this forum is not enough. Some readers are less inclined to write than others, or are less likely to write on one side of an issue than another or are less likely to write on some subjects than on others. So the editor must seek to diversify opinion on the editorial page in other ways as well. Syndicated columns for 50 years or so have been a traditional source of some diversity, as we will note in Chapter 15, "Columns and Cartoons." They have their limitations, however, since most syndicated columnists write on national and international news, often writing about the same topics they wrote about the day before. Editors need to bring to their pages writings from irregular sources who have knowledge and insight on matters of public interest. Who some of these sources may be and how they can be presented will be explored in Chapter 16, "Innovations in Makeup and Content." The addition of an op-ed page on an increasing number of papers has expanded opportunities for publishing material that could never have been squeezed into a single editorial page already jammed with editorials, letters, columns and cartoons.

Editorials on any one newspaper can't be expected to replicate faithfully all of the viewpoints of today's newspaper readers. But, with a little help from friends, and adversaries, newspapers should be able to create opinion pages that make readers feel that their views are being taken into account even if the newspapers' own editorials come to entirely different conclusions.

THE TUNE PLAYER

Finally we come to editorial writers themselves, the players of the tunes. What types of men and women are they, and should they be, at a time when audiences are diverse and distracted by other demands on their time and attention? Obsequious, bland editorial writers who are content to mouth a harmless editorial policy, as many did during the corporate era, will not do. They will bore readers to death with platitudes. They may never arouse the ire of their business-minded associates, but they certainly won't arouse the ire, or the enthusiasm, of readers either.

Opportunities to speak out forcefully may not come immediately to beginning editorial writers. Many beginners come from the news side of their papers, where they have been conditioned to keep opinion out of the paper, at least their own opinions. Those with editorial writing experience who come from other papers find themselves working for a new, unfamiliar employer. In both instances, being junior members of a staff, and feeling junior even on a one-person staff, they are not likely to push their bosses toward a more aggressive, outspoken editorial policy or to feel that they are in a very strong bargaining position. But, if they allow themselves to remain indefinitely in such a weak position, they ought to change newspapers or change jobs. Editorial writing is a job for someone who has the ability to dig into a subject and to figure out something meaningful, and often controversial, to say about that subject. Now, every novice editorial writer ought not to be given license to put into print anything he or she comes up with. The art of writing editorials is a demanding and subtle one. It can take quite a few months, even years, for a writer to get the hang of blending fact, interpretation and opinion into a piece that is likely to prove interesting and convincing—and not too long. Beginning editorial writers are likely to write editorials that have either weak conclusions or strong conclusions unsubstantiated by facts and arguments. The roots of both problems are similar. The novice suffers from a lack of experience in using facts and arguments to produce and support conclusions. The only way to correct this common failing of apprenticeship is through experience, preferably under the guidance of a competent, demanding editor.

Once editorial writers fully grasp the subject matter they are writing about and get the feel for putting fact and argument together to support conclusions, they should be able to begin increasing the strength of their positions on their editorial page staffs. We will talk more about this in Chapter 6, "Relations With Publishers," but it seems important to say now that, if editorial pages are going to hold their readers and attract readers of coming generations, they must address the world of readers as it is. Reality and reason, not pure ideology, must be the basis for any editorial policy that stands a chance of addressing the real needs and concerns of readers. If editorial writers know what they are talking about, the odds are that they will convince readers, or at least cause them to rethink their opinions, and that they can convince their editors, general managers and publishers that their ideas merit publication. On many, too many, newspapers editorial writers must restrict their published opinions to narrowly defined policies determined by someone who is not actively engaged in the day-to-day determination of editorial stands. The trend for setting short- and medium-range policy, however, seems to be moving from the corporate level to the editorial page staff, or at least to the editorial conference. We will be talking more about the workings of staffs and conferences in Chapter 8, "The Editorial Page Staff." Ironically, perhaps, the trend toward group ownership seems to be contributing to this increased autonomy of editorial staffs. Sensitive to charges of monopolization of news and opinion, executives of most large groups stress that news and editorial decision making is the function of the local newspaper. Under such circumstances, the corporation's business representative at the local level, whether called a publisher or a general manager, is likely to be more concerned with profit and loss than with news and editorial policies. Within limits, this preoccupation of management with the bottom line provides opportunities for editorial writers to exert influence on policy that may not have existed when a local editor-publisher checked the editorials after, if not before, they were set in type. Even on the diminishing number of independently owned papers, editorial writers who can hold their own in policy discussions are earning respect and the opportunity to influence policy.

Editorial writers are also being given opportunities to establish their credentials through more public identification. Anonymous editorial writers are being replaced by men and women whose names appear in the masthead and in by-lined interpretive and opinion pieces on the editorial and op-ed pages and whose faces, either in pictures or sketches, appear from time to time with these pieces. Editorial writers are not only getting out into their communities to find out what is going on, but they are also going out to make themselves known among their readers. They make speeches and appear on panels, belong to civic organizations and show up for public events, where they may be among the most widely recognized persons present. In many communities, the women and men who write editorials are regarded, whether deservedly or not, as important, influential persons. This recognition, coupled with sound editorials, provides the makings of the power to persuade readers and to influence a community.

Because of the unique role that an editorial page plays in a community, it has become fashionable in editorial writing circles to describe the page as the conscience of the community, the soul (or heart or personality) of the newspaper, the moral substructure of the paper. Editorial writers should hope that their pages are all of these and more. But writers who set out to be the conscience/soul/heart of the community/paper risk committing one of the follies of editorial writing. At a time when philosopher-kings and prophets are rare and the credibility of institutions is low, the role of truth-seeker should be a humble one. Modern readers don't want truth through revelation; they want to feel that they are discovering it for themselves. Writers who would lead must become servants of those readers. There is a role, and a most needed one, for editorial writers of that kind today.

The view of the editorial writer as one who reacts more deliberately and views more broadly than most of those about him was described in the story of Ol' Ed, told at a workshop of the Pacific Northwest editorial writers by R. S. Baker, assistant professor of humanities at Oregon College of Education at Monmouth. There was trouble in Prairie Gulch. A drought had left the wells dry and the sheep dying. Rustlers had taken many of the cattle; there had been mysterious fires, and the church bell had developed a crack. "Into a disturbed town wanders a Chinese lesbian deaf-mute midget—an ideal scapegoat," Baker related. The townspeople quickly gather as a lynch mob. But Ol' Ed steps forward, and a hush falls.

> Surveying the mob, he casts a steely glance at the leading hot-heads, drags his toe in the dust, and speaks: "You folks go right ahead. If the Good Lord hadn't meant for us to lynch Chinese lesbian deaf-mute midgets, He wouldn'ta growed hemp for rope nor cottonwoods to string 'em from. You gotta right to do it. That's freedom which is what I suppose all that fuss in Lexington back in '76 was all about. (Pause.) But just remember, folks (judicious spit no. 2), the last time we lynched a poor innocent Chinese lesbian deaf-mute midget, the next day a whole passel of 'em rode over the hill and burnt the town and poisoned the wells."

To further illustrate the editorial writer as "uniquely equipped to stand at the corner of life and represent us all," Baker described "the man in the Piazza." He said he had often wondered how the Italians, who read very few newspapers, could be so well informed. The mystery was solved, he said, when he observed the buzzing chatter, the exchange of information and gossip and the constant movement of people in the piazza, the public square. Over a period of days, you could spot the person who is the equivalent of the editorial writer. He described the person in this manner:

He is usually middle-aged with a face made grave by experience yet softened by flickers of humor. Most of the time his head is inclined in attentive listening while his eyes scan the square, alert and skeptical. But when he speaks he is listened to. He does not orate. He does not preach. He does not even adopt a tone of outraged innocence. Softly but clearly, he suggests how the matter appears to him. In his words there is a ring of wisdom based on his balancing of claims of past, present and future, the claims of the ideal and the actual, the desirable and the probable. If he lived here he would have your job—would, from his station in the piazza, keep one eye on the new-book shelf in the library and the other on City Hall, on the till.

Baker urged the writers to drop the pose of divine authority and accept simple humanity. ''Do not aim to be Zeus the Thunderer (your 19th- and early-20th-century crusading editor) nor even Jove the All-seeing (your cool, shrewd commentator on legislative/administrative matters). Rather, you should settle for being wily Odysseus, content to be—in all its terror and glory—a man among men, *primus inter pares*.''[19]

CONCLUSION

So how does the editorial writer become the man or woman in the piazza instead of a publisher's mouthpiece, an ivory tower dweller, an impersonal penman or a judgment imposer? No secret magic will cause such a transformation. The chapters that follow are intended to offer suggestions for the writer who may not have all the answers but, like the man in the piazza, wants to be listened to when he or she speaks.

QUESTIONS AND EXERCISES

1. Examine newspapers in your area for a period of several days. Do you get the impression by reading the editorial pages that the editors are trying to find a wide variety of opinions to present to their readers? In what forms do these opinions appear?

2. Examine the editorial pages of these papers for evidence of the personalities and individual opinions of editorial writers. Are the writers faceless persons, or do their names appear in the masthead or over bylined articles?

3. What seems to be the general tone of the editorials on these papers? Are the writers issuing bugle calls or something more subtle and complex? If a mixture, is the tone chosen for individual editorials appropriate?

4. Put in your own words what you think R. S. Baker meant by likening the editorial writer to the man in the piazza.

The Who of the Editorial Page

—Don Addis
Evening Independent
St. Petersburg, Fla.

Anybody for Editorial Writing?

CHAPTER
3

Here we are, the practitioners and champions of a profession which, we modestly like to think, assists the sun to rise and set—and we are doing very little, seemingly, either to seek out the young people with brains and judgment who we hope will be our successors or to interest them in the virtues and satisfactions of editorial writing.
—Robert Estabrook
Washington Post[1]

Why would anyone want to become an editorial writer? What kinds of people make the best editorial writers, and where do they come from? These are some of the questions raised in this chapter, which is intended to give prospective editorial writers some idea of what it is like to be an editorial writer.

In the 1950s and early 1960s, when I was beginning my newspaper career, few young journalists gave much thought to becoming editorial writers, at least not until they had had their fill of walking a news beat. So I was surprised when, at age 28, a friend and former professor asked me if I would be interested in an editorial writing job he knew of in Des Moines, Iowa, on the *Register and Tribune*. Having left my native Nebraska and taken a job in the Pacific Northwest only three years before, I was not keen on returning to the Midwest. But the editor of the editorial page in Des Moines, Lauren Soth, had recently won the Pulitzer Prize for editorial writing, and I had enjoyed writing editorials on my college newspaper. So I applied for the job, got it and never looked back. Editorial writing became my new life.

My professor-friend said something else when he was trying to interest me in that editorial writing job. "Someday," he said, "you ought to have an editorial page of your own.'' I could not possibly have dreamed that five years later the publishers I had been working for in Washington state would hire me back as editorial page editor of their newspaper. I had my own editorial page at age 33.

THE ATTRACTIONS OF EDITORIAL WRITING

What have I and other editorial writers found so attractive about working on an editorial page? Editorial writing offers the chance to step back a pace, to take a broad view of the stream of news that rushes through the pages of a newspaper. Reporters, from time to time, have opportunities to write interpretive articles that attempt to put news into perspective, but only editorial writers spend their entire working day trying to understand what's happening in the world. In order to interpret the news, editorial writers must have enough time to do a high quality job of researching and writing. Editorial writers, at least on some papers, can take half a day if need be to dig out information for an editorial that, when set in type, might be only five or six inches long. Editorial writing tends to appeal to people who take pleasure in careful writing; of all the duties writers may be pressed to perform the one they are likely to enjoy the most is turning out the one or two editorials that must be written each day.

Another attraction of editorial writing is having a ready-made "soap box" from which you can explain and persuade. Readers, of course, don't always fall in line with the editorials they read in their local newspapers, but over a period of time an editorial page with credibility will influence the thinking and direction of the community. It is exciting and rewarding to be a part of the decision-making process of a community.

As noted earlier, the job of editorial writer carries more importance at the newspaper and in the community than it did not so many years ago. Editorial writers may not get their names in print as often as star reporters, but the position tends to be one of the most prestigious on the paper—in surveys in the 1970s writers rated their occupation as high as tenth out of 40 in terms of prestige. An increasing number of papers are providing opportunities for writers to become known to the public, perhaps most frequently through signed articles on the editorial page. While most editorial writers don't spend as much time out in public as reporters, they can, if they wish, get out and become acquainted with the community.

From a financial standpoint, editorial writing also has its advantages. Editorial writers generally are better paid than reporters and newsroom editors and their job tenure is usually longer. In a 1962 survey of 222 writers, 71 percent thought they were earning more money than those of the same age and experience in the newsroom. That figure went up to 84 percent in 1971 but dropped to 75 percent in 1979. The professor who conducted the 1979 survey, G. Cleveland Wilhoit of Indiana University, concluded that, even though inflation had eroded some of the salary gains of editorial writers between 1971 and 1979, the three surveys conducted over two decades "show a remarkably stable, highly educated and highly principled professional group of journalists."[2]

These, then, are some of the reasons that editorial writing appeals to those who have tried their hands in the field and liked the work. Surveys have found that most editorial writers are happy in their jobs. The 1962 survey showed that 73 percent of them would keep their current jobs if they had a choice. Only 7 percent preferred to be columnists, 7 percent executive editors and 7 percent other newsroom staff.[3] A survey in 1971 found 30 percent satisfied and 67 percent very satisfied with their jobs,[4] and a 1979 survey of 650 writers found only a 1 percent change from the 1971 figures.[5]

Despite these attractions, a 1963 survey of newsroom staffs showed that only about 30 percent of news reporters and editors were interested in the possibility of going into editorial writing.[6] Interest was expressed primarily by men under age 30 who had pursued more formal education. The most frequently mentioned reason for not going into editorial writing—mentioned by about 20 percent of those who responded—was personal disinterest; editorial writing just did not appeal to them. Almost as many saw too many restrictions and a lack of freedom of expression; they felt that publishers might require them to write editorials they personally disagreed with. Smaller numbers saw the job as too confining, too removed from reality (too much ivory tower). Some saw themselves as lacking the necessary scholarship or experience.

The survey caused William W. Baker of the *Kansas City* (Mo.) *Star* to conclude that "our little niche in the profession does not command the respect that it might among our fellow workers across the room." He wondered whether news staffs had the impression that editorial writing was "dull, uninteresting and downright boring." To overcome that impression, he suggested that editorial writers come out of their ivory towers and into the newsroom more often, work at creating more stimulating writing and frown "a bit less frighteningly when we tackle our typewriters."[7]

The Qualifications for Editorial Writing

The surveys suggested that it was not just discomfort with the editorial ivory tower, but also the demanding qualifications, that led newsroom people to shy away from editorial writing. A significant 58 percent of the respondents to the 1962 survey thought that the qualifications for a competent editorial writer were different from those for a competent news staff writer, pointing in particular to the need for more education and knowledge as a prerequisite to becoming an editorial writer. Also mentioned were the need for more analytical skills, more experience, sharper insights, better grasp of issues and trends and better writing.[8]

What qualities are required for editorial writers? First, they need a wide variety of interests. Editorial writers on large staffs may have opportunities to specialize in their subject matter, but those on most papers need to be able to write on almost any subject on almost any day. Even those who specialize need to understand how their topics fit into the broader world. Writers need to know about economics, politics, history, sociology, the arts and the sciences. In stressing the catholic interests of editorial writers, Warren H. Pierce of the *St. Petersburg* (Fla.) *Times* said that writers "should know more about all these subjects than any except a specialist in one of the fields, and enough of each so that even the specialist will not scoff" at their opinions.[9]

Second, editorial writers need to be good reporters. They must be able to dig out information and to recount accurately what they find. No editorial is stronger than the facts behind it. Previous experience as reporters can help editorial writers know where to go and whom to talk to when they need information.

One might think that, because editorial writers deal with opinion, they require less of the ability to be objective than do reporters. But the capacity to fully understand an issue or situation may be even more important for editorial writers. In arguing for the need for objectivity, Professor David Manning White of Boston University wrote: "To the editorial writer is given the power to exercise the most unrestrained use of language in the name of rhetoric and persuasion," and for this reason editorial writers must check and double-check that what they write "conforms as closely as possible to objective, examinable truth." Editorial writers have more time than reporters to check for errors. White wrote: "Any failure to examine all sides of an argument because of a partisan bias is unalterably against the spirit of objectivity as it applies to editorial writers." But achieving objectivity and overcoming biases and prejudices that they have grown up with does not come easily for anyone, including editorial writers. White said:

Unlike John Milton, who at the age of 10 decided that his life work would be to write a great epic poem, most newspapermen come into the profession by chance or circumstance. When we are born we certainly have no idea that 20 years later we are going to be newspapermen. So for the next 175,000 hours (from the time the doc gives us life's first slap on the posterior until the day some hardboiled city editor tells us, "You probably won't be worth much to us, but we'll put you on and see how it goes"), we live in a world which pays little attention to seeing things objectively *per se*.[10]

A third qualification needed is good writing. Editorial writers must write succinctly, since the editorial page is usually tighter for space than the news pages. They also need to be able to write in an interesting and convincing manner. Newspaper readers may have to read the news columns if they want to know about news but they don't have to read the editorials, and they won't if editorials are dull and don't say anything.

Fourth, editorial writers need a quality that is sometimes called a sense of fairness or justice, sometimes called a spirit of the reformer, or a commitment to principles, or integrity. The subjects they write about should be approached with a sense of purpose.

A fifth qualification is the desire to express an opinion. Hoke Norris of the *Chicago Sun-Times* saw reporters who became editorial writers as moving "from the sidewalk to the parade, from the press table to the speaker's table." As participants, Norris said, editorial writers "must study, weigh, deliberate, contemplate, meditate, judge, discuss, talk over, think through and generally know all there is to know about any given subject, and . . . must be capable, at times, of completing the entire process in five minutes."[11]

Another desirable quality is the ability to reason cogently. Warren Pierce was referring to one aspect of this ability when he quoted the philosopher Arthur Schopenhauer as saying that geniuses share one characteristic: an ability to proceed from the particular to the general. Pierce thought that editorial writers need that ability, as well as the reverse ability. Editorial writers must be able to go from one specific case of juvenile delinquency to the general causes of such delinquency, and "from one deep-freeze or white convertible Oldsmobile to a proposition of ethical conduct in public office." Equally they should be able to give meaning to reciprocal trade agreements in terms of a clothes-pin factory in their community or of cotton or corn growers in their state.[12]

One view of what an editorial writer's qualities should be is expressed by Irving Dilliard, editorial page editor of the *St. Louis Post-Dispatch,* who compiled an impressive list in an article entitled "The Editor I Wish I Were." His principal points were these: Editorial writers should know their community, state, nation and world and read a great deal. They should be courteous, treating readers as individual human beings. They should be cooperative, working with associates to produce the best possible newspaper. They should be curious, perhaps not the first to learn everything in the community but they at least should know more new things than anyone else. They should have imagination, seeing opportunities for improving the press in content, service and leadership. They should be persons of conscience and courage, with the ability to stand up to interest groups or a superior editor or publisher. They should have judgment, avoiding "the heavy artillery . . . if a spatter of birdshot will suffice." They should know that it is impossible to know too much to do their jobs well. They should be able to criticize others, but also be able to accept criticism. They must take care to avoid activities that might prove embarrassing or detrimental to editorial independence. According to Dilliard, writers should even be "sparing" in friendships because friendships outside their newspapers "may at any time force the hard choice between personal kindness to a friend and devotion to duty as an editor." Editorial writers should have what editor William Allen White called "intelligent discontent," as well as enthusiasm—a zest for life.[13] Dilliard also prescribed a prodigious reading list, a qualification that we will look at in the next chapter.

Another editor, Frederic S. Marquardt of the Phoenix *Arizona Republic,* was so overwhelmed by Dilliard's description of the ideal editor that he asked: "Doesn't the guy ever have any fun?" The need to find out about so many places in the world "would give most newspaper auditors acute melancholia," Marquardt wrote. The reading requirements would make an average person nearsighted at age 30 and blind at 40. "I would need at least 72 hours [a day] to keep up with Dilliard, even if I didn't stop for a short beer now and then." Marquardt was especially critical of the admonition to be sparing in friendships. "Show me an editor who bends an elbow in a neighborhood tavern once in a while, or who occasionally sees if he can fill an inside straight, or who goes to a football game without the slightest intention of improving his mind, and I'll show you an editor who knows more about life than all the Ivory Tower boys," Marquardt said. If editors allow their friendships to cloud their judgment, they'd "better quit the newspaper business and start selling bonds."[14]

Who are these journalists who become editorial writers? Surveys show that they tend to be male and white. They also tend to be college-educated, middle-aged and lean politically toward the Democratic Party.[15] One survey found eight black editorial writers and four Hispanic writers among editorial staffs on 70 papers. "Editorial pages run a close race with the church as being the nation's most segregated enclaves," Professor Sam Adams of the University of Kansas wrote after looking at the results of that survey.[16] The figures prompted the Minority Opportunity Committee of the National Conference of Editorial Writers (NCEW) to conclude that "the status quo in minority representation on the editorial pages of America is not acceptable."[17] It offered no easy answers for solving the problem.

The first woman editorial page editor of a major newspaper may have been Molly Clowes. She joined the editorial page staff of the *Louisville* (Ky.) *Courier-Journal* in 1940. It took her 26 years to become editor. One survey conducted in 1979 found that only 7 percent of editorial writers who responded were women,[18] while another survey the same year found 14 percent were women.[19] In an attempt to gain insights into how women editorial writers have been treated, editors of *The Masthead* asked editorial writers to share their professional experiences in a symposium published in the quarterly. All those who participated expressed confidence that their sex had not kept them from meeting all of the requirements of the job, but several told of difficulties in getting to be an editorial writer and in dealing with the public after they became editorial writers.[20]

Jane Reid of the *Burlington County* (N.J.) *Times* thought that the chief disadvantage of having a woman editorial writer on a staff "is the same one which for many years barred women from radio and television broadcasting—the belief that the audience would not accept a woman's voice as authoritative." If readers think about it at all, chances are they will assume the writer is a man. Once a member of the National Rifle Association came stalking into Reid's office, "with fire in his eye, ready to take a swing at the fellow who wrote that editorial supporting gun controls." But he simmered down when he saw the writer was a woman and meekly asked if she would read some of his literature. Reid said he apparently regarded arguing with a woman as "beneath his dignity." She added: "Frankly, the feeling was mutual."

Elisabet Van Nostrand of the Vancouver (Wash.) *Columbian* wrote in the symposium that a common response when she answered the telephone was: "I don't wanna talk to no secretary. I wanna talk to the EDITOR!" Hysterical readers who sometimes called to complain about an editorial or a "racy column" by Nicholas von Hoffman were slowed down when they found themselves talking to a woman. "When they learn that the person responsible also has children, especially daughters, it tends to subdue them somewhat," she wrote, "although I have upon occasion been asked, 'What kind of mother are you?' " Van Nostrand said the big problem for her was not so much being an editorial writer or editor but convincing editors and publishers that a woman could be a competent editorial writer.

WHERE EDITORIAL WRITERS COME FROM

Because editorial writing requires so many skills and qualities, it is not surprising that editors and publishers despair when they face the task of finding an editorial writer. Any publisher or editor who has found the right person will say without a doubt that such success is one of the most satisfying experiences in the field of newspapering. I know; I have experienced both despair and success.

It is infinitely more difficult to predict the ultimate ability of a would-be editorial writer than it is to decide whether a candidate will make a good reporter. Few guidelines exist for judging whether a former reporter, a college professor, a recent liberal arts graduate or an editorial writer from another newspaper will do the job a publisher or an editor has in mind. For one thing, most people who hire editorial writers, no doubt thinking of some of those qualities mentioned above, are not certain whether editorial writers are born or made. Some editorial writers seem to have it, and some seem not to. Professor James H. Howard of the University of California, Los Angeles, thought that editorial writers probably had innate talent but that "those not blessed with the talent at birth" could be taught to improve their research, sharpen their writing and "present readable results of logical thinking."[21] Donald L. Breed of the *Freeport* (Ill.) *Journal-Standard* said his experience on small newspapers showed that adequate editorial writers were usually found "only by accident."[22] Since they were not likely to have had previous editorial experience, there was no way to predict from their past whether they could do the job.

One of the dilemmas faced by an editor looking for a new writer is whether to look in the newsroom for a person with no editorial page experience or to search outside for a person who has had editorial experience in another community. Most of the editors who were asked in a *Masthead* symposium what they did said they looked first in the newsrooms of their own papers but were not especially optimistic about finding exactly the person they wanted. As John Cline of the *Washington Star* said, although the paper in his time had tried hiring an editorial writer from outside the paper, "our preference, in event of a vacancy, is to bring in someone from the news side." The results were mixed, however; reporters tended to have trouble making the transition from reporting facts to commenting on facts. Furthermore, Cline was interested in editorial writers, not people who were good at rewriting copy.[23]

An employer identified only as "an editor in the West" was discouraged by what happens to good reporters "who can pound out several thousand words of news copy a day" when they sit down in front of the editorial typewriter. "That clear, decent prose becomes stilted, 'literary' or arch. They grasp at the editorial 'we.' Why can't they relax?" One reporter who started on Monday ran out of things to say by Thursday. Another didn't work out because of lack of background. "I don't think he's read a book since he left college," the editor said. Still, he hesitated to go outside the newsroom for an editorial writer for fear of hurting staff morale. "Also, how long would it take to develop in a new editorial writer the valuable traits that a good reporter on our staff has already?" he asked.[24]

One editor who found talent in the newsroom, Theodore Bingham of the *Dayton* (Ohio) *Journal Herald,* said that "at times it seemed easier to find an astronaut who was afraid of heights."[25] Paul McKalip of the *Tucson* (Ariz.) *Daily Citizen* found an editorial writer on that paper's sports staff. George Burt of the *Louisville* (Ky.) *Times* tried to spot potential editorial writers while borrowing reporters from the city staff for vacation duty on the editorial page. Grover C. Hall of the *Montgomery* (Ala.) *Advertiser* was surprised to find himself hiring a young Harvard graduate who had never considered a newspaper career. Hall reported that the writer couldn't spell or punctuate but had read "everything from Melville to Nabokov."[26]

William D. Snider of the *Greensboro* (N.C.) *Daily News* said he found that good editorial writers often come from non-journalistic backgrounds. He cited Ed Yoder, who had come to the *Daily News* after majoring in English and then studying philosophy, politics and economics as a Rhodes Scholar at Oxford. He had been editor of his college paper. Between stints at the *News* he taught college history. From Greensboro Yoder went to Washington, where he became the last editorial page editor of the *Star.* Snider himself had been secretary to two governors before returning to the newspaper world.[27]

The *Detroit News* received 55 replies to its want ad in the *Wall Street Journal*—from journalists, professors, public relations people, management consultants, a bank president and a plant equipment operator at a dam. In the end the *News* hired the only woman applicant; she had a Ph.D., lived in Detroit and had been an assistant professor.

A survey of editorial writers found that 72 out of 86 of them thought a background in reporting essential or desirable for applicants. Most who responded to the survey expected that the new writer would be selected after a search of the newsroom or through talks with other editors. The writers generally anticipated that the person for the job would be between 30 and 45 years old, have a liberal arts degree, be a proficient writer and be prepared to represent the newspaper in a public relations capacity. After examining the results of the survey, Robert Estabrook of the *Washington Post* said, with tongue in cheek no doubt, that the survey group expected the new writer would have "emphasized the study of English, history, political science, economics, natural science, sociology, languages, psychology and philosophy, with perhaps some attention to newspaper editing, law and history." Estabrook placed much of the blame for less-than-adequate applicants on the "haphazard methods of selection" by the newspapers and the tendency to "fob off 'hacks' on the editorial page." Fewer than half the papers reported making any effort to interest young people in editorial writing as a career or conducting any training program of their own for new editorial and news employees. He scolded his fellow editors for doing little to seek out young people with brains and judgment to interest them in editorial writing.[28]

I must acknowledge that, in seeking new editorial writers on the *Columbian,* we did no more planning ahead than the majority of the papers in that survey. My first search represented a classic case of frustration. An ad in *Editor & Publisher* elicited more than 100 applications. Few came close to the type of person we wanted. As we closely examined each of the most promising, we found that, for one reason or another, none of them was quite right for the job. Many were the "hacks" Estabrook mentioned. Many were acquainted with neither editorial writing nor the territory. Almost in desperation, we allowed a *Columbian* reporter, who eagerly wanted the job, to try out for it. Here was the exact opposite of the reporter who has trouble moving from fact to opinion, but fortunately, after a few weeks of overexuberant expression of opinion, she settled down to become a fine, if still flamboyant, editorial writer. In the next search for a writer, we hired a person who had been an editorial writer, in fact the editor, on a small daily newspaper in California. He knew how to write editorials, and it didn't take him long to learn the territory.

My first editorial writing employer hired me when I knew very little about editorial writing and even less about Iowa. But my return to the Vancouver paper represented an almost ideal set of circumstances. I had become acquainted in that community during three years of news reporting. I had had five years of editorial writing experience under a respected editorial page editor and excellent teacher. To make my situation even sweeter, I was brought back to Vancouver six months before the retiring editorial page editor was due to leave the paper. I had six months to get acquainted again in the community and write occasional editorials as I felt moved to do so. I recommend this combination of experiences but recognize that one's experiences do not often come together in this fashion.

CONCLUSION AND A WARNING

My comments and results of the surveys of editorial writers may suggest that editorial writers think highly of themselves. They think that they practice the prince of professions (not many princesses yet), and many feel pretty princely themselves. The jobs they hold require all those "fantastic" qualities discussed above. Thus if they hold those jobs, editorial writers reason, they must be fantastic themselves.

Some of this self-esteem is merited. Some of the best informed, most talented, incisive, conscientious people I know are editorial writers. In my experience, nothing can be more stimulating than bringing editorial writers together, at an editorial page staff meeting or a meeting of writers from several papers. But as praiseworthy as these wordsmiths generally are, perhaps a warning about too much self-congratulation is in order as a conclusion to this chapter.

Editorial writers may be well-educated, draw good salaries and have their own offices, but they are still newspaper people. Newspaper people tend to be held in high esteem these days—higher than half a century ago certainly. But much of this esteem comes from the jobs they hold, not from their own individual qualities. I learned that lesson when I went into college teaching. When I was an editorial writer, people wanted to know what I thought. Except possibly for readers of this book, who wants to know what a professor thinks? And even these readers are likely to be more interested in what the former editor, not the professor, has to say.

Press critic Ben Bagdikian has warned that, with newspapers becoming "a respectable institution and editorial writers the most respected of all," newspaper people shouldn't forget where their predecessors came from. "Newspapers were born and raised in the bloody arena, kicking and gouging their newspaper competitors in the ring while the crowd screeched and now all of a sudden all of the fighters were carried out on stretchers and there was the audience in their Sunday best, hands folded primly, waiting for a lecture on the Manly Art." Editorial writers should avoid the temptation to think of themselves as totally respectable.[29]

Among middle-aged and older members of NCEW, perhaps the best remembered call for humility came from Jonathan W. Daniels, editor of the *Raleigh* (N.C.) *News and Observer,* who delivered an address entitled "The Docility of the Dignified Press" to a convention of the NCEW in 1965. He spoke at an evening banquet at an exclusive country club on the outskirts of Milwaukee, Wis. Daniels told the writers that the editors and publishers who gathered for meetings of the Associated Press and the American Newspaper Publishers Association at the Waldorf-Astoria Hotel each spring were "indistinguishable from bankers." He quickly added: "You look pretty impressive yourselves." He reminded them that they are courted by senators, cabinet members and generals. "You really cannot blame the press for wanting a little dignity," he said. "Its members, as their social positions improved, naturally did not want to seem to be like Horace Greeley, who before he founded the famous *Tribune* was fired from one paper because its owner wanted 'only decent looking men in the office.' " Why shouldn't members of the press like their "pants pressed—sometimes striped?" He acknowledged that, "if [the press] didn't appear full-armored from the brow of Jove, it doesn't twist genealogy more than some other people do in suggesting that it is descended from the Bill of Rights." But he reminded his listeners that there were other ancestors. "There was the guitar player on the back of the patent medicine salesman's wagon. Also there was the ink-stained impertinent fellow who began long ago to put embarrassing reports on paper." He said it was then more fashionable to look like Walter Lippmann, then a distinguished columnist, than Heywood Broun, a disheveled-looking columnist of the 1920s and 1930s who had rankled publishers by trying to organize labor unions in their newsrooms.

Perhaps it was at this point in Daniels's speech that one of the editorial writers suddenly rose from his table, lurched drunkenly toward the right side of the room, uttered a profane epithet at Daniels and staggered out, never to be seen at an NCEW meeting again. Daniels bade him farewell and continued with his speech. "There is, of course, something disreputable about any business devoted to prying into matters," he said. "It is a nosey business. And it should remain so. Anybody who would never wish to hurt anybody's feelings, who never wishes to make anybody mad, should stay out of the newspaper business. The editor who deserves the respect of his community can be no respecter of persons in his community. He must be nosey and often a public scold."[30]

So when editors and publishers want to hire a new editorial writer, all they have to do is find a man or a woman who is a writer, a thinker, a scholar, an objective viewer, a critic, a scold and a person with humility. Is it any wonder that good editorial writers are hard to find—or any wonder that, once found, they think pretty highly of themselves?

QUESTIONS AND EXERCISES

1. What are the reasons for trying to find a new editorial writer in an editor's own newsroom?

2. What are the reasons for looking elsewhere?

3. How do you account for the slowness in opening editorial page positions to women and racial minorities?

4. Are there women editorial writers or members of racial minorities on editorial pages in your area? How long have they been editorial writers? What education and experience did they have when they became editorial writers?

5. What do you regard as the most important qualities of an editorial writer?

6. What aspect of editorial writing would appeal to you most? What would appeal to you least? Why?

7. If you wanted to land an editorial writing position on a major newspaper within 10 years, what route would you attempt to follow?

8. On what newspapers with which you are acquainted could you feel philosophically comfortable writing editorials?

WORDSMITH

—Tim Menees
Universal Press

Preparation of an Editorial Writer

It is hard to imagine any discipline that would not benefit a journalist.
—*A response to a questionnaire concerning college curricula*[1]

Everybody has a sort of reading anxiety neurosis.
—*Robert B. Frazier*
Eugene *(Ore.)* Register-Guard[2]

Preparing oneself to be an editorial writer is like preparing oneself for life. Everything that the potential editorial writer thinks, learns or experiences is likely to become pertinent someday in the writing of some editorial. The same is true of journalists who are already editorial writers. Every word they read can provide an idea or information for an editorial. Compulsive readers who find themselves reading the sides of the breakfast cereal box may write an editorial that day, or another day, about the dangers of the sugar content in children's breakfast foods. A casual conversation with a household domestic may provide an unexpected insight into problems involving social security or the minimum wage. More than any other job in journalism, perhaps more than any other job in the world, editorial writing encompasses universal concerns.

In this chapter a discussion of the unending education necessary for editorial writing is limited to five areas: undergraduate education, continuing education, firsthand experiences, reading and culture. A sixth area, professional experience, was discussed in the previous chapter.

UNDERGRADUATE EDUCATION

Bring an editor and an educator—or even two editors or two educators—together and you will have a debate on how best to prepare students for careers in journalism.

Journalism schools are a rather recent invention, and many editors before World War II saw little need for them. They hadn't gone to journalism school—and perhaps not even to college. Reporting and editing, they knew from experience, could be learned on the job. But the world was becoming more complex, and readers were becoming more knowledgeable and sophisticated. To the GI Bill, which provided educational and other benefits for World War II veterans, must go much of the credit for sending more Americans than ever before to college. Students poured into journalism and every other field of study. Before many postwar classes had graduated, the competition for jobs made a college degree a necessary ticket for many positions.

Skills vs. Liberal Arts

With the legitimacy of journalism programs gradually becoming accepted, the debate turned to skills courses versus liberal arts. How many courses in journalism were necessary to prepare students to write a news story? How many courses in "academic" subjects were necessary to prepare students to know what they were writing about? Out of that debate came general acceptance of the 75/25 ratio set by the American Council on Education for Journalism, the national accrediting agency in journalism. In other words, 75 percent of graduation credits should be in liberal arts and related areas and not more than 25 percent in journalism.

Green Eyeshades vs. Chi-Squares

Next came arguments over which journalism courses should be offered and required. The protagonists in these arguments were sometimes referred to as the "green eyeshades" and the "chi-squares."

"Green eyeshades" was a reference to the transparent green bills that copy editors used to wear to cut the glare of overhead lights. "Chi-square" is a mathematical procedure used in statistics to measure differences in sets of numbers. The green eyeshades feared that journalism schools were shifting from old-fashioned skills to theory and research. They wanted the schools to concentrate on courses in reporting, news writing, feature writing, copy editing and editorial writing. They wanted attention paid to spelling, grammar, punctuation and style. The chi-squares were interested in creating courses in communications theory, communications research, surveys of mass communications, and mass media and society. One of their goals was to make journalism and communications academically respectable among their research- and theory-oriented colleagues in other university departments.

In 1964 John Tebbel, writing in *Saturday Review,* noted that the journalism schools had gained professional standing but that there seemed to be "some danger" of the educators' "wandering away into an unprofessional jungle where the shadow [had] grown larger than the substance."[3] Journalism educators, he said, were becoming preoccupied with research, the techniques of sociology and statistics. One result was "the Ph.D. in Journalism, a degree that once would have been laughed out of court but now has achieved a respectability in the new field it represents, communications research, a specialty that may have its own value but is far removed from journalism," Tebbel wrote. The new studies had a lot of numbers and fancy words, but they didn't have much to do with putting out a newspaper.

Editors didn't care whether new reporters knew about the formula for testing for chi-square or about the "two-step information model," which theorized that information was passed to the public through intervening opinion leaders. But they did care about hiring employees who could spell and write decent news leads. Some educators were also concerned about the trend toward theory and research. Nathaniel Blumberg, dean of the School of Journalism at the University of Montana, complained that, in concentrating on research, "high-powered, high-salaried" professors were neglecting the teaching of undergraduates, leaving that task to teaching and research assistants.[4]

But the trend was to continue toward research. Supporters of the trend argued that too many schools of journalism had become vocational trade schools, concerned with turning out reporters and copy editors but not truly educating students. Also at work was an effort by journalism professors to prove to colleagues in the traditional academic disciplines that they should no longer be treated with what Professor Norval Neil Luxon of the University of North Carolina described as "amused condescension." Luxon agreed that a good university demands research from all of its departments and that research "immediately strengthens teaching" and can play "an important role in the search for truth." He argued further that research was benefiting the communications business and that industry was hiring consultants from among those researchers.[5] To name only a few areas under study, this research has involved readership preferences, readership profiles, analysis of readability of news and editorial writing, influence of editorials, layout design and advertising impact.

In 1978 a survey by the National Conference of Editorial Writers found that, in the decade and a half since a previous survey, non-skills courses had increased at most journalism schools while skills courses had decreased. Limited by the 25 percent regulation of the accrediting agency, educators were forced to drop the requirement for a skills course if they wanted to add a requirement for a course in theory or research. One of the courses that NCEW found was being de-emphasized was editorial writing.[6] Since then, both NCEW and the Association for Education in Journalism and Mass Communication (the organization of journalism professors) have passed resolutions urging journalism schools to restore editorial writing to their curricula.

Non-Professional Courses

The non-professional education of would-be journalists has also been criticized. Referring to job applicants, one publisher complained that "we're getting too many hopefuls who lack a background in economics, literature, philosophy, sociology and the natural sciences," and that "they know little of government." Otis Chandler, publisher of the *Los Angeles Times,* deplored the inadequate exposure given journalism students in ecology, energy, land-use planning and economics, as well as the physical sciences, birth control and bureaucracies.[7]

In surveying colleges in the NCEW study, LeRoy E. Smith and Curtis MacDougall found that, because most journalism students must meet requirements for both journalism and a liberal arts degree, they were left with few opportunities for taking courses in other areas. Smith and MacDougall asked NCEW members to recommend how students should use the opportunities they do have to expand their knowledge beyond the required courses. The poll showed courses preferred in the following order: U.S. history, composition, state and local government, introduction to sociology, principles of economics, critical writing, constitutional law, comparative economic systems, geography, history of political thought, political parties, history of modern Europe, economic history of the United States, public financing, urban and regional planning, and philosophy. One respondent could not conceive of any discipline that would not benefit a journalist.[8]

Some educators have concluded that, because of the need to know about so many things, the journalism program should be a five-year one. Such a program might lead to a master's degree.[9] Other educators think that four years is enough to produce a working newspaper person, that he or she can grow on the job and later pick up additional education on the side or return for a master's degree, perhaps in another discipline.[10]

Because reporting and commenting on the news are becoming more specialized as the world becomes more complex, the student who comes to a newspaper with training in a particular field—economics, the arts, the health sciences or the criminal justice system, for example—can prove to be a valuable asset to a news or editorial staff, especially when a newspaper seeks to fill a beat or an editorial writing position that requires knowledge in that field.

Writing Skills

Almost every meeting of editors and educators evolves into a debate over whether journalism schools are doing what they should be doing to teach the basics of language and writing. The editors say that they can put their trust only in a journalism program that turns out students who come to their papers with the basic skills. The educators argue that they are charged with teaching a lot of other things, not just spelling and grammar, and that those skills should have been learned in elementary and secondary school.

Any student who enters a journalism program with problems in spelling, grammar and punctuation is certain to have problems in the program. Any graduate who comes to a city news room with these problems unresolved will have problems in a career in journalism. Having been both an educator and an editor, I can attest to both of these statements.

Internships

One method of impressing students with the need to learn basics—and to teach them at the same time—is through an internship on a newspaper or with another news operation. If interns have at least a couple of news writing and reporting courses, within the course of a three-month internship they can acquire the ability to substitute on several of the regular beats, handle most stories that walk into the newsroom and write a simple feature story. The internship experience helps when applying for a job after graduation. The prospective employer knows that the applicant has had some practical experience and that the internship supervisor can provide an evaluation of the applicant's work. Often a successful internship can lead to a job on the paper on which the student worked as an intern.

Another valuable experience is reporting and editing on a campus newspaper, especially if the work is supervised and criticized by faculty advisers or knowledgeable senior staff members. Even work on a mediocre paper can give the student a feeling for deadlines, accuracy and space limitations.

CONTINUING EDUCATION

Editorial writers, and would-be editorial writers, should never stop trying to expand their educations. The world, in nearly every field, is changing rapidly; science, mathematics, agriculture, medicine, politics, geography, education—all have vastly changed from the days that many of today's editorial writers were in college.

Year-Long Studies

The most formalized way for writers to recharge themselves intellectually and psychologically is through educational programs. The most extensive are those in which journalists remove themselves to a college campus for a semester or a year and study one specific field. An editorial writer for the *Boston Globe,* Anson H. Smith Jr., was given a year's leave of absence to study law at Harvard Law School. "I cannot urge too strongly the desirability, for editorial writers particularly and working journalists generally, of a good dose of formal legal education," Smith said. "It sharpens the mind, provides valuable sources of information and advice on legal issues in the news, and generally enhances one's understanding of the legal process."[11]

A more likely possibility for a newspaper person is a fully funded program such as a Nieman Fellowship at Harvard or a Professional Journalism Fellowship, which until recently was funded by the National Endowment for the Humanities. After completing such a fellowship at Stanford University, Sig Gissler of the *Milwaukee* (Wis.) *Journal* said the experience gave him the chance to think about "the big, tough questions that editorial writers seldom have time to dig into deeply." He added: "Think how rewarding it would be to spend nine months at a great university contemplating these concerns—without deadlines, spats with the boss, phone calls from ired readers; without mandatory term papers or exams; without significant restraints on your freedom to explore and reflect."[12] Most journalism schools can provide current information about programs that are available to working newspaper people.

Shorter Courses

Among programs of a briefer nature, the best known is probably at the American Press Institute (API) in Reston, Va. For more than 30 years API has provided seminars, most of them two weeks long, in almost all phases of newspapering, including sessions on editorial writing and editorial pages. The seminars are financed through tuition fees. Participants meet in small groups to criticize and praise each other's editorials and editorial pages and in larger groups to discuss current issues with experts in journalism and other fields.

From time to time various universities and colleges offer short courses in specific areas of newspapering or possibly in state government or business. Editorial writers who feel the need for more education can enroll in one or more courses in a nearby college. Evening courses in such areas as economics or public administration can give editorial writers knowledge that might improve their editorials.

Visiting Professorships

One way to learn is to teach. Possibilities exist at some universities for editors and writers to return to the campus as visiting editors or visiting professors. The William Allen White School of Journalism at the University of Kansas, for example, has brought a series of editors to campus. The University of Montana, which from time to time has money for a professional visitor, invited me to teach during the fall quarter of 1976 while I was an editor. The experience was so satisfying that, when a few months later I had a chance to teach an entire year at Washington State University, I accepted the offer.[13] Teaching forces you to think about what you have been doing as a matter of unreflective habit.

FIRSTHAND EXPERIENCES

The editorial writer who hopes to address a changing world must get out of the office. "There is no real substitute in journalism for the face-to-face confrontation," Terrence W. Honey of the *London* (Ontario) *Free Press* wrote in an article entitled "Our Ivory Tower Syndrome Is Dead."[14] Unfortunately for some editorial writers it is not dead.

Local Level

Busy editorial writers are often tempted to write editorials on local topics on the basis of what has appeared in the news columns, interpreted in the light of past editorial policy, rather than attend meetings of city councils and local citizen bodies that can become an every-evening job. For editorial writers, who are not there to report the action, most of the time spent at these gatherings may seem boring and unproductive. So writers tend to put off going to local meetings until a hot issue comes along. Attending only at crucial times is better than not attending at all. But most of the work of local government bodies is done in regular, humdrum meetings in the absence of the eyes of the public. Editorial writers who want to know how a council or council member functions under normal circumstances should attend at least some of these dull assemblages. In addition to gaining knowledge, editorial writers can boost their credibility with members of local organizations and with anyone else who happens to be at these meetings.

More informative than public meetings are private ones, perhaps over lunch, with the key persons involved. If there are two or more points of view on a volatile issue such as a teachers' strike, editorial writers, or the editorial board, might find it advantageous to meet separately with members of the opposing sides. On other occasions inviting representatives from all sides to discuss an issue might prove to be an effective way of gaining insight.

To make certain that such conferences are not limited to times of crisis—and that lethargy does not win over good intentions—some editorial boards schedule a weekly meeting to which they invite one or more sources on a topic of current interest. Writers should meet, from time to time, with labor officials (as well as rank-and-file members), Chamber of Commerce leaders, other business groups and individuals, environmental groups, utility officials, energy interest groups, consumer groups, education groups (professional and citizen), religious leaders, sports people, transportation people and even people from rival media. And, of course, writers should not forget local judges and bar association officials.

State Level

Face-to-face confrontation can be more difficult at the state level. Unless a newspaper is located in a state capital, legislative sessions and committee hearings are difficult and extremely time-consuming to attend. Most provide little concrete information for editorials, since the legislative process is spread over extended periods of time. But much of what was said about local meetings applies here too. Writers need to get a feel for the process at its usual slow pace to see how it works and how its practitioners function. Editorial writers need to show their faces and make their presence known, at least among their local legislators. Credibility with the legislators, as well as knowledge, is the goal.

It was easier to follow legislatures when they met for short sessions every two years. Now critical moments in the process are spread out, and opportunities for strategically directed editorials become more difficult to spot. Some of the difficulty can be alleviated if a newspaper has skilled reporters assigned to the legislature who can keep editorial writers informed about the timing of bills as well as track down information for editorials.

Maintaining contact with the executive branch of state government is even more difficult from a distance. Decisions can come at any time and often without public notice. Probably the best approach to establishing contacts in the executive branch is through people at the assistant level—governors' aides, assistant attorneys general, the elections supervisor in the secretary of state's office, a key assistant in the state planning office, a high-level career employee of the tax commission. These second-level people are more likely to be expertly informed than their bosses and, even more important, are usually easier to get on the telephone when you need them.

Another way to keep abreast of state affairs is to watch for statewide conferences of such groups as county commissioners and city officials and conferences on specific issues, such as taxation, education and legislative or judicial reform.

National Level

For national issues, most editorial writers must rely heavily on the news services and newspapers such as the *New York Times* and the *Washington Post* or *Congressional Quarterly*. These and other sources will be discussed later in this chapter. Editorial writers with Washington bureaus to call on can get help from their bureaus. Close contacts with the offices of the state's two senators and that of the local representative may also be useful. Most of these officials will have offices in the district or the state, but sources there are likely to prove beneficial primarily on matters of local interest or subjects relating to the committees on which the senator or representative serves.

A visit to Washington, D.C., may seem even less productive for an editorial writer than a trip to the state capital. But through periodic visits to the capital, a writer can begin to cultivate sources in the federal government, especially in departments that deal with issues pertinent to the writer's own locale or region.

From time to time the Department of State invites editors and editorial writers to Washington for briefings on world affairs. I found the first one I attended fascinating because of the opportunity to see the famous personages. But by the second briefing I began to realize that the presentations offered little more than I could have obtained by reading any number of publications readily available to the editorial writer.

Attendance at national political conventions can benefit an editorial writer, although not as much as it did in the days before television. The principal benefit is probably in getting some of the flavor of the proceedings and watching the home state delegation.

International Level

The American Association for the United Nations sometimes invites editorial people to meetings and briefings at the United Nations headquarters in New York City. Again, the principal value is in getting a feel for the personalities and the atmosphere. Probably more productive are visits to foreign countries—that is, if the writer has made substantial advance preparation; a quick tourist- or host-conducted visit may distort rather than provide insight into affairs abroad. In recent years NCEW has sponsored and organized a series of overseas tours for members that provide participants with background information about and interpretation of what they are seeing. Of course, these trips are expensive; the cost may be prohibitive for small papers.

One of the most productive tours I have taken was sponsored by the *Wenatchee* (Wash.) *World*. I traveled with a plane load of natural resource and newspaper people on a barnstorming tour of western Canada and Alaska. Most of the stops were short, but during each stop participants received background information on the geography, natural resources, political situation and personalities. On that trip, we heard the first rumors of the soon-to-be-revealed oil find in Prudhoe Bay. My newspaper paid the way.

Two years later, I paid my own way and devoted a family vacation to driving up the Alaska Highway. While mainly for personal satisfaction, the trip did provide further insights into the far north that proved of benefit to me as an editorial writer. For one thing, I came away convinced that the environmental doubts that had been holding up construction of the Alaska pipeline would not stop the pipeline. Seeing stack after stack of pipes at several locations along the proposed route told me more than anything else I had seen in the press or heard from politicians about chances for the pipeline.

Professional Level

Associating with journalists with similar interests can help rejuvenate editorial writers' enthusiasm for their work and challenge them with ideas for doing a better job on the paper. One of the main purposes of NCEW is to improve the quality of editorial pages by bringing editorial writers together for sessions of mutual enlightenment and criticism. A most valuable and consistent feature of NCEW's annual meeting has been the day-long critique session in which participants, having studied the editorial pages before arriving, analyze, praise and criticize one another's pages. Held at some time in nearly every section of the country, the NCEW meetings have given members a firsthand (though brief) look at other communities. Also, participants have heard many interesting speakers: President Harry Truman and President Lyndon Johnson, Barry Goldwater before he ran for president, George Romney while he was running in the primaries, pollster George Gallup, press critic Ben Bagdikian, editor Jonathan Daniels and CBS president Frank Stanton, as well as expert speakers and panelists who have delved into automation, the space program, the automobile industry, the South, the Pacific Rim and the arts. For editorial writers who don't mind having their blood let twice a year or for those who find it hard to make an annual national conference, regional conferences are held in several sections of the country.

EDITORIAL SHELF

Robert B. Frazier of the *Eugene* (Ore.) *Register-Guard* surveyed 100 editorial writers in 1962 to determine their reading habits.[15] In the following year he wrote an article for *The Masthead* entitled "The Editorial Elbow," in which he offered a "more-or-less compleat [sic] listing of reference works useful, day by day, to the editor, reporter and copyreader."[16] From the two studies Frazier concluded that writers consistently thought they read too little, that probably no other group in the country "read more or more catholically" and that writers on smaller papers, with smaller editorial page staffs, followed a more varied reading diet than writers on larger staffs.

Non-fiction was more popular than fiction. Only about 40 percent said that fiction accounted for a quarter or more of their reading. Half said they read essays, poetry or plays. About 10 percent read often in a foreign language. Some bought only two or three books a year, but one bought 200. Forty percent were regular patrons of libraries.

A quarter of them said they read in bed. Two got up and read in the middle of the night. Three read early in the morning. Four admitted to being bathroom readers. One had read Gibbon and one Spinoza. Shakespeare appeared on several lists.

Columnist James J. Kilpatrick wrote that editorial writers don't begin to read enough, and it shows up with painful transparency in the superficiality, the shallowness, the gracelessness, of our editorial writing."[17] He advised writers to read the Bible and Shakespeare and to read heavily "in the older classics" —Thucydides, Plutarch, Homer, Aeschylus, Disraeli, Gibbon, De Quincey, Spinoza, Voltaire—and then the more recent works of Thorstein Veblen, William James, John Dewey, Alfred North Whitehead and Peter Finley Dunne. To this assignment, Kilpatrick added a list of poets, from Pope to Edna St. Vincent Millay, and fiction writers, from Dickens to O. Henry. Irving Dilliard of the *St. Louis Post-Dispatch* said an editorial writer should be "familiar with the monumental publishing projects of his time in biography, in history, in the social sciences, regional life, in the messages and papers of the great Americans—Franklin, Adams, Jefferson, Lincoln."[18]

Magazines and Newspapers

In moments when they are not reading the classics, where should editorial writers turn for help in writing their daily assignments? Most editorial writers today probably subscribe to *Time, Newsweek* or *U.S. News & World Report.* These magazines provide a more comprehensive account of some news than daily news stories and, just as important, provide essays and reports on such areas as religion, science and the arts, which are not covered well in most newspapers. Back sections of these magazines often provide ideas for nonpolitical editorials. Information on current events that appears in the review-opinion section and the magazine section of the *New York Times* may also prove helpful.

Writers should seek out varying points of view on public issues, if only to know what the opposition is saying. One way is to subscribe to, say, the *New Republic* or the *Nation* for the liberal side and the *National Review* for the conservative. *Business Week* publishes not only easy-to-understand articles on business and economics but some fine editorials that discuss issues beyond a narrow business orientation. The monthly in-depth interviews in *Playboy* are full of information on pertinent topics and provide an excellent example of the technique of interviewing. *Foreign Affairs* offers writing by recognized experts in international matters. The *Economist* and the weekly edition of the *Guardian* offer British points of view. Other magazines worth considering are *Harper's, Atlantic,* the *New Yorker, Scientific American, Omni, Science, Rolling Stone, Mother Jones, Consumer Reports* and *Architectural Digest.*

In his 1962 survey Frazier was surprised to see how many read women's magazines, including *McCall's, Ladies' Home Journal, Better Homes and Gardens* and *House Beautiful.* This was before the days of *Ms.* and the transformation of *Cosmopolitan.* One writer said that half or more of all readers are women, so why shouldn't editorial writers know what women wanted to read?

Editorial writers should be devourers of newspapers. They should read every newspaper in their community, even those that circulate among a small portion of the population, and their own paper meticulously. They should read the local minority press, if there is one, and the *New York Times,* the *Christian Science Monitor* or the *Washington Post* daily. Another important newspaper, the *Wall Street Journal,* offers not only business news and well-written editorials but one or two in-depth front-page articles every day on subjects that often are worthy of editorial comment.

Writers should also subscribe to the major state or regional paper in their area. From time to time they should look at papers from other regions, among them the *Los Angeles Times,* the *Boston Globe,* the *St. Petersburg Times,* the *Chicago Tribune,* the *St. Louis Post-Dispatch* and the *Louisville Courier-Journal.*

Without subscribing to them, an editorial writer can get a glimpse of other editorial pages through exchanges sponsored by NCEW. Many of the editorials reprinted in this book were obtained through the NCEW exchange.

Periodic Research Materials

Available on a weekly or more frequent basis are the following periodicals:

Facts on File, a weekly service that boils down the essential elements of the news into a ready-reference form. It is a good source of elusive facts. Facts on File, 119 West 57th St., New York, N.Y. 10019.

Congressional Quarterly and *Editorial Research Reports.* It is possible to subscribe to either or, at a reduced rate, both.

Congressional Quarterly offers background material that can be used as bylined articles for editorial or op-ed pages. Each week, newspapers receive a digest of congressional activity—voting records, content of major bills—which can be bound in temporary covers. In or around February a hard cover book is published to replace the loose-leaf material. *Editorial Research Reports* comes in two principal parts. The daily service reads like an editorial, and some editors, not to their credit, print it as though it were a locally written editorial. Included with the daily service is a reminder service of possible topics for editorials. In-depth reports are published four times a month. The daily material and the reports are reprinted in a well-indexed volume semi-annually. 1414 22nd St., N.W., Washington, D.C. 20037.

Committee on Economic Development publications. This committee provides a wide-ranging series of authoritative and detailed reports on economic matters—labor, foreign trade, monetary policy, agriculture. CED publications can be obtained at little or no cost from 711 Fifth Ave., New York, N.Y. 10022.

Congressional Record, which can be obtained through your senator or representative in Congress. This publication provides a day-to-day account of what happens in Congress (and some things that don't happen but that legislators wish had happened). The *Record* also contains a large amount of reprinted material, including editorials. The daily volumes present a storage problem and far too much material for most editorial writers. One way to get at least a glimpse into the *Record* is to glance through the index that arrives every 10 days or do. It does not take long to look up state and local legislators to see what they have said or inserted into the *Record*. Current, and especially regional, topics can also be checked quickly, as can the names of the editorial writers' newspapers and the cities in which the editorials are published. It is nice to know when you have been reprinted in the *Record*.

Permanent Reference Materials

Every editorial office needs a supply of reference materials, including an encyclopedia of fairly recent date; *Webster's Third International Dictionary*—or the Second if the writers are purists; a quality atlas; *Who's Who in America;* probably *Who Was Who;* a regional *Who's Who;* a geographical dictionary; a medical dictionary; probably a legal dictionary; a thesaurus; foreign language dictionaries; a music dictionary or encyclopedia; the *Congressional Directory;* one or more annual almanacs; the annual *Statistical Abstracts of the United States;* a biographical dictionary; a book of quotations; the Bible; perhaps the works of Shakespeare; the *U.S. Official Postal Guide* (plus a book of ZIP codes); city directories going back as many years as possible; and telephone books from assorted cities.

A convenient and inexpensive guide to reference materials of all kinds, in all types of areas, is *The Basic Guide to Research Papers,* edited by Robert O'Brien and Joanne Soderman (New York: New American Library, 1975, paperbound). Another is *The New York Times Guide to Reference Materials* by Mona McCormack (New York: Popular Library, 1971, paperbound).

Books on Language Usage

Here are a few books on language use that are high on the lists of editorial writers:

The Elements of Style. Third Edition. William L. Strunk Jr. and E. B. White (New York: Macmillan, 1979, paperbound).

Modern English Usage. H. W. Fowler. Rev. by E. Gowers. (Oxford: Oxford University Press, 1965).

A Dictionary of Contemporary American Usage. Bergen Evans and Cornelia Evans. (New York: Random House, 1967).

Modern American Usage. Reissue, Jacques Barzun, ed. (New York: Warner, 1977, paperbound).

Writer's Guide and Index to English. Sixth edition. Wilma R. and David R. Ebbitt. (Chicago: Scott, Foresman and Co., 1978).

Watch Your Language. Theodore M. Bernstein. (New York: Atheneum, 1976, paperbound).

CULTURE

Editorial writers should know something about and be comfortable at a symphony concert, whether the orchestra is playing Beethoven or some composer whose work features only drums, cymbals and whistles. Writers should be somewhat knowledgeable about art and be comfortable at an exhibit of Monet or some local artist. They should know something about different religions and the divisions among religions even though they may not be comfortable at services that are much different from their own, if they attend them.

Editorial writers may scoff at television as trivial and entertainment-oriented. But nearly every family has at least one television set, and one show may be watched by as many as 60 million Americans. If editorial writers want to know what their fellow citizens do and think about in their leisure hours, they had best watch the tube enough to know what's on. They should watch the three network news broadcasts and local broadcasts enough to know the types of news their readers are getting. They will never know when television is presenting quality programs unless they read *TV Guide* or the daily TV listings. Columns by television critics are also worth following.

Much of radio is an intellectual wasteland. News is sketchy, except for all-news stations. But writers should know the types of songs the younger generation is listening to. They may never write an editorial about any of the top-40 tunes, but they almost certainly will write about the current generation of radio addicts. Public radio and public television offer more stimulation, with more extensive news coverage and programs on topics worthy of editorial comment. One worthwhile program on public radio is "All Things Considered," an hour and a half of news, comment and reports on a variety of topics, aired in the early evening.

Writers also need to keep abreast of the movies—not necessarily seeing every major show but making certain they are aware of what is being seen by their readers. And the newspaper comics should be followed. While some comics are pure escape, others provide insights into human nature or into what is troubling the younger, or older, or middle generation. Some are technical works of art. Some even carry political messages that are as forthright as any editorial on an editorial page.

CONCLUSION

Perhaps more than anything else, editorial writers must come to editorial writing equipped with curiosity and a good memory. They must want to find out about everything that comes within touch or sight or hearing. Editorial writers who hope to address the human condition must know about that condition in all its aspects. The specific list of books or newspapers or television programs that writers tackle is not as important as the open, searching attitude good writers bring to whatever they approach. If they are restless, energetic and curious, enough material worth examining will come to their attention to keep them on a productive search for truth that will last a lifetime.

If what writers find in their quest goes "in one ear and out the other," the time they have spent will have been wasted. Writers must assimilate and remember—or at least remember where they can find what they want. Shakespeare and the Bible may be worth reading and rereading, and so may a few other books. But demands on the time of editorial writers are too great, and life is too short, to have to spend time searching for information and ideas that they should have tucked away in their heads or for materials that they should have at their editorial elbows.

QUESTIONS AND EXERCISES

1. What do you regard as the ideal undergraduate preparation for a potential editorial writer?

2. In your view, what is the proper role in journalism education for the "green eyeshades"? For the "chi-squares"?

3. The American Council on Education for Journalism, the national accrediting agency for journalism schools, is reluctant to allow a school to give more than a minimum number of credit hours for internships because the council considers that most of the journalism credit hours should be earned under close supervision of faculty members. Do you think that this limitation is reasonable? Why?

4. Among the periodicals you are acquainted with, which do you think would prove most beneficial to an editorial writer? In what ways?

—Herman Auch
Rochester (N.Y.) *Times-Union* for *The Masthead*

Who Is This Victorian "We"?

CHAPTER

5

Who would not be an editor? To write
The magic we *of such enormous might;*
To be so great beyond the common span
It takes the plural to express the man.
—J. G. Saxe in The Press *(1855)*[1]

When the *New York Tribune* published an editorial in the mid-1800s, readers knew who wrote it, or thought they did. As we noted in Chapter 1, subscribers read the *Tribune* to find out what Horace Greeley had to say, and, if someone else on his staff wrote it—as in the case of "On to Richmond!"—everyone assumed that it expressed Greeley's point of view. When the days of the great editors began to pass, following the Civil War, it became less clear who was writing the editorials and for whom the editorials spoke. As the era of corporate newspapers emerged, editorial writers retreated anonymously into their ivory towers and took to writing what a publisher or an editorial board asked them to write. When Greeley had said "we," he meant "I." When these writers used "we," they may have meant the collegial views of the writing staff, the views of a publisher who might be equally anonymous or perhaps the views of some mystical entity called "the newspaper."

A good deal of confusion exists among readers, and even among newspaper people, over the identity or identities behind the editorial "we." That confusion is reflected in a humorous piece that *The Masthead* reprinted from *Quill* magazine. It was written by Fred C. Hobson Jr. of the University of North Carolina. Here is a portion of it:

It was not intended this way, but when I started to write we got so pronounly—er, profounly—confused we changed my mind.

Besides, when we sat down at my typewriter, I first-personally felt singular.

Hopefully now, what I say, you see—in an editorial, why am I we? Enough poetics. Now for how I—er, we—got confused.

We had an interview the other day. It went fine until we wondered if the person I was interviewing were plural too. If so, then I was we and he was they. But if I am we and he is they, then how the hell is *he*?

And should was be were, if I be we? Or is be are, if she be they? . . .

After all this, I've decided to stick to the editorial I. You should too. After all, there is an old adage . . . we Southerners espe-

cially like. . . .
You can't legislate plurality.[2]

The purpose of this chapter is to discuss who are the speakers of editorials on American newspapers today and to examine competing arguments over for whom editorials ought to speak.

THE CASE FOR THE UNSIGNED EDITORIAL

Surveys that show that a large majority of editorials are published anonymously suggest that the owners and publishers of most newspapers want their editorials to speak for someone or something other than an individual writer. A survey in 1975 found that more than 70 percent of 178 editors who were questioned said they never signed editorials. Sixteen percent said they signed them occasionally; 14 percent said they signed regularly. More signatures appeared in smaller papers than in larger papers.[3]

The first reason usually advanced for unsigned editorials is that, even if written by one person, they generally represent something more than an individual's personal opinion. Often they directly reflect policy set by the paper's owner or the publisher. Supporting this line of reasoning, Robert U. Brown, editor and publisher of *Editor & Publisher,* asked: ". . . whose name should be put on the editorial when the owner-publisher—whose prerogative cannot be questioned—says 'tomorrow we will endorse such-and-such candidate and I want a strong editorial endorsing him'?"[4] An editorial writer may write all of the words of an editorial, but the editorial in this instance would speak for the publisher. Supporting the role of the publisher, Floyd Bernard of the *Port Huron* (Mich.) *Times Herald* wrote that no editorial writer, on the basis of his or her own convictions, "has a right to demand a share of ownership's private forum."[5] We will see later in this chapter that a growing number of editorial writers today disagree.

I have seen no recent studies that indicate how prevalent the practice is of having editorial policy set strictly by a publisher. A publisher may set a general policy and hire writers who agree with that policy; the publisher may then give those writers considerable freedom to write daily editorials. In a somewhat different approach, a publisher may impose his or her views only occasionally on major issues, leaving the writers to decide what to say about other matters. In these cases, it is not a simple matter to define who the editorial "we" is.

The most often heard explanation for unsigned institutional editorials is that editorials do express more than one person's opinion. Brown pointed out that many times an editorial is not the product of one writer's opinion "but the amalgam of thought pounded out in an editorial conference of several people." He wondered what purpose it would serve to attach to the editorial "the name of the technician (a skilled editorial writer, albeit) who was assigned to express in words the agreed-upon thought or policy?"[6] The opinion might be a general one worked out over time among writers on a paper, or it might be worked out on a single issue during a morning editorial conference. In any case the writer would be expressing a combination of ideas. It might then make as much sense to put every staff member's name on the editorial as that of the actual writer. Sometimes the actual writing of an editorial will end up being the work of more than one person. Most editorials must pass through an editor or a publisher before they go into print. Since the editor or the publisher has the final say, the end product may be slightly, or greatly, different from the original version. Whose name, or names, should go on in this case? The original writer might not want to be identified with the editorial after the editor or the publisher has made substantial changes.

Sometimes defenders of unsigned editorials argue that a paper's editorial policy is something more than the sum of the opinions of the members of the editorial page staff. In this vein, George C. McLeod of the *Tucson* (Ariz.) *Daily Citizen* wrote: "Editorial writers come and go, although as a group our longevity record with one paper no doubt surpasses [the records] of news gatherers. But The Paper stays in the community for decades, through depression and prosperity."[7] Charles G. Strattard of the *Saginaw* (Mich.) *News* saw "we" as "an expression of a single newspaper speaking to its readership." An editor "must be willing to live" with the paper's policies—"if not always in total comfort," he said.[8]

Some defenders of unsigned editorials contend that these editorials carry more weight with readers because they are not just the personal opinion of an individual. "A signed editorial carries about as much punch as a letter to the editor," Ann Merriman of the *Richmond* (Va.) *News Leader* wrote in arguing that signed editorials have no place under the masthead of a newspaper's editorial page, "even though it would be a good thing if every editorial were written as if it were to be signed."[9]

With more and more newspapers being bought by the multipaper groups, the question arises: For whom does the unsigned "we" speak—the headquarters of the newspaper group or the policy-makers at the local level? In 1974 a survey of 12 groups found that, with one exception, the answer was the local publisher or editor, not a corporate official at central headquarters.[10]

Calvin Mayne, a representative of the Gannett Co., owners of more daily newspapers than any other group, reported that local editors and publishers are free to determine their own editorial policies. Gannett asks local executives a lot of questions about business and technology, "but how the newspapers stand on this or that editorial policy is *not* one of the queries because that would violate the local autonomy that has been a keystone of the Group policy ever since the late Frank E. Gannett began accumulating newspapers in Upstate New York more than a half century ago."[11] One of the other large groups, then known as Knight and later to become Knight-Ridder, "chooses its editors carefully and gives them their heads," Reese Cleghorn of the *Charlotte* (N.C.) *Observer* reported. He said the group had no "corporate line" or "group line" on editorial policy, "but neither does the top management of the organization have a 'don't-give-a-damn' view of the individual paper's editorial policies." The group did not tell editors whom to endorse or what to support but headquarters executives did have "a healthy interest in the way editorial policies are pursued—with attention to tone, quality of reasoning and respect for the readers." Cleghorn said that for months editorial writers would not hear from headquarters. When they did, comment was informal, and editors who disagreed with the comment were free to state their views and go on about their business.[12]

The only decidedly different report came from Merrill Lindsay, president of Lindsay-Schaub Newspapers, who said that local papers had full responsibility for policy on local issues. On state, national and international issues, however, a group of editorial writers at a centralized office researched and wrote the editorials. Editorial policy was set by the group editor, but, except for state and national endorsement editorials, local editors could decide whether or not to run the editorials from the central office.[13]

An article published in *Journalism Quarterly* following this survey of groups questioned whether local papers were as autonomous as the respondents to the survey had insisted. After studying presidential endorsements from 1960 through 1972, the authors of the article found that the vast majority of groups had generally homogeneous endorsement patterns in those elections[14]—data that "would appear to contradict clearly" the proposition advanced by representatives of the groups that they were independent in their political endorsement policies. As we noted in Chapter 1, however, that finding could have applied to newspapers in general, not just to group papers. In presidential elections, far more than in other elections, American daily newspapers stick together, endorsing Republicans over Democrats by four or five to one.

Further evidence of local autonomy in policy setting among chain papers was provided by a survey in 1980 that showed that 85 percent of group editors did not ever consult with group headquarters before taking a controversial editorial stand; 11 percent said they did consult. In contrast, 71 percent of editors on independently owned papers said they consulted with owners, compared to 27 percent who did not consult.[15]

In my 12 years on the *Columbian* in Vancouver, Wash., we ran editorials that were not signed, presumably to indicate to readers that they represented the opinions of the newspaper, not of just one person. But I would have counted myself as among those who did not consult with the owners in most cases. My publishers and I had spent considerable time before they hired me sounding out each other's views. When they decided we were compatible, they, in effect, handed me the editorial "we" to use as I wished (subject of course to cancellation at any time they thought we should go our separate ways). There were occasions when the publishers were not wholly pleased with what I had written, but for the most part they kept silent. At one point one of my publishers thought the paper should be taking a stronger stand in favor of legalizing marijuana, but he made no attempt to change the policy. On another occasion I found out several months after the fact that this publisher had not been in sympathy with the paper's strident opposition to plans to expand Portland International Airport onto a square mile of fill in the Columbia River. But he made no effort to soften or change our editorial stand.

You learn who the real "we" is during elections, especially presidential ones.

In the 1972 election the co-publishers had their minds set on endorsing Richard Nixon for re-election, and neither the other editorial writer on the paper nor I could budge the publishers from their decision. We argued for no endorsement, since we saw neither Nixon nor George McGovern as worthy of an endorsement. I wrote an editorial pointing out the weaknesses of both candidates but the publishers wouldn't consider it. I suggested that it be published as a signed article elsewhere on the editorial page. The publishers said No; readers might be confused by conflicting viewpoints on the page.

Neither the other writer nor I was required to write the Nixon editorial. A semiretired former managing editor, who had written many editorials over the years, was given the assignment.

The only other disagreement over who was "we" in those 12 years on the *Columbian* also involved an election, this one for a local judgeship. The publishers had their candidate. Two other editorial writers and I preferred another candidate, though we would have settled for kind words for both. In this instance the publishers agreed to look at an editorial that said either candidate would be a good judge. What emerged in print, however, was an editorial that used many of the words I had written but that also contained added praise for the publishers' choice and a firm conclusion backing their candidate. That was one occasion when it would have been impossible to have put one person's name on an editorial.

In even the most compatible relationships between editorial writers and publishers, writers are almost certain to find out from time to time that, as smart and knowledgeable as they think they are, they are not the final boss.

THE CASE FOR THE SIGNED EDITORIAL

The most persistently heard objection to unsigned editorials, and the most frequently heard argument for signed editorials, is that editorials are generally the work of individuals and that, while they may reflect some broad newspaper policies, the thinking and the words that go into them are more important than any general philosophy. A flamboyant argument along these lines, in the form of an attack on "editorial transubstantiation," was made by Sam Reynolds of the *Missoulian* in Missoula, Mont. In Roman Catholic and Eastern Orthodox rites, bread and wine are transubstantiated (or converted) into the body and blood of Christ although the appearance remains unchanged. "I view editorial transubstantiation with less awe," he wrote. "Editorial transubstantiation is the basis for editorial anonymity. It is not a miracle; it is nonsense." He argued that "flesh-and-blood human beings" write editorials, and usually it is only one of them that does so. How does the work of a human being become the product of an institution? "The answer must lie in faith, not fact," Reynolds said. In the end transubstantiation "is merely a lie; a lie eloquently defended by its many priests, but in the end a complete lie."

When Reynolds switched from unsigned to signed editorials, he found that he was no longer blamed for editorials that someone else had written and that the advertising staff no longer had to ''fend off attacks from persons aroused by my editorials.'' He also found his editorials had more influence, and he felt that signing editorials was more honest than pretending that editorials represented an institution.[16]

A similarly rewarding experience was reported by George Hebert of the *Norfolk* (Va.) *Ledger-Star,* which began attaching writers' names to opinion pieces in 1976. The switch attracted wide attention in editorial writing circles. In announcing the change, the editors said readers had told them that they wanted to know who was writing the editorials. ''There will be real people with real names on our end of what we hope will be a continuing exchange of views between us and our readers,'' the editors said. They hoped to give their writers freer rein and an opportunity to ''have more time to probe issues and sharpen their comments.'' The change elicited almost unanimous approval. The paper added to this emphasis on its writers by inserting sketches of their faces alongside the editorials.[17]

In 1971 editors of *The Masthead* asked 11 editorial writers to describe who was the ''we'' for whom they spoke. Nine remained firmly committed to speaking anonymously for the newspaper, two expressed some interest in departing from anonymity, but only one took a strong stand for signed editorials. That one, Ray Call of the *Emporia* (Kan.) *Gazette,* argued that writers who sign their names are likely to take more pride in their work and make more effort to check their facts than writers who know they will not directly be associated with what they write. He also thought that, in a time when people feel overwhelmed by institutions and readers see newspapers as corporate units, signing editorials helps readers relate more closely to their newspapers. While the *Gazette* had gained a name for personal journalism in the early 20th century when William Allen White had become editor and publisher, the practice of signing editorials came much later, following publication of an anthology that was supposed to include only editorials of William Allen White. After the book was published, White noticed that about two-thirds of the editorials in the last section had not been written by him but by his son, William L. White. ''Since then,'' Call wrote, ''initials have been used at the end of editorials that appear in the *Gazette.*''[18]

The most elaborate case for signed editorials was a two-part series in *The Masthead* written by Professor Warren Bovee of Marquette University. Bovee set out to debunk what he saw were seven myths about editorial anonymity. The first was that newspapers traditionally have run unsigned editorials. Our look into the history of the editorial page in Chapter 1 has shown that anonymity is only about a century old. The second myth was that editorials represent the views of the paper, not an individual. Bovee argued that, ''until the time arrives when editorial positions are decided by the total personnel of a newspaper . . . , it is misleading to attribute those positions to 'The Paper' . . . '' While publishers might set broad guidelines, he likened them to ''the ball field within which the editorial writers must still decide how to play the game.'' He said that ''editorial writers say more than most publishers would ever think of saying.''

The third myth, that editorials represent an editorial conference point of view, could be resolved by all members signing the editorial, he argued. A fourth myth, that "anonymity is necessary to protect the writer from verbal and physical abuse," Bovee saw as the "real, secret reason" why readers think editors do not sign editorials. His comment was that writers ought to be as subject to "phone calls, crank letters, crosses burned on the lawn and stones thrown through picture windows" as readers whose signed letters also appear on editorial pages. My own experience is that this fear of personal abuse figures minimally in editorial anonymity. Most editorial writers I know would appreciate more public recognition.

A fifth myth is that, if an editorial is signed, it becomes only a personal article or column. But Bovee contended that signed pieces by William Randolph Hearst and Jenkin Lloyd Jones are regarded as editorials. As to a sixth myth, that unsigned editorials carry more weight, Bovee argued that the impact depends more on what the editorial says than on who signs it. To the seventh myth, that there are no good reasons for signing editorials, Bovee argued that signing might help overcome reader mistrust of newspapers, giving writers greater freedom to write. "If the occasion demands it," he said, "the signed piece can be as personal and informal as a love letter, or it can be as formal and impersonal as a doctoral dissertation." Finally, he argued, when a paper has a number of editorial writers, there are bound to be occasions on which the writers disagree with one another. By allowing each, with a byline, to offer his or her view, the paper would have a more interesting editorial page.[19]

A COMPROMISE—BYLINED ARTICLES AND COLUMNS

Some of the fire may have been taken out of the debate over signed editorials by an increasing use of articles and columns bearing the names of editorial writers. Publishers have been able to give their writers public recognition and increased opportunities to express their individual views without giving up the principle of the institutionalized editorial. A survey of editorial writers in 1972 found that almost all of them wrote signed articles on at least an occasional basis.[20]

The advantages most cited in the survey were that signed articles help make the editorial page more human, allow for more casual and informal writing and provide more space than editorials for background or firsthand accounts, especially about local matters. Less often mentioned was the function of the signed article as an expression of a writer's views that might be at variance with the paper's editorial policy. This function can provide an outlet for frustrated editorial writers, but it can also cause problems. For example: James P. Brown, an editorial writer for the *Providence* (R.I.) *Journal-Bulletin*, had been writing a signed column during the early months of 1967. Then, following a column on Martin Luther King and the Vietnam War, publisher John C. A. Watkins stopped the column, not because of Brown's expressed views but because the column had become "shrill, hortative and dogmatic." A staff member wrote a letter to Watkins contending that a publisher is not sufficiently omniscient "to decide for our readers which opinions are proper for them to read" and that a paper is public property to the extent that it should present all views. Watkins replied that he didn't think he had an obligation to publish any particular person's column on any particular subject, but that he did have an obligation to present as many facts on a problem as are available and to make reasoned arguments available to readers. The arguments, he said, should be presented by informed writers "who respect the judgment and opinions of others" and not those who are "contemptuous of those with whom they disagree."[21] This incident suggests that, while publishers may recognize the principle that editorial writers may express dissenting opinions, the ultimate decisions about time, place and writer remain with the publisher.

Most publishers probably would have no objection to the balance between signed and unsigned pieces that we maintained. In my later years on the *Columbian,* when there were three of us writing for the editorial page, I urged the other writers to write bylined articles and on occasion to write pro-con articles, with each person signing one of the articles. I tried to hold to a schedule of writing at least one bylined article each week. We did not use those articles to express opinions directly opposed to the official editorial policy, but through the use of the byline we gained a greater feeling of editorial freedom for ourselves.

If most newspapers have been reluctant to give up the anonymous editorial "we," they have at least largely abandoned the "we" in personal columns and in obvious references to individuals. The change in philosophy on this point can be illustrated by the case of David V. Felts, who wrote a personal column for half a century for the Lindsay-Schaub newspapers. After his retirement Felts wrote an article for *The Masthead* in which he said: "I chose to use first-person plural 'we' in order to avoid the capital I, which seemed at the time . . . to suggest a vanity I did not care to confess, or an arrogance I would deny. So I rejected Teddy Roosevelt's 'I' and instead went along with Queen Victoria's 'We.' " However, Felts acknowledged, logical extension of the "editorial we" can be embarrassing and even ridiculous. He recalled that on one occasion a radio disc jockey, who was a friend of his, quoted from his column. Felts wrote: "I had written, so he read, 'When we stepped on the bathroom scales this morning. . . .' Then my friend observed: 'Oh, well, couples who weigh together, stay together.' " Felts then wrote: "Should I someday be assigned to one of those golden typewriters in the great city room in the sky to write celestial chit-chat, I will use the first person singular pronoun, even if only a modest, chastened lower-case i. Queen Victoria probably will not be amused, but Teddy Roosevelt surely will be 'dee-lighted.' "[22]

There is no historical evidence, or even a suggestion, that Horace Greeley could have done what Dave Felts did—look back years later and laugh at a ridiculous use of "we." Greeley's editorials abounded with "we's." In 1846, for example, Greeley was recalling the first election in which he had taken an interest, the presidential race of 1824: "We were but thirteen when this took place. . . ."[23]

CONCLUSION

The pendulum that had swung so far from the personal journalism of Horace Greeley to the anonymity of the corporate newspaper has begun to swing back. A growing, but relatively small, number of newspapers publish signed editorials. Many more promote the identities of editorial writers through signed articles and columns. Some of these writers are allowed to express opinions contrary to their newspapers' official policies.

Editorial writers are getting out of their offices and becoming better known in their communities (see Chapter 9, "Relations With the Community"). Editorial writers are also strengthening their positions on editorial boards (see Chapter 8, "The Editorial Page Staff"). A survey in 1980 showed that editors on group newspapers thought they had more independence from management in setting editorial policy than did editors on independent papers (see Chapter 6, "Relations With Publishers"). On all papers, personal expertise provides the best opportunities for editorial writers to achieve stronger and more public voices. In an era of complex issues, writers who know what they are talking about stand a good chance of convincing not only their readers but also their editors and publishers. They stand a good chance of getting a piece of the editorial "we."

QUESTIONS AND EXERCISES

1. Find a newspaper with signed editorials and read them for three or four days. Compare them in terms of tone and style with unsigned editorials on the same subjects published in other newspapers. Try to judge the differing impact, if any, that the types of editorials might have on readers.

2. Look through a number of editorial and op-ed pages of papers in your area. Try to find bylined opinion articles by editorial staff members. Do these articles express opinions that differ from the paper's editorials? Analyze how a reader is likely to respond to specific editorials and opinion articles that express different views.

3. Select an editorial with which you disagree and write an opinion piece that would be suitable to publish alongside the editorial.

4. Select several editorials that use the editorial "we" in referring to the newspaper's opinion. Does the "we" clearly convey the impression of a corporate opinion behind the editorial? Rewrite the sentences to make the same point without the use of "we."

5. Can you find a column in which the writer refers to himself or herself with the Victorian "we"? Could "I" have been used just as well?

6. Write a letter to an editorial writer on one of the papers in your area to ask about specific instances in which he or she and the editor or publisher might have disagreed on issues. How were the disagreements resolved? Did the writer end up producing an editorial he or she disagreed with? Was he or she allowed or encouraged to write a dissenting opinion? How often and on what kinds of issues has disagreement occurred?

7. Can you uncover, perhaps by reading *Editor & Publisher*, instances in which editorial writers have resigned or moved to non-editorial positions because of disagreement over editorial policy?

shoe

Relations With Publishers

In any kind of business you have clashes of personalities, but that does not seem to explain the talk that so often takes place about how are [editors and publishers] going to get along together. There must be something in this relationship between publisher and editor that is unusual.
—*Bernard Kilgore*
Wall Street Journal[1]

When they drew up the Bill of Rights in the late 1780s, the Founding Fathers did not have to worry about whether they intended freedom of the press to apply to publishers or to editors because most of the printers who produced periodicals, books, pamphlets and handbills were owner-editors. In the view of Hugh B. Patterson Jr., publisher of the *Arkansas Gazette,* the authors of the First Amendment believed "that the editor would most likely be the owner whose resources as well as reputation would be at stake; that newspapers would be vigorous critics and advocates on public questions; that newspapers would generally be locally owned and controlled; and that readers would have available from different publications a variety of views, sometimes directly competitive, from which to choose, whether the question was local, regional or national in scope."[2]

Today the editor and the publisher, however, are most often not the same person. Bernard Kilgore, editor and later publisher of the *Wall Street Journal,* described the relationship between publisher and editor as "a new kind of problem." With the demise of the owner-editor "comes the job which is that of the publisher," Kilgore said, and "the question which somebody is likely to ask [is] whether publishers are necessary."[3] In any other industry, he said, the job parallel to that of publisher would be clear: He or she would hire and fire. But in the newspaper business, "that's where we get into all the trouble. . . . A publisher just does not hire and fire editors because our business is not that kind of business." The difference is that the product a newspaper sells is "a completely intangible thing." Newspaper people should remind themselves that all the physical plant and machinery around the newspaper business provide only the package or container of the product, "just something to wrap up the ideas that editors have" and carry these ideas to the public. But the newspaper business has become "a great big manufacturing operation and a great big selling operation," Kilgore said. Consequently, "the general management of a newspaper has more and more come to be regarded as a job for a manufacturer or a salesman, and the editorial function . . . has tended to become a secondary consideration."[4]

FAMILY VS. GROUP OWNERSHIP

The era of the family-owned newspaper may look rosier in retrospect than it actually was. Many papers did not make enough profit to produce a good product. Some of the owner-publishers did not know what a good journalistic product was, and some didn't care. But the publishers were products of their communities and those who wished could do what they wanted with their papers without worrying about satisfying a bigger boss somewhere else. The publisher-editor who runs the whole show "in theory . . . is the happiest of mortals, if he can keep his separate selves from warring with one another," wrote Donald L. Breed, editor-publisher of the *Freeport* (Ill.) *Journal-Standard*.[5] Even those owner-publishers who did not write editorials tended to dominate their papers. Editorial writers, on the other hand, were "anonymous wretches," as Ralph Coghlan of the *St. Louis Post-Dispatch* referred to those who attended the first meeting of the National Conference of Editorial Writers in 1947. Indeed, a survey of editorial writers in 1951 found that fewer than 50 percent thought they could stand up for what they believed without risking financial disaster and 63 percent said they wrote opinions that were not always their own.[6]

In the three decades since then, group ownership has come to a majority of cities with daily newspapers, changing the nature of publishers. Most of the publishers are not home-grown; often they have been sent in for a few years, then transferred somewhere else, and other publishers brought in. Many are strictly business people.

Nevertheless, results of a 1979 survey suggest that group ownership may offer some advantages for editors and editorial writers. A survey sponsored by the American Society of Newspaper Editors found that editors on group newspapers thought they had more freedom in determining editorial policy than did editors on independently owned papers. Before taking a stand on a controversial issue, 85 percent of group editors said they did not consult with group headquarters, while only 27 percent of independent editors said they did not consult with the owners. Of course one reason may be that editors on independent papers have only to go to the next office to find out the views of management, while the editor on the group paper has to contact group headquarters hundreds or thousands of miles away. When asked what happened when they disagreed with management, 32 percent of the group editors said they wrote what they wanted to, while only 8 percent of independent editors did so.[7] These figures suggest that out-of-town ownership and a non-newspaper-oriented publisher may provide opportunities for editorial writers on group newspapers to emerge less cautiously and more outspokenly from publishers' offices and editorial conference rooms.

Hoke Norris of the *Chicago Sun-Times* said he had a friend who thought he had discovered a new law of journalism: "That the quality of the editorial page varies in inverse proportion to the degree of interference from the publisher, because publishers these days, with a few noteworthy exceptions, are not newspapermen but businessmen."[8]

The trend toward groups, however, is not the only change occurring in newspaper ownership. When publishers or groups own all or most of the newspaper, they can determine the profit levels that seem proper and desirable. But more groups and major newspapers are going public, selling stock on the market. Immediately the entrepreneur becomes concerned about the price of the stock. If profits lag, the stock is likely to fall in value. If the newspaper ventures into an area of controversy in its news or editorial columns—and perhaps stakes its reputation when tackling a sensitive public issue—the paper's stock may skid in value.

Spokesmen for groups contend that ownership of several papers allows them to use their numerous resources to enable an individual paper to stand up to the pressures of advertisers or other special interests. That may be true if the owners are sufficiently dedicated to the newspaper business to be willing to forgo some of the profits while the paper fights its battle. But, if the publishers and groups must answer to stockholders who are interested in profit, not journalism, it may not be possible to be so idealistic.

Robert Pittman of the *St. Petersburg* (Fla.) *Times* saw "a basic conflict" between an editor's responsibility to readers and the responsibility of an investor-owned newspaper to its stockholders. "What's good for Media General stock isn't necessarily what's good for the country," Pittman said.[9]

David Halberstam, in his book *The Powers That Be,* noted that the Washington Post Co. had gone public only two days before publisher Katharine Graham had to decide whether to defy the government and publish the Pentagon Papers. "The shadow of the stock hung very much over the editorial deliberations," Halberstam wrote. "The timing for everyone concerned could not have been worse. In addition to everything else, there was one little clause in the legal agreement for the sale of the stock that said that the sale could be canceled if a catastrophic event struck the paper.'' If the government halted distribution of the *Post,* that might be such an event; so might an indictment for contempt of court. The effect on the stock, then, was one of the matters considered by the *Post* in making its decision whether or not to publish the papers.[10] The *Post,* following the lead of the *New York Times,* did begin to publish the papers. Court injunctions obtained by the federal government temporarily halted publication, but a 6-3 decision by the U.S. Supreme Court removed the injunctions and allowed the newspapers to resume publication.

In a growing number of instances newspapers and other media have become only minor parts of corporations with investments in many industries. At best, the media owned by these conglomerates are viewed as business operations that must produce their share of the corporation's revenue. At worst, the conglomerate may view profitable media as sources of funds to shore up its weaker operations—or, as ABC, Inc., did with ABC News, a conglomerate may chop funds from a media operation because of weaknesses elsewhere in the system.[11] Corporations that were once primarily newspaper-oriented have become involved in telephone book publishing, timber, cable television, billboards, Bibles, television, radio and magazines. Diversity may help ensure profitability and stability, but it also tends to produce a corporation hierarchy that is primarily business- rather than newspaper-oriented. Basic decision making is farther removed from the editor and editorial writer. When these large corporations are committed to doing a good job in news and editorial operations, they have the resources to do so. But when they are not committed to doing a good job, chances are slim for changing their editorial priorities.

THE PUBLISHER'S ROLE

Weighing on the publisher's mind almost as heavily as making a profit is what Frank Taylor, managing editor of the *St. Louis Star-Times,* called ''harmonious relations'' with other employees.[12] Publishers like to run smooth operations and do not like to employ personalities that clash. Publishers dislike friction between news and advertising or between news and editorial operations. In short, publishers are comfortable with the philosophy expressed in *The Economics of the American Newspaper,* which suggests to news and editorial people that the whole newspaper staff is in this together and that no one can benefit without everyone helping. So why doesn't everyone cooperate and forget differences of opinion and interest?[13]

One of the threats to the why-can't-everyone-be-friends atmosphere is posed by the publisher's responsibility to negotiate with the labor unions. Most editorial writers do not have to worry about coming into conflict with the publisher in contract negotiations, since most are excluded from newsroom organized labor groups. But a publisher who is worried about a threatening strike or angered by what he or she sees as an unfair tilt of federal or state labor relations laws may hold a strong opinion on what editorial writers ought to be saying about organized labor. More than one newspaper has departed from its moderate-to-liberal social philosophy when the subject of labor arises.

Since a publisher's first concern is often to function successfully in the economy, he or she is also likely to have firm views on how the economy should operate. "There is one special interest always present, and that is the pro-capitalist bias of a newspaper," publisher-editor Breed wrote. "Privately-owned and operated newspapers are expressions of newspaper enterprise, and they must make a profit to survive. . . . Therefore, it must be taken for granted that American newspapers will support the free enterprise system."[14] Breed's assumption no doubt is true for the vast majority of papers. But the economic system has grown to be extremely complex. Mixed in with free enterprise is substantial government support and protection of business, direct and indirect government intervention in the economy and a growing amount of control by huge corporations. Commenting intelligently on the economy these days requires a lot more information and sophistication than it used to (see Chapter 13). Publishers may have some ideas about how the economy should be managed, but many of these are likely to be rooted in introductory economics classes attended 30 years ago. Publishers may be up to date on economic matters affecting their own businesses and fellow local merchants, familiar with property and income taxes, state and federal health and safety requirements, unemployment and workmen's compensation, and perhaps local zoning and building regulations. While experiences in these areas may provide publishers with some insight for editorial comment, they should recognize that they are parties with special interests and (probably) narrow views in economic matters.

If publishers have contributions to make in evaluating economic issues, they probably have fewer to make in other areas. It is not that publishers, given time and resources, are not smart enough to hold their own with editorial writers. But most publishers have neither the time nor the frame of mind needed for knowledgeable editorial writing, while an editorial writer must be constantly alert to topics that might merit the expression of opinion.

Publishers are often hard-pressed to find time to read their own newspapers thoroughly. One of my publishers, acknowledging this difficulty, asked that his staff tell him personally about any news or editorial items that were likely to bring him a phone call or personal comment. He wanted to be forewarned to avoid the embarrassment of not knowing what the caller was talking about. Publishers simply do not have the time to be editorial writers. Therein lie the makings of both conflict and a good working relationship between publisher and writer.

If publishers think, however, that they are editorial writers, the resulting intervention is likely to drive the editorial staff out the door, up the wall or into the closet. A weak and submissive staff that stands no chance of putting out a vigorous editorial page will result. On the other hand, if publishers allow themselves to be too busy to think about the editorial page or to discuss ideas and issues with the writers, conflict is likely to occur at some point. The publisher should exercise leadership continuously and cooperatively, rather than intermittently and imperiously. Almost as annoying as having a publisher constantly breathing down the necks of editorial writers is having him or her descend suddenly and unpredictably into the editorial department.

Unless a publisher is news-oriented, news and editorial sides may get little attention compared to other departments. Many editors, in fact, encourage this type of distant relationship with their publishers by trying to run their departments with as little publisher contact as possible. This tactic entails some risks, as I will discuss at greater length later in this chapter.

One result of a lack of communications between publishers and editors is what might be called "frozen issues." If a publisher and an editor have not discussed a subject, the editor may keep silent on that subject even though it may deserve editorial comment. Or the editor may speak softly on the subject, fearful that strong opinion will offend the publisher. If writers find themselves in such a position, they have as much responsibility as the publisher to come forth and, if necessary, battle the issue out. A battle or a good vigorous discussion now and then is healthy for both parties. Of course, if battles have to be waged often to unfreeze issues, publishers and writers may need to recognize that their philosophies are not sufficiently compatible to allow for a good working relationship.

One of my publishers used to say that he expected disagreements to arise between us, though he expected me to convince him of my point of view most of the time since I (presumably) knew more about the subject than he did. That usually proved to be the case, or at least he let me think so. The degree of freedom that an editor achieves thus lies partly within his or her own control. As author Robinson Scott has said, the editor owes whatever freedom he or she enjoys to "force of character, . . . knowledge and the strength of [his or her] convictions."[15]

THE CASE FOR THE EDITOR

A strong case can be made for the argument that, once the editorial page editor gets the job, he or she should determine a newspaper's editorial policy. Hugh B. Patterson Jr., publisher of the *Arkansas Gazette,* contended that editorial page editors ought to be given room to set policy, and owner-publishers should support them completely. He thought that, just as career politicians are generally best suited to hold high public office, so "career newspaper editors are best qualified to run newspaper editorial pages."[16] Frank Taylor, of the *St. Louis Star-Times,* saw publishers as "God-fearing, decent men who would much rather push a cash register button than pull a tiger's tail." He thought that "a majority of editorial writers would measure up well on the God-fearing test but would come through 100 percent plus on pulling a tiger by the tail."[17]

Sevellon Brown III, editor of the *Providence* (R.I.) *Journal-Bulletin,* saw three reasons why "the editor *ought* to be the one—and only one—to make final decisions on editorial policy." First, the editor "is relatively uncluttered by other professional duties and responsibilities." The publishers, with all the other duties they must perform, can give only limited time and energy to the editorial page. Editing an editorial page is a full-time job. Second, the editor is the person "in closest, broadest touch with the news," one of the primary ingredients in editorial policy making.

Third, the editor is best qualified because he or she is, or ought to be, "*relatively* disinterested, *relatively* uncommitted to any particular cause or faith or point of view." The publisher, properly so, comes from the business side and represents only a business point of view. With brains, "moxey" and endurance, the editor can become a lightning rod for all points of view—for business, labor, politicians of all parties, enthusiasts for public education or world trade "or what-have-you, do-gooders of all kinds." The editor, in dealing with a specific issue, can sort out and synthesize the varied pressures and interests "into something like a reasoned, intelligent conclusion"—and there is the paper's editorial policy.[18]

An editor who has fortitude and convictions can attain a strong, unique position in relations with a publisher. As Kilgore pointed out, much to the chagrin of some editorial writers, ". . . you cannot make a five-year-old eat. No amount of force or physical violence will work. . . . Authority, you see, does not accomplish things. With editors it is somewhat the same thing." You can't force an editorial writer to write, and even more fundamental you can't force an editorial writer to think. The relationship between editor and publisher, Kilgore said, is "a case where you have a boss who is not really a boss, and a case where you have a workman who is not really a workman."[19]

Yet, when it is necessary to make basic policy and settle disagreements, someone must assume the final authority, and it is a rare newspaper where that final authority does not rest with the publisher, general manager or representative of ownership. "Ownerships generally last longer than editorships," William H. Heath, editor-emeritus of the *Haverhill* (Mass.) *Gazette,* wrote. "Therefore, policy made by ownership is more stable. There is a rock-of-ages quality about a newspaper that is distinguished by editorial policy. This quality strengthens public confidence in the paper."[20]

GETTING ALONG WITH THE PUBLISHER

Relationships between editors and publishers probably vary as widely as do the personalities of editors and publishers. Some publishers and editors are easy to get along with; some are not. Some personalities work better together in an editor-publisher relationship than others. The relationship depends partly on the rules that are set when a publisher hires an editor. Consequently, the recommendations that follow may or may not be appropriate for specific editors and publishers.

The first thing that editors need to recognize is that, even when the most congenial relations exist between an editor and a publisher, from time to time decisions are certain to go against the editor. When disagreements go all the way to the mat, the publisher almost always has the authority to win.

So what can editors do to minimize those occasions, which may become traumatic and shake editors' confidence in themselves? The best advice, of course, is for editorial writers to choose their papers and publishers carefully. Editors need to know enough about the personality of a prospective publisher to have a pretty good idea that they can get along despite disagreements. They need to know enough about the prospective newspaper's editorial policy so that they can, in most cases, feel comfortable writing editorials expressing that policy.

Throughout the country editorial writers looking for a job will find a lot of middle-of-the-road (apple pie and motherhood) newspapers on which writers of moderate convictions might be able to muddle through a lifetime of editorial writing. Kenneth McArdle of the *Chicago Daily News* may have had these papers in mind when he said, referring to publishers, "Generally speaking, it would be hard to be utterly out of synch with them unless you, yourself, were on the kooky side, because they tend to be rational people."[21] But some newspapers, to their credit, have stronger editorial convictions, and, fortunately, so do some editorial writers and would-be writers. Nevertheless, unless a writer's views fall within the middle 50 to 60 percent of the political spectrum, opportunities for signing on with a congenial editorial page are limited.

The task of finding a congenial editorial page may also be more difficult today than in earlier times because journalists don't seem to hop around the country from newspaper to newspaper as much as they once did. They get married, raise a family, buy a house and try to find a decent school system in an attractive community. They put their roots into the community and may develop as deep a concern for it as any publisher. Their concern for and knowledge of the community, in fact, may go deeper than a publisher's because some newspaper groups make a practice of moving their publishers around. Hence the writer or would-be writer may feel that he or she has a bigger stake in the community than the representative of ownership. Such feelings are not likely to ease the working relationship with publishers who have different ideas for the direction of editorial policy.

Dialogue helps to keep editors and publishers from suddenly being surprised to learn that they hold differing opinions on important issues. If publishers and editors can talk about issues before it is necessary to make decisions, chances of compromise improve greatly. Kilgore perceived that misunderstandings between publisher and editor sometimes result because of editors. He suggested that editors should "get into the business side of a newspaper and try to see what the thing is all about."[22] Editors who want a bigger slice of the corporate budget might stand a better chance of succeeding if they could convince the business side that they understood the problems of producing income and holding down costs. On occasion my publishers took several department heads out to solicit new subscriptions. My principal memory of those occasions concerns all the reasons that people had for not taking the paper. For a greater understanding of the community as well as for purely pragmatic business reasons, editorial writers should keep abreast of circulation and advertising lineage figures. If they have a head for figures, so much the better. Most journalists don't, or think they don't. One of the ways I scored points with one of my publishers, who prided himself on his business acumen, was through coming up with accurate figures on my slide rule faster than he did on his calculator. If editorial writers can talk the publisher's and the circulation manager's languages, they are more likely to project an image of having their feet on the ground—and stand a lot better chance of selling their editorial ideas.

One of the principal functions of editorial writers may be to educate their publishers. "If the editor is willing to educate everybody, including the world, and foreign countries, then it is also necessary for the publishers and the owners to be educated," Kilgore said. However, the writer must educate the publisher with what Hoke Norris of the *Chicago Sun-Times* called "a certain tact—even a tenderness." Norris described an editor friend who saw his function in "the care and feeding" of the publisher: "His publisher always believes that he originates the ideas and holds his own opinions. This is perhaps a harmless deception and it might even save a publisher, on occasion, from making a damn fool of himself."[23] A writer who is more educated and informed than his or her publisher must handle the boss with special care. Otherwise, the writer may run the risk of making the publisher feel resentful or intimidated rather than favorably impressed. As Frank Taylor of the *St. Louis Star-Times* put it, "More than one inferiority complex parades the precincts of publishers."[24]

Publishers might feel less intimidated if they availed themselves of opportunities to keep abreast of current events, took time to dig deeply into local issues or enrolled in a course at a local college. Houstoun Waring, publisher of the *Littleton* (Colo.) *Independent,* warned that it is "only partially effective to educate the reporter and the feature writer if the arteries of the man who calls the tune continue to harden. . . . Publishers may feel they are omniscient, but adult education programs are good for them, too."[25] He had in mind such formal programs as the Nieman Fellowship and other sabbatical opportunities, local press councils and discussions over breakfast with local sources.

Nathaniel Blumberg, dean of the School of Journalism at the University of Montana, recalled in an article in *Montana Journalism Review* "A. J. Liebling's essentially accurate aphorism that without a school for publishers no school of journalism can have meaning."[26] The API offers two-week sessions for publishers, but the topic of setting a service-oriented editorial policy for a community, if it appears at all, is likely to rank far down the line on the agenda after more directly business-related subjects.

Methods generally available to editors for educating publishers, however, are likely to be much less formal. Editors can send memos and background articles (although probably not books) across the publishers' desks to help them understand issues before decisions are made, though busy publishers, of course, may not find time to read the material. Editors can also invite publishers to go to public meetings, speeches, panel discussions and workshops where a variety of points of view are likely to be aired. And editors can invite publishers to lunch to exchange, in a less formal atmosphere than that of the editorial conference, ideas about what their newspapers should be doing and saying.

Publishers who want a hand in editorial policy ought to understand that they have as much responsibility as editorial writers to sit and plow through all the material necessary for making intelligent decisions. Publishers also need to understand that no one appreciates being descended upon at the last minute, after all the hard work is done, to give an opinion, even if the opinion is a modest one.

To avoid unexpected, last-minute opinions or decision changes, editorial conference members should try to establish the habit of delaying decisions on important matters until everyone has aired his or her opinions and the issue at hand has been fully discussed. Once a person—especially a publisher, who could lose face before employees—declares even a tentative position on an issue, moving off that position becomes difficult. An editorial page staff that anticipates disagreement with the publisher might find it advantageous to meet before the editorial conference to plan a strategy. If the writers anticipate that they might not be able to convince other conference members of their opinion, they might try to agree beforehand on a compromise that they would find acceptable. (The workings of editorial conferences are examined in more detail in Chapter 7.)

Editorial writers need to be especially sensitive to special requests from publishers. These come in two forms. First, publishers may ask editors and writers—or reporters, for that matter—to use their professional contacts or knowledge in an area to perform a favor for them. Favors that coincide with what clearly seems to serve community interests present no problems. Those that do not should be avoided at all costs; performing them would compromise editors with their sources and with their own sense of integrity. For example, one publisher enlisted the aid of one of his editorial writers in lobbying Congress to increase appropriations for research into a disease that had struck a member of the publisher's family. The cause was a good one, and probably no great harm was done. But did the writer lose some of his credibility with the senator whom he was principally lobbying and become just another favor-seeker? A more clear-cut case of conflict of interest might involve a publisher's asking an editor to help move the company's expansion plans more quickly through municipal red tape.

The second type of request is for a specific editorial. Again, if the editorial idea is a good one and is in the interests of the community, the writer should produce it—posthaste. If the request is obviously self-serving or out of character with the paper's policy or contrary to reason and common sense, the editorial writer has a problem. The best course is to dig into the subject, document arguments against writing the editorial and present them to the publisher boldly and positively. Confidence and facts are the best weapons. By no means should a writer ignore or delay action on such requests—even if he or she thinks that an idea is so far out of line that the publisher couldn't be serious about it. Chances are, just as a writer is congratulating himself or herself on successfully having avoided doing anything about the request, the publisher will issue a sharp reminder. At that point in the game the publisher has the upper hand. The writer is embarrassed, apologetic, off balance and in a very poor position to convince the publisher of the lack of the merits of the idea. I found myself in that position when a publisher asked me to write an editorial on certain practices of labor unions that offended him. In addition to convincing him that the idea was not a good one, I faced the task of convincing him that I had not intentionally ignored him. A writer stands a better chance of fending off undesirable requests by confronting the publisher and risking an argument than by ignoring the request. Publishers don't like to be ignored.

To the publisher who has a yen to write, editors might be tempted to suggest a personal column. But editor-publisher Donald Breed of the *Freeport* (Ill.) *Journal-Standard* warned that publishers who write "should have exceptional capacity for self-criticism" and for evaluating the criticisms of others. "It is perfectly obvious that many publishers who write editorials or 'columns' have no power or will to step aside and look at themselves and their work," Breed said. "Publishers who write columns about their personal friends, their daily lives, their travels can sometimes be interesting, but the balance of experience is against them."[27] Writers who have a disagreement with their publishers or editorial boards might seek to express their dissident opinions in a signed article or column on the editorial or op-ed page. But many publishers, and some editors, are reluctant to open this avenue for contrary opinions from staff members.

Some articles in *The Masthead* have suggested that editorial writers as a group "take on" their publishers. One of the first rallying cries came in 1970, in an article by Curtis D. MacDougall, then professor of journalism at Northwestern University. He quoted with approval a statement that had been made by one of the founders of NCEW a couple of years earlier: "During our first two decades we have educated ourselves. Now let us devote our energies toward doing the same for our publishers."[28] MacDougall did not identify the originator of the quotation.

Over the years editorial writers have carried a lot of ideas back to publishers from conferences of NCEW. At the following years' meeting writers often report that suggestions that emerged from critique groups were accepted back home and that the editorial pages were the better for them. That is one way of bringing the collective enlightenment of editorial writers to publishers. But ideas are not always accepted. Editorial writers on some papers receive criticism for the same deficiencies year after year. When asked why they don't change, the answer is usually that the publisher (or editor) "wants it that way."

At least one editorial writer has issued a battle cry for a full-fledged offensive against the publishers. In 1977 Sam Reynolds, editorial page editor of the Missoula (Mont.) *Missoulian,* wrote: "We must lay down standards of what is good in a publisher, and what is bad. We must, as an organization, sharply criticize shabby publisher performance." Reynolds suggested using *The Masthead.* "It must be done because nothing so retards healthy editorial comment in America as lame-brained, narrow-minded, unimaginative, cowardly, sluggish, dogmatic, and imperial publishers. . . . Until the vital step of ripping up publishers who sit like slugs upon editorial spirit and quality is taken, this organization is simply bird-doggin' it, a representative group of aggressive slaves, or hired guns." He called on NCEW to encourage good publisher practices and to attack the bad. "Growl! Snap!" he wrote; "it's time we blew the whistle."[29]

Reynolds's call for NCEW to "blow the whistle" seems to have gone unheeded. *The Masthead* carried no further reference to his proposal. Perhaps editorial writers did not know what they wanted to put into a code of ethics for publishers. How should the ideal publisher behave? For starters, writers might look to their own statement of principles, especially the portions dealing with personal favors and conflicts of interest. A code might include a provision emphasizing the integrity of the editorial decision-making process—the need for previously agreed-upon procedures to be followed in setting editorial policy. It might contain some variation of the NCEW statement that says that an editorial writer "should never write anything that goes against his or her conscience." The same statement also emphasizes that "sound collective judgment can be achieved only through sound individual judgments," and it implies that editorial policy should evolve through discussion, not be imposed from the top. A code might state that a publisher should participate in editorial decision making only if he or she has participated in the information-gathering and discussion phases of the process.

Perhaps many members of NCEW were reluctant to take on the publishers because they faced a tough enough task back home dealing with publishers who didn't pay a lot of attention to them. They might have feared that, if they stirred up trouble, they would end up with a bigger battle on their hands. The way most American newspapers are run today, publishers may lose a skirmish now and then, but they rarely allow themselves to lose the big battles.

CONCLUSION

Publishers do have the final say on most newspapers. But on many papers editors and editorial writers have more say than they did several years ago, as differences in responses to the surveys conducted in 1951 and 1979 suggest. Editorial writing is increasingly regarded as a career, not just a job that a news person from some other part of the paper has wandered into at a late stage in his or her working life. The job on many papers is beginning to lose its image as a mouthpiece for the bosses. Publishers are hiring editors and giving them increased editorial freedom. One reason for this new confidence is that editorial writers and editors are better prepared for their jobs. In recent years they have become better educated, more interested in their communities and more willing to speak up for what they know and believe. Knowledgeable, confident writers these days can expect to win a considerable amount of freedom from publishers, at least from those publishers who recognize the value of strong, enlightened editorial pages.

QUESTIONS AND EXERCISES

1. If you were a publisher, what role would you choose in regard to the editorial page? If you were an editorial page editor, what would you want the role of the publisher to be?

2. Should the role of publisher vary with the size of the newspaper? Should whether a paper is owned locally, by a distant owner or by a group make a difference in the role of the publisher?

3. Judging from the newspapers with which you are acquainted, what chances do you think you have for working for a publisher with wholly compatible views on issues? Under what circumstances might you agree to write editorials with which you disagreed?

4. Among the group-owned newspapers that you are familiar with, have you detected any evidence of control of editorial policy by the group headquarters? Have you seen any evidence of similar editorial policies among newspapers of the same group?

5. What do you think are the most effective ways for an editorial writer to keep a publisher happy and to achieve a maximum sphere of freedom?

6. If editorial writers were "to take on the publishers," as suggested in *The Masthead* articles mentioned in this chapter, what steps might they take?

—Jeff MacNelly,
Reprinted by permission of Jefferson Communications, Inc., Reston, Va.

Relations With the Newsroom

Historically the relationship between the newsroom and the editorial page has been a one-way street. The newsroom produces the news. The editorial writers sit back in Olympian reflection, rearrange their dandruff into new patterns, and then write comments on or interpretations of that news.
—Clifford E. Carpenter
Rochester *(N.Y.)* Democrat and Chronicle[1]

Most American newspapers subscribe to a firm policy of trying to keep editorial views out of the news columns. But that policy should not keep editorial writers out of the newsroom or, at least according to some editors, reporters out of the editorial offices. Reporters and other news persons can provide a great deal to editorial writers—tips, insights, facts, contacts. But, because of jealousy, antipathy or misunderstanding, much of that potential help never gets past the partition that separates the newsroom from the editorial offices.

This lack of contact results partly from a healthy tradition on most newspapers that editorial policy should not influence what goes into the news columns. But the separation can go too far. Reporters, who pride themselves on reporting news without concern for the opinions of management, may try to avoid editorial writers for fear that, if they are seen with them, their colleagues in the newsroom may think they are being influenced. News people may view editorial writers as simply management's "hired guns."

As we noted in Chapter 3, the jobs of reporting and editorial writing, with differing functions to be performed, require persons of contrasting skills and temperaments. These differences tend to reinforce the tendency of each group of journalists to associate with its own kind and to avoid fraternizing across the news-editorial boundary, a tendency that may result in distorted perceptions. "In the eyes of some editorial writers," wrote Edward M. Miller of the *Oregonian* of Portland, "the news department is manned by fugitives from the world of intellect. The news department is notable for misjudging the news. It is concerned with trivialities at the expense of Things that Really Matter." To news people, the editorial page is staffed by "fugitives from the world of reality." Editorial writers "commune with God, and do that with considerable reluctance," Miller said.[2]

Another source of news-editorial trouble is the resentment sometimes felt by news personnel who disagree with a paper's editorial policy, especially policy involving endorsement of candidates. The public, they believe, assumes that editorials speak for the entire journalistic side of the paper, when in fact editorials represent the views of only a few policy makers. On occasion newsroom people will purchase advertisements in their own paper to state their support of policies or candidates different from those supported by the editorial page.

Sometimes relations between news and editorial people can be soured by an excessive amount of competition. Editorial writers may take delight in scooping the news department—finding a story and writing an editorial about it before the story appears in the news columns. Once in a while reporters may find sardonic pleasure in reporting a story that makes the editorial staff look as though it didn't know what it had been writing about. Repeated efforts on one side of the news-editorial partition to embarrass the other can be destructive to the morale of a newspaper staff and can harm the credibility of the paper. But a little friendly competition between news and editorial can help keep both departments on their toes; it may provide the only such competition in one-newspaper communities.

Problems of a different sort arise when a firm partition is not maintained between news and editorial content, when a publisher does not insist that editorial writers hold complete responsibility for policies expressed in the editorial columns and that news personnel have complete responsibility for the news columns. The editorial staff must not expect the news department to produce articles aimed at bolstering an editorial viewpoint, and the news staff must not allow its opinions to filter into news articles.

REPORTERS AS SOURCES

Whatever the reason, reporters and editorial writers have tended to go their own ways. Reporters produce the news; editorial writers comment on it. Reporters do the spade work; editorial writers do the pontificating on what reporters dig up. They may operate without speaking to each other.

In many cases in which editorial comment is called for, editorial writers have no need to talk with reporters. They have their own sources; or the subject of the editorial may already have been fully explained in the news columns. But editorial writers who ignore reporters miss a chance to get quick, expert advice. Since a newspaper invariably has more reporters than editorial writers, the news people are likely to have more sources of information and spend more time in the community than editorial writers. They may have information, not yet ready for print, that might make a big difference in how editorial writers evaluate an issue. Clifford Carpenter of the *Rochester* (N.Y.) *Democrat and Chronicle* found during his years in the newspaper business that reporters generally know more about a story than they can put into print. "But much of it isn't always admissible as news in the normal concept of a newspaper," he said. "This unused information can be invaluable to the editorial writer who has much more latitude."[3] This information may also be essential, since, as William J. Woods of the *Utica* (N.Y.) *Observer-Dispatch* pointed out, reporters "are invaluable in keeping the egg of silly mistakes off the editor's chin."[4]

At the simplest level writers who want to tackle a subject in which they are not experts can ask a knowledgeable reporter to brief them on the subject. If, for example, the subject is a proposed zone change that is coming before the city council, the reporter should be able to recount the history of the case, from the developer through the planning staff and zoning commission. The reporter may also be able to provide technical information on zoning procedures. At the next level a writer may ask the reporter to clarify the issues involved—using our example, to state the arguments of the developer, the protesting neighbors and the zoning commissioners.

REPORTERS IN THE OPINION PROCESS

At the most crucial, and controversial, level, the editorial writer might ask the reporter for a personal opinion on the issue. In the zoning change instance, the reporter might reply that, in comparison with other similar changes, this one does not seem out of line—or perhaps that the change does seem far out of line. In seeking opinion, however, the editorial writer should be wary. Reporters are responsibile for maintaining the appearance of fairness in reporting the news as well as fairness in their writing. A city editor, who is concerned about the credibility of reporters, may not appreciate having reporters offer opinions to an editorial writer on subjects that they write about. A reporter's relations with a news source can be adversely affected if it becomes known that the reporter has voiced an opinion. To think public matters through to editorial conclusions is the job of the editorial writer, not the reporter.

Some editors—on both news and editorial sides—are receptive to the practice of encouraging reporters to express opinions, in print and personally. Desmond Stone of the *Rochester Democrat and Chronicle* reported that inviting reporters to participate in editorial board meetings for a period of two weeks was one way that his paper and its sister paper, the *Times-Union,* tried to make news personnel feel more a part of the editorial decision making.[5]

Rufus Terral of the *St. Louis Post-Dispatch* suggested a more extensive use of news personnel in the editorial function. In describing his ideas for an ideal editorial staff for a city of 100,000, Terral recommended picking two promising writers in the newsroom to contribute editorials from time to time. He hoped that they could fill in when members of the editorial staff were on vacation or ill and eventually become full-time editorial page staff members when a replacement was needed.[6] Some papers make a practice of asking reporters to write editorials or bylined opinions on a regular basis on particular subjects on which they are experts.

These practices could provide one solution for the problem of finding new editorial writers. But bringing reporters into the editorial-writing process blurs the line between reporting and commenting. Can a journalist be a news writer one day and an editorial writer the next and still keep the two functions separate— or perhaps more important, maintain the appearance of keeping them separate?

David H. Beetle of the *Albany* (N.Y.) *Knickerbocker News* once asked several Washington reporters to write a 500-word appraisal of the current administration. The reporter from the Albany paper responded that writing a signed opinion article on the editorial page would brand him as biased forever. As a reporter, he dealt only in facts; he was proud that, in public, he had no opinions. Beetle asked other editors what they thought. They were divided. "Ridiculous," said one editor. "Our city hall reporter writes straight news daily and once a week tells what he thinks of it all. No one believes he is biased." But another editor argued, "If a city hall reporter writes opinion, he'll instantly become 'suspect' when he gathers news."[7]

As an editor, I personally did not encourage reporters to write articles that expressed opinion about the subjects they were reporting. I did, however, encourage them to write in-depth, analytical articles for use in either the daily news columns or the Sunday opinion section. My experience as both a reporter and an editorial writer convinced me that something happens inside a writer when he or she writes a piece that expresses an opinion. As an editorial writer, I often ended up having much stronger opinions on a subject after I had written an editorial about it. Once a writer has thought through the arguments and embraced one of them, his or her attitude on an issue will never be the same again.

EDITORIALS IN THE NEWS COLUMNS

Two ideas for introducing editorials into the news pages were considered in the early issues of *The Masthead.* Neither idea has been given much credence by editors.

The first is the front-page editorial. Such editorials have become rare in recent years. But Professor Nathaniel Blumberg of Michigan State University found enough page-one editorials during the 1952 election that he wrote an article for *The Masthead* entitled "The Case Against Front-Page Editorials." Blumberg argued that the reader is likely to be confused about what is news and what is opinion when a paper publishes its opinion on any page except the editorial page. "Furthermore, front-page editorials are most bitterly resented by those who do not share the views endorsed by the newspaper," he said. "Simultaneously, editorials on the front page increase suspicions that the news coverage might not be impartial."[8]

Some papers still summarize election endorsements in a front-page box, and some editorial page editors use front-page teasers to call attention to editorials on the editorial page. Many of the criticisms of front-page editorials could be applied to these practices as well.

The other suggestion for bringing opinion into the news columns came in 1935 from Douglas Southall Freeman, editor of the *Richmond* (Va.) *News Leader*. While going through old files in the early 1950s, James J. Kilpatrick, then of the *News Leader,* found the original proposal that Freeman had submitted to his publisher. Freeman argued that the news needed interpreting when and where it was printed. The reader should not have to wait until the next day, "when his interest in it has been diminished or has been distracted by some new event." Freeman went on to propose that the editorial page be abolished and that interpretation and comment be appended at the end of news stories that merited opinion.[9] Kilpatrick's resurrection of the proposal prompted the laboratory newspaper at the University of Michigan, the *Michigan Journalist,* to try what Freeman had proposed. Students found that one advantage of tacking an editorial on the end of a news story was that the editorial did not require so much space; there was no need to rehash factual information. But the experiment posed problems. The professor who worked with the students on the idea, James C. MacDonald, said he feared that readers would think that news sources had not been "given a square shake if the newspaper proceeds to bludgeon those views editorially in the same news column." He also feared that the instant editorial would encourage off-the-cuff reactions and discourage the double-checking, the digging for more information and calm reflection required by first-rate editorial comment.[10]

EDITORIALIZING ABOUT NEWS POLICIES

One occasion on which lowering the bar between news and editorial can be justified is the use of editorial columns to explain news policies and practices—and editorial practices for that matter. An editorial or a signed article on the editorial page can be a proper forum for telling readers why certain types of news and not others are covered in the news columns or why new features have been added and others dropped. Robert S. Bates of the *Meadville* (Pa.) *Tribune* used an editorial to explain why his paper had not carried a story about a prominent local citizen who had been arrested in a nearby city. When Terry Greenberg made a substantial number of changes when he became editor of the *Redlands* (Calif.) *Daily Facts,* he ran a series of six explanatory articles in the news columns, but he used a bylined piece on the editorial page to report the public reaction to the changes and the further changes he had made in response to readers' objections.

In the last couple of years in which I was on a newspaper, I regularly wrote a Sunday op-ed column, which I usually devoted to a journalistic issue. Some of the columns dealt with my own paper's policies and practices; others concerned matters of more general interest, such as protecting the confidentiality of news sources, libel, invasion of privacy and the signing of editorials. Reader response seemed good. Subscribers wanted to know more about their newspaper, and the press in general.

Some newspapers assign a full- or part-time person to respond to complaints of readers. Often readers' commentary is published on the editorial page. When the remarks of these media critics have pertained to the newspaper industry in general, they have been given considerable freedom to draw conclusions. On some newspapers, when criticism comes too close to home, however, critics find that they don't have as much freedom as they may have thought.[11]

CONCLUSION

The newspaper that wants to maintain the credibility of its news and editorial columns needs to draw a line between the two and take every opportunity available to remind readers of this line. But news and editorial are two parts of the same package. It may be possible to produce an outstanding news product without a good editorial page. It is virtually impossible, however, to produce an outstanding editorial page without the support of a good news product. Editorial writers need reporters more than reporters need editorial writers: They simply don't have enough arms and legs and eyes and noses to do their jobs all by themselves.

QUESTIONS AND EXERCISES

1. Why do you think that editorial writers have tended to ignore reporters and newsroom editors?

2. Do reporters, in your opinion, have a legitimate complaint when the editorial page expresses views with which they strongly disagree? What steps should be open to them?

3. Should news persons be allowed to purchase advertising space in the newspaper for which they work to express views contrary to those of management?

4. Should reporters be invited to write editorials on subjects with which they are familiar? Or to write signed opinion pieces for the editorial and op-ed pages?

5. Do reporters on papers in your area write editorials and/or signed articles for the editorial or op-ed pages?

6. Should editorial writers ask reporters for their opinions on issues that the reporters are covering?

7. Are there occasions when a page-one editorial can be justified? How about page-one election endorsements?

8. What do you think of the idea of tacking editorial comment to the end of news stories?

EDITORIAL PAGE
- EDITOR
- WRITER
- JANITOR
- WAITER
- RESEARCHER
- LETTER EDITOR
- PROOF READER
- TYPIST
- OILER OF TROUBLED WATERS

—Herman Auch
Rochester (N.Y.) *Times-Union* for *The Masthead*

The Editorial Page Staff

CHAPTER 8

Many editorial pages in this country's newspapers are wretchedly understaffed.
—Laurence J. Paul
Buffalo Evening News[1]

Mine, by damn, all mine.
—Don Shoemaker
Asheville *(N.C.)* Citizen[2]

Ask editorial writers if they need more help in putting out the editorial page and chances are they will answer Yes. But ask a writer who puts out a page all by himself or herself—or better yet one who used to put one out alone—and chances are you will get a lecture on the freedom and rewards, and misery, of doing the whole job by yourself.

Perhaps an editorial page staff, no matter how large or small, never quite seems to be the right size for all members. The writer on the one-person staff knows that he or she is overworked and doesn't get as much time to write editorials as desired. Writers on some two-person and three-person staffs, especially on larger papers, think they need more help. On some days, on papers with large staffs, a writer wishes that not so many colleagues were competing for space, promotion and community recognition. Members of large staffs think back fondly to the days when they wrote all the editorials, handled the letters, and still found time for a Chamber of Commerce luncheon. I know that I did when the editorial staff on the *Columbian* grew from one to two, and then from two to three members.

Just as there is variety in staff size, so is there a variety of opinion among editorial staffs regarding how much freedom each member of the staff should have and how much emphasis there should be on formal communication among members through editorial staff conferences. These are some of the topics of this chapter.

ONE-PERSON STAFF

A survey of editorial writers in 1979 found that the one-person staff is the most prevalent on U.S. daily newspapers. Almost 27 percent of all papers had a single editorial page person. Seventeen percent of all papers had no full-time person at all; another 17 percent had two persons; 14 percent had three; 10 percent had four; 8 percent had five; 6 percent had more than five.[3]

Putting out a page by yourself has its advantages. You can write what you wish if you have a good relationship with your publisher. You don't have to worry about disagreements among staff members. You can take full credit, or discredit, for whatever you do. Your readers know whom to praise or blame. You can go home at night and point to what you have accomplished.

"I should confess that I still recall with pleasure some of the aspects of those years when I wrote editorials for a semi-weekly and later a small daily newspaper without conferring with anybody in advance," recalled Wilbur Elston of the *Detroit News*. "I won't say those editorials could not have been improved. Obviously they could have been. But they were all mine. Whatever praise or criticism I heard from readers was especially pleasant to my ears." Unfortunately, Elston also recalled, most of the editorials "were, I fear, written off the top of my head."[4]

The one-person show is a tough one, and it's not for everyone. In the words of Don Shoemaker of the *Asheville* (N.C.) *Citizen,* it's like being "the keeper of the zoo." Shoemaker, who was the inspiration for the leading character in Jeff MacNelly's cartoon strip, "Shoe," saw the single editorial writer as "more put upon" than any other person in the field of newspapering. The writer had to please "crotchety and sour-bellied" printers, select and edit editorial page features that would complement the locally written editorials and satisfy the publisher, and know all about proofreading, page layout and makeup. The writer had to worry about "any novice journeyman who happens to be around the shop" fouling up the page. At the same time the one-person staff had to "keep a weather eye cocked for the passions and prejudices" of the community, the state and the region. "As any fool kin plainly see, the curator has an impossible, a thankless, a miserable job," Shoemaker wrote. But mostly the "fool" loves it. "I (ugh!) do," he concluded. "But there are moments."[5]

One of the big pluses is satisfaction of the ego. Shoemaker spoke of the "complete identity with a whole product— . . . come gripe or praise." When you are a one-person staff, you don't have to worry about bylines. Readers who are familiar with your page will know who wrote the words they agree or disagree with. The letters to the editor that comment on editorials are written to you. Members of the community who want support from the editorial page know whose door they should knock on.

Turning out the letters, the columns, the cartoons and the page layout, while handling telephone calls and office visitors, can account for a good share of the working day. But, once you get into the swing of it, composing one thoughtful, researched editorial and another quick one every day turns out not to be impossible at all. Topics always abound. William H. Heath of the *Haverhill* (Mass.) *Gazette* saw no reason for amazement or pity for the one-person staff. If the writer has the courage of his or her convictions, talent for writing clearly and forcibly, the hardest part of the task, Heath said, is finding room for all the editorials the writer is impelled to produce.[6]

Some editors—in fact, some editors who also double as publishers or managing editors—are able to produce two, three or four editorials a day and say something significant in each of them. They seem able to cover an unlimited range of topics. But my experience has been that single writers make the best use of talent and time if they concentrate on one topic a day, a topic they know a great deal about. They probably make their greatest contribution in explaining and commenting on local affairs. Once editorial writers have established their reputations on local matters, they can begin to expand their attention to state and regional levels. If writers pick their issues carefully and dig into them, state legislators, governors and other civic leaders outside their circulation areas will begin to read and cite the editorials.

IF NOT ONE, HOW MANY?

The 1979 survey of editorial writers cited earlier in this chapter did not relate the number of staff members to circulation size of newspapers. But a survey made eight years earlier found that 54 percent of dailies with less than 100,000 circulation had only one full-time editorial writer or a part-time writer. "Is it any wonder that performance occasionally falters?" asked Laurence J. Paul of the *Buffalo* (N.Y.) *Evening News* after reviewing the findings. "Apparently all this ink-stained Solomon is expected to do, in addition to whatever other sideline duties he may have, is to comment stylishly, thoughtfully and consistently on a broadening array of complex subjects in 15 to 25 lucid editorials a week," Paul wrote. "And after the value judgments are made, Solomon, don't forget the waste baskets before you leave." Paul found it scarcely more reassuring that 16 percent of the writers on papers of more than 100,000 circulation worked on staffs of no more than two full-time members. The deficiencies that he saw included superficial analysis, clumsy style, convenient subject matter, padded editorials and "even the canned editorials (God save us)."[7] (Canned editorials are opinion pieces supplied by editorial writing services or representatives of interest groups that a newspaper passes off as its own editorials.)

One of the tendencies of an editorial staff that is overworked is to write about national and international issues, which generally are well researched and summarized in the national media, news magazines, the *New York Times* or supplemental wire services. It is no trick to turn out several editorials in a few hours. But information is not likely to be so easily available on local, regional and state topics. There are likely to be fewer editorial voices to listen to and imitate. Consequently these issues tend to get left out when time starts to run out.

Paul thought it ought to be possible to set some guidelines for the size of the editorial page staff based on a newspaper's circulation. He suggested that the National Conference of Editorial Writers recommend that any paper with a circulation of 100,000 or more should employ at least three full-time writers and that any paper with 150,000 to 200,000 circulation hire at least four. He thought that papers between 50,000 and 100,000 should have a minimum of two writers.

In one sense, the circulation of a newspaper has little to do with the size of the staff needed to turn out a high-quality editorial page. There are editorials to write, columns and letters to handle and callers and visitors to deal with. An editorial page in a paper with a small circulation is the same size as in a larger paper. One difference, of course, is that a larger paper may produce seven editions a week instead of five or six, may have two opinion pages a day instead of one and publish an opinion section on the weekend. But the main reason that larger papers should maintain larger editorial page staffs is that they have greater resources with which to do so. They have more circulation, more advertising and more money to spend.

There is another reason: Larger papers tend to serve not just a local community but a region or an entire state. These papers thus have the opportunity to provide leadership in public affairs in the areas they serve. But they will not make full use of that opportunity unless they provide their writers with the time and the incentive to do their own research and their own thinking on the issues.

DIVISION OF DUTIES

A one-person staff doesn't have to worry much about how to split up the duties of producing an editorial page. He or she does whatever needs to be done. But help, primarily with letters to the editor, might be available from a newsroom secretary, copy clerk or someone with clerical skills. This person could check addresses of letters, enforce any rules the paper has concerning letters and retype them, if possible, for easy editing, on video display terminals. The person might be encouraged to try writing headlines for letters. Assistance with letters is probably the greatest help that a one-person staff can get. Next best is with messages and phone calls.

On a two-person staff one member is almost certain to be assigned the task of handling letters and perhaps the columns and cartoons as well. The other person (the editorial page editor) will devote time to writing editorials and meeting with the public and the newspaper management. The person doing the letters and columns will write editorials as he or she finds the time.

On a three-person staff the editorial page editor may ask one of the staff members to handle the letters and the other one to take care of the columns and the layout of the page. If the paper has a weekend opinion section, that may be the responsibility of one of the staff members.

On larger staffs, with a greater volume of letters, handling the mail may require a full-time person. A paper with an op-ed page may also require a full-time person to find and edit material for that page. The larger the staff and the more consistent the duties, the greater is the degree of specialization of the writers. When I was on the staff of the *Des Moines* (Iowa) *Register and Tribune,* most of the nine editorial page staff members had their own area of interest and expertise. All generally knew before the morning editorial conference what they would write about that day. Of course a nine-member editorial page staff is unusually large, even for those papers that publish both morning and evening editorial pages, as the *Register and Tribune* did before it became a combined operation in 1982.

Specialization can produce a more knowledgeable editorial writer, and thus more knowledgeable editorials. If an editorial is directed primarily toward experts in the subject, it may fully serve its purpose. But specialization has limitations. First, writers may become so engrossed in their speciality that they may not write an editorial that is comprehensible to the average reader. Second, when a paper's specialist on a subject is sick or on vacation or has left the staff, an editor may find that no one on the staff is capable of writing on that topic. Editorial writers should be able to write about many subjects, including their specialty.

THE TYPICAL DAY

A "typical day" for editorial writers on most papers is a contradiction in terms. Editorial writers who have contact with the outside world, or with other members of the staff, are not likely to *have* a typical day. It is hard for writers to plan their day and stick to that schedule. The smaller the staff, the greater the difficulty. Here is the day that John Sanford of the *Reno* (Nev.) *Evening Gazette* would like to have had:

First thing, the stack of newspapers to be scanned—all the Nevada papers, representative Western ones, with the *Wall Street Journal* and the *Christian Science Monitor* for topping. Then there's the morning mail, but that doesn't take long. Most of it hits the wastebasket.

Then along comes the day's editorial proofs, followed by close watch on the editorial page make-up, and a page proof for a double check.

Selection and editing of features and columns for tomorrow's page follow, for this material has to be in the backshop by noon.

That should leave the afternoon open for editorial meditation and writing.

This is a beautiful schedule—if it would ever work. It hasn't for the last 20 years.

Sanford said that, with interruptions and other demands, editorial writing usually occupied only an hour or two a day, and the trick was to find that free hour or two.[8]

Interrupting this ideal schedule are phone calls from everyone—from pests to big shots—unanticipated talks and conferences with other staff members and the boss, a cry of anguish from the composing room about missing copy, people who wander off the street to talk or sell an editorial idea. Then there are speeches, lunches, meetings, the stroll down Main Street (dreamer!) and after-hours cocktails that help keep the ivory tower from becoming too isolated—but may keep a spouse waiting at home with a no-longer-hot dinner. Some hard-pressed editors find they have to wait until most of the staff has gone home to find time to write their editorials.

David E. Gillespie of the *Charlotte* (N.C.) *Observer* kept a log one day to see how he spent his time. During the morning he had been able to find a few minutes to pick a topic for an editorial and to assemble some facts from a clippings file in the newspaper library. The time that remained for writing the editorial was from noon until 12:40 p.m., when he was due at a luncheon. During those 40 minutes he also managed to straighten his desk. The only other writing he did that day was 15 minutes devoted to paragraph-long shorts.[9]

On the *Buffalo Evening News* LeRoy E. Smith said that he usually spent three hours each morning catching up on the news and mail, correcting proofs and attending an editorial conference. The amount of time he spent in the afternoons on editorials, he said, depended on the prewriting research required. Digging into local, regional and state matters took longer than digging into national and international subjects.[10]

A schedule that many writers might envy was sketched by William G. Peeples of the *Louisville Courier-Journal*. First thing in the morning, he said, he read various newspapers and drew a list of possible editorial topics. He might check the library for information on the topics before a 10:30 a.m. editorial conference. The conference lasted from 30 minutes to an hour. He might do some research or make a phone call before lunch at 11:45. Thirty minutes later he was at his desk ready to write. That left him 2 hours and 15 minutes until his 2:30 deadline for the next day's page. After the deadline he might work on a different piece without pressure, or see visitors or just read. He left the office around 5 p.m.[11] That type of routine may be possible on a paper where someone else handles the letters, columns, walk-ins and call-ins and worries about fitting the page together in the composing room.

EDITORIAL CONFERENCES

Editorial writers and editors divide sharply over the value—or lack of value— of regular editorial board conferences. Proponents argue that they provide an opportunity to bring the thinking of several people to bear on topics, that give-and-take discussion can produce ideas that might otherwise not emerge. Discussion can also show that a topic needs more research or possibly ought to be dropped entirely as unworthy of comment. John G. McCullough of the *Philadelphia Evening Bulletin* said that when his staff skipped the morning editorial conference he and the other writers missed it. "When the free give-and-take of these conferences is missing, I feel it shows in an editorial," he said. "They seem to have a structural narrowness reflecting the absence of other, counter, views. Such editorials come through as a whoosh of heated opinion." He said those editorials lacked the persuasive logic that is provided by "the extra ingredients fed into the mix during the editorial conference." He argued that, if an editorial is to represent more than one person's point of view, it should reflect a blending of various shades of opinion.[12]

Some of the critics of conferences contend that this blending contributes to bland editorials. Hugh B. Patterson Jr. of the *Arkansas Gazette* of Little Rock acknowledged that discussions helped clarify and sharpen arguments but they could also produce no more than "the lowest common denominator of mutual agreement."[13] In the same vein, William P. Cheshire of the *State* of Columbia, S.C., quoted the dean of Guilford, who blamed the committee approach of his colleagues of the Church of England for language he called "graceless parson-speak." "A committee," said the dean, "however talented its members, can no more be expected to write a poem or become joint authors of a new Hamlet than the Board of British Rail can be expected to dance Swan Lake at Waterloo Station in the rush hour." The quotation prompted Cheshire to ask: "Could the board, I ask, write an editorial?"[14]

Pat Murphy of the Phoenix *Arizona Republic* contended that his staff members did not need editorial conferences. "Our staff is made up of self-starters who spin out ideas and suggestions and hit the ground running every morning,'' he said. Instead of a conference, he made the rounds of staff members first thing in the morning to suggest ideas and listen to their proposals. "Fie on daily conferences," he said. "They're a waste of time."[15] Robert B. Frazier of the *Eugene* (Ore.) *Register-Guard* said he and two other writers didn't need to meet, since they were "really in perpetual conference," checking constantly with one another.[16] Sam Laird of the *Courier-Post*, Camden, N.J., thought that, while daily meetings were a waste of time, meeting once a week, on Monday morning, was adequate.

Various combinations of people involved in setting editorial policy might be tried. Staff members who do the writing of the editorials might meet each morning with the editorial page editor to discuss that day's topics. At less frequent intervals the editorial page editor might meet with the newspaper editor or the publisher to talk about paper policy as it affects the editorial page. Daily meetings, coupled with the editorial page editor conferring with the editor, were what we followed when I was on the *Des Moines* (Iowa) *Register and Tribune.* On the *Columbian,* in Vancouver, Wash., the pattern that evolved consisted of a daily meeting of editorial writers and a bi-weekly meeting of the editorial board, which included all the editorial staff members, the co-publishers and two or three representatives of other departments of the paper. Another possibility, of course, is for the representative of management, whether a publisher or a general manager, to sit in on all daily conferences. This last arrangement helps assure that the publisher is informed on editorial issues, but it probably also has an inhibiting effect on discussion of the issues.

The principal purposes served by the daily conference in Vancouver were two: to coordinate assignment of topics and to discuss, perhaps only briefly, the merits of the arguments that might be made. With two writers and an editor, no one covered particular areas. One of the purposes of the meeting therefore was to decide who got a topic when both of the writers had it on their lists.

Sometimes, after the assignment was made, the topic might not be discussed. But because of some differences in experience and philosophy—and some friendly competition—one of us would ask, "What do you intend to say about it?" or sometimes more pointedly, "You're not just going to say such-and-such, are you?" Usually the result was that the writer, who may have planned to dash off something that had come quickly to mind, was slowed down enough to take a more careful look at the issue. The final product was usually a piece with more perspective and a more convincing conclusion. If that stabbing question had not come at the morning conference, the editorial might have been an off-the-cuff product.

Four years after I left the *Columbian,* I sat as an observer at the paper's morning conference. The three staff members conducted the conference in much the same way as when I worked there. One interesting aspect at the beginning of the meeting was that most of the possible editorial topics mentioned related to national and international events, items that had been in the paper that morning. These topics got very little discussion, partly because staff writers had previously commented on these or similar topics and they all knew the paper's position.

It was when the local topics emerged that discussion got under way. A proposed local expressway did not get much attention; after all, it had been discussed when I was on the paper. Lengthy and heated discussion, however, arose over a rumor that congressional redistricting might put Vancouver and Tacoma, 140 miles apart, into the same district. The writer who eventually was assigned that topic spent almost an entire day tracking down a reliable source on the subject and writing the editorial. Some discussion at the meeting focused on a local weekly open-air market that was about to fold, a topic that seemed of interest to two of the writers. At the end of the conference the editorial page editor said that, since the writer who had suggested the subject already had a topic for the day, he, the editor, would write about the market. A story in a rival newspaper that morning prompted discussion about the county auditor's charges that unforeseen costs justified a re-evaluation of a proposed new county jail. The arguments about the project got a thorough airing at the conference, but the writer who was assigned the topic, one he had written on before, eventually concluded that the project should proceed and that these were likely to be only the first of unforeseen costs in the project.

The national and international topics were not addressed in editorials that day, although several of them might have been if all the writers had not spent several hours later in the day with a subdivision developer who had a project he wanted to discuss and in one of the bi-weekly editorial board meetings.

I did not attend that board meeting, but the general format remained unchanged from the days that I was there. The editorial page editor reported that the meeting had gone well. No major disagreements had arisen. He said that one reason he had been satisfied with most of the board meetings was that he made a point of establishing the agenda and researching his topics thoroughly ahead of time. I know from my experience with that board that, when the agenda was not set, some of the non-editorial members were likely to bring up matters of interest to them, usually topics that the editorial writers were not prepared to provide definitive answers on. The writers sometimes found themselves agreeing to look into subjects that they were not interested in or that they viewed differently from the non-editorial members. We counted ourselves fortunate when we emerged from the meetings without being saddled with any of these topics. The board meetings hardly ever provided the real thrashing out of issues that took place in the smaller morning sessions.

Editorial writers, even those who hold regular meetings, need to step back a pace or two from time to time. Gilbert Cranberg of the *Des Moines Register and Tribune* found that putting out two editorial pages a day kept his staff so occupied that it had no chance to examine how it really operated or how the pages could be improved. Cranberg tried a 90-minute luncheon for the writers and found that the session produced ideas for improving use of syndicated features, increasing locally written material for the pages and instituting a proposed sabbatical leave program.[17]

When I was on the *Columbian,* the three of us left the office early on a couple of afternoons, with a six-pack of beer, to talk about the broader issues, some minute details and the inter-workings among our own personalities. The result was a clearing of the air that could not have taken place in a hurried morning meeting and some ideas for improving the page that did not spring full-blown from the mind of any one of the participants.

CONCLUSION

There are no ideal sizes for editorial page staffs. The size that editorial writers are likely to regard as ideal may depend on their own prior experience. To writers who have run a one-person show, a two-person staff may look like a luxury. To writers who have worked on a larger staff, two persons are likely to seem wholly inadequate. Although some attempts have been made to prescribe staff sizes for papers of varying circulation sizes, the results seem to show that the circulation of a newspaper has little correlation to the work that needs to be done on an editorial page. The page must come out every day, whatever the circulation; columns and letters must be edited; a certain number of editorials must be written; visitors and callers must be dealt with; meetings, editorial conferences and research must be attended to.

All things being equal, a larger editorial page staff should be able to turn out a better product. If writers have an opportunity to spend a lot of time thinking about one or two specific areas of editorial writing, instead of having to render the judgments of Solomon on all issues, they ought to be better editorial writers. If they write only one editorial a day, they should be able to do a better job than if they have to write three. However, if they overspecialize, they may work themselves out of their jobs. Editorial writers must never stop being generalists.

QUESTIONS AND EXERCISES

1.   Recent surveys suggest that editorial page staffs on the average have not been growing in size. What does this seem to say about the attitudes of publishers and other holders of the newspaper budget purse strings?

2.   What are the advantages of a one-person editorial page staff? The disadvantages? Do you think the disadvantages outweigh the advantages?

3. Determine the number of editorial page persons on papers in your area. How do these staffs compare in size with the staff sizes mentioned in this chapter?

4. How are the editorial duties distributed among the staff members of these papers?

5. How do the editorial conferences—if any—work on these papers? Who attends? How often do they meet? How are assignments made? Does the editor, the publisher or the editorial board make the final decisions?

—Tony Auth
Philadelphia Inquirer for *The Masthead*

Relations With the Community

I suspect that from the smallest daily to the largest, the editor is hooked for service on various boards, commissions and committees, and . . . cannot wiggle out of these commitments without damage to the community image of [the] publishing corporation.
—James J. Kilpatrick[1]
Syndicated columnist

I choose to remain virginal.
—Norman Cherniss
Riverside *(Calif.)* Press-Enterprise[2]

Some of the toughest decisions faced by editors and editorial writers involve the degree to which they allow themselves to participate in civic, business and political affairs. Involved in these decisions is the question: How can editorial writers be a part of a community without becoming biased, or appearing to be biased, through associations with groups with special interests? Closely related to this aspect of maintaining integrity and the appearance of integrity is the problem faced by all journalists—to what extent, if any, can you accept drinks, meals and trips from persons with whom you deal without compromising yourself?

These questions have provoked a lot of conscience-searching among editorial writers and have led several organizations in the newspaper business to conclude that consciences need help through codes and guidelines. In this chapter we will see how editorial writers have tried to work out what they see as proper relationships with groups in their communities and with those who would like to do them favors.

TO PARTICIPATE OR NOT TO PARTICIPATE

Those who defend participation in community affairs contend that editorial writers should recognize that they are part of their community and should feel a responsibility to help make it a better place in which to live. But others contend just as strongly that, if writers become involved, they compromise their credibility in commenting on community affairs.

If editorial writers were to subscribe wholeheartedly to either philosophy, decision making would be easy. If they thought that working through organizations was as appropriate for them as molding opinions through their writing, they would say Yes when asked to participate in a worthy cause. If they thought they should undertake no obligations, they would say No. Most editorial writers, however, seem to think that there are some occasions when they can or should become involved and some occasions when they cannot or should not. Places for drawing the line are almost as numerous as editors and writers themselves. When 13 editorial writers participated in a 1966 *Masthead* symposium on the question of proper community involvement, they gave 13 different answers.[3]

Civic Activities

The argument in favor of working through local groups and causes usually begins with the premise that editorial writers have the same stake as anyone else in making their communities better places in which to live. Most communities are not so blessed with potential leaders and activists that they won't be affected adversely by the absence of representatives from one of the major institutions. Especially in smaller communities, newspaper people may be among the relatively small number of people with the educations, income, leisure time and civic interest needed for community leadership.

Robert M. Hitt Jr. of the *Charleston* (S.C.) *Evening Post* said he thought that newspaper people "have an obligation to assist worthwhile civic endeavors, including sitting on policy-making boards and holding high office." He ruled out political offices and what he regarded as public or quasi-public bodies such as banks and savings and loan associations. But he thought his interests would only be sharpened by such activities as serving as director of the Chamber of Commerce, vice president of the United Fund or an officer of the Family Agency.[4]

James J. Kilpatrick, while on the *Richmond* (Va.) *News Leader,* said the policy on that paper was that no editor should accept a position with a group that might be the subject of editorial comment. But "in actual practice it tends to get bent around the edges," he said. What is an editor to do when asked to serve on the board of the local library, or the symphony orchestra, or the community college, or the art museum? Or perhaps a committee on public parks or race relations? Sometimes, he said, editors can get away with saying No, but inevitably requests catch up with them. Editors cannot become completely detached from the community. Accepting some of these requests may leave an editor's "editorial purity something less than that of Ivory soap," but they also are likely to make the editor "a better informed and more useful citizen of the community on which the paper depends."[5]

An effort to observe the line between topics that are and are not likely to be subjects of editorial comment was made by Hal Burton of *Newsday,* on Long Island, when he accepted appointment to the Adirondack Mountain Authority of the State of New York. When he took the job, he told the governor that he would consider himself free to criticize activities of the authority as he saw fit. He did not regard the actions of the authority, whose sole concerns were ski centers and mountain parkways 300 miles north of Long Island, to be of interest to his paper. But, he said, if he had been asked to serve on the Long Island State Park Commission, a local agency or the State Thruway Authority, whose activities came under the scrutiny of his paper, he would have declined the appointment.[6]

Kilpatrick recounted that he had accepted an appointment to a state commission that seemed at first to be innocuous enough but that eventually came to embarrass him. For eight years he had served on the state Commission on Constitutional Government, an agency organized to encourage states to defend their reserved powers under the federal government. He also was chairman of publications for the commission. But when the commission came under attack in the Virginia General Assembly, Kilpatrick said he found himself in a trap. "I could not defend the Commission's publications without appearing to be saying what a great guy am I." In the end, he said, he wrote a "lame piece" to the effect that the incident ought to have taught him a lesson about becoming involved with boards and commissions.[7]

Two embarrassing experiences were described in the symposium by Jameson G. Campaigne of the *Indianapolis* (Ind.) *Star.* He agreed to serve on the publicity committee of the Family Services Association, which seemed to him to be "a noncontroversial organization doing some good." But within months the association took a stand against disclosing information about welfare programs that both he and his paper thought ought to have been disclosed. He resigned from the association. Later he accepted a position on the board of the Indianapolis Servicemen's Center, which he thought was not likely to become involved in a public issue. But shortly thereafter the Community Fund, which financed the center, decided to abolish it. Campaigne wrote "a stinging editorial blasting the Community Fund and its directors." The conflict of interest proved to be double-edged. He had forgotten that the *Star*'s assistant general manager was head of the Community Fund and that the managing editor was head of its publicity committee.[8] Here clearly were examples of newspaper people allowing themselves to be drawn into worthy community causes that turned out to be more controversial than they had at first seemed.

That these editors agreed to serve on publicity and publications committees seems especially surprising. Helping to publicize an organization seems to be in direct conflict with a journalist's commitment not to give special favors to one organization over another. Newspaper people are constantly asked to help with publicity. Here they should be able to draw a definite line.

Some writers have tried to draw the line between themselves and newspaper management people. Worth Bingham of the *Louisville* (Ky.) *Courier-Journal* suggested that it might help insulate editorial writers from community interests "by having their bosses take on the civic and charitable duties."[9] E. L. Holland Jr. of the *Birmingham* (Ala.) *News* said his paper's management generally shied away from memberships but had not been able to avoid getting involved. Executives, Holland said, may serve "with relative ease," while people generally honor the editor's decision to remain uninvolved. He said it was possible for an editor to comment on agencies on which a newspaper's executive serves, but "I would not—and few would—write a caustic piece about the results of an agency's work, efficiency, etc., when the chief mover of such an agency was just down the hall."[10]

Clearly, civic commitments made by publishers and other non-news, non-editorial executives on a newspaper can make credible editorial writing hard for staff members and hurt the overall credibility of the newspaper.

Jonathan Marshall, publisher of the *Scottsdale* (Ariz.) *Daily Progress,* said that he attended meetings of civic groups and fraternal organizations, but "I don't join them so that I can be impartial when they want a story."[11] Another publisher, Donald Breed of the *Freeport* (Ill.) *Journal-Standard,* warned that being independent of groups is "not a luxury; it's work," but is "not too much to ask." He acknowledged that neither the publisher nor editorial writers can live in a vacuum, "without friends or follies, residing on both sides of the tracks at the same time, indifferent about political parties, religious affiliation or other group or personal interest." The real trick, Breed said, was "to step out of groups and parties and view them with an appraising eye." It requires the same type of detachment required of judges. "Many judges are equal to the demands made on their intelligence, and so are many publishers and the editorial and news writers," Breed said.[12]

Robert Pittman of the *St. Petersburg* (Fla.) *Times* referred to the process of remaining independent as finding one's way "through the jungle of social and civic clubs." In the end, editors will have to struggle whether they "fraternize and fight off the requests for special attention" or "stay aloof and fight off the requests for attention." He wrote: "Either way, the objective editor must be alert to the fact that the modern threat of editorial seduction is more social than economic or political."[13]

The social pressures come not only through formal memberships but informal associations as well. Joe Stroud of the *Detroit* (Mich.) *Free Press* reminded readers of a *Masthead* symposium that editorial writers "like to be liked," especially by the "right people," those with expense accounts, club memberships and "a manner polished through the years of bellying up to the Press Club bar with newspaper types in tow." He advised writers to listen to the public relations people but to "keep them at arm's length and then go out to see for yourself."[14]

Business and Labor

Some of these public relations people represent civic activities; more of them are likely to represent business interests. No editorial writer can expect exemption from the influence of the business community. For one thing, the newspaper is a business; one of the publisher's first concerns, as we noted in Chapter 6, is to make a profit. One of the editorial writer's concerns is to make enough money and have a steady enough job to live securely and comfortably. To a larger extent than many businesses, the profitability of a newspaper is tied to the growth and prosperity of the community in which it is located. When a community expands, a local supermarket cannot expect to keep its monopoly; another market moves in. The same can be said about service stations and real estate offices, even radio stations. But the result for the newspaper is likely to be more circulation and more advertising but not a new competitor. The temptation to ally a newspaper with whatever brings growth and income to a community has been a fairly consistent one in many communities. Perhaps in recent years the temptation has seemed easier to resist, evidenced by a more sophisticated understanding of the financial and environmental costs of unplanned growth that has begun to work its way into the editorial pages of American newspapers. Still, it remains difficult not to get excited editorially when a major industry, especially a "clean" electronics industry, chooses your town for a new plant.

When I was on the *Columbian* in Vancouver, Wash., such a plant was announced for construction, in three phases, in our community. The company would start in an existing building, with modest employment, then build a larger interim facility while making plans for a giant plant for future construction on the edge of the city. The *Columbian* enthusiastically welcomed this new citizen to the community, through its editorials. Just for fun, I also wrote a second editorial, a satirical one, suggesting that the new industry would disrupt the community, interfere with existing land use plans and cost it a lot of money. I circulated the piece only among other newspaper executives, and we all laughed. The company was a good company. It did not pollute; it paid well; its employees participated extensively in community affairs. The interim plant was occupied, and the necessary rezoning and the building of new sewers and roads proceeded apace. Land values in the area of the proposed plant rose. Then suddenly the company announced that it was phasing out the type of equipment that it was making in Vancouver. The long-range plant would not be built, and the interim plant would be closed. The company left town, and the community was left with open sewer trenches, partly built roads and empty positions on many community agencies.

If there is a lesson for editorial writers here, it is probably that, in looking at economic as well as political issues, they need to cast a wary eye on what other members of the community may see only in black-and-white terms. Writers need to remind their readers, and local business and political leaders, that growth may carry a price that is not always immediately apparent.

Closely related to the temptation to look favorably on growth is a tendency among editorial writers toward what might be called local or regional provincialism. Writers should take pride in their city, their state and their region and should want to see their area prosper and become an attractive place in which to live. But it is hard sometimes for them to see beyond their own circulation areas—and such provincialism can become a vested interest. For example, a writer may condemn a proposed federal dam halfway across the country as a congressional boondoggle but praise a proposed local dam as an economic necessity. Another editor, living in Northern California, may argue that water located in the north should stay there. One of the challenges for editorial writers is to lift their sights and those of their readers beyond the city limits and the near bank of the next river.

Another concern for editorial writers in the economic arena involves the ever-present threat of a clash between business interests and news or editorial policy. What does a newspaper do when a major advertiser threatens to withdraw advertising because of something that has appeared or might appear in the paper? Does the publisher stand firm and let the advertiser pull out? What does a newspaper do when it learns that an advertiser has been caught in an unfair trade practice or a sex discrimination practice? Does it publish its findings and condemn them on the editorial page? What happens when a local supermarket wants to build a new store in an area that the community had previously designated as non-commercial? Do the editorial writers feel free to come out against this advertiser if they think the proposal is wrong?

These are some of the questions that can face editorial writers and publishers. Taking a strong stand against business interests can be tough, especially if the financial well-being of the newspaper itself is at stake. In the long run, newspapers probably serve themselves best if they take a firm stand at the beginning of a confrontation. A publisher who refuses to back down to an advertiser's threats will let it be known to other potential threateners that the paper will stand firm against them as well. A paper that can take an editorial stand against its own immediate financial interests can gain public respect that may eventually help not only its credibility but its economic condition as well.

Labor associations can pose conflicts for editorial writers as well. Some publishers and editors see membership in an organized labor group as interfering with an editorial writer's ability to write objectively. In the view of Sylvan Meyer of the *Gainesville* (Ga.) *Daily Times,* an editorial writer who belongs to a labor organization is almost certain to run into conflict between the "responsibility to comment on current history" in an unbiased manner and a "desire to maintain the strength" of the organization.[15] Many editorial writers are spared having to decide whether to join a labor group by the terms of employee-management contracts; editorial writers are excluded on the grounds that they speak for management. Some editors see no cause for concern over union membership of editorial writers. "The only policy reason for barring them, so far as I can see," wrote Robert Lasch of the *St. Louis* (Mo.) *Post-Dispatch,* "would be a fear that they would permit their union affiliations to color their writing on labor or political issues." But if editorial writers cannot be trusted to be honest, they ought not to be editorial writers, he said.[16]

Politics

We noted in Chapter 3 that of the editorial writers who responded to a survey those who considered themselves Democrats slightly outnumbered those who thought of themselves as Republicans. But if there is one community activity about which most editorial writers agree they should not become actively involved it is partisan politics. The 13 writers who participated in the 1966 symposium agreed unanimously on this point. But editorial writers, and certainly editors and publishers, have not always avoided partisan entanglements. The editor of the *Redlands* (Calif.) *Daily Facts,* Frank E. Moore, told me that he and his brother, publisher William G. Moore, were often contacted by Republican members of Congress, in the 1950s and 1960s, when they wanted advice on local political appointments. William Moore served as county Republican chairman for a time, headed the county campaigns for William F. Knowland and Richard M. Nixon and served as a delegate to the National Republican Convention. Other editors and publishers could tell similar stories. Knowland himself was a newspaper publisher, of the *Oakland* (Calif.) *Tribune.*

The trend seems strong these days, however, for editors and publishers to avoid formal ties to political parties and generally to avoid close associations with nonpartisan local political races. The most frequent exceptions probably occur in smaller communities, where getting people to serve on the school board or the town council may be sufficiently difficult that the editor or the publisher feels a responsibility to take a turn.

Sometimes in small, and even not so small, communities editors are drawn into a community position when they would prefer to remain on the outside looking in. In Wichita, Kan., Martin Perry of the *Wichita Eagle* concluded at one time that government had become so bad at city hall that he wrote an editorial calling for formation of a citizens' committee to set things straight. The next day a community leader called him to say, in effect, "Okay, you say we need a citizens' organization. Let's form one." It was "put up or shut up," Perry said. So the two of them called several other citizens, organized, eventually elected a three-person majority to the city commission and achieved some of their goals. "You can write your own lessons from this," Perry said. "Perhaps you'll conclude that—as I always thought before—editorial writers should stay out of direct involvement in 'politics.' Or, maybe you'll decide, as I did, that special circumstances sometimes dictate otherwise."[17]

Personal Experiences

In the nearly two decades in which I was associated with an editorial page, I tried to limit my civic activities to those that required little time and seemed to pose little risk of conflict with editorial policy. Looking back, I think I should have limited myself even more.

I inherited a Rotary Club membership from my predecessor on the *Columbian,* faithfully attended luncheon meetings for nearly 12 years and never encountered any conflict of interest that I recognized. I was never asked to serve on the publicity committee. I never had an occasion to write an editorial either praising or criticizing the club or its activities. Membership benefited me, I thought, because it brought me into contact with leaders of the business community whom I would have found difficult to get to know otherwise. Rotary provided me the one community fellowship, aside from my church, that I allowed myself. I think my membership benefited the newspaper too. Instead of being an unknown person in an ivory tower, expressing opinions more liberal than most of those of the club's members, I was a fellow member whom they could poke fun at over typographical or other errors that appeared in the paper. The club had a policy of fining a member whenever his name appeared in the paper; it seemed to be a rare week that someone didn't figure out a way to impose a dollar fine on the editor as well. The good-natured ribbing that came with my membership almost became a club tradition. I tried as hard as I could to avoid such activities as the club's rummage sale and selling tickets for an annual travel series.

Another organization in which I was not so successful in avoiding conflict was called Design for Clark County. It consisted of civic-minded citizens who wanted to ensure good government and a good environment for the community. The conflict began when I agreed to head one of four goals committees, the one on government. The committee proved to be the most active of the four, partly because goals can be expressed more specifically in government than in other areas of the community. Because of the attention the committee received and because the goals generally coincided with the *Columbian*'s editorial policies, some members of the community began to think that the newspaper and I were running Design for Clark County. I later backed off sharply in my participation in Design, but the association between the paper and the organization had been established so strongly in people's minds that it was several years before the effect of my initial involvement was forgotten. During those years Design might have been more effective in achieving its goals if it had been perceived more as an independent voice.

I served for a short time on the board of the Washington Environmental Council, a private non-profit organization. No problems resulted as long as the council remained concerned with general environmental policies, but when it began to talk about supporting and opposing candidates for the legislature, I got out of there fast.

I found myself in Kilpatrick's shoes when I agreed to serve on the Washington State Planning Commission. It was not a real planning commission; I would never have served on an official state policy agency. It was a two-year ad hoc committee of citizens and officials charged with proposing a new state planning act. Mostly it held hearings on what other people thought the state should do. Eventually the staff, with some help from commission members, drew up a model act to submit to the legislature. The act didn't get very far—or I probably would have encountered greater conflict than I did. I thought I should not comment editorially on the proposal, though I did write an article for the op-ed page trying to explain the model act—with an editor's note pointing out my connection with the commission. Participation on the commission made for an interesting and informative two years, but if the act had been seriously considered for adoption a conflict of interest would have prevented me from commenting editorially on it and would probably have hurt the credibility of anything the *Columbian* said even if the writing had been done by someone else.

I feel less concern about the four years that I served on the Washington Commission for the Humanities, a private, non-profit organization that awarded money mostly to local groups to bring the ideas of humanities scholars to bear on public issues. Some of the awards were controversial among the commission members, but I don't remember any award that would have called for editorial comment in my newspaper. Perhaps that says something about how lacking in radicalism the funded projects were, or perhaps I avoided facing the bigger issue by concentrating on the modest requests for $2,000 and $9,000. Toward the end of my term some members of Congress and other critics began questioning the value of the activities of the National Endowment for the Humanities and the state commissions, and the method for funding became an issue.

One reason I enjoyed the commission was the chance to know and associate with the other members. It was a stimulating group and one, like the Adirondack Mountain Authority, that was concerned with matters far enough away from my circulation area to present few chances for conflict. Besides, I told myself, an editorial writer needs to have some stimulating, continuing associations beyond those of family and religious ties. Editorial writers aren't supposed to be hermits.

TO ACCEPT OR NOT TO ACCEPT

The second general topic of this chapter concerns the problem of what to do about "freebies," the gifts, large and small, that people with views to push are only too willing to share with newspaper people. In this area in recent years government and business, including the newspaper industry, have tended to become more sensitive to possible conflicts of interest. Tighter codes have been written for public officials, and in many instances editorial writers have written in favor of the tougher restrictions. If newspapers expect public officials to observe a higher standard, should not newspapers themselves observe an equally high one?

In 1974 and 1975, following a lead set by other journalistic organizations, NCEW took steps to tighten its code on conflicts of interest. The conflict portion of an original statement of principles, adopted in 1949, had merely said: "The editorial writer should never be motivated by personal interest, nor use his influence to seek special favors for himself or for others. He should hold himself above any possible taint of corruption, whatever its source.'' At the NCEW convention in 1975 members approved revisions in the statement, substituting the following:

> The editorial writer should never use his or her influence to seek personal favors of any kind. Gifts of value, free travel and other favors that can compromise integrity, or appear to do so, should not be accepted.
>
> The writer should be constantly alert to conflicts of interest, real or apparent, including those that may arise from financial holdings, secondary employment, holding public office or involvement in political, civic or other organizations. Timely disclosure can minimize suspicion.
>
> Editors should seek to hold syndicates to these standards.
>
> The writer, further to enhance editorial page credibility, also should encourage the institution he or she represents to avoid conflicts of interest, real or apparent.

The Professional Standards Committee and the Executive Committee of NCEW had wanted stricter language on freebies. They had proposed: ''Gifts, free travel and other things of value can compromise integrity. Nothing of more than token value should be accepted.'' This restriction was not included because a majority of NCEW members thought that the organization should not be substituting its judgment for the members' own consciences.

Free Trips

The wording regarding travel was softened partly because NCEW officers at that time were hoping to arrange a trip for members to the People's Republic of China and a trip partly paid for by the Chinese was seen as the only way to get there. The trip finally materialized a few years later.

The only participants in a *Masthead* symposium on junkets were six whom the magazine's editors call scoffers. Basically they argued that the benefits of subsidized trips abroad outweighed any dangers that might arise from possible conflicts of interest. H. Brandt Ayers of the *Anniston* (Ala.) *Star* said he never would have been able to travel to the Soviet Union and meet leaders firsthand if the trip had not been subsidized. ''What we wrote is a better standard for judging independence, intelligence and integrity than who paid for the trip,'' he said.[18] John Causten Currey of the *Daily Oklahoman* and *Oklahoma City Times* said that familiarization trips offered by the armed services provided the only way that editorial writers could see what the defense budgets bought. He said a paid trip to Israel as an official guest provided him a picture of the Middle East he could not have obtained as a private citizen.[19] Smith Hempstone, a syndicated columnist, contended that any problems involved in accepting a subsidized trip could be overcome by letting readers know who paid for the trip.[20] Richard B. Laney of the *Deseret News,* Salt Lake City, wondered how free travel could be compromising to those who accepted it, since he suspected that invitations are extended only to those known, or thought to be, friendly. "The persuasion of those already persuaded may not be gutsy PR," he wrote, "but it's hardly an attack on editorial morality either."[21]

One of the earliest statements of the dangers of accepting free trips was made more than 20 years before NCEW tightened its code. In 1952 Robert Estabrook of the *Washington Post* wrote:

> At least a respectable argument can be made that the public interest is served in making available to newspaper readers more information about governmental programs, particularly programs abroad. The plain fact is that many newspapers, if left to their own resources, would neglect these areas and their readers would be the poorer for it. . . .
>
> If we expect to persuade our followers there is something wrong with unreported political funds or junkets by Congressmen at the taxpayers' expense, then we have an obligation, it seems to me, to pay our own way. We properly criticize "influence" with public officials, but I wonder if our readers, if they knew of the all-expense tours, would see much difference.[22]

Stricter codes, unless one stays home and makes no junkets, cost more money. However, in general newspapers and the media are more prosperous than they were when Estabrook wrote. If editors and publishers think their staff members should be sent off somewhere for a story, they should pay as much of their way as they possibly can. What they pay out in money they will regain in credibility with readers.

Gifts

When newspaper salaries were notoriously low, some reporters reasoned that free liquor and tickets to shows and games helped make up for the bucks they didn't get. Today salaries are up, and gifts are down. Some newspapers have attempted to stop the flow of gifts, however inconsequential it may be. But in line with the arguments supporting expense-paid trips, some editors contend that, if writers can be bought for a bottle of whiskey or a lunch, they have no integrity worth buying. Most of the debate among editorial writers over freebies has been over travel, not gifts.

The argument against the need for strict rules was presented in this manner by Mark Clutter of the *Wichita* (Kan.) *Beacon*: Why should newspaper people "be offended by gifts of whiskey, ham or similar items?" Sometimes the gifts are a matter of "public relations routine"; sometimes they are "expressions of genuine friendship or admiration," he said. "Whatever the motive, it would be churlish to refuse." He thought that one way to maintain contact with sources of information was to let these people do nice things for one. "No one can give payola to a man of integrity," he concluded. "To a man who has no integrity, practically everything is payola."[23]

On the other side, Jack Craemer of the *San Rafael* (Calif.) *Independent-Journal* said people on that paper sent everything back to donors, even though they "look upon us as goof-balls. . . . I wish organizations like NCEW, Sigma Delta Chi and ASNE would take a strong stand against the journalistic counterpart of payola," he wrote. "I would like to get over the feeling that I'm alone in my opposition to and criticism of gifts-for-influence."[24]

CONCLUSION

That was written in 1960. About a decade and a half later the three organizations that Craemer named took such stands, of varying strength. NCEW, as we noted, recommended against accepting gifts, travel and other favors that could "compromise integrity, or appear to do so." The Society of Professional Journalists, Sigma Delta Chi, prescribed that "nothing of value should be accepted." The American Society of Newspaper Editors said that newspaper people "should neither accept anything nor pursue any activities that might compromise or seem to compromise their integrity."

In spite of these admonitions, if the *Independent-Journal* is still sending freebies back to senders, it is, if not exactly alone, at least very lonely. Many newspaper people are still accepting freebies, some of which are not consequential. Some newspaper people relish getting tickets worth a few dollars or a free book in the mail. They like a hosted bar; the paper manufacturers have been great hosts over the years. Newspaper people like hard-to-get reserved seats when the Goodyear blimp comes to town. To the credit of NCEW, it has refused to accept hosted functions, but it does rely on host newspapers to help defray convention expenses.

Probably very few editorial writers, and newspaper people in general for that matter, are directly influenced by the gifts, travel and other favors they receive. The publicity over tougher codes has made many of them sensitive to the most blatant forms of handouts. They know that they are not being influenced by the ticket or the drink. But do their readers know? Editorial writers may know that they have made every effort possible to report objectively on a free trip they have taken. But do their readers know? If they were told, would they believe it?

When conflict of interest is involved, appearance can be as important as reality in maintaining credibility.

QUESTIONS AND EXERCISES

1. If you were an editorial writer, where would you draw the line on participation in civic affairs? Would the size of the community make a difference?

2. Does an editorial writer or editor have a responsibility to participate in the life of the community in addition to contributing through work on the paper? Again, might the answer depend on the size of the community?

3. Should an editorial writer feel freer to accept a civic task that is less likely than other tasks to affect the community in which the paper circulates? Does distance, in other words, make a difference?

4. Should newspaper management people feel freer to participate in community affairs than news and editorial people?

5. Should a newspaper establish a code that spells out what freebies, trips and other perquisites news and editorial people can accept? If so, where should the paper draw the line?

6. If a newspaper does not establish a code, how should it avoid conflict of interest or the appearance of conflict of interest?

7. How do you respond to the argument that, if journalists are not honest and trust-worthy, no code will make them so?

8. If you were an editorial writer, what trips would you regard as acceptable?

9. Have you seen evidence in the columns of newspapers in your area that indicates the writers do or do not accept free trips? If they do, do they explain the circumstances to their readers?

10. Do the papers in your area have official codes concerning professional conduct? If so, what do they prescribe?

The How of the Editorial Page

'Dear, from my right I'd like you to meet . . . Righteous Indignation, Stinging Rebuttal, Agonizing Reapprisal, Thunderous Fury, and Pretentious Crowing.'

—Tom Innes
Calgary (Alberta) *Herald* for *The Masthead*

Nine Steps to Editorial Writing

CHAPTER

10

I would not suggest that writing editorials can be codified like a law book or that anyone can learn to write good editorials by learning a few rules. But . . . it would be possible, I submit, for editorial [writers] to advance their craft by giving a little more thought to . . . what would . . . not be rules but intelligent guides.
—Vermont Royster
Wall Street Journal[1]

An experienced editorial writer, on occasion, can turn out a quality editorial, from idea to finished form, in an hour or so. On another occasion, it may take the same writer all day just to do the research necessary to begin writing. Sometimes the actual writing of an editorial will take only a few minutes; the ideas flow freely onto the paper or into the video display terminal. At other times the ideas come hard; the words falter; the arguments don't support the conclusion. The writer must slowly and painfully grind out the editorial.

Yet, no matter how long it takes to write an editorial, or how hard or easy it is to write, the editorial-writing process is basically the same. Producing an editorial, from start to finish, requires a succession of steps. An experienced editorial writer may not be conscious of going through all of these steps each time he or she writes an editorial. Some of the steps may require no more than an instant of reflection. But the steps, generally in the same order, are taken. The purpose of this chapter is to walk the editorial writer or would-be editorial writer through these steps, one by one. The steps might be defined in different ways, but for our purposes let us identify these nine:

1. Selecting a topic.
2. Determining the purpose of the editorial.
3. Determining the audience.
4. Deciding on the tone of the editorial.
5. Researching the topic.
6. Determining the general format.
7. Writing the beginning of the editorial.
8. Writing the body of the editorial.
9. Writing the conclusion.

To provide an illustration of each of these steps, we will select a topic for an editorial and carry it through the nine steps of writing an editorial.

SELECTING A TOPIC

Usually the problem in selecting a topic is deciding which among many possible subjects should be written about on a particular day. Editorial writers typically scan the morning newspaper for ideas. Any one day's paper is likely to carry international, national, regional, state and local stories that are worthy of comment, plus some off-beat stories that can provide topics for change-of-pace editorials.

On a several-person staff, where writers have their own specialties, some of these topics may automatically fall to certain writers. Selecting a topic may be more difficult on a small, especially a one-person, staff. Where writers are few, topics should be selected from day to day that will provide readers with a variety of subjects at different levels, from local to international. Where writers have only limited time for editorial writing because of their other duties, a topic should be selected that can be researched and written in the time available. Just as writers on larger staffs tend to gravitate toward their own favorite topics, so hard-pressed writers on smaller staffs find themselves tempted to pick familiar topics or those on which someone else has done the research. When time runs short, it is often easier to write about a national or international issue than about a regional or local one.

Questions a writer might ask in deciding on a topic include: Can I make a significant contribution to public understanding on this topic? Do I have information or insights that are not generally held among my readers? Is discussion of the topic timely; does it come at an appropriate time for public discussion? Some of these questions may overlap with our next steps, determining the purpose and the audience of the editorial, but they are part of the process of picking a topic.

For the example in this chapter, let us decide that among the topics available to write about on this day we will select a story about the unsuccessful efforts of a nearby newspaper, the *Riverside* (Calif.) *Press-Enterprise,* to get the courts to open hearings in the selection of a jury in a murder-robbery case. The story that catches our attention reports that the U.S. Supreme Court for the second time has declined to hear the paper's appeal from lower court decisions that upheld the closing. During the early stages of the murder-robbery trial, a Superior Court judge held closed hearings for 82 days while prospective jurors were interviewed. We select this topic partly because we have an interest in, and some knowledge of, conflicts occurring over free press vs. fair trial and partly because we think that our readers should understand that the issue involved is important to the public, not just to the courts, the parties involved or newspapers.

The picking of editorial topics by itself is an important part of the process of trying to persuade readers. Communications research shows that the mass media may exert their strongest influence through helping set the agenda for public discussion. *What* the media choose to write and talk about is seen as having a more significant effect on the public than what the media *say* about the chosen topics.[2]

DETERMINING PURPOSE AND AUDIENCE

As we will see when we consider the topic we have chosen, determining the purpose and determining the audience of an editorial are interrelated. The purpose of an editorial is to convince a certain audience to do something or think something. The purpose may not be to persuade all of our readers. We may want to urge all readers to vote for a certain candidate for office, or we may want to direct our editorial primarily toward convincing readers who are not inclined to be favorable to this candidate. We may want to urge readers in general to turn out for a public hearing on a proposed freeway through the city, or we may want to convince members of the highway commission that the freeway is not a good idea.

In fact, we may have more than one audience in mind for an editorial. We may want both to convince the highway commission and get people to turn out for a hearing. On occasion this type of editorial will appear to be addressed to readers in general but will contain sufficient technical information to speak to the experts as well. On other occasions an editorial will be directed specifically at the narrower group. In this two-level type editorial writers should be careful not to become so involved in the fine points of the topic that they lose their general readers. "School Board Must Mature" (p. 146) is an editorial, from the *Oregonian* of Portland, that, while discussing a matter of community-wide concern, specifically addresses five members of a school board—and ultimately, as the last two paragraphs indicate, one of those members in particular. However, most readers should have little difficulty in following the editorial.

School Board Must Mature

Portland School Board Chairman William Scott Saturday sounded a public call to the board to outgrow its ill-disciplined adolescence, to end the destructive vendetta by some members against Superintendent Robert Blanchard and to start coming up with answers for pressing school problems that only the board can resolve. Hallelujah and amen.

The Oregonian's reading of Scott's essential points is that:

—Portland's school problems will become more serious if they are allowed to fester.

—The board, whose majority has served less than a year, has not shown itself sufficiently knowledgeable, able and willing to act in key areas.

—The board has not passed the minimum competency test of earning public trust and confidence with a recent record of successes. It has shown only that it has an oversupply of member-critics—guides who claim to know the way but have not demonstrated they can drive the car.

—Until the board builds its own record of achievement, firing the superintendent (which will be discussed in executive session Monday night) would be a dangerous, scapegoating descent into the politics of personalism.

Based on a four-year contract granted Blanchard a year ago, on a generally favorable evaluation given him by the board only weeks ago and on the strong support extended him last week by the Portland Association of Teachers, a firing—actually, a purge—would show that board is continuing the largely futile second-guessing of the prolonged desegregation debates. It would tell the public that the board, like a compulsive owner of a professional sports team, is willing to squander money to buy out a manager's contract for trivial reasons. In this case, though, there is no money to spare.

—A breaching of the contract with Blanchard would mean that the board is more willing to indulge in non-essential demolition than the difficult craftsmanship required now. In practical terms, the board would have to delay for a year, while searching for a new superintendent, vital decisions on how it will adjust to rapid enrollment declines and to the special needs of non-English-speaking immigrants and the handicapped; how it will provide and preserve quality education in the face of a looming financial crisis compounded by a growing, unfunded pension liability; and how it will monitor and ensure the success of the new desegregation plan it must implement.

Board grievances with Blanchard, in essence, come down to personal relationships, issues of style rather than of substance and priorities. This personal malaise ought to be insignificant, absolutely trivial, when measured against the agenda of important work facing the board.

Portland School Board members reportedly are deadlocked over Blanchard's fate. The swing vote seems to rest with Sarah Newhall.

A vote to break the superintendent's contract would be an endorsement of delay and chaos for the Portland School District. It would be an irresponsible decision to spurn acting on the major issues, rather than acting in the responsible manner called for by Chairman Scott. The ball has been hit to Ms. Newhall. For Portland's sake, she cannot afford to fumble it.

The Oregonian (Portland, Oregon)

The purpose of an editorial and the audience for it will depend partly on our understanding of how persuasion through editorials takes place. Half a century ago mass communications were thought to exert a strong, direct influence on audiences. The Bullet Theory, or Hypodermic Needle Theory, popular then, suggested that information and opinion from the media flowed directly into the heads of recipients. Editorials, presumably, would be read and acted upon by readers. Then in the 1940s researchers began to find that audiences were not paying as much attention as had been thought and were not being persuaded to the degree anticipated.[3] To explain this apparent inattention, researchers came up with the Two-Step Flow Theory. It maintained that ideas tended to flow from the media to a select group of opinion leaders, who in turn passed ideas on to the general population. Thus, if only 20 percent of readers read editorials every day, this theory suggested, that was all right, since presumably these few were the opinion leaders. But that theory didn't last long either. Further research showed that information flow is much more complex. The population is not neatly divided into leaders and followers. Much information goes directly to users of the media, not through a middle level.[4] Reader surveys show that relatively large percentages of readers read editorials at least once in a while.[5]

Current theory suggests that it is upon this general audience that a newspaper's editorials have the most effect over a long period. The effect is produced not so much by the persuasion of specific editorials as by the day-to-day dripping of the editorial writer's ink on the stone of the public consciousness. It is the members of a community who decide elections and decide whether to stay or move to another city or feel good or bad about their community. All these people are the editorial writer's principal audience, even when an editorial calls on a school board to fire a superintendent or criticize a city manager for a mistake. Public officials are as likely to be motivated by an aroused public as by an editorial's eloquent logic.

In selecting our topic on open court hearings, we have already indicated at least one purpose for our editorial: to help the public understand the importance of the issue. And we have identified an audience: the general, non-expert public. It is not likely that the editorial can be expected to have a direct effect on the case involved, even if the judges and other parties in the case should read it. The judicial process will run its course regardless of what we say. Might there be another purpose or another audience for our editorial? One possibility might be other judges and attorneys who, if we present a strong enough argument, might give more thought to keeping courts open in cases in which they are involved in the future. Another possible audience is the state legislature, which only a few months earlier had passed legislation aimed at keeping preliminary hearings open to the public. Legislators might be interested in how the laws are being interpreted and implemented. But, since we are not legal experts or writing for a law journal, our principal audience will be the general public and our principal purpose will be to help lay persons understand the issues involved.

DECIDING ON THE TONE

At least as far back as Aristotle, writers have been concerned with how they can best persuade their audience. Aristotle identified three basic avenues available to the persuader: the character of the persuader, the attitude of the hearer and the arguments themselves.[6] The more credible the persuader, of course, the more likely an audience will be persuaded. If an editorial page has attained credibility with its readers over the years, editorials on that page are likely to be viewed favorably. Aristotle thought the communicator needed good sense, good will and a good moral character—appropriate prescriptions for an editorial writer.[7] Concerning the attitude of the audience, Aristotle saw that "persuasion is effected through the audience when they are brought . . . into a state of emotion." For example, "pain or joy, or liking or hatred" can have an effect in changing attitudes. Concerning the third avenue, the arguments, he saw that "persuasion is effected by the argument themselves."[8] Thus, at least from the time of Aristotle, persuaders have recognized that they can appeal to the emotions or to the rationality of their audience in their arguments.

When editorial writers select a tone for an editorial they have many choices, ranging from deeply serious to satirical and humorous. Concerning the choice between an appeal primarily to emotion or one primarily to reason, some recent research suggests that emotion and reason may not necessarily be in opposition to each other and that simultaneous appeals to both may serve to reinforce persuasion.[9] For the purposes of most editorials, however, writers choose between making an appeal based mainly on feelings, values and symbols and making one based mainly on information, evidence and logic. The decision will depend on the subject matter and the occasion as well as the writer's own preferences. On the day following the assassination of a prominent political figure, a writer might use an emotional tone to express outrage and grief over the tragedy. The next day the writer might take a more rational approach to talk about what contributed to the killing and how to prevent such incidents in the future. An emotional approach might be appropriate to provide entertainment, to arouse readers to action, to chastise or to praise someone. A rational approach might be more appropriate to explain to readers something they don't know or to convince them of the correctness of the editorial writer's conclusions.

Emotion undoubtedly plays a smaller role in editorial writing today than several decades ago, when daily newspapers were numerous and subscribers could take the paper that came closest to expressing their own opinions. Readers relished reading emotional, partisan appeals, and, if opinions were not changed, they were at least reinforced. Today's editorial writers must appeal to readers with a much broader spectrum of opinions. A rousing editorial based mostly on bombast may please a small group of partisans but leave other readers unconvinced or repulsed. Today's readers are better educated than readers of a hundred years ago and people as a whole are better informed; they should be better able to recognize incorrect or incomplete information. It may be more fun to dash off an editorial that attacks a person or policy without mercy, and perhaps without much thought; such an editorial may draw the strongest, most immediate response from readers. But what value does the editorial have beyond giving a momentary emotional high to some readers and long-term pain to others? Henry M. Keezing of the *New Britain* (Conn.) *Herald* said that one of his prized possessions was a letter to the editor lauding a flamboyant editorial he had whipped up in a matter of minutes. The letter was highly complimentary but it "was written in pencil, in a scrawling longhand, on a piece of paper which a beer distributor gives to cafes and taverns for use for menus." Keezing had made a hit with someone in a tavern. But he said he would have much preferred to hear from a community leader, a legislator or a person of influence.[10]

Columnist James J. Kilpatrick, who writes with about as much indignation as any American newspaper writer, has described how the complexities of today's world have inhibited him from just sounding off. He noted that writing about something you know nothing about is easy; "when research fails, prejudice is there to prop you." But "what raises the sweat and paralyzes the fingers on the keys is to grapple with an issue in which the issues are divided," he said. "It is a maddening thing, but damned little in the editor's world is all white or all black; the editor's world is full of mugwump grays."[11]

The time has come now for us to decide on the tone that we will take in our editorial about the courts. That should be an easy decision after the discussion above. Subjects relating to First Amendment rights might, on occasion, be written in an emotional manner. It might be necessary to raise a public outcry against the trampling of journalistic or religious freedoms. If one of a newspaper's reporters had been held in contempt of court and jailed for trying to report a trial, we might sound off in loud protest against the actions of the judge. But our case is one in which a great deal of explanation will probably be necessary. While we will hope to convince readers of our point of view, we will not be asking them to take up pickets and march around the courthouse. A rational approach seems the obvious one in this case.

RESEARCHING THE TOPIC

When we decide whether our editorial will be primarily emotional or rational in tone, we also determine the type of research we will have to do to write the editorial. If we can write the piece off the tops of our heads, we can skip research. If we are going to present only one point of view, about which we will say more when we discuss the next step, we can limit our research to the arguments on one side. The amount of research conducted by writers depends to some extent on how much time they have and the availability of resource materials. Very few writers have the luxury of going to the public library or a law library or the city hall or the courthouse to dig out information for that day's editorial. A telephone call—to an office across town or to the state capital—may provide a writer with the only opportunity to obtain information that is not immediately available in the newspaper office. So the kinds of reference materials mentioned in Chapter 4 need to be nearby.

In our court case example, we start with the story in the morning paper. It seems to provide the details we will need to talk about this particular case. We will probably want to put the case into the context of a series of decisions on trial closures that have been handed down by the courts in recent years. A beginning point for obtaining this background information might be the state publishers' association. Many associations provide continuing reports to members about legal developments around the state. In California we can turn to *FOI California* (a quarterly bulletin) and weekly newsletters published by the California Newspaper Publishers Association. If we had not already known that the most pertinent U.S. Supreme Court decision on this subject came in *Richmond Newspapers* v. *Virginia,* the quarterly bulletin would have told us, since it carried an article on court closures in its most recent issue. The bulletin also tells us that the California case that has progressed the farthest in the courts has been appealed to the Supreme Court after an unfavorable decision for the *Sacramento Bee* in the federal court of appeals. We also note a similar case being appealed from a state Supreme Court decision in Washington state. We note another California case that is similar to the one we are concerned with. Our case also is mentioned.

Our next check might be *Editorial Research Reports* to see if one of its weekly analyses deals with the subject. We are not so lucky. An issue dated Oct. 26, 1979, mentions the topic, but the only case mentioned is an earlier one, *Gannett* v. *De Pasquale,* handed down a year before *Richmond Newspapers.* *Gannett* held that courts could close preliminary hearings in criminal cases. We need a more up-to-date report. We might check ERR's sister publication, *Congressional Quarterly.* Here in the annual volume for 1979 we find the *Gannett* case given a full page in the section summarizing the year's court decisions and in the 1980 volume we find *Richmond Newspapers* given a scant three paragraphs. It provides no direct quotations from the decision. Our next stopping place is *Facts on File.* A weekly report in 1979 provides about half a page on *Gannett* and one in 1980 provides about a third of a page on *Richmond Newspapers.* Fortunately *Facts on File* offers us several quotations from the decisions. It might be that our office has another service from *Facts on File,* called *Editorials on File.* If it does, we will find that it reprinted 10 editorials that were written following the *Richmond Newspapers* decision. Reading them might give us some idea of how the decision, which favored open courts, was viewed at the time. We note that all of the editorial writers seemed overjoyed with the decision, but they didn't offer much insight. The editorial in the *Richmond* (Va.) *News Leader,* for example, was only four short paragraphs in length, and it presented only that newspaper's side of the case.

We will have to turn to other sources to obtain expert legal opinion on the two cases. Here a mass media law book or two can come in handy. One of the mass media textbooks that I have found helpful, *Mass Media Law* by Don R. Pember, devotes seven pages to closed hearings, including references to the two Supreme Court cases. Another text, *Mass Media Law and Regulation* by William E. Francois, has nine pages on the subject. Both discuss public reactions and the legal significance of the cases.[12]

On many topics research can go on and on. The writer who is a scholar or an investigative reporter at heart may find it hard to close the books, decide against making one more phone call and start writing the editorial.

DETERMINING THE GENERAL FORMAT

Deciding whether to be basically emotional or rational in our editorial does not determine how the editorial will be written, especially if we decide on a rational tone. Communications researchers have devoted a lot of effort trying to discover how arguments can be presented in the most persuasive manner. Among their concerns have been (1) one-sided versus two-sided arguments, (2) the ordering of arguments and (3) the degree to which opinions can be changed.

Research going back to soldiers in World War II suggests that the one-sided versus two-sided decision largely depends on the audience being addressed. One-sided arguments were found to be more persuasive when the receivers of messages were in agreement with the arguments and when receivers were of lower intelligence or less educated. This approach was also found to be more effective when the receivers were not familiar with the issue being discussed and were not likely to be exposed to opposition arguments in the future, and when the topic was not controversial.[13] Presentation of opposing arguments was more effective in persuading when the receivers were initially hostile to the persuader's view, were highly educated, were accustomed to hearing both sides of an argument and were likely to hear the other sides eventually anyway.[14]

Concerning the order of the arguments, the researchers have come up with contradictory findings. Both primacy (the favored argument first) and recency (the favored argument last) have been found to be persuasive. The primacy approach has the advantage of drawing an early favorable opinion from the audience, an opinion which may remain unchanged during the remainder of the presentation. The recency approach has the advantage of providing the last impression with the best chance of being remembered. One line of reasoning suggests that, if you have arguments that are likely to be received favorably by your audience, present them first to establish a favorable setting for less favorable arguments later. If you have a solution for a problem or a need, it may be better to present the problem or the need first, then suggest your solution.[15] Researchers agree that the weakest spot for an argument is in the middle of the message, so you might put arguments unfavorable to your position there.[16]

The third aspect of communications research involves the extent to which readers can be persuaded to change their opinions. It seems clear that readers' first inclinations are to seek and perceive information that reinforces their present viewpoints. Some studies suggest that reinforcing opinions is about all that can be expected of editorials. Readers, they point out, tend to ignore, disbelieve or reinterpret information that does not conform to their own beliefs. Still, some research shows that readers sometimes seek out information that is contrary to their beliefs and, within limits, are willing to modify their beliefs. It is surmised that a person is able to feel comfortable with a different opinion if it is perceived to fall within a certain comfort zone. The closer the offered opinion is to the outer edge of that zone, the greater the change that is likely to take place in the person's opinion. If the offered opinion is barely outside the zone, however, it is likely to be perceived as more divergent than it actually is. The trick for the editorial writer is to know enough about a newspaper's readers to be able to push for a maximum amount of opinion change without going so far as to antagonize readers with demands for too much change.

In terms of presenting one or two arguments, our court case would seem to be an example of a subject about which our readers are likely to know little and are unlikely to read an opposing side later. It might be an occasion for a one-sided editorial, presenting in this instance the case for letting the public into the court. But at least three factors ought to be considered before we take this route. First, one of our hoped-for audiences includes the legal and legislative community. If we are to persuade these experts, we will need to give credence to arguments on both sides if we can. A second factor is that this type of editorial will probably be read primarily by readers who are among the more highly intelligent and better educated, the audience that is likely to be persuaded by presentation of both sides. A third factor is an inclination on the part of some readers to take a skeptical attitude toward the press on matters involving the mass media. Arguments that might appear to be self-serving are not likely to be persuasive with this group. To some extent we face a situation in which some readers hold views contrary to those that we wish to push. The task facing the writer of this editorial, then, is to convince readers that the public, not just the press, stands to gain if trials are opened. These three factors suggest the need for a two-sided argument in favor of opening trials.

WRITING THE BEGINNING

The beginning of an editorial may be the most important part. First, it has to provide a sufficient attraction to readers so that they will start reading the editorial. A dull opening paragraph is a certain turnoff. Second, the writer has to decide whether to let readers know at the beginning what the conclusion of the editorial will be. Stating the conclusion at the beginning may offer the best chance of influencing reader opinion if the majority of readers tend toward that opinion already or have no opinion. But it also could turn off readers who disagree; they may decide not to read any farther.

The most frequently used beginning is a brief statement of the proposal, incident or situation that has led to the writing of the editorial. It may be a simple restatement of information that has been reported in the news columns. This approach is especially appropriate for readers who have no previous knowledge of what the editorial writer is talking about. It also provides a way into the editorial without antagonizing readers who may hold views different from the editorial writer's.

Sometimes a writer needs to present an even broader approach than a statement of the facts of the situation. Beginning with the background of the subject might help readers understand how the immediate topic relates to more general information that they may be familiar with. Sometimes an effective way to get readers to modify their opinions is to begin with the statement of a generally accepted point of view. After readers have become comfortable with what the editorial writer is saying, the editorial can take what I call a "Yes, but" switch to try to convince readers that another point of view makes even more sense. This approach might be particularly effective in an editorial that seeks to debunk commonly held views or takes a stand that may surprise readers. This approach is not the same as building up an artificial argument that can easily be knocked down. The opening argument needs to be credible. "Yes, but" might be useful when a newspaper wants to change or modify its editorial stance on an issue. This type of editorial can be readable and persuasive, especially if the writer sneaks up on the reader and presents the counter-argument unexpectedly.

An editorial sometimes can be started with a question. This can serve to focus on the point of an editorial immediately and tell readers that they can expect to find the answer by reading the editorial. A question that arouses curiosity can be effective in attracting readers. But, if a question asks, "What should be done about such-and-such?" and the reader answers, "I don't care," the editorial writer has lost a reader. Questions need to be real, not rhetorical.

In any case, opening paragraphs must catch the readers' attention. "It's 'Grass Roots' Politics Time" (p. 154) and "Now Is the Time . . ." (p. 155) are two editorials on the same subject; they urge voters to do exactly the same thing: participate in precinct caucuses. The former starts in a traditional manner, simply telling voters to attend—strictly a community-service editorial. In the other, the writer uses an imaginative approach that disguises the mundane message for the reader until well into the fourth paragraph. In the meantime, the reader has enjoyed some clever writing.

Sam Reynolds, an editorial writer on the *Missoulian* in Missoula, Mont., was faced with trying to say something in an editorial to appear the morning following an election. He came up with this opening: "Writing an editorial on election day is like kissing your sister (or, if you are a sister, kissing your brother). The election is the consuming interest, but no results are in. Within 24 hours there will be a dozen things to write about. But there's nothing right then."

Readers must get confused and exasperated reading about congressional spending, so a *Wall Street Journal* writer took the line that members of the *Journal*'s staff too had been confused. The editorial opened in this manner: "We try our best to keep up with Congress's schemes to spend money that isn't there, but even we often underestimate its ingenuity at finding new shill games. It is starting to look as if congressional spenders slipped another one by us on Social Security and now it is probably too late to save the taxpayer from the consequences."

It's 'Grass Roots' Politics Time

No matter which political party you support, next week finds you as an individual citizen in the driver's seat in your neighborhood.

You will carry more political clout on March 7 than at any other time of the year—if you so choose. For that night has been set for precinct caucuses by members of both the Democrat and Republican parties.

The precinct caucus is unique to the United States. It is the usually all-too-small neighborhood gathering where area residents meet—Republicans at one site and Democrats at another—to conduct such party business as choosing delegates to county and state conventions. In addition, those at the caucus frequently formulate resolutions to send to their party political headquarters. Sometimes, money is volunteered by those attending.

By far the most important feature of the caucus, however, is the give-and-take discussion of anything anyone attending wishes to bring up for party consideration. An agenda to be accomplished usually is sent to each precinct committeeman from the party's county headquarters. A poll on questions of national, regional or local issues sometimes is requested by party headquarters. But discussion is by no means limited to the agenda. In exchanging ideas, better understanding of all issues affecting the party and the nation is gained for all attending.

The caucus is the idea springboard for the county and state conventions. Often planks for the platform are drafted in rough form in precincts where those attending have a viewpoint they wish to put forward. And, out of the caucus come the elected delegates who go to county conventions knowing first-hand the ideas of their neighbors and friends. In turn, out of the county conventions come delegates to the state conventions. There is a direct line of communication, therefore, from the neighbors who meet in caucus on to the county conventions and ultimately the state conventions, where national convention delegates are named.

That direct line of thought remains strongest when it has the broadest possible base—heavy attendance at precinct caucuses. Spokane's record probably is much like that of most cities in the U.S. Too many people stay home. A drizzle of rain, a day that left them tired, a wish to see a concert or a play that night deter all too many from attending. Those may be the same citizens who later complain that their ideas are never aired or echoed in the party. The reason: The complainers did not express the ideas because he or she was not at the caucus.

Summary: The "grass roots" political system of America is built on the citizen's interest in the precinct caucus. Participate in yours.

Spokane (Wash.) *Spokesman-Review*

Let us turn now to how we will begin our editorial on closing court trials. Among other considerations we need to recognize that the issue we are talking about is a complex one, that few readers are directly affected by it or even interested, and that one of our tasks is to make open courts a public, not just a press, issue. A standard opening for our editorial might be:

For the second time, the U.S. Supreme Court has refused to look at the lengthy closed-door questioning of prospective jurors in the Norco murder case. The *Riverside Press-Enterprise* had asked the court to review the exclusion of the public and the press during 82 days in which 250 jury panel members were questioned in secret.

Now Is the Time . . .

"Now is the time for all men to come to the aid of their party."

As a typing exercise, we normally tend to prefer the quick brown fox jumping over the lazy dog's back. Not only is the imagery more colorful, but one isn't likely to get in trouble with the message. Sure, it's an unfair stereotype of the canine quadruped as a shiftless creature. But the canine movement so far hasn't advanced enough to have a barksperson to complain about such disparagement of man's best friend.

The other typing drill is clearly sexist, however. We hasten to revise the message to say that "now is the time for all men and women to come to the aid of their party."

Considering the shape the political organizations are in—especially the Republicans—any time is appropriate for a sympathetic citizen to get involved in the process. But the time factor is especially relevant now. Meaning tonight. If it's nearly 8 o'clock, in fact, you'd better start putting on your coat if you've been think-

ing that maybe you should do something to support the two-party system.

This is the night of the precinct caucus in Washington state. That's when the ordinary citizen who considers himself a Republican or Democrat is supposed to make his influence felt by expressing opinions and by electing delegates to the county conventions who reflect those opinions.

It's the grassroots, man! And woman!

Granted, not many persons turn out. And in the past, such caucuses have been vulnerable to maneuvering, particularly in a presidential election year when a small number of ideological activists can "stack" the meetings on behalf of candidates or positions not favored by most voters. But that's exactly why it would be a good thing for more "ordinary" citizens to take part instead of just complaining about the results.

Caucus meeting sites were listed on Page 14 of Sunday's Columbian. You probably can get to one in your neighborhood quicker than it takes for that brown fox to jump over that lazy hound's back.

Columbian (Vancouver, Wash.)

This basically factual approach might attract readers already interested in the case but probably not many others.

We might try a question beginning, such as:

Should the public and the press be excluded when prospective jurors are questioned in murder cases in this state?

This question focuses squarely on the issue. The next paragraph might explain what has most recently occurred. This approach has merit: By taking a view that is broader than this individual case the likelihood that readers will be interested increases. Suggesting that the public and the press have been "excluded" introduces an element of conflict and controversy, always good for an opening sentence. As we noted earlier, of course, the reader may say, "I don't care whether trials are open or closed'' and read no further. We would then have missed our chance to convince the reader that trials should be open.

If for no other reason than that question openings should not be used too often, let us try another angle, still maintaining the element of conflict:

> "The appearance of justice can best be served by allowing people to observe it,'' the chief justice of the U.S. Supreme Court wrote two years ago in a decision supporting open trials. Yet this week the court refused to consider the Norco murder-robbery trial in which prospective jurors were questioned in secret for 82 days.

This beginning sets the stage for the broader issue of open trials, then almost immediately focuses attention on the specific case. And it introduces conflict—between what the court said and what it has now done. You may say that we have telegraphed our conclusion, that the court was wrong in turning down the Norco case, and that thereby we have reduced our chances of convincing those who start out disagreeing with us. That is a risk. But by posing the apparent contradiction in such clear terms, we may succeed in enticing readers into sticking with us long enough to see if the court is in fact being inconsistent.

One of the weaknesses of this opening is that it contains a direct quotation. I discourage professional and student editorial writers from overusing the quotation opening. Usually the writer's own words can make the point more sharply and succinctly. But in this case the quotation is short and states precisely the standard we will want to uphold during the remainder of the editorial. It provides a nearly perfect contrast to the immediate mention of 82 days behind closed court doors. Quoting from a Supreme Court decision should have some persuasive effects on members of the legal profession.

Another possibility might be a more dramatic approach, which may bring readers into an editorial on an otherwise dry, difficult subject:

> For 82 days over a period of five months the door of Superior Court No. 4 remained closed while 250 Riverside County residents were individually questioned to serve as jurors in the Norco murder-robbery case. The *Riverside Press-Enterprise* has contended that the closure violates the principle of open criminal trials, but thus far it can't get the U.S. Supreme Court to consider the case.

This type of approach may be a little too sensational in this instance, however. The editorial would be fun to write. But remember that we are addressing our editorial to lawyers, judges and legislators as well as to the general public. Logic, not melodrama, is likely to be our most effective tool.

WRITING THE BODY OF THE EDITORIAL

The steps we have discussed thus far, starting with picking a topic, have covered a number of pages and involved quite a lot of explanation. Except possibly for research, most of the steps may in practice, however, be taken quickly. Not more than a few seconds may be required for an experienced editorial writer to select a topic, decide on the purpose and the proper audience, determine the tone and select the general approach. Much of the process takes place without conscious reflection. After writing editorials for a few years, editorial writers get a feeling for the right way, for them, to write an editorial. With the beginning determined, at least tentatively, and all the other steps behind them, they are ready to write the body of the editorial—the explanations, the arguments and the analysis. Here is where they either will or will not convince their readers to agree with them. Here is where they win or lose in the battle to persuade.

To illustrate three basic approaches to the body of an editorial, let us look at editorials based on the same news event, a speech by Chief Justice Warren Burger in which he criticized the lack of qualifications of some trial lawyers. "Incompetence in the Courtroom" (p. 158), from the *Chicago Tribune,* uses a standard, two-sided editorial that allows the writer to present information and arguments in an orderly, understandable manner to readers who are not already well informed on the subject. The writer tells the reader what the editorial is about (designated as S, meaning the statement of the situation), then provides background (B) before developing the argument on one side (A_1) and the argument on the other side (A_2), followed by a discussion of the merits of the arguments (D) and the conclusion (C). If the writer presents both sides of the argument fully and fairly, this type of organization offers a chance to persuade the reader who may have started out disagreeing with the conclusion that is eventually drawn in the editorial. This might be considered the standard editorial, in terms of these symbols, an SBA_1A_2DC editorial, one that presents the situation, the opposing arguments, a discussion of the arguments and the writer's conclusions.

Incompetence in the Courtroom

S { Chief Justice Warren Burger has been complaining for some time that too many trial attorneys do not know their craft. Their incompetence, he asserts, causes delays and does a disservice to clients.

B { When Mr. Burger brought this message to the American Bar Association's midyear meeting in New Orleans, the response of at least part of that organization was lawyer-like to a fault.

In effect they wanted the ABA to tell Mr. Burger to prove his charge or shut up. Led by the Illinois State Bar Association's delegation, a group of delegates introduced a resolution calling upon the chief justice to retract his criticisms or produce evidence to support them.

The House of Delegates wisely rejected the proposal after many members argued that the chief justice has the right of free speech and that he has long been a good friend of the organized bar.

A₁ { It is hard to imagine that Mr. Burger's solution to the problem he sees in American courtrooms would work. He proposes a system of certification for lawyers doing litigation and other specialty work. A lawyer would have to take special training and pass some sort of test beyond the bar examination before he could appear in court on behalf of a client.

A₁ { The trouble is, being a lawyer is something of an art. Standardized tests don't measure well such skills as concentration, articulateness, quickness of mind. And these are the litigator's most important tools.

A₂ { Nevertheless, it is hard to deny the validity of Mr. Burger's criticism. One has only to spend a day meandering through the courtrooms at 26th and California to reach the same conclusion he has. Direct and cross-examinations are often poorly prepared and indecisive. Confusion over simple points of procedure and evidence gobbles up time and sometimes works injustice. The law takes on a haphazard and fickle appearance. Justice becomes a matter of plea bargaining—simple barter—and the resulting product is of bargain basement quality.

D { Mr. Burger has said in the past that only about half of the practicing trial lawyers in the United States are competent. His numbers may well be exaggerated and his solution may not be the best one. But having rejected the idea of challenging Mr. Burger to put up or shut up, the Bar Association ought to accept his challenge and think seriously about the problem he raises.

C {

A more direct presentation is illustrated by "Burger Hits a Homer" from the *Los Angeles Times*. This is the one-sided editorial (SAC), which starts with the statement of the situation (S), presents an argument on one side (A) and reaches a conclusion (C) based on that argument. This approach will serve if an issue is so clear, at least to the editorial writer, that only one argument is necessary. It might prove effective in convincing a reader who is not familiar with any other side of the issue and is not likely to encounter it later. Of course, this editorial runs the risk of antagonizing readers who hold different points of view.

The strongest presentation involves starting the editorial with a conclusion and then proceeding to present arguments in favor of it, as the *Washington Post* did in "Courtroom Incompetents." The editorial (CSCAC) is structured in the following order: the conclusion (C), a brief statement of the situation (S), amplification of the conclusion (more C), arguments in favor of the conclusion (A) and finally a reiteration of the conclusion (C). Many writers like such editorials.

Burger Hits a Homer

The chief justice of the United States is not the most diplomatic of men. When he has something to say, he is inclined to lay it out cold. Addressing a midyear meeting of the American Bar Assn. in New Orleans, Warren E. Burger said that as many as half the nation's trial lawyers lacked the professional competence to try cases in court.

The vibes from the audience were not good, but the white-haired chief justice, standing there so splendidly erect and handsome that he looked as though he had been chosen for the part by Central Casting, pursued the subject with relentless zeal.

One of the major reasons for court congestion, delay and high costs, he said, "is the inadequate performance of many lawyers who come into the court. . . . In 23 years on the bench, I have reviewed in whole or part literally thousands of trial records. A large percentage of the trials under review consumed double or more time (than that) which well-trained lawyers would have required. . . . We are several generations behind in training of advocates for courtroom performance."

Lawyers incensed by Burger's criticism wanted the ABA to tell him to offer more proof or to withdraw his statement, but a Washington, D.C., attorney sank the effort by reminding the outraged minority that it was putting on a bad show by publicly arguing over the percentage of incompetents in their midst. "What utter nonsense," he said. The delegates laughed, recovered their balance, and voted down the resolution.

William B. Spann Jr., ABA president, called Burger's evaluation "grossly disproportionate" but conceded that perhaps 20% of trial lawyers are unqualified. Burger, seeing that big, fat, lazy ball float up to the batter's box, knocked it out of the park. He replied, "If . . . 20% are incompetent, we ought to be doing a great deal more about it than we have up till now."

That has been the chief justice's essential point all along, and the ABA should meet his criticism for what it is worth.

Los Angeles Times

When they have strong opinions on a subject, they may write this way even when logic tells them they risk antagonizing readers who disagree. If a newspaper has a stated position on a subject or if the lines of opinion are already well drawn among readers, writers may think that they might just as well indulge themselves in this type of editorial.

Courtroom Incompetents

THE OUTRAGED-INNOCENCE response to Chief Justice Warren E. Burger's New Orleans remarks about incompetent trial lawyers was, as Lee Loevinger rightly put it, "utter nonsense." The chief justice may have exaggerated a little when he said at an American Bar Association meeting that a third to a half of the lawyers who appear in court perform incompetently—it may be only a quarter or a tenth. But those Bar Association members who criticized him on the grounds that his comments reflected badly on all lawyers missed the point: It is the legal profession's tolerance of its incompetent members—whatever their precise number—that reflects badly on good lawyers. As for solving the problem, it is hard to see how that can be done *without* discussing it.

You don't have to be the chief justice, or even a high-powered lawyer, to spot incompetency in the courtroom. All you need do is to sit for a while and listen to what goes on. You learn the difference, quickly, between cases that are well presented and those that are not. We've observed incompetence in police courts and known people to go to jail because of it. And we've observed incompetent arguments before the Supreme Court and wondered if decisions might have been different if the cases had been properly argued.

The trouble is that many inadequate lawyers will not admit—and no one seems to want to tell them—that they lack the skills an advocate should have. There are real differences, too, between preparing a case for trial and preparing a brief for the Supreme Court, between trying a case before a jury and arguing one before the justices. Few lawyers are good at all these tasks. Some seem to be good at none of them.

If it takes the kind of blunt criticism the chief justice has been dishing out to force the organized bar to look more closely at itself, so be it. It is true that some corrective steps have been taken; some states now require lawyers to renew their education periodically in order to retain their licenses; there is a trend toward permitting lawyers to develop (and advertise) specialties. These are helpful, but more needs to be done. The chief justice is right in contending that a license to practice law in an office should not necessarily be a license to mangle cases in court. The idea that the lawyer is one of the few remaining generalists who can handle anything has been overwhelmed by the law's own complexity. The trouble with incompetence is that when it exists the victim is rarely the lawyer or the court, but rather some individual (or corporate) victim who may not even realize what happened.

Copyright *The Washington Post*

What should we say in the body of our editorial on the closing of the court? One thing we must do is to be sure to explain what we are talking about. Readers tend to let legal issues frighten them, partly because editorial writers neglect to translate legal terms into lay language. Another thing we should do is to frame the issue we talk about in broad terms. The case we are talking about is important, but helping readers understand the need for open judicial processes in general is more important. In effect, we are using this case to make a larger point. After all, as we noted earlier, whatever we say about this case will not affect its outcome.

Probably the first thing we need to do after our opening paragraph is explain the Norco case in more detail—the circumstances of the closed sessions and the series of refusals by appellate courts to consider the pleadings of the *Press-Enterprise*. Assuming that we use the opening approach that we tentatively picked, we might explain the circumstances in which Burger wrote the statement that we used to start the editorial. This will lead us into describing the *Richmond Newspapers* case. We will have to decide whether to discuss the *Gannett* case also. Probably, to avoid unnecessary detail and make our presentation as simple as possible, we will not mention this case. It dealt only with preliminary hearings; our case involves the beginning portions of the trial itself.

To produce an editorial that stands a chance of convincing judges, lawyers and legislators, we will need to recognize the concerns of those whose interests lie in providing a fair trial for the defendants. One of the ways to try to convince someone of your point of view is to acknowledge the validity of that person's point of view.

So, with these thoughts in mind, we write our editorial.

Keeping the Public Out

"The appearance of justice can best be served by allowing people to observe it," the chief justice of the U.S. Supreme Court wrote two years ago in a decision supporting open criminal trials. But this week the court refused to consider the Norco murder-robbery trial in which prospective jurors were questioned in secret for 82 days.

Attorneys for newspapers in Riverside and San Diego had asked the court in the Norco case to hold that Superior Court Judge So-and-so did not have to hold closed-door sessions to protect the rights of three men charged with 46 crimes, including the murder of a deputy sheriff. The charges arose out of a bank robbery in Norco followed by a 50-mile chase in which police and the alleged robbers exchanged shots.

The California Supreme Court held in 1980 that, in cases such as this, when the death penalty could be imposed, prospective jurors must be questioned separately when asked about their attitudes toward the death penalty. The purpose is to keep the answers of one person from influencing those of other persons in the sensitive matter of capital punishment. The court ruling did not cover other aspects of the questioning process, but the judge in the Norco case took it upon himself to extend the ruling in two ways. He ruled that prospective jurors should appear separately to answer all questions, not just those related to the death penalty, and that the public as well as the remainder of the jury panel should be excluded.

The Supreme Court has held that, if it is necessary to protect a defendant's rights to a fair trial, criminal trials or portions of them can be closed to the public and the press. A judge might have reason to close a portion of a trial in which disclosure of certain information might impair the defendant's rights or in which testimony might be offensive to the public or a threat to the safety of one or more individuals. A judge might close a trial in which the communications media were printing and broadcasting sensational or irresponsible accounts of court proceedings. A judge might impose tight security conditions if a defendant's life were in danger.

But the Supreme Court ruled very clearly in *Richmond Newspapers* v. *Virginia* in 1980 that judges should exclude the public and the press only when "an overriding interest" requires closed sessions. Chief Justice Warren Burger wrote for the majority: "We hold that the right to attend criminal trials is implicit in the guarantees of the First Amendment; without the freedom to attend such trials, which people have exercised for centuries, important aspects of freedom of speech and of the press could be eviscerated." He said that "a presumption of openness inheres in the very nature of a criminal trial under our system of justice."

In the Norco case, while the judge was required to question jury panel members separately on the death penalty, what "overriding interest" was served by isolating the entire questioning process from the public view? The questioning of jurors is as much a part of the trial as any other part.

The purpose of open trials is not just to give the press an opportunity to recount court proceedings for its readers or to provide the public the opportunity to listen to titillating testimony. One purpose is to keep judicial proceedings open to scrutiny by the public. In an earlier case, Justice Harry A. Blackmun described "secret judicial proceedings" as "a menace to liberty." He argued that the public guarantee of a public trial "ensures that not only judges but all participants in the criminal justice system are subjected to public scrutiny as they conduct the public's business of prosecuting crime."

In the *Richmond* case, Burger spoke of an "unbroken, uncontradicted history" of open criminal trials in this country. Can that history remain unbroken when the Burger court itself refuses even to consider whether an "overriding interest" required 82 days of secret sessions in a major criminal trial?

We have written what is basically a two-sided editorial with the main emphasis on our preferred side. It seems clear at the beginning that we will end up critical of the court's inaction. After the opening paragraph we provide more information on the case in question and on earlier pertinent cases. Then comes one side of the argument (our A_1), which recognizes that there are occasions when court sessions might be closed. We try to present these statements in as favorable a manner toward the courts as possible in an attempt to convince those who disagree with us that we are taking a reasonable, middle-of-the-road position. Then we turn to the other side (A_2), primarily using words from the court itself to make our case. The quotations are good strong ones. In the conclusion we cite another Burger quote, then tie a reference to this quotation to the earlier one about "overriding interest" and apply them to our case. The overall result is an attempt to use the words of the court to judge the court.

To provide an opportunity to view the editorial in its entirety, we have attached the conclusion before discussing conclusions in general. Now we proceed to the ninth and final step.

WRITING THE CONCLUSION

Well-written beginnings help attract readers. Well-written endings help convince readers. Possible conclusions for an editorial are as infinite in number and variety as the manner in which the editorial is written. Conclusions vary according to the purposes of an editorial and a conclusion should express what the writer intends the editorial to accomplish. Conclusions also vary according to the degree of firmness that is intended by the writer. I have found it helpful in acquainting would-be editorial writers with possible varieties of conclusions to think of them as coming in six general forms. Within each form are variations that primarily reflect degree of firmness. In order of descending firmness, the six categories are: urge, approve, disapprove, conclude righteously, take consolation and come down softly. Explained below are the categories, ranked in that order. The examples within each category are also ranked in descending order of firmness.

Urging

The most specific and direct conclusion is one that urges readers, a government official or a private party to do something. An editorial may urge voters to support or oppose a candidate or ballot proposition; it may urge the president or Congress to compromise on tax cut proposals; it may urge a city council to lower the speed limit on a street or fire the city manager; or it may urge readers in general to support something, such as a nuclear arms freeze.

1. _Do_—write or vote or give (to the United Way, for example). This conclusion urges readers to perform some specific action. When the _Missoulian_ of Missoula, Mont., decided that a development proposal called Ski Yellowstone "would court disaster," the editorial writer concluded: "Protests against this potential boondoggle should be written today (the deadline) to Lewis Hawkes, Forest Supervisor, Gallatin National Forest, P.O. Box 130, Bozeman, Mont. 59715."

2. _Must_—intended to leave no doubt in the mind of the reader what the editorial writer wants done. The _Daily World_ of New York City concluded an editorial on deferral of production of the neutron bomb in this manner: "The N-bomb must not merely be deferred. It must be defeated."

3. _Ought_—less forceful than "must" but still a firm stand. A _Montana Kaimin_ editorial contended that a state constitutional provision requiring reclamation of mineral lands was not being enforced, then concluded: "Someone ought to tell the legislature about this law, unless perhaps there is a confidentiality clause prohibiting politicians from learning the exact location of the document." (There is, of course, a little satire here, too.)

4. _Should_—slightly less emphatic than "must" and "ought." The _Columbian_ of Vancouver, Wash., noted a Supreme Court ruling that broadened the doctrine of judicial immunity from lawsuits. The editorial said that disciplinary measures are available to deal with poor judges and concluded: "So long as such remedies are available, the judiciary should remain free from the threat of lawsuits." Another firmly stated example comes from the _Minneapolis_ (Minn.) _Tribune_ in an editorial arguing for state control of dredging by the U.S. Army Corps of Engineers: "What should be done? One: The state should pursue the issue to the U.S. Supreme Court. Two: The next Congress should amend the Water Pollution Control Act to force the corps to observe the high standards set by states like Minnesota. At the same time, Congress should provide funds so that the corps can do the job correctly."

"Should" can have two meanings, and editorial writers need to make certain their readers know which they intend. The manner in which "should" was used in the two preceding examples implies obligation, necessity or duty. The other usage implies expectation or anticipation of an occurrence. "The sun should come out tomorrow" is an example. To avoid possible confusion, some writers prefer to stick with "ought" to express obligation and reserve "should" for expectation.

5. _We hope_—a much overused phrase that seems to temper a recommendation by suggesting that it is only the newspaper's opinion. Some newspapers try to avoid, or even forbid, the use of "we." Usually the point can be made without "we." However, when the _Miles City_ (Mont.) _Star_ noted that a "significant dent [had been made by Congress] in the OSHA [Occupational Safety and Health Administration] statute which American businesses have found so difficult to comply with," the editorial concluded: "We hope the fight to trim

OSHA's autocratic reign is renewed in the next Congress." The writer could easily have said: "The fight to trim OSHA's autocratic reign must be renewed in the next Congress." (Note: Although you will find "hopefully" in the conclusions of editorials, it is not an acceptable substitute for "we hope." "Hopefully" is an adverb and, as such, modifies a verb or an adjective.)

6. *We can hope*—a slightly softer version of "we hope." The *Livingston* (Mont.) *Enterprise* expressed concern that Jimmy Carter might resemble "a young and ambitious political candidate" portrayed in a movie by Robert Redford. It concluded: "So we can hope that Jimmy Carter is not that Redford candidate, and that he knows what to do next."

Approving

Sometimes no specific action is expected on a public or private issue. Perhaps some action has already been taken that deserves praise, such as a contribution an individual has made to the community or a decision by a governmental body. Sometimes an editorial writer may want to commend a proposal without going immediately to the next step to urge its approval; additional study or changes may be needed. The following, in descending order of enthusiasm, are variations of positive editorial endings.

1. *To be commended*—an appropriate phrase when the writer wants to compliment someone for some action. When the Utah Supreme Court voted a temporary stay of execution against the wishes of Gary Mark Gilmore, the *Spokane* (Wash.) *Spokesman-Review* praised the court, concluding: "Criminal Justice . . . has recorded many cases of false confessions and the Utah court apparently wants to avoid any possibility of error at any point. For that the court can be commended."

2. *Should be proud*—sometimes used when a community or a group has cause to compliment one of its members. Two days before the 1976 election, a black clergyman was denied entrance to the church that Jimmy Carter attended. The *Minneapolis Tribune* praised Carter for not doing the "expedient thing" and resigning in protest. Instead, he stayed and helped pass resolutions affirming the church's open door. Concluded the *Tribune*: "Later a gracious Carter said: 'I am proud of my church.' For the wisdom, patience and compassion he brought to helping his neighbors understand the meaning of 'freedom of worship,' his church—and his country—should be proud of Carter."

3. *Good thing*—a solidly positive phrase for announcing a paper's approval of something. A *Billings* (Mont.) *Gazette* editorial approved everything about a downtown redevelopment proposal, concluding on this note: "Let's keep Billings downtown area a viable asset. It's good for everyone."

4. *We agree*—indicative of a positive, though not wildly enthusiastic, reception. The same Billings paper disagreed with some of the recommendations of the Commission on the Review of National Policy Toward Gambling but concluded: "We do agree that the states should determine what gambling will take

place within their borders.''

5. *Deserves a hearing*—suggestive of only lukewarm approval. The *Minneapolis Tribune* examined some proposed changes in the rules of the state senate and concluded: ''The proposed rules deserve a favorable hearing when the majority DFL caucus meets next week.''

6. *But in the long run*—a phrase useful when a writer thinks that the immediate effects of something don't look very good but that eventually things will work out for the best. The *Minneapolis Tribune* sympathized with the legislative majority's reluctance to tackle a lot of difficult issues that tend to get lost in debate: ''That kind of work might not make headlines—but in the long run it would be a major service to the state.''

7. *Despite the difficulties*—an expression that suggests that something deserves approval in spite of major deficiencies. This is illustrated in the next example.

8. *Taken as a whole*—an indication that the good outweighs the bad, but maybe not by much. A *Minneapolis Tribune* editorial noted that, while black enrollment in colleges had increased dramatically, recruiting of minorities in the highly selective private schools was waning. The conclusion stated: ''We think that, despite occasional difficulties, minority-recruiting programs and educational-opportunity programs, taken as a whole, have given solid support to minority hopes of 'catching up.' ''

9. *Better than*—a suggestion that something is only the lesser of two evils, not such a good thing in itself. A *Billings Gazette* editorial argued that high standards should be imposed on new coal-fired steam plants and that customers who buy the electricity should pay the additional cost. Having all users pay, the editorial concluded, was ''better . . . than dumping the crud on those who happen to live downwind.''

10. *But no cause for complacency*—generally approving what has happened but warning readers that all is not well. When a MiG25 Soviet interceptor was found not to incorporate the latest metallurgical and electronic technology, the *Oregonian* of Portland said in an editorial: ''What the findings are telling the world is that the best of the Soviet fighter machines reflects the backward technology in the Soviet Union. But there should be no cause for complacency in the United States, because the Soviets have been determined to make up technical deficiencies by producing larger numbers of weapons than are stockpiled in the West.''

11. *But at least*—a sense of approval that is getting quite weak. A *Livington Enterprise* editorial noted that a new congressional measure would put severe tax limitations on out-of-country business meetings. ''There will be new loopholes, there always are. But at least the new law plugs a couple of the old ones for a little while,'' the *Enterprise* said.

12. *But only if*—approval only under certain conditions. A *Denver Post* editorial, commenting on federal financing of political campaigns, concluded: ''. . . the federal reform effort initiated in the 1974 campaign law can only be fully effective if congressional elections are also brought under the law.''

Disapproving

The types of editorials that end in disapproval are basically the same as those that end in approval; the editorial writer decides to come down on the negative rather than on the positive side of an issue. My search through a large number of editorials suggests that disapproving editorials are not nearly so abundant as approving editorials and that they come in only a few identifiable forms. Here, in descending order of disapproval, are five examples.

1. *We can hardly believe*—a strong expression of disapproval suggesting that the writer can scarcely comprehend what has happened. When a prominent member of the shadow cabinet of Britain's Conservative Party expressed total opposition to sharing power between Eire and Northern Ireland, a *Chicago Tribune* editorial concluded: "Mrs. Thatcher, Mr. Heath's successor as Tory leader, has let Mr. Neave's statement pass without comment. If Mrs. Thatcher does not speak out and denounce it, she runs the risk of seeming a party to it. We can hardly believe that Mrs. Thatcher seeks parliamentary majority built on bigotry and renewed bloodshed."

2. *A disservice*—a controlled but absolute statement of disapproval. When a Washington state senator was arrested on a charge of soliciting for prostitution, the *Columbian* of Vancouver noted that he might have been making only an off-hand remark, as he claimed, but it concluded that the public expects "the highest form of behavior from a man in [his] position" and that he "has done a disservice not only to himself, but to the Washington State Legislature as well."

3. *Makes no sense*—a fairly strong suggestion that something generally lacks merit. The *Missoulian* editorialized in favor of shorter presidential and congressional political campaigns. The conclusion: "Campaigns which last close to 300 days and campaigns which require every major candidate to raise enormous sums to win office make no sense. They do not, in the end, serve the public interest."

4. *Must be a better way*—suggesting that the idea may not be all bad but not good enough. The editorial may conclude that there must be a better answer even though the writer may not have it. A *Washington Post* editorial that examined the state of automobile liability insurance came to this conclusion: "There has to be a better way of compensating those to whom reparations are due than the clumsy and expensive mechanisms that exist today. . . ."

5. *Would have been wiser*—suggesting that a better idea does exist. A *Minneapolis Tribune* editorial raised questions about an all-expense-paid trip to Taiwan by members of Congress and their aides. Concerning the Minnesota member of the delegation, the *Tribune* said: "It would have been wiser—in the view of the questions being raised—if he had listened to a colleague on the House Ethics Committee. . . ."

Concluding Righteously

One of the ministers I knew in Vancouver, Wash., used to call me "the village preacher." Being a preacher himself, he must have intended this epithet as a compliment. I accepted it as such, since I thought I was upholding the moral standards of the community. But the adjectival form of "preacher," when applied to an editorial, is not particularly complimentary; readers may resent preachy editorials. Still, one of the purposes of an editorial page is to serve as a community conscience, and one of the duties of an editorial writer is to protect and promote the public good, as he or she perceives it. So, if editorials take on a high moral tone from time to time, perhaps no one should complain about a little preaching.

1. *Let that serve as an example*—a very strong form of the type of conclusion that I refer to as righteous. The editorial writer wants readers to learn a lesson from something that has happened. When Patty Hearst was sentenced to seven years in prison as a bank robber, the *Oregonian* concluded: "The Patty Hearst case should serve as a lesson to any young, impressionable person who believes that the acknowledged wrongs of society can be cured by violence."

2. *The public's rights*—a favorite touchstone for the editorial writer in making a case against government secrets or private interests. Writers find particularly gratifying the invocation of rights involving the First Amendment and freedom of information. Newspapers can perform a worthwhile function speaking up for these rights, but it is easy to allow them to become a cliche. The public gets tired of being preached to about its rights, especially when these may seem to benefit editors and reporters more than most readers. In Montana the Bureau of Land Management released the names of persons and companies that had "nominated" (proposed) various federal lands for coal leasing but refused to reveal who had nominated what lands. Concluded the *Missoulian*: "The public has a right to know who wants to glom onto what public coal. It has a right to have coal development carefully controlled." In this instance, the paper was contending that the public should know these names, but some of those who opposed publication might have argued that the *Missoulian* wanted the names for the purpose of publishing an interesting news story.

3. *Preservation of liberties*—another strongly righteous conclusion. In an editorial entitled "Freedom's Protector," the *Los Angeles Herald Examiner* noted "the never-ending assault on liberty itself by powers that protect themselves— or seek to—by forbidding public criticism of their actions." The editorial saw "the best protector of existing human liberty as a free press, whose importance cannot be overstated," then concluded: "Preservation of these liberties is critical to the health and even the survival of any true democracy. Keep that in mind the next time another judge tries to interfere with full press coverage of a public trial."

Taking Consolation

When events don't go exactly the way an editorial writer wishes, an alternative to disapproving is taking some consolation that the outcome isn't all bad. Here are four specific types of these endings.

1. *Yes, but* . . .—a conclusion acknowledging that something untoward has

occurred but insisting that things aren't so bad as they seem. When Montana voters turned down an initiative that would have restricted nuclear power plant development in their state, the *Missoulian* concluded: "Industry beat Initiative 71. That means people do not want a ban. But that does *not* mean the people want nuclear power development."

2. *... but ... heartening*—suggesting that things are bad but may improve. This is exemplified by an editorial in the *Denver Post* that noted increasing enrollment of minority students in the nation's colleges: "The Civil Rights Office's statistics do not touch on the quality of educational offerings, and on the rise in academic performance, which certainly must be an essential goal. But for now, the rising minority enrollment is heartening indeed for the students and for the nation."

3. *Not a trend, but ...*—pointing to a bright sign but warning not to make too much of it. The *Denver Post,* after noting the political instability of many African nations, pointed to "a few hopeful signs that this gloomy picture may be brightening" and concluded: "These are modest gains, to be sure, and should not be interpreted as indicating a trend. But they do suggest that the democratic spirit will not forever be denied in independent Africa, if and when the conditions are right."

4. *Some day ... some time*—a way for editorial writers who do not see much hope at the moment to take the long view and find consolation in thinking that eventually right will triumph. The *Wall Street Journal* used such a view in an editorial that lamented the 1976 presidential candidates' "adjusting their positions to the instant answers found in the polls, not to a sense of where the public is headed." The editorial concluded: "The irony is that the voters ultimately know what they want, and if the candidates won't provide an informative debate, then the voters will go by code-words, symbols and whatever clues they can pick up to the candidate's basic outlook. The voters know how elections work; experienced politicians feel it in their bones, and maybe some day the candidates' poll-takers and media advisers will learn, and stop taking their product so seriously."

Coming Down Softly

As any reader of the editorial page knows, not every editorial reaches a firm or clear conclusion. In fact, many editorials purposely remain inconclusive. (Others, unfortunately, arrive at no conclusion in spite of the writers' efforts to reach conclusions.) Writers might use this type of ending when they want to interpret what is happening or to bring their readers information and insights that have not appeared in the news columns. Writers may also resort to this form if they can envision no solution to the problems at hand. Editorial writers, after all, don't have to know all the answers. Here are some examples in decreasing order of firmness.

1. *It would appear*—a fine phrase to weaken any conclusion an editorial

writer might feel uncomfortable with, as in this *Denver Post* editorial: "Trudeau's dream of a comfortably bicultural Canada in which all citizens pursued consonant goals has been shattered irrevocably, it would appear."

2. *You can also argue*—a way to end an editorial in which the writer thinks that there are two reasonable ways to look at an issue. Usually this construction seems to favor the second alternative, as in this editorial from the *Minneapolis Tribune*: "You can argue that Peru shouldn't be the first to introduce Soviet fighters into South America or that it really doesn't need them. You can also argue, as we would, that the governing error was the [earlier] sale of F5's [by the United States] to Chile."

3. *Makes no difference*—an admission by an editorial writer that he or she can't see much difference between alternatives. The *Wall Street Journal* commented on how candidates Carter and Ford might affect New York City's financial problems: "The Carter campaign in New York City sees the two candidates as day and night. Yet, beyond a difference in rhetorical tones, and wishful thinking in City Hall, we can't see why. Chances are that when New York returns to Washington in January with its plea for more help, it will get about the same reception, regardless of who is in office."

4. *These are the questions*—a fitting conclusion when an issue raises only questions for which the editorial writer has no answers. Even when writers do have an opinion, they sometimes will seek to raise an issue merely for community discussion. They may be trying to avoid the reaction of "That paper can't tell me what to do!" This reaction is not uncommon when a newspaper from a larger city tries to tell a nearby smaller town, or a neighborhood within the city, what it should do. Sometimes editorial writers recognize that a community has to work its way slowly to answers that may seem self-evident to the writers themselves. Answers can't often be handed down on tablets of stone, even by writers who believe "Truth" has been revealed to them. In a *Chicago Tribune* editorial the conclusion notes that the deaths of eight tannery workers raised questions about what steps should be taken to prevent future disasters: "These are the questions that federal and local officials, manufacturing and business associations, and labor unions should address jointly in the wake of the tannery tragedy and in the hope of preventing other fatal accidents in the future."

5. *No easy solution*—when no answer seems to be a good one. For example, when sheriff's deputies were searching students attending concerts at the University of Montana, the *Montana Kaimin,* the student newspaper, said that "people should be safe from injury [from thrown bottles and cans], but they also have the right to be safe from a random search without a warrant." The editorial concluded: "There is no easy resolution to the problem. UM students and officials should attempt to devise an equitable way to ensure safe concerts."

6. *No solution*—when an editorial writer has no solution at all to offer. Lamenting previous studies aimed at eliminating duplication in the Montana college system, the *Helena Independent Record* concluded: "We thus hesitate to advocate another study. Nor do we offer any solutions. Meantime—uneasy rests the head wearing the crown."

7. *No issue*—the final step toward softness. These are editorials that don't even attempt to present an issue. Noting changing fashions in slang, the *Montana Standard* of Butte said that things used to be cool and neat but now were weird, and that "type" is being attached to a word to create an adjective. "Many newspapers today use a photo-printing process that yields something called 'cold type,' to distinguish it from the actual 'hot metal' type of days gone by. So far, we haven't heard anybody refer to cold-type type, but it's bound to happen. We've got no particular reason for discussing these things. We just did it to be weird."

CONCLUSION

Editorial writers are not likely consciously to turn to such devices as those listed in this chapter each time they decide how to start, organize or conclude an editorial. The categories mentioned here are not intended to provide a stock of elements from which editorial writers can choose to come up with effective editorials. Form cannot substitute for logic, facts and insight. But editorial writers who pay attention to form—their own and that of other writers—can become more aware of their own writing. By being aware of the elements of an editorial, writers ought to be able to organize editorials in a manner that is clear to their readers. And by becoming sensitized to a variety of beginnings, middles and endings used by others, writers can provide themselves with many more options for attracting and convincing readers.

QUESTIONS AND EXERCISES

1. Find editorials on the same subject that are written in at least three different formats. How are the facts (background information, etc.) handled differently by the writers? What seem to be the writers' assumptions concerning the pre-existing attitudes and prior knowledge of their readers? In what ways are these assumptions different? The same?

2. Find editorials on the same subject that are different in tone. How would you describe the tone of each? Would the approach of any tend to antagonize readers? Cause readers to identify with the writer? Put readers to sleep?

3. Pick a topic and write two editorials using distinctly different formats, for example, SA_1A_2DC and CSAC. Which do you think would be more convincing to most readers in this instance?

4. Select an editorial on a topic that interests you. Then rewrite it in an entirely different tone. Use any of the formats you like. Which editorial is likely to convince more readers?

5. Find several examples of each of the six major types of editorial conclusions. Can you find endings that would fall into categories other than these six?

6. Without substantially changing the editorial, rewrite a coming-down-softly ending to create a conclusion expressing firm approval or disapproval. Do the reverse with an editorial that has a firm conclusion.

7. Select an editorial that is directed toward a single audience and rewrite it as two-level editorial (addressing a dual audience). For example, pick an editorial that seems directed primarily toward a city council and rewrite it so that general readers will understand how the issue being discussed will affect them and what they ought to do about it.

"MUST BE THE NATIONAL CONFERENCE OF EDITORIAL WRITERS . . ."

—Draper Hill
Copyright 1978 *Detroit News*

Nine Steps to Better Writing

CHAPTER
11

By "good writing," I mean writing that is first, clear; and second, clear; and third, clear. I would have sentences that go snap, crackle and pop. . . . [Unless] they convey meaning, and add something affirmatively to the development of an idea, I would strike them out.
—James J. Kilpatrick[1]

Now that we have taken a look at the basic steps in writing an editorial, let us turn our attention to some of the finer points of turning out an editorial that is convincing, terse and well written, concentrating on the following nine areas.

1. The right amount of fact.
2. Logical conclusions.
3. Consistent point of view.
4. Clear referents and antecedents.
5. Sentences of appropriate length.
6. Economy of words.
7. Correct grammar.
8. Absence of cliches and jargon.
9. Proper use of individual words.

To provide examples of how editorials can be improved in these nine areas, I will refer to two editorials reproduced here, "File Flap Offers Object Lesson to Other City Department Heads" and "Fair Taxes Shared Fairly." These two were among editorials evaluated at an NCEW critique session in which I participated. Some of the comments made about these editorials were offered by members of the session. Newspapers and editorial writers will remain anonymous.

File Flap Offers Object Lesson to Other City Department Heads

Two weeks ago, H---- City Council turned thumbs down on the proposed purchase of a fancy automated file system for the Police Department. The city fathers did so after being told by Councilman H---- F---- that the only problem with the current filing system was that it was overloaded and, after being purged of hundreds of pounds of records, now was working fine and didn't need to be replaced.

In the wake of council's action, Police Chief O---- A---- arranged a first-hand visit to the police record room for the council members—and made sure that members of the news media were invited too.

At the session in the Police Department's basement HQ at City Hall, the staffers who regularly use the system detailed its problems and voiced a plea for its replacement. But it was A---- himself who delivered the coup de grace vowing that its replacement was his "top priority" and warning that in the event of another breakdown, many vital records would be unavailable until the system was repaired "and it could be a life or death situation."

Once A---- said what he did, there was little question that City Council would reverse itself and approve the purchase of the new $9,000-plus file system. And this, at Monday night's session, is exactly what happened. In the absence of F----, council voted unanimously to purchase the new system.

The object lesson here for other city department heads should be clear. If City Council refuses to buy some piece of equipment that you want, just invite the council members to your department for a first-hand look at the problem. Make sure you invite the press too and tell them to be sure to bring their cameras and their microphones.

Then get your staffers to tell everybody how much the new equipment is needed. And, if you can manage it, look very somber and warn that failure to buy the equipment in question "could be a life or death situation."

It worked for A---- and—who knows?—it may just work for you too.

Fair Taxes Shared Fairly

Based upon our study of the matter, it seems to us that the under-assessment enjoyed by the S--- fairground disclosed in Thursday's Herald is less an indictment of the property owners than of the system which permitted it to continue over five years.

The cost in lost property taxes to the county, the S--- municipality and the re-

gional school district amounts to more than $8,000. There is little likelihood the money can be recovered by the taxing bodies involved.

Because they received annual grants from both the county and the state, a case can be made that they stockholders who own the fairground should have noted the radical decline in their 1974 assessment to

$6,250 from the previous year's $30,650 and directed inquiries to the county tax assessment bureau ~~questioning the accuracy of the new figure~~. The bureau is responsible for the assessments used by virtually all taxing bodies in the county to determine taxes due them.

That they did not is understandable, if ~~morally questionable~~. What property owner is likely to invite more taxes by informing the assessor of a mistake—and particularly on the low side? *only on the low side*

Thus, we are ~~forced~~ to the conclusion that the prime responsibility for this error must be placed ~~at the feet of~~ the county assessment (bureau) and the county commissioners, whose duty it is to oversee the operation of the (office.) The (agency) determines the value for tax purposes of some 65,000 individual properties, and it says it lacks the manpower to police each one to insure current accuracy. Until it finds, or is alerted, to a change in a parcel's status— as in this case—it has no reason to act. The bureau, incidentally, already has moved to bring the fairground's assessment more in line with its true market value.

The chances are that ~~there are~~ many other such discrepancies (still) undiscovered *remain* in the bureau's files. The case of the fairground should alert the bureau to seek them out and to make the necessary corrections as quickly as possible.

~~There are those who~~ will see in this case *Some* favoritism and an exercise of political influence; we find no evidence to support this. Instead, what we find is a need for the assessment office, its heavy clerical burden notwithstanding, to take ~~those~~ steps ~~necessary~~ to insure that the principle of fair taxation fairly shared is not further abused.

40

50

THE RIGHT AMOUNT OF FACT

Editorials should contain only those facts that are necessary for the purposes for which the editorials were written. "Facts are precious things, and to be thoroughly enjoyed must be tasted sparingly and drooled over leisurely," Vermont Royster of the *Wall Street Journal* advised editorial writers.[2] Usually the detail required in an editorial is less than what would be needed in a news story on the same topic. In many cases editorial readers will have read the news reports and will not want a repetition of the facts before finding out what the editorial writer has to add. Still, editorial writers cannot assume that most readers know all of the facts. So a compromise between a brief reference and a full factual account must be worked out. In this matter, editorial writers have to rely on their judgment; but they should try for brevity. Space in editorial columns is far more limited than in news columns.

The two editorials included here are fairly brief, both between 300 and 400 words, and seem not to be overburdened with unnecessary information. But some of those who criticized the "Fair Taxes" editorial thought that the writer assumed too much about readers' knowledge of the subject. If the disclosures that the *Herald* had made had been spelled out early in the editorial, readers would have found the editorial easier to follow. Some of the needed facts are in the second half of the editorial, in lines 36 through 59.

LOGICAL CONCLUSIONS

One criticism of the "File Flap" editorial was that it did not attempt to reach a conclusion on the basic question posed by the incidents: Was a new system really needed? The writer offers no evidence or arguments against the contention of the council member that the problem was simply unpurged old records. Nor did the writer attempt to judge the arguments of the users of the equipment. The editorial concludes, in effect: "Well, that's the way it is." If the users' presentation had convinced those who were present or had directly responded to the council member's point, the editorial should have said so. If it did not, it should also have said so.

In "Fair Taxes" the writer carefully comes to a specific conclusion: The paper does not find evidence to support suggestions that the loss of property taxes resulted from political influence; rather, the assessment office needs to pay more attention to fair taxation. This conclusion seems to be thoroughly supported by what precedes it.

It is not always easy to judge whether an editorial presents logical arguments that lead to an appropriate conclusion. Whether the arguments work depends on the point of view of the person doing the judging.

CONSISTENT POINT OF VIEW

By consistent point of view, I mean that the editorial writer should use a consistent first-person ("we"), second-person ("you") or third-person ("he," "she," "they") approach in an editorial. When we talked about the editorial "we" in Chapter 5, we noted that some papers discourage or forbid the use of "we" in editorials. Other papers regard the usage as appropriate. In any case, care should be taken to use "we" infrequently. If you use "we" to refer to the paper, do so consistently; don't switch back and forth between "we" and the name of the paper.

On occasion writers find it appropriate, especially when writing on informal topics, to address editorials to the readers with a second-person "you." Once adopted, this form of address must be maintained throughout the editorial. Use of "you," of course, can be overdone in an editorial. Writers must be careful not to switch suddenly to a "you" point of view in the middle or at the end of an editorial.

Another inconsistency to avoid is a shift in the intended audience. Unless there is a clear reason, a writer should not start an editorial talking to one audience, then switch to another.

Until the last three paragraphs in "File Flap," the editorial seems to be recounting, in the third person for a general audience, the flap over the file system.

Then the writer turns to talk specifically to city department heads and refers to them as "you." The "you" point of view continues through the conclusion. The writer could easily have continued in the third person.

CLEAR REFERENTS AND ANTECEDENTS

To avoid repeating words in a boring fashion, writers use pronouns to refer to the nouns they are talking about. To avoid repeating phrases and sentences, even whole paragraphs, they use "that" or "that idea" or "that concept" or "that development." Sometimes readers become confused by this shorthand. Professor R. Thomas Berner of The Pennsylvania State University referred to pronouns as "those unemotional, ambiguous, spineless parasites we use to refer to other parts of speech somewhere else in the same sentence, or, on occasion, in another sentence in the same paragraph, or, the worst of all possible contortions, in another paragraph." Berner cited the following sentence as an example of what he was talking about: "The city collects only swill from the university, and because of it, it has determined that the rate was higher than it should have been."[3] The only unambiguous "it" in the sentence is the last one, referring to the rate. But what do the first two refer to? According to the rules of grammar—a pronoun should refer to the nearest preceding logical referent—both of them should refer to university. But the first "it" apparently stands for the whole idea that only swill comes from the university, and who knows whether the second "it" means the university or the city?

In our "Fair Taxes" editorial we have two examples of vague references. In line 14 readers come across a "they" that is not made clear until two lines later. Clarification could be made in this manner: "Because fairground stockholders received annual grants from both the county and the state, they should have noted. . . ." At the beginning of the fourth paragraph, in line 26, the writer says: "That they did not is understandable, if morally questionable." That they did not *what*? The reference is to "the stockholders . . . should have noted the radical decline in their 1974 assessment . . ." two sentences back. In this case it seems desirable to repeat the key words: "That they did not report the underassessment is understandable. . . ." An appropriate, if redundant, use of "it" occurs in lines 38–42, where "it" is used four times to refer to the same agency.

SENTENCES OF APPROPRIATE LENGTH

If readers and editors were polled, probably most would say that they thought sentences in editorials tended to be longer and harder to understand than those in news stories. Yet at least two studies made 20 years apart showed that readers found editorials easier to understand than news stories. In 1969 Professor Galen R. Rarick of The Ohio State University, who made the second study, speculated that this apparent anomaly occurs partly because most editorial writers have been in the writing business longer than most reporters. Another reason, he suggested, was that news writers may be better at reporting and investigating than at writing. Editorial writers also have a longer time to rewrite and polish their products than most reporters, and so should produce better writing.[4]

The earlier of the two studies was based on a book called *The Art of Readable Writing* by Rudolph Flesch. This book and a subsequent one by the same author, *How to Test Readability*, attracted considerable attention among writers in the late 1940s and 1950s.[5] Since longer sentences were considered harder to understand than short ones and longer words were considered more abstract than short ones, Flesch came up with a scale based on two factors—average sentence length (number of words) and average word length (number of syllables per 100 words). Using the scale, a "standard" rating of 65 (seventh or eighth grade level) could be obtained by various combinations. If sentences were short, words could be longer; if words were short, sentences could be longer. A "standard" rating could be obtained by sentences that averaged 15 words in length if 100 words had no more than 149 syllables but only 10 words if 100 words had 157 syllables. Although Flesch himself warned against taking the scale too seriously, response to his books was such that Francis P. Locke of the *Dayton* (Ohio) *Daily News* felt moved to write an article for *The Masthead* entitled "Too Much Flesch on the Bones?" "We have created a cult of leanness," he wrote. "The adjective is packed off to a semantic Siberia. The mood piece, if tolerated at all, must be astringent and aseptic." He feared "the growing pressure to water everything down to the thinnest possible pablum for the laziest possible minds."[6]

Writers should realize that readers, even of editorial pages, are usually in a hurry. Today's readers are not likely to labor over the type of heavy prose that an E. L. Godkin or a Charles Dana gave to his readers a century ago. Yet simplistic writing can be boring, and if a writer has a fairly complex thought to express, a complex sentence may be necessary to express it. The complexity of the writing should depend on the editorial and the concepts that are discussed in it. But a good rule is to try to keep the writing simpler than you are at first inclined, since it is still likely to be perceived by most readers as more difficult than you expect.

So how do our two editorials rate on the Flesch scale? "Fair Taxes" has sentences that average a little more than 26 words in length and has 159 syllables for every 100 words. On Flesch's scale this would earn a rating of about 48, a little closer to "fairly difficult" than to "difficult." "File Flap" has sentences that average 25 words in length and 142 syllables for every 100 words, earning it a 62, a little closer to "standard" than to "fairly difficult." Most of the difference between these two editorials results from the length of words rather than the length of sentences. But average sentence length is long in both editorials, and both contain several extremely long sentences. The second sentence in "File Flap" has 46 words, and the sentence beginning in line 20 has 48 words. The first sentence can easily be split in two by placing a period after "overloaded" and starting a new sentence: "After being purged of hundreds of pounds of records, F—— said, the system was working fine and didn't need to be replaced." (We will rewrite the latter sentence when we look at the use of individual words.) In the section on clear referents we had some suggestions for the 57-word sentence beginning in line 14 in "Fair Taxes." After some additional work on it, here is one possibility: "Because fairground stockholders received annual grants from both the county and the state, they should have noted the radical decline in their 1974 assessment and directed inquiries to the county tax assessment bureau." (The actual dollar figures could go in a separate sentence.) That trims the sentence to 33 words, still fairly long.

ECONOMY OF WORDS

Long sentences are a tip-off to wordiness, as we have seen. But wordiness also shows up in words and phrases that may be part of short sentences. Let us examine our two editorials for ways to tighten the writing.

In "File Flap," in line 27, "Once A—— said what he did" can become "Once he said that." In lines 31–32, "And this, at Monday night's session" can become "This is exactly what happened." The following sentence makes clear that the action came at the meeting. In line 35, "The object lesson" becomes "The lesson." In neither line 12 nor line 40 is "first-hand" needed. Are there such things as second-hand visits and second-hand looks?

In "Fair Taxes," in line 1, "it seems to us" is not needed; the meaning can be carried by changing "is" in line 4 to "seems." You don't have to tell readers that it is "us" who is saying these things. In lines 21–22, the writer says the obvious in the words "questioning the accuracy of the new figures." Directing inquiries adequately suggests a questioning of the figures. In line 33, we can replace "at the feet of" with "before." In lines 57–58, "those steps necessary to insure" can become simply "steps."

Two words that often signal wordiness and the use of the passive voice are "there is" and its various forms (there are, there will be, etc.). Usually you can strike "there is" and insert a stronger verb elsewhere in the sentence. We have three examples in "Fair Taxes." In lines 11–12, "There is little likelihood the money can be recovered" can become "The money probably cannot be recovered." In line 46, "The chances are that there are many other such discrepancies undiscovered" can become "The chances are that many other such discrepancies remain undiscovered." In line 52, "There are those who" can become simply "Some."

CORRECT GRAMMAR

A person who attains the august position of editorial writer should not have to worry about correct grammar. Yet errors creep into the best of editorial pages. Jumping right out at us in "Fair Taxes" is a common grammatical error: the dangling participle. In line 1, the phrase beginning with "based" has nothing to modify in the following clause. Correct grammar would require that the subject of the main clause be "we" or "this newspaper." In any event, the opening phrase, whether in dangling or correct form, is unnecessary. If a writer's conclusions aren't based on a "study of the matter," what are they based on? When we get to the section on individual words, we will have more to say about this opening sentence, so we will wait until then to rewrite it.

The only other grammatical problem I have spotted in these editorials occurs in lines 41–42 of "File Flap." This is a matter of agreement between noun and pronoun. The writer has "the press," which is singular, coupled with three plural pronouns. Now no doubt more than one camera and more than one microphone showed up. Usually problems such as this can be solved by changing "them" and "their" to "it" and "its," but in this case such a change would suggest that a single journalist brought several cameras and several microphones. The simplest solution is to insert "members of" in front of "press." We could change "press" to the plural "media," but I consider this a pretentious word for an editorial. "Press" is fully understood by readers.

ABSENCE OF CLICHES AND JARGON

Cliches and jargon, in a sense, are at opposite ends of the spectrum in terms of comprehensibility by the general reader. Cliches tend to be used in everyday conversation by the sophisticated and the unsophisticated, the educated and the not-so-educated. Jargon is a special set of words used by a specific group of people. Everyone understands cliches; only the in-group fully understands jargon. The editorial writer must resist the easy temptation to use both—jargon, because many readers will not easily understand what the words mean; cliches, because good editorial writing should use fresh terms, not hackneyed phrases. While at times cliches may be appropriate—these expressions have been around for a long time, and they do "ring bells" with readers—in most cases a little more thought can produce a more exact phrase than the cliche. Instead of "ring bells," we could have said "easily understood by readers." Problems with jargon tend to increase with the specialization of editorial writers. When writers associate with educators, lawyers, doctors, sociologists, government bureaucrats, politicians or farmers, they pick up their language and tend to forget that many words that are full of meaning to these people are either incomprehensible or lacking in meaning to many readers. Writers must constantly be on guard against such words sneaking into their writing.

Some of the words that tend to get overworked by editorial writers include,

alarming trend	on closer examination
amazing	only time will tell
basic	problem
broadly speaking	program
factor	remains to be seen
gratifying	responsible observers
incredible	the economy
in fact	thoughtful people
in order ("A new examination is in order.")	to be deplored
in terms of	underlying ("underlying causes")
major ("major event")	unquestionable
obvious	would seem

In 1955, long before the widespread use of computerized machines, the *Wall Street Journal* suggested that editorial writers might find a use for IBM's gadget called a Wordwriter. It could store up to 42 words or phrases and all the writer would have to do was punch a letter on the machine and out would come the word or phrase. The *Journal* cited the following list as possible entries:[7]

"A": will be for "As we have reminded our readers time and time again. . . ."
"B": "Both sides of this question have merit. . . ."
"C": "Considering all the factors involved. . . ."
"D": "Doubtless some will disagree with this view. . . ."
"E": "Except for the particular circumstances surrounding the case in question. . . ."
"F": "Fortunately, things are not always as they seem. . . ."
"G": "Generally speaking. . . ."
"H": "However, the public believes the facts are. . . ."
"I": "Indeed, there is no gainsaying. . . ."
And so on, to the inevitable conclusion that must follow.

From a short stack of editorials, I came across these cliches:

"It'll soon be time to fish or cut bait."
"Montanans can breathe a sigh of relief. . . ."
"Inflation has reared its ugly head."

"Time marches on."

"The country went absolutely bananas. . . ."

"That's a real can of worms."

"By 1986 it will be time to stir the pot again."

". . . the computer . . . coughed up the latest . . . report."

"A natural tendency to 'let George do it.' "

"Into the breach lept the Jaycees."

Even less defensible than the use of the cliche is the use of the jargon of government, education and any other field with its own vocabulary. Noting the efforts of the National Council of Teachers of English to fight government jargon, the *Milwaukee Journal* published an editorial, "Gobbledygook," to poke fun at bureaucrats. It is reproduced here.

Gobbledygook

It's good to know that somewhere in the sprawling government bureaucracy is an employee with a sense of humor. That useful commodity often withers in the criticism heaped on public officials, or is buried in the jargon with which such people often communicate.

Take as a modest example the terms face-value consensus, content validity, concurrent validity and predictive validity that recently fuzzed up an HEW memorandum. They probably mean something to someone, but who knows what to whom? In an effort to get officials to say what they mean in terms everyone can understand, the National Council of Teachers of English presents Public Doublespeak awards, whose wry purpose is to uncover the absurdity of communication that doesn't communicate.

The latest honor went to the State Department for an announcement that its consumer affairs coordinator would use the consumer communication channel to review existing mechanisms in order to improve linkages of consumer input, thruput and output. Its author, surprisingly, stepped right up to claim the award. It was a compliment, he said, considering the "normal inability of the bureaucracy to do anything in a manner which would merit an award for anything." Maybe the answer to gobbledygook is requiring bureaucrats to talk with their tongues in their cheeks.

Milwaukee (Wis.) *Journal*

What do we find in our two editorials? In line 4 of "File Flap," we see "city fathers," one of the most overworked expressions used to talk about city officials. How the current city authorities could have fathered the city is hard to comprehend. In line 11 appears "in wake of"; in line 12, as we noted previously, is "first-hand visit"; in line 21, "coup de grace"; in line 40, also noted before, "first-hand look." "Staffers" in line 18 is a bureaucrat's word for staff members, and reference to City Council or council in lines 28, 32 and 36 without a preceding "the" is a habit of insiders and is not the way people talk on the streets.

In "Fair Taxes," in lines 15–16, we have "a case can be made," and in line 31, "forced to the conclusion" (why not just "conclude"?). We have already noted "at the feet of" in line 33.

PROPER USE OF INDIVIDUAL WORDS

After all of these potential writing traps have been checked, we may also have to check for the use of weak or inappropriate words. In "Fair Taxes," in line 6, "which" properly should be "that." "That" is the word to use when the dependent clause that follows is necessary to make clear the identity of the noun it modifies. A "that" clause is not set off by commas. In this case, without the clause, readers would have no idea what system the writer was talking about. If a clause is not needed for clear meaning, "which" is appropriate, and the clause should be set off by commas. Also in line 6: Journalism stylebooks prefer the use of "more than" instead of "over" when the writer means that something exceeds something else. One more point should be made concerning this sentence. Can a fairground "enjoy" something? The writer attributed human feelings to an inanimate object. Why not say "under-assessment of the fairground"? Now we are ready to rewrite the sentence that has been more discussed than any other in this chapter: "The under-assessment of the S—— fairground disclosed in Thursday's *Herald* seems less an indictment of the property owners than of the system that permitted the practice to continue more than five years."

In line 29 of the same editorial, use of the word "particularly" raises a question about the logic of the phrase, "and particularly on the low side." If a mistake in assessment had been made on the high side, the owners would not be inviting higher taxes by informing the assessor. They would be asking for lower taxes. So the phrase is both redundant and illogical. In lines 34 and 36 the writer jumps from "bureau" to "office" to "agency" to refer to the same assessment bureau. The writer is trying too hard to avoid repeating words. Simpler wording might be: ". . . the county assessment bureau and the county commissioners, who have the duty to oversee it. The bureau. . . ." Eliminated are several unneeded words: "it is" and "the operation of."

In "File Flap," in line 9, we have the joining of "now" with a past tense verb, "was." "Now" can be dropped. In line 21, "vowing" seems a little strong. Both "vowing" and the cliche "coup de grace" can be eliminated and the meaning made clearer in this manner: "A—— himself offered the most convincing argument. He warned that, in the event of another break-down, many vital records would be unavailable until the system was repaired 'and it could be a life or death situation.' He said replacement of the system was his 'top priority.' "

CONCLUSION

Simply following all of these steps, and those described in the preceding chapter, will not guarantee a good editorial. Thought, imagination and lively writing, none of which can be reduced to a simple how-to formula, are even more essential than the format of the editorial or the correctness of the use of words. No matter how technically correct or skillfully organized, an editorial is not likely to be effective unless it also carries hard-to-define qualities that attract and persuade readers.

James J. Kilpatrick has described the goal of the editorial writer "to be, in 300 words or less, temperate, calm, dignified, forceful, direct, catchy, provocative, stimulating, reasoned, logical, literate, factual, opinionated, conclusive, informative, interesting and persuasive. And put a live head on it."[8]

That's all it takes to write an editorial.

QUESTIONS AND EXERCISES

1. Find an editorial with what you regard as an overabundance of factual information. Rewrite the piece using only those facts that are necessary to make the subject understandable.

2. Apply a heavy editing pencil to an editorial to remove unnecessary words and phrases.

3. Try to find an editorial in which the arguments and evidence presented do not support the conclusion. With the information that is contained in the editorial, can it be rewritten to bring the conclusion into line with the supporting material?

4. Count and average the number of syllables for every hundred words and the number of words per sentence in the editorials of several newspapers. How do the editorials compare in terms of word and sentence length? Are the editorials with longer words and sentences more difficult to understand? If not, why not?

5. In examining these same newspapers, do you find a general trend in individual papers toward long sentences and long words, or short sentences and short words, or do editorials vary within the papers?

6. Find an editorial in which the simplified style of the writing seems condescending to readers. Can you rewrite the editorial to overcome this problem?

7. Scan a handful of editorials for cliches. Which—if any—can you justify? How could you eliminate the remainder?

8. Rewrite an editorial that relies excessively on government or other types of jargon. Translate the offending language into understandable English.

9. Examine several editorials for euphemisms and for more difficult words and phrases than are necessary to convey meaning.

10. Find improper and ambiguous uses of "it" and "that" as referents. Rewrite to clarify the meaning.

11. Find several sentences that begin with a form of "there is" and rewrite them in a clearer and more direct manner.

WHAT'S THIS I HEAR ABOUT YOU PUTTING **HUMOR** IN YOUR EDITORIALS?

—George Fisher
Arkansas Gazette for *The Masthead*

Subjects That
Deserve More Attention

CHAPTER
12

Is it necessary or desirable to fill the editorial columns with pieces on government and politics to the virtual exclusion of all else . . . ?
—Creed Black
Nashville Tennessean[1]

When editorial writers assemble in small or large groups to assess each others' work, a frequent criticism is that they spend too much time writing about government and politics. They do this, for one reason, because the news business seems concerned primarily with public affairs, and much of public affairs involves government. They may also follow this tendency as a matter of least resistance, since their own interests are likely to lie in this direction. But there are other reasons why some topics, while generally recognized as appropriate for editorial comment, get less attention. Writers regard some subject areas as too difficult to write about, or too easy to merit more than a minimum of writing effort or not of sufficient seriousness to warrant taking time from the "great issues of the day." This chapter will look at three types of these editorials: subjects that are tough to write about, subjects that are deceptively easy and subjects that editorial writers ignore.

SUBJECTS THAT ARE HARD TO WRITE ABOUT

Any subject can be hard to write about if you don't know what you are writing about. Over the years, I have found that, because of the fear of not knowing enough about the topic, writers have tended to shy away from seven subject areas: economics, legal issues, international affairs, culture, medical and health topics, religion and sports.

Economics

For the writer who wants to write more than cliches, the editorial on economics is one of the hardest to write. Of all the topics that I assign my students, economics is the one that they most resist writing about. The minds of those who have taken introductory economics courses are filled with bewilderment at all the theories and laws and graphs. The minds of those who have not taken these courses are filled with horror at the thought of writing about what has been called "the dismal science." Part of the reluctance of both groups stems from their impressions that editorials on economics are boring and filled with numbers. If they have read editorials on the subject, they probably think of them as dealing with taxes (too high), government spending (too much), unemployment (too high) or inflation (too rapid). Or they think that editorials on economics deal with the theories of John Maynard Keynes, Milton Friedman or Arthur Laffer. None of this seems to have much to do with daily life.

But economics does relate to how readers live their lives. For example, the supply and price of gasoline affect nearly every American, so editorials about decisions made by the OPEC nations stand a good chance of being read if they talk about how these decisions will be reflected at the local gas pump. Editorials about tax credits for installing solar facilities, the lifting of inheritance taxes, the imposition of rent controls or a requirement for fire-resistant roofs can be written about in a manner that will make readers understand how and why they are affected. So how does a writer produce an editorial on economics that does not end up simply saying the government shouldn't be spending so much money or labor unions should hold down their demands for wage increases?

Lauren K. Soth of the *Des Moines Register and Tribune,* a veteran at writing editorials on economics, has made a number of suggestions. Editorials, according to Soth, should explain and interpret, not merely spout official newspaper policy. They should discuss "what is happening here and now" and concentrate on how current economic phenomena actually affect people's well-being. This means avoiding the temptation to "pontificate on every little economic event in terms of . . . grand ideologies." Soth emphasized that organization of the subject matter is extremely important, that the writer needs to proceed in a manner that seems logical to readers—from the known to the unknown, spelling out each major step of reasoning from the beginning to the conclusion. Each editorial should concentrate on one central idea and drive it home, avoiding getting involved in side issues.

While Soth did not contend that economics can be made simple and entertaining, he believed that the writer can, and should, arouse interest by talking in terms of what people are interested in—people. "Instead of saying, 'Wheat acreage increased 10 percent,' why not say, 'Farmers planted 10 percent more acres of wheat'?" Without oversimplifying complex issues, the writer can make them understandable. For instance, instead of stringing facts and figures together in prose comparisons, data can be organized in tables and rounded off for easier comprehension.[2]

What Soth was espousing—that the writer should speak in terms of people and should simplify numbers—is illustrated by an editorial in the *Wall Street Journal*, "The Gold Rush." Notice the personal manner in which the editorial begins. The writer depicts New Yorkers as "raiding their jewelry boxes and heading for 47th Street to see how much they can get from old-gold buyers." Later the writer talks about home owners cashing in on rising residential prices. These are real actions by real people. No reference is ever made to dollar amounts. The writer must have decided that quoting specific prices of gold was not necessary to make the points of the editorial and would only have made it more difficult to read. The sentences are relatively short—an average of 22 words, compared to 25 and 26 in the two editorials we examined in Chapter 11 (pp. 174–175). There are about 160 syllables for each 100 words, placing the editorial between difficult and fairly difficult on the Flesch scale, which is comparable to "Fair Taxes Shared Fairly," the more difficult of the two editorials.

The Gold Rush

With the price of gold bouncing up and down like a yo-yo—but mostly up—New Yorkers have been raiding their jewelry boxes and heading for 47th Street to see how much they can get from old-gold buyers.

It's a form of savings liquidation, which we've been seeing a great deal of over the last year. Elsewhere, people have been cashing in on rising home prices by borrowing against their expanded equities. As to saving in general, or more to the point, total capital formation, the outlook is not good. Figures released by the Commerce Department yesterday reveal that personal savings last year averaged only 4.5% of income, the lowest level in 30 years, and that the savings rate slumped to an incredible 3.3% in November. The implications of this for U.S. capital formation help explain, as much as war fears in the Middle East or whatever is happening to sales of new gold, why the gold price has soared this past year.

It has soared because the U.S. dollar is fundamentally weak. The dollar is funda-

mentally weak because the American economy is fundamentally weak. The American economy is fundamentally weak because for some time now government policies have encouraged spending and discouraged saving.

The inflation that has resulted further aggravates the problem by encouraging individuals to spend their money before it can be eroded away, and by raising the government tax take which also is quickly translated into demand. To raise cash, the old-gold sellers are falling back on items they had never thought of before as savings. The buyers are figuring that things will probably get worse before they get better.

Gold is not the only item that has been rising in dollar terms. The Dow Jones spot commodity index is up 13% from a year ago, a rate which coincides roughly—and not accidentally—with the general rate of inflation. This means that the underlying factor in the gold rush remains the devaluation of currencies, and the dollar in particular, relative to goods.

The reason why so many people doubt

this will improve much can be glimpsed by looking at the financial markets forecast for 1980 prepared by Salomon Brothers. On the savings side, the internal cash generation of corporations (profits and depreciation allowances less deductions) will fall in 1980, mainly because federal corporate taxes will rise. This will be happening in an economy where total private domestic investment in real terms is only slightly above the level it reached just prior to the 1973–75 recession. During that seven years, personal consumption expenditures in real terms have risen some 18%.

As to the demand for credit during the coming year, the big item will be a whopping increase, some 44% according to the Salomon projections, in federal borrowing. Much of this will go to support transfers from the capital markets to unproductive Americans, whose demands for support are expected to rise as a result of recession.

The combination of rising taxation, a continuing high rate of inflation, rising federal demands on the nation's capital supply and a low rate of capital generation relative to demand makes for a dire situation. The economic base that backs the dollar as it performs its vital duty as a national and international currency is being eroded. Americans can see the physical evidence of this in potholed streets, faltering railways, shabby public buildings and idle or unproductive human capital.

The most troublesome thing, something that the markets are no doubt reading quite accurately, is the evidence that the nation's putative economic policy makers, in the administration and Congress, have no idea what is happening. They prefer to blame the gold gyrations on greedy speculators or irrational fears.

The market knows that this administration intends to keep on raising taxes, through bracket creep and the huge oil industry levy currently being touched up by a conference committee in Congress. It knows that this money taken out of the capital generation stream will mainly go for consumption, through income transfer programs designed to buy votes. It knows that even this won't be enough for the Washington spenders and that they will also make big demands on public credit markets. And it knows that no nation can continue this process without eventually causing its own ruin.

Wall Street Journal

Despite the difficult to fairly difficult rating, most of the words in "The Gold Rush" are part of simple, everyday language. Where something is referred to that readers might not know about—for example, the Dow Jones spot commodity index (up 13 percent in a year)—the writer quickly explains: "This means that the underlying factor in the gold rush remains the devaluation of currencies, and the dollar in particular, relative to goods." In an attempt to explain clearly what the editorial is about, the writer uses three short, direct sentences in the third paragraph: The price of gold "has soared because the U.S. dollar is fundamentally weak. The dollar is fundamentally weak because the American economy is fundamentally weak. The American economy is fundamentally weak because for some time now government policies have encouraged spending and discouraged saving." What could be more succinct or better written? The editorial is also made more accessible by its reference to a yo-yo in the first paragraph, to potholed streets, to faltering railroads and to shabby public buildings. Again, the writer is talking about things that affect people. Whether or not would-be writers on economics agree with the *Journal*'s point of view in this editorial, or with its general editorial stance, they can find worthy models of economics editorials in the newspaper.

While the *Journal*'s editorials tend to be relatively long—"The Gold Rush" has about 660 words—editorials on economics do not have to be that long. "Free Lunch," from the *Milwaukee* (Wis.) *Journal,* is an example. The editorial identifies one specific aspect of a proposed change in the capital gains tax and argues that the social benefits of the tax savings would be lost. The editorial seems to be directed at one audience, the House of Representatives.

Free Lunch

There's sense in using the tax system to stimulate investment as a way of creating new jobs and increasing productivity. The House Ways and Means Committee lost sight of that goal in one proposal to reform the capital gains tax.

Homeowners, once in their lives, would be allowed to pocket the profits—up to $100,000—on the sale of a home without paying any tax. That's unjustified.

We agree that a case can be made for not taxing a capital gain at all *if* the gain is reinvested, if the tax exclusion serves a larger social purpose. But the logic for special treatment disappears when a gain is simply converted into spending money. The full House should remedy the committee's extravagance.

Milwaukee Journal

Writing about taxes of any kind can be touchy, since taxes affect individual interests more directly than most other economic matters and, as was apparent in the first years of the Reagan administration, can become highly partisan. Writers must be fair, and they must know what they are talking about. Information about proposals for changes in federal taxes can be obtained from sources noted before, including the *Congressional Quarterly* and *Editorial Research Reports*. Information about the effects of taxes on state and local levels may be difficult to find. The writer often must dig out information, digging that may make the editorial all the more convincing and worthwhile. At the state level people working in the tax commission or for such groups as the state labor organization or state business association are possible sources. At the local level the county assessor is likely to be a good source for information about property taxes.

The writer of "Severance Tax Is Off Base" (p. 192), from the *Wichita* (Kan.) *Eagle,* was faced with finding out not only what impact a proposed tax on oil would have but also why the proposal was being advanced in the first place. The editorial attempts to put the proposal into the perspective of a declining state industry that would be reduced even further by the tax. Rather than stick with the economics, the writer also brings in the political angle—there is speculation that the proposal is being made to gain support for a power plant to be fueled with something besides gas or oil. The editorial is mostly free of unneeded details, though using the exact figure 124,467,713 in the opening sentence has a deadening effect. The writer could have, as Soth suggested, rounded the figure to 124 million and thus made it easier for readers to compare that number with the 56 million in the next sentence. The $10 million figure, the amount the tax would raise, is needed, if only to compare with the $55 million tax benefit that previous proposals had coupled with earlier efforts to levy the tax. Perhaps including the value of the coal-fired plant is not necessary. Only in the next-to-last sentence does the writer talk about the effects on the general public—higher fuel prices for consumers; readers might be more inclined to read the editorial if this impact had been mentioned much earlier.

Severance Tax Is Off Base

It would have made some sense 23 years ago, when Kansas crude oil production peaked at 124,467,713 barrels, to put a 1 percent severance tax on oil and gas. But now the state's wells pump only about 56 million barrels a year, the idea is highly questionable. Yet the House Ways and Means Committee has voted to introduce just such a bill.

The $10 million it would raise would be earmarked for power plant improvements, energy conservation and easing the impact of rising utility bills at state institutions—all commendable goals. But the committee has to consider what such a discriminatory tax would do to the state's declining oil and gas industry.

Nearly 80 percent of Kansas' oil production is from stripper wells that produce an average of 2.9 barrels a day. A severance tax would put a heavy burden on these wells, and no doubt would force the plugging of many of them earlier than they might have been otherwise. The oil they would have produced probably would be lost forever.

It isn't the first time a severance tax has been before the Legislature. Numerous bills have been introduced and defeated over the past dozen years or so. Some of them have included a provision removing the ad valorem tax the industry now pays—about $55 million last year. No such provision is in the proposed Ways and Means bill.

Speculation in Topeka is that the bill is a pressure tactic on the part of legislators who favor an $18-million coal-fired power plant at Kansas State University over plants that might use other fuels—natural gas, for example.

The Legislature has appropriated money for a study of the plant, and it is complete. It should be the basis for decisions on what kind of plant is to be built.

The introduction of a bill to influence these decisions can only confuse things. And there is always the danger of its actually making it through the legislative process and into the law books.

The inevitable result would be hastening the decline of the state's oil industry. And, because about half of the gas produced in Kansas is consumed in Kansas, a severance tax could have an adverse effect on consumers, who no doubt would be paying more for fuel.

If the Ways and Means Committee proceeds with the bill's introduction, the proposal should be defeated when it comes up for consideration by the full membership.

Wichita (Kan.) *Eagle*

Legal Issues

Discussion of a legal issue can become so involved that readers may stop trying to understand what an editorial writer is talking about. Writers need to keep in mind that most readers know little about legal matters, so legal terms should never be used when plain English will do. If a legal term is used, it should be defined in the simplest language possible. Writers should keep a pocket law dictionary handy. Simplifying complex and technical legal matters, however, may distort information or mislead readers. So care must be taken to include enough of the complexities to persuade those knowledgeable of the subject. In "Is It Up to the Host?" the *Spectator* of Hamilton, Ontario, acknowledged that the issue being discussed could become so complex that "trials involving alcohol-related offences [*sic*] may become nightmares." In this instance the writer ignored the legal complexities in dealing with social and moral values, concluding that people who drink are responsible for their own actions and should not expect other people to look out for them. The writer did not get tangled up in legal points but turned directly to a broader issue—the implications of the verdict. To speak in such a firm manner, a writer must have confidence in his or her knowledge of the subject.

Is It Up to the Host?

If an Ontario Supreme Court jury decision handed down in Kitchener last week becomes the norm, the question of who is responsible if an individual becomes inebriated and subsequently causes death or injury will become so complex before the law that trials involving alcohol-related offences may become nightmares.

The jury awarded damages totalling $387,000 to two children who were injured and whose parents were killed in an accident caused by a drinking driver. The jury decided that the Woodstock Legion was responsible for paying 15 percent of the damages because it allowed the driver of the car to drink to excess.

While there is no argument with damages being awarded, there is a serious question about how much responsibility—if any—a tavern owner should take for the state of his customers. Under current Ontario law, the owner of licensed premises can be fined if he serves a customer who is obviously inebriated. But the jury decision making a tavern owner partially responsible for any damage his customer may cause after leaving the tavern is a different matter.

The law, although not strictly enforced, is reasonable. The Ontario Supreme Court jury's damage award is open to challenge.

Some time ago, the state of California passed a law that in effect made a tavern owner or party host share responsibility with guests if the guest drank too much and subsequently caused damage or death. The most wide-spread effect of the law was a spate of damage suits—many of them fraudulent—attempting to collect from both the drinker and the man who had served him too many drinks.

California, after experimenting with a law designed to water down personal responsibility of the excessive drinker, was forced to repeal the statute.

It would be unfortunate if the Kitchener decision—which implies that everyone is his brother's keeper—became the norm. It didn't work in California, and it will not work in Ontario. Even people who drink to excess must ultimately accept responsibility for their own actions.

The Spectator (Hamilton, Ontario, Canada)

Newspaper writers are especially likely to become involved in issues concerning the press and "the people's right to know" about government. "Courtroom Camera Ruling Benefits the People's 'Right to Know' " (p. 194) is an editorial on a decision of the Florida Supreme Court to allow television and newspaper cameras in the courtroom. The headline and the first sentence echo the familiar slogan. Does the editorial live up to the promise of the headline to explain the benefits for the public of cameras in the courtroom? In the second sentence, the editorial makes its bold assertion supporting the court's ruling: Cameras and microphones serve as the public's eyes and ears. Then the editorial explains and justifies that assertion: First-hand exposure can correct the incorrect impressions that much of the public has about trials and allow voters a better opportunity to judge the officials they must elect, without interfering with a fair trial. At the end the writer suggests that putting court officials on camera might also improve the business of justice. One problem (as we noted in Chapter 10 in writing our editorial about closed courts), in editorials that show readers how open meetings and open courts help the public, is the appearance of self-interest. In "Courtroom Camera" the writer does try to convince readers that they have a stake in the issue, but the press is barely mentioned.

Courtroom Camera Ruling Benefits the People's 'Right to Know'

In a victory for open government and the people's right to know how their public officials and criminal justice system operate, the Florida Supreme Court has unanimously ruled that TV and newspaper cameras and tape recorders belong in the courtroom.

Cameras and microphones serve as the eyes and ears of members of the public who don't attend in person.

Winners of this legal battle are not the newspapers and TV stations who will use the cameras in court, but the people themselves—for they will get a close-up view of the reality of a trial in action.

The public's perception of how a trial is proceeding, or how the criminal justice system operates, is twisted by lack of first-hand views:

Real trials are greatly unlike how most TV shows portray them. When voters choose judges, prosecutors, court clerks, and public defenders; when they are asked to support a bond issue for a new jail; when they form their opinions of a jury verdict or a judge's decision, the more knowledge they have, the better.

A year-long experiment, ending last July, showed that the presence of cameras could be controlled so that it did not interfere with a fair trial and distract trial participants.

A survey showed that two-thirds of the jurors, one-half the witnesses and many of the lawyers and judges involved felt cameras were not a problem.

The new court ruling provides strict rules to prevent the kind of disruptive "circus" coverage that marked trials years ago.

Some trial participants may "play to the cameras," but the experiment shows this behavior is not widespread. After the initial novelty wears off, cameras are largely ignored.

Any potential for distraction could easily be removed if cameras and photographers were placed behind partitions with one-way glass, so no one will see them.

One result of the presence of cameras—in addition to educating and informing the public—could be to improve the performance of both judges and attorneys, make them stop playing courtroom games and tend more to the business of determining guilt or innocence of the defendant.

Sun-Sentinel (Fort Lauderdale, Fla.)

International Affairs

International subjects may be both the hardest and the easiest topics to write about. They are easy in the sense that, when you write about a far-away country, you will not have your mayor, governor and next-door neighbor calling to say you don't have your facts straight, as they might on a local topic. Writers used to say that the safest editorial was a hard-hitting one about Afghanistan. That led to the term "Afghanistanism," a label generally thought to have originated in a speech that Jenkin Lloyd Jones, of the *Tulsa* (Okla.) *Tribune,* gave to the American Society of Newspaper Editors in 1948. He said that local readers "bark back, and you had better know your stuff." But you can pontificate on a situation in Afghanistan, he said, since "you have no fanatic Afghans among your readers," and nobody knows or cares about what you write.[3] The term "Afghanistanism" stood for more than 30 years—until the 1979 Soviet invasion of Afghanistan. Since then editorial writers have had to search for another obscure country to write a safe editorial about. But, as events in Afghanistan have shown, we live in an age when no country is totally unconnected with any other country. The writer thus must be prepared to write about events anywhere in the world—and that is the hard part of tackling a foreign subject.

How can a writer know enough to comment intelligently without parroting someone else's opinion? Writers must read a lot—and not just the daily press and the weekly news magazines. *The Economist* of London provides reliable reporting and perspective on all parts of the world. *Foreign Affairs,* a quarterly journal, provides background and perspective. *Atlas* magazine shows what the press around the world is saying. Listening to speeches by visiting persons from other countries and talking personally with them can provide new points of view. Local world affairs councils can provide information programs and opportunities to meet knowledgeable visitors, as well as local citizens who are concerned with international affairs.

Except for the hottest topics of the day, writers are faced with the problem of how to interest readers in foreign subjects. Most surveys show that foreign news ranks well down the list of readers' preferences. The issues have to be made extremely clear. Interesting details—specific events, personalities, colorful quotations—can help attract and hold the reader. One enticement can be a catchy headline, such as "Sleazy Doings in Namibia" (p. 196), from the *Des Moines Register.* The use of "sleazy" suggests that the writer and the person who wrote the headline are trying to tempt readers into reading something about a country they may never have heard of and almost certainly do not care about. The task is not an easy one, since the editorial is concerned with complications of an election involving several organizations with long names and not generally recognizable abbreviations. The writer has kept sentence length short—about 17 words on average, well below those we have examined before—making reading easier. But because of so many multi-syllable words—diplomacy, territory, guerrilla and Namibia itself—the syllable average is about 170 for every 100 words. On the Flesch scale the writing is closer to difficult than to fairly difficult.

Sleazy Doings in Namibia

The new interim assembly in Namibia (formerly South-West Africa) has been under pressure to agree to United Nations-supervised elections before declaring its independence. So, the assembly last week accepted the idea, in principle. Then it imposed a set of conditions that would make such supervision almost nonexistent.

As an example of cynical humor, the action deserves a sardonic grin. As an example of diplomacy, it fell flat on its face.

The assembly is dominated by the Democratic Turnhalle Alliance. The DTA is the chosen political instrument of South Africa, which has been running the territory since 1920 and only recently (and reluctantly) set up pre-independence elections won by the DTA.

The election was a sham, since it was run by South Africa and boycotted by the South-West Africa Peoples Organization, the territory's dominant guerrilla organization. South Africa knew that SWAPO could not ready itself for a political campaign before the spring. That's why the elections were held before the end of the year, when the DTA was sure to win.

The DTA's plan for a second election is as sleazy as the election that brought it to power. It stipulates that no South African troops would leave until SWAPO ends its guerrilla resistance and that U.N. peacekeeping forces would be stationed in neighboring Angola, from which SWAPO forces operate. In essence, the DTA wants the U.N. to safeguard a SWAPO surrender while South Africa runs another election the way it ran the first. That is, it wants a second rigged election to ratify the results of the first rigged election.

Namibia deserves an election worthy of the name. That requires, among other things, supervision by a multi-national group of neutrals, namely the U.N. It requires the withdrawal of South African forces, which are bound to constitute an intimidating presence. It requires enough time to permit all political groups to organize and campaign.

Only such an election can achieve international recognition and reflect the desires of the people of Namibia.

Des Moines (Iowa) *Register*

The writer uses one other device, in addition to short sentences, to try to make the reading easier. Besides using "sleazy" both in the headline and in the editorial, phrases such as "cynical humor," "a sardonic grin" and "flat on its face" appear as promises that what transpired is understandable in familiar terminology. The election is labeled a "sham" and "rigged," terms that readers should also feel comfortable with. Finally, the editorial is clear in what it proposes: an election run by the United Nations with South African forces withdrawn.

The writer on Namibia had a tough subject to write about. It is hard to find an angle that promises to have an impact on many readers in Iowa. But, if the topic is important in terms of international significance, as Namibia is, the issue should be addressed. While circulating far from the centers usually thought to have international ties, the Des Moines papers, especially the *Register,* have stressed for many years news and editorial comment on world topics such as this one. Perhaps the papers had something to do with the interest in international matters that I found among Iowans when I lived in that state. As we noted in Chapter 10, one of the most important roles of the press is to set the public agenda. Providing editorials to readers on international topics should by itself increase their interest in such topics.

Surveys show that newspaper readership of news about the arts ranks low compared to most other features. Few daily newspapers have good arts and music coverage, even though the surveys have encouraged papers to expand and beef up their "life style" sections. "The prevailing attitude seems to be that the arts are of interest to only a few," wrote Professor John M. Harrison of The Pennsylvania State University, "that they exist in a rarefied atmosphere, and that if they are touched on at all it must be done with kid gloves and a properly respected attitude."[4] But there is an audience for news and comment about the arts, and there might be a bigger and more appreciative audience if editorials about cultural topics appeared as often as those about other types of public issues.

Editorial writers may be afraid to appear ignorant about culture. But dealing with any topic for the first time makes most writers feel ignorant; that does not keep them from reading background material and checking sources—and even appearing less than fully informed at first. In any event, not all cultural editorials require expert commentary. Some involve pitches to readers to give, go or join. Others involve public policy: How far should museums go in becoming retail stores or in licensing commercial firms to market imitations of their collections? How much should the federal government pay to support the arts and the humanities?

Any writer with historical perspective knows that art and politics, and almost every other field of human endeavor, traditionally have been closely related. When exhibits such as those of the treasures of Tutankhamen or Alexander the Great come to this country, the editorial writer who likes politics and history can mix them with comment about the visiting shows. The writer of the editorial "Culture Is Basic, Too" may not have had detailed knowledge of stringed instruments, but that didn't stop him or her from writing an editorial, and one with strong opinions, on a threatened cutback in a music program.

Culture Is Basic, Too

The possibility . . . or is it probability? . . . that Hampton public schools will severely curtail its string music program for lack of money is distressing.

Not merely for the sake of the youngsters who will be deprived of the exposure and training, but for the memory of a very charming, dedicated woman—Elizabeth Chapman—who was such a vital part of the Peninsula's music life when the area was essentially a cultural wasteland.

Mrs. Chapman was the inspiration for and, indeed, the physical force behind the schools' string music program, which was

a model of its kind locally. The value and success can be seen in her pupils' devotion, the number who went into musical careers and the decision to continue the program after her death.

It's easy to forget how recently the Peninsula and Hampton Roads as a whole have achieved a semblance of cultural stature. Today's volume of concerts, operas, dramatic performances were unknown as recently as 10 years ago.

A decade ago, few nationally known artists came to the area and then, usually, as guests with the few existing local groups, such as the Peninsula Symphony, Jewish Community Center and Governor's Palace series.

Now, we have an opera company in our backyard, one with rising national acclaim, and frequent visits by highly-regarded artists either in solo performances or as guests with the area's orchestras.

We also have the possibility of the Peninsula and Norfolk Symphony orchestras combining their talents for even bigger and better musical achievements.

There are an increasing number of local groups producing and sponsoring performances of very creditable quality.

Acceptance and demand for the best in music and theater have been nurtured of late by public television's live and filmed broadcasts of operas, concerts, ballet, orchestras and drama from the great halls of the world.

But we also think the seeds were planted far earlier by the likes of Elizabeth Chapman, who believed music and culture is appreciated at very early ages, especially when there is actual participation.

We regret sincerely the likelihood the string program will be cut back, perhaps eliminated, in Hampton's schools.

Much is made of the need to get back to the basic in education. We suggest there is something very basic about culture, too, in the striving for quality of life.

Times-Herald (Newport News, Va.)

Medicine and Health

The health sciences represent another area in which editorial writers feel ignorant. Unlike the arts, they don't have the excuse that not many readers are interested in the subject. Nearly every daily newspaper carries a medical column, which usually ranks high in readership, and an even more popular advice column that often deals with health matters. An editorial on a medical issue generally would not offer advice or explain an ailment, as these columns do. Rather, the opportunities for comment lie in the medical, moral and legal issues that seem to arise increasingly as science discovers new things that can be done to and for human beings. The topic of abortion, for example, touches all of these areas, as does euthanasia, artificial insemination, artificial life-preserving treatment, radiation therapy, holistic medicine and decisions relating to victims of Down's syndrome. Questions sometimes arise concerning the role that should be played in medical treatment by nurses, midwives, naturopaths, chiropractors and physicians' aides. Readers need to know about these issues, about the decisions that are being made continually in medical and health areas at national, state and local levels. They need to know more than the news columns generally explain about medical choices and the arguments for and against each choice.

Since medical topics are no different from other topics, they need to be framed in a manner that cuts through to readers. In "Laetrile," the *Buffalo Evening News* discussed a subject that had received much attention in the news. It accepted the judgment of medical research. Yet, while not backing down, the editorial writer concluded that there are other grounds than strictly medical for setting public policy in the health field. In this instance the writer has taken a broader perspective than might be expected on the basis of scientific evidence. That, after all, is what commenting on public policy aspects of an issue is all about.

Laetrile

"Laetrile has been tested. It is not effective."

Those words by Dr. Charles Moertel of the Mayo Clinic in Rochester, Minn., are in no way surprising. It would have been a great boon, of course, if the drug Laetrile had been shown to have value in the treatment of cancer. But the finding should have a beneficial effect by convincing cancer sufferers not to put their hope and money in a treatment that is, according to the best scientific judgment, worthless.

The newly announced findings come as a result of a study begun last July, sponsored by the federal government and the National Cancer Institute. The 163 persons enrolled in the test were advanced cancer patients with no hope of cure through conventional medical treatment. Of these, 104 patients have already died. In only one case did there appear to be a partial response, and that was questionable. The doctors concluded that Laetrile has no medical effect in slowing the advance of cancer.

The National Cancer Institute and the Food and Drug Administration have long held that Laetrile is worthless. One purpose of the recent study was to make a convincing case in order to persuade people not to pin their hopes on Laetrile and then forsake standard treatment, such as chemotherapy, which has proved effective in many cases. "Too many lives have been sacrificed to blind faith in the many Laetrile promises that can't be kept," the American Cancer Society emphasized in commenting on the findings. Advocates of Laetrile, however, do not accept the results, claiming that the substance tested was not pure Laetrile and that the study was made only for the purpose of discrediting their treatment.

While we fully accept the study findings, we continue to believe that the law should not deny the terminally ill the right to use Laetrile if they insist upon it, if they have exhausted accepted therapies and if they acknowledge in writing warnings that the government regards Laetrile as worthless. Dying patients should not be deprived of the right in such circumstances to make their own choices, however unwise and futile.

Buffalo (N.Y.) *Evening News*

Religion

Most editors assiduously avoid allowing readers to become involved in denominational or scriptural arguments in the letters columns. Some editors just as assiduously avoid religious topics in their editorial columns. But as the barriers and suspicions that have divided Christian and Jew, Christian and Moslem, Catholic and Protestant have weakened, more editorial writers have begun to deal with religious subjects. There is an increasing ease in talking about religion and religious differences. In addition, many current religious subjects hold broad public interest: citizens have had to deal with controversies over prayers and scripture in the public schools, the placement of crosses and manger scenes on public property, solicitations by Hare Krishna in public airports. The controversy over the rights of women and of homosexuals in the churches is an integral part of the broader transitions our whole society is passing through. Similarly, current arguments over whether churches and income-producing properties of churches should be taxed relates directly to the current reassessment of First

Amendment rights and of tax exemptions in general. Whether churches should turn over their financial records to the courts in the event of a lawsuit is a question that goes to the heart of the traditional separation of church and state. When a pope tours a nation and draws crowds in the tens of thousands on the streets, in the parks and in public arenas, a religious and media event takes on national significance as well. When students hold foreign hostages in the name of Allah, the event becomes an international one. The positions of various religious groups on the abortion issue and on the Equal Rights Amendment have taken on strong political and social significance. Writers can discuss all these subjects without becoming embroiled in a denominational morass—but only if they use a great deal of care, accuracy and charity.

In "Creationism," the *Louisville Courier-Journal* notes without surprise that a judge has ruled that creationism is not a science and gives no credence to the claims of its advocates. Yet the editorial treats these advocates gently, carefully attempting to explain why the appeal to a sense of fair play is not valid. The editorial cites the creationists' own insistence on certain claims to show why creationism is not open to the scientific method. The writer reserves admonishment not for the creationists but for "cynical politicians" who may have been taking advantage of the controversy.

Creationism

There was little surprise in the ruling that Arkansas can't force its schools to teach fundamentalist religious doctrine as an alternative to scientific theories about the origin and development of life and the universe. The nation's courts have preserved through two centuries the principle that the power of the state may not be used to impose *any* kind of religious indoctrination.

The surprise, if any, was that the nine-day trial illuminated the issues so effectively. Tennessee's 1925 Scopes trial, in which a teacher was prosecuted for informing students about the concept of evolution, was mostly a circus. The Arkansas trial dealt with issues, not personalities, and thus stripped away much of the confusion.

The issue in Arkansas was new in only one respect—the disguise in which this particular form of religion was attempting to enter the classroom. The aim was essentially the same as that of the now-void Tennessee law that prohibited teaching any scientific theory that conflicted with "the story of the Divine Creation as taught in the Bible." It was no different from later state laws, which fared no better in the courts, that attempted to bar evolution from the classroom without mentioning religion.

As the trial clearly showed, the new and somewhat more confusing tactic amounts to claiming that the Bible is itself a scientific text, intended to provide guidance on physical facts as well as spiritual matters. An elaborate doctrine called "scientific creationism" has been constructed to couch the biblical language in scientific terms.

The claim that this doctrine should be taught as a rival to generally accepted scientific findings in biology, geology, astronomy and several other sciences appeals at first glance to a sense of fair play. If there are two sides to a story, why not tell both?

That view is valid only if "scientific creationism" is science. The trial found otherwise. As Judge William Overton observed in his ruling, nothing that starts with a conclusion and rejects evidence that may stand in the way can be called scientific.

The Creation Research Society, a principal developer of the creationist ploy, requires members to believe that the Book of Genesis is "historically and scientifically true in all of the original autographs." So it follows, in this reasoning, that the earth and all its living species were created at the same time, 6,000 to 20,000 years ago, and that living creatures haven't changed since.

Acceptance of this view as the route to scientific knowledge leads to pernicious consequences. If the Arkansas law were accepted, students would be asked, in effect, to choose between a religious creed and science as accepted by scientists. The creationist doctrine implies that evolutionary theory presupposes the absence of a creator or God—which is distinctly untrue. Scientists may be religious or non-religious. But as scientists, they study the natural, not the supernatural.

The choice between science and religion implied by the Arkansas law surely was one of the reasons that led a coalition of leaders from major religious denominations—Catholic, Episcopal, Methodist, Presbyterian and Southern Baptist—to join in the suit against it. Some of these leaders may have had varied views on the proper height of the fence between church and state. But none could relish a law that offered the state's young people the implication that one must choose between science and religion.

The logic and facts in the court decision surely won't stop the creationist movement. Even as the judge issued his ruling, Mississippi's Senate was voting for a similarly unconstitutional law in that state. In fact, cynical politicians will feel all the more safe in voting for such laws, confident that the courts will overturn them.

But the Arkansas trial has at least removed the excuse of ignorance among legislators who vote for "scientific creationism" laws to appease comparatively small but highly vocal groups of supporters. It may even have awakened voters who don't normally put pressure on legislators to the pernicious choice the creationists are trying to impose on the schools.

Louisville (Ky.) *Courier-Journal*

Sports

Overall readership figures show that sports ranks relatively low among newspaper sections. But those figures do not tell the whole story. While many readers may pay little attention to sports, the followers of the sports section are faithful and avid. Perhaps one reason that few editorials are written about sports is a feeling that, since sports fans have their own section of the paper, the editorial page should cater to the more general reading public. A few newspapers, in fact, publish editorials and letters from readers in the sports section. Another possible reason for the lack of sports on the editorial page is that most editorial writers fear venturing into a field in which it seems that even the fans are experts. Woe to writers who get in over their heads in this subject area.

But there is no reason why editorial writers should not consider sports as they would any other subject, discussing relevant issues and personalities when occasions arise. Readers who don't regularly follow sports might be surprised to find events that merit thought and analysis occurring in the sports world, and readers who do follow sports might find affairs that interest them occurring on the editorial page.

Sometimes an editorial writer may simply want to say how great the hometown team is, even when that team isn't so great. That's fine. Such an editorial

Wings: Our Team Skated and Stick-handled Its Way into Our Hearts. Thanks

The Red Wings are out but not down.

They played like winners in what turned out to be the last game in their quarterfinal series against the Canadiens in Montreal; that they were not winners almost seems irrelevant.

There were many "miracles" along the way as the season skated by, but miracles in sports do not happen without skill, and the Wings increasingly exhibited that.

Bobby Kromm, Ted Lindsay—and their never-say-die team—may and should take pride in what they accomplished with an organization that seemed early on to have left its best days in old and yellowed record books.

They have delighted their fans, and their fans have delighted the team.

The city is left with good feelings and high hopes.

It will be hard to wait for next year.

Detroit (Mich.) *Free Press*

is "Wings" from the *Detroit Free Press*. The writer does not try to cover up the team's dismal record for the year, but does take pleasure in the team's apparent "never-say-die" attitude and the delight that local fans felt. Perhaps it is the duty of the editorial page, from time to time, to offer that old cliche about "it's not whether you win or lose. . . ." Sometimes an editorial writer needs to talk about events in sports that aren't so great. When the University of New Mexico was one of a series of universities charged with providing improper benefits to athletes, the *Albuquerque* (N.M.) *Journal* took a tough stand concerning the actions taken by the university in "Scandal Damages UNM." Using the occasion to speculate beyond the specific situation, the editorial traced the problem to the demands of fans for winning at any cost.

Scandal Damages UNM

We would like to regard action taken Friday by the University of New Mexico as part of the thorough housecleaning we advocate for the athletic department. Trouble is, it is not.

Suspension of head basketball coach Norman Ellenberger and assistant Manny Goldstein came in reaction to FBI disclosures. University president William "Bud" Davis had little choice in the matter.

But for several weeks Davis and other UNM officials have known the Lobo men's basketball program was under investigation by the National Collegiate Athletic Association. Among the allegations: transcript and grade alterations. Among the information turned up by the FBI: possible transcript alterations.

The institution has until February to answer allegations that UNM committed some 90 violations of NCAA rules.

The seriousness of the NCAA allegations—which never have been revealed publicly—surely was cause for immediate action by the administration. Instead, the institution has hid behind the February deadline and tried to stonewall its eventual responses.

The basketball scandal has at its heart the constant demand by fans that the team win. The success of a collegiate athletic program, unfortunately, is measured in the win-loss column.

Those demands, however, do not excuse anyone who winks at the rules and laws.

The university cannot afford to wait until the deadline to begin an immediate cleanup of the athletic department. Regents must take a close look at UNM's athletic program and any administrative structure that would allow such a scandal to develop.

The win-at-any-cost syndrome can blunt the primary purpose of any institution of higher learning—to educate. The longer the basketball scandal is allowed to persist, the more damage it will do to the University of New Mexico.

Reprinted courtesy of
Albuquerque (N.M) *Journal*

SUBJECTS THAT ARE DECEPTIVELY EASY

A second category of editorials that deserves more attention consists of editorials that can be turned out without much thought. Although the lines between the subcategories may not be absolutely sharp, I will discuss four of these deceptively easy areas: obituaries, the local pride piece, the favorite subject (or "easy shot") and the "duty" piece.

Obituaries

De mortuis nil nisi bonum is not a good rule for writing editorials about persons who have died. Speaking nothing but good of the dead may be fine for funeral orations, but telling readers only some of the facts has no more place in an obituary editorial than it has in any other kind of editorial. Relating the full story is relatively easy for a national, or even state, figure. Information is often readily available and indisputable. The family of the deceased is not likely to see the editorial, at least not immediately after publication, so the writer can feel free to tell the good and the not-so-good. But when the person is a local figure, inhibitions take hold. The temptation is to stick with the favorable facts and throw in a dash of "he'll be missed." This is no time to add to the family's bereavement, the reasoning goes.

And undeserved praise is no praise at all, since those likely to care the most about what is written will know that the words are hollow. In my experience, families often respond very favorably to obituary editorials that mention the less-than-perfect, human side of the deceased. When I wrote that a civic activist had a booming voice and had been something of a glad-hander (not quite in those words), his widow told me, "That was Bob, all right." Another time I wrote that a woman who had been involved in many activities was something of a character and that she sometimes had said things that other people didn't understand. Shaking his head, her son told me, "That's the way Mother was, and we loved her for it." Of course, in small and medium-sized communities, if not in larger ones, there are limits to telling the full truth. You would not want to dig up something especially embarrassing from a person's past, particularly something that the person had lived down.

The trick to writing an obituary editorial is to catch some detail—words, behavior, description—that makes the person seem unique and human, something that distinguishes him or her from everyone else, something for which the person can be remembered. You don't always have to write about a widely known person. Fitting subjects might be a person who had taught a long time in the local schools, someone who had been quietly helpful to neighbors and friends, a mail deliverer, someone who had clerked in the same store for many years, a person who had sold newspapers on the same corner ever since anyone could remember.

When comedian John Belushi died, typical editorials used the occasion to denounce abuse of drugs and cite horrifying figures about the increased use of cocaine and heroin. Few made more than passing comments on Belushi himself—what kind of person he might have been, what kind of personal tragedy he might have faced. One exception, a very brief editorial, was "John Belushi" in the *Detroit* (Mich.) *News*.

John Belushi

Headlines announced the other day that John Belushi died, not of natural causes as originally reported, but of cocaine and heroin.

We're sure the warning implicit in those news reports wasn't lost on Mr. Belushi's thousands of young fans, and we have no wish to belabor the obvious here.

One report that did catch our eye, however, quoted the actor's Beverly Hills doctor. Mr. Belushi knew better than to take cocaine, the unidentified doctor said. "On the other hand," he added, "let's say he got drunk, *which we all have a right to do,* and somebody gave it to him."

Well, a high tolerance of substance abuse—including alcohol abuse—is one of the hallmarks of Hollywood culture, where many important fads and fashions are said to originate.

God only knows what miscalculations or private torment drove Mr. Belushi to self-destruction. But one thing's certain: His social *milieu* had no behavioral brakes to offer.

Detroit (Mich.) *News*

Local Pride

Second cousin to the obituary editorial is the local pride editorial, which comments on the activities of local people, local teams or local organizations. As with obituaries, there are ways to make these editorials more than sheer puffery. Sometimes, for example, an editorial may be called for to boost the spirits of someone or some organization in the community after a disappointment; such seems to have been the purpose of "Wings," cited earlier (p. 202). Sometimes residents of a community need to take a realistic look at how they appear to others. Is the community as friendly as its promoters say it is? Does it have residential areas that those concerned with its image do not talk about much? Are residents going elsewhere to shop because they can't find what they want in local stores? Are building and development restrictions keeping out all but a selected, privileged class of citizens?

Editorial writers cannot be expected to be able to view their communities completely objectively. After all, if these writers didn't think their communities were pretty decent places, why would they be living there? Writers should take pride in their communities and should work hard to make them better places. But without a true understanding of the limitations, as well as the advantages, of the area, no writer can help his or her community deal with its problems and successes.

"Big (?) and Beautiful" is an editorial in which the writer, on the *Eugene* (Ore.) *Register-Guard,* responded to an article that ranked Eugene second among the 10 best American cities for "a good life." The writer acknowledged

Big(?) and Beautiful

Family Circle magazine has decided that Eugene ranks second among the 10 best U.S. cities "in which to live a good life." The magazine doesn't try to define a good life.

The selections were based on a combination of objective and subjective criteria—low rates of crime, disease and unemployment; adequate "modern housing"; plentiful recreational facilities; nice cultural amenities and "esthetic appeal."

It's nice that Eugene did well in this semi-scientific survey after having done even better—Number One among the nation's medium-sized metropolitan areas—in the statistically elaborate study done two years ago for the Environmental Protection Agency.

Most of the cities in the Family Circle top ten also rated high in the earlier study. Portland was Number One among larger metro areas in the EPA standings; it ranks sixth for Family Circle. LaCrosse, Wis., best of the smaller cities in the EPA study, is ranked eighth by the magazine. Seattle is first in the Family Circle survey. It was third among larger metropolitan areas in the earlier report.

Although the results are flattering for the winners, these kinds of city ratings will not affect the thinking of many individuals. People judge cities in highly personal, subjective ways. There are people who hate Eugene and there are people who love Newark.

The Family Circle study itself can be faulted for less than scrupulous attention to detail. The narrative on Eugene has us "blanketed above by what is considered the cleanest air in the nation." Considered by whom? Surely not Eugene residents. It also has Bill Bowerman still turning out long-distance runners at the University of Oregon.

The oddest part of the article is its population citations. Eugene is listed as having a population of 241,800, close enough for our standard metropolitan statistical area, which by Census Bureau definition includes all of Lane County. But Seattle is shown as having 503,013 people and Minneapolis 397,421. Those have to be populations just within city limits; Seattle has a metropolitan population of 1.4 million, Minneapolis more than 2 million.

The magazine citations for Denver, San Francisco and Honolulu appear to cover the metropolitan areas, but that for San Diego has to be for the city only. In no case are these differences noted or explained.

Our Christmas present for the editors of Family Circle will be an Almanac.

Eugene (Ore.) *Register-Guard*

that "it's nice" that Eugene did so well in the survey but, after providing a little background, he or she spent the last half of the editorial questioning the findings and procedures of the survey. In doing so, the writer was saying that Eugene residents shouldn't take the compliment entirely seriously; the community isn't that good.

A test of the credibility of local-pride editorials comes when something occurs that reflects negatively on a community. The editorial "Brought to Judgment" is how the *San Diego Union* responded when a former "Mr. San Diego" fell from his pedestal. The editorial spells out in some detail the charges against, and the defiance of, the subject of the editorial. While the editorial stands firmly behind the verdict and the sentence, it also begins and ends with words that try not to judge too harshly. A view of "Mr. San Diego" that might enlist sympathy is given and some of his past contributions that are likely to endure are mentioned. An effort is made to put the event in perspective. The judgment seems tempered with a little mercy, and I found that welcome.

Brought to Judgment

Though the mills of God grind slowly,
yet they grind exceeding small;
Though with patience He stands waiting,
with exactness grinds He all.

Retribution
Henry Wadsworth Longfellow

An 80-year-old man whose life and works are in ruins, who has been adjudged a crook by his peers, who is almost universally reviled, and who has been sentenced to spend his final years, or a large part of them, in confinement would, ordinarily, still gain some sympathy because humanity is basically humane.

But C. Arnholt Smith, who has just been found guilty of the blackest of white-collar crimes, defiantly repels any kindly impulse that anyone might harbor toward him. "I cannot say I'm sorry," because, he insists, no crimes were committed. It was merely that "the district attorney was interested only in prosecuting me." And the U.S. National Bank, which Mr. Smith looted, "did not collapse, it was beaten to death by unprincipled bureaucrats." The jury was confused.

Such paranoiac breastbeating convinces no one, of course, that Mr. Smith is an innocent victim of a gross miscarriage of justice; it only compounds his disaster and his tragedy.

The mills of justice have ground slowly indeed since 1972 when the collapse of Mr. Smith's bank made manifest his monumental misdeeds, which had robbed his trusting investors and his employees as surely as though they had been held at gunpoint. The $30,000 fine and three-years probation Mr. Smith received in 1975 in U.S. District Court on federal charges of bank fraud, to which there was a no-contest plea, was little more than a reprimand which justified the widespread outcry about how wealthy criminals escape punishment.

Now, after more than two years of preliminary hearings and an eight-month trial, unprecedented in this county's history, Mr. Smith has been brought to judgment. "The jury, by its verdict, found Mr. Smith was a crook and that's my verdict," said Superior Court Judge Robert W. Conyers on Thursday as he handed down a sentence of three years in confinement, five years probation and restitution of $681,000 in income taxes owed the state.

As judges and juries are to be criticized, so are they to be praised. We believe the vast majority of San Diegans regard the verdict and sentence as proper and just—that justice has been served. And, finally, District Attorney Edwin L. Miller Jr. and his competent colleagues deserve the highest marks for preparing and prosecuting this case to its successful conclusion—a result which goes far toward vindicating our system of jurisprudence at the local level.

How are the mighty fallen! The rise of a struggling young bank clerk to become a widely respected civic leader and a nationally known financier and his subsequent disgrace are not without poignancy. The very qualities which accounted for Mr. Smith's remarkable financial achievements were, in the corruption of power, responsible for magnifying the damage he did.

And let it be said that the one-time "Mr. San Diego" made contributions to this city which will, we believe, endure beyond the awful effects of his downfall.

Reprinted by permission.
The *San Diego Union*

Favorite Subject

Editorial writers cannot be expected to produce fresh wisdom, certainly not on every topic, each day. Reiterating a message is one solution to the lack of more inspiring topics. Since most readers don't read the editorial page every day, remaking a point is not likely to seem repetitive. Another, and less defensible, solution is writing on a subject on which the writer has to do little or no research and do little or no new thinking. Sometimes the subject is a favorite target. I call this type of editorial "an easy shot."

An example of an easy shot taken every year by some editorial writers is the editorial that appears on the day that the average taxpayer has stopped "working for the government" and started earning money to keep for himself or herself. Every year some tax association notifies newspapers of this date and usually points out that it falls one or two or three days later this year than last year. The first time that editorial appeared it had merit; the idea is clever as a piece of propaganda. Since then, the editorial has become a cliche.

Another perennial piece is the one that criticizes the salaries being paid state legislators or members of Congress. This editorial is usually accompanied by an attack on the legislative body for not doing its job and for letting personal interests and pleasures interfere with the public's business. The editorial writer often adds something to this effect: "It is no wonder the voters have lost faith in government." No doubt some legislative bodies deserve criticism for the sneaky ways in which they slip benefits for themselves into legislation and for the seemingly petty politicking that frustrates the legislative process. But an editorial written to condemn a specific misdeed should stick to the particular subject and avoid generalizing about all the wicked ways of government officials. One strange thing about this tendency of editorial writers to pick on legislative bodies is that when it comes time for endorsement of candidates all of the past sins are forgotten. Congress is bad, it seems, but our own local member is good enough to merit another term.

Closely related to the let's-jump-on-Congress editorial is the pork barrel piece. It is not uncommon for an editorial page that persistently calls for cuts in the federal budget and in unnecessary federal projects to issue a stirring defense of a desperately needed local project. A pork barrel project in another part of the country becomes a fully justified investment in a home community, an investment needed to provide jobs or to prevent a flood.

If editors are pressed for a topic, they can pull out the old national-debt piece, or the how-much-is-a-billion bit. That is always good for helping readers understand the complexity of the political issues of the day! It may get a rise out of readers who think the government is spending too much money, but if they want less spending, what are they willing to give up in government benefits? This type of editorial never seems to address the latter question.

Some editors like to pick on the courts: Lenient judges are the cause of today's criminal-infested society. Some like to pick on the schools: No wonder kids can't read; the teachers are just interested in easy jobs and high salaries and don't know how to spell themselves. Some like to pick on environmentalists: If it weren't for these Sierra Club do-gooders, we would have a lot less inflation and a lot more jobs. Some like to pick on the oil companies: Big oil wants to force prices up so that it can profit from all that oil it has stashed away. Some like to pick on developers: All they are interested in is the fast buck.

Another favorite target is bureaucracy, especially the boards and commissions in Washington. The Office of Safety and Health Administration (OSHA) has been a favorite for years. The classic way to start editorials of this nature is to cite a very specific and ridiculous application of a regulation or threatened regulation. Not content to stick to the subject, the writer wanders off into condemning an entire agency or a whole branch of government or even the government itself.

One of the agencies that gets its share of editorial criticism is the postal service. "They've Got Your Number" is probably typical of editorials that showed up when the nine-digit ZIP codes were proposed. It made no attempt to explain the purpose of the code or to acknowledge that the new code might improve service. ZIP—ZAP! If one number went wrong, the mail might end up in Eugene, Ore. Meanwhile, in Eugene, the writer on the *Register-Guard* began "Tougher ZIP Codes," an editorial on the same subject, in the same tone, but

They've Got Your Number

As if the new postal contract, guaranteed to result in higher postage rates in the future, weren't enough, mail users now have to look forward to learning longer ZIP code numbers.

If the Postal Service has its way, in the next two and a half years your ZIP code will grow by four numbers. Instead of 32901, it could be 329014673.

That is not only a mouthful, it is a brain-clutterer. And we question whether its intended purpose—to let machines sort the mail more efficiently—won't actually hinder getting mail to the right destination.

Get your number wrong, and your mail could end up in Eugene, Ore. You may think that eight out of nine ain't bad, but try telling that to a ZIP code machine.

Fort Myers (Fla.) *News-Press*

Tougher ZIP Codes

You say you can't remember your Aunt Jane's ZIP code? Well, the Postal Service is now about to provide one almost twice as hard to remember for every one of your correspondents.

Though an arbitration agreement has forbidden the firing of any present postal employees, ever, the nation's mail managers say they're being forced to replace five-figure ZIP codes with nine-digit area designations in order to reduce mail handling staffs.

The change, which will be made over the next 30 months, is supposed to enable the mail sorting now done by 20 workers to be done by 8. We'll all be grateful, of course, if the 12 left over are put on jobs that will speed mail deliveries.

But it's hard not to remember that the ZIP code system was introduced in 1963 to speed the mails and hold down costs. In those days, a first-class stamp cost only a nickel, and letters rarely took longer than a day or two to get to the most remote parts of the country.

It's also hard not to recall that this country used to have twice-a-day mail deliveries—back in times when penny postcards actually cost a penny.

So the most difficult thing is not to be pessimistic about the success of nine-digit ZIP codes. Or to complain about the almost-impossible memory feats their regular use will require.

These block-long serial numerals are supposed to permit sophisticated computerization of mail handling that will facilitate sorting for delivery in big cities, sharp-shooting delivery areas perhaps as small as one square block, or even one large building. But here in the boonies, who needs them?

This latest Postal Service "improvement" will be justified only if it really results in shortening the time it takes to communicate by mail and offsets the costs of paying postal workers wages exceeding those many workers with comparable skills are paid in private industry.

Eugene (Ore.) *Register-Guard*

quickly moved to deal in greater depth with the issues involved. The first editorial, short and to the point, was fun to read and probably expressed the response of most readers. Perhaps the nine-digit code should have been immediately zapped. But the second editorial, which may have pleased fewer readers, offered some editorial insight that readers might not have found elsewhere.

This fault-finding with "easy shot" editorials about the deficiencies of government, or about anything else, must not be misinterpreted. One of the responsibilities of a newspaper, and of an editorial writer, is to keep an eye on the government and public activities in general. If some agency or some activity deserves criticism, the writer should speak out clearly. But the editorial should stick to the subject at hand, should be fair and should make some attempt to enlighten readers, not just inflame them.

One other favorite subject of editorial writers is the computer. It is easy to dash off a standard piece about a check for $1,000,395.43, bills that won't stop coming, computerized telephone solicitation or the computerized "personal" letter. After a while the subject must get tedious to most readers, who have their own equally frustrating experiences. But, in "Dear Dr. Computer . . . ," a *Los Angeles Times* writer uses imagination and whimsy to turn a couple of not-unusual mistakes into an editorial that is a delight to read.

Dear Dr. Computer . . .

It seems that each new day brings further wondrous word of what computers are capable of doing. Slip the right program into the right machine and the sky's the limit, anything goes, and the world's your oyster, whatever that means. Computers can catch tax cheaters, years after their transgressions would have been forgotten in a more civilized society. Computers can louse up bank statements beyond the wildest imaginings of the human mind. Computers can even write and address personal letters. Not necessarily correctly, but then no one is perfect.

An envelope landed on our desk the other day, its contents obviously computer-processed. Inside was an invitation:

The President and the
Board of Governors of
THE NEW YORK ACADEMY OF
SCIENCES
cordially invites
Dr. Los Angeles Times
to apply for membership.

The covering letter, naturally, was headed "Dear Dr. Times."

We replied, in a letter addressed to Dr. The New York Academy of Sciences and headed "Dear Dr. Sciences"—a lack of acquaintance ruled out our use of the more intimate "Dear NY"—regretting that Dr. Times was unable to accept the kind invitation. His membership in so many other organizations—the auto club, the book club, etc.—currently precluded him from assuming any further obligations. But Dr. Times was flattered by this, the first invitation of its kind that he (or it) had ever received.

We mentioned this curious occurrence to a colleague of ours, who then proceeded to relate at tedious length his own continuing experience with binary-code dysfunctionalism. It seems that a computer at Columbia University is under the laughable impression that our friend is an honored alumnus of that distinguished institution, on whose campus he has never so much as set foot. Regularly, mail arrives not only expectantly asking for contributions to keep the old alma matering, but offering such goods as reduced rent-a-car rates if ever he should be so foolish as to visit New York, discounts on books and periodicals, lecture tickets and the like.

Our friend hasn't taken advantage of these offers. He is, though, toying with the idea of writing to Columbia and announcing that he seems somehow to have lost his doctoral diploma—the one in Oriental philology, mind you, not the other one in planetary physics—and he would appreciate it if the university would send him a replacement copy. That request could well send the errant computer into delirium tremens. On the other hand, it might just get our friend a classy new diploma.

There is, as we said, no end to what computers can do. Just feed the right information in, and there's no stopping them.

Los Angeles Times

The "Duty" Piece

"For tomorrow's page we're going to need an editorial on _____. Who's going to write it?" Fill that blank with "Thanksgiving," "the Fourth of July," "the annual United Way campaign," "the state high school basketball championship" or "a highway safety campaign," and you will understand what is meant by a "duty" piece. It is an editorial that you think you ought to run to mark an occasion or boost a good cause, but it is almost impossible to think of anything more to say than you did the last time you wrote on the subject. Most editorial writers dread being asked, or expected, to write "duty" pieces; they prefer to spend their time on more worthy efforts. But at least two points ought to be made on behalf of these editorials. The first is that, while an endorsement of an annual fund drive may be repetitious to the veteran editorial writer, whatever is said is usually appreciated by the promoters of the drive. If an editorial doesn't actually raise any more money, it at least serves to legitimize the cause. Second, an editorial writer can regard a duty editorial as a challenge to say something creative or imaginative on an old topic. This type of assignment can bring forth some excellent writing, since how the editorial is written may have more effect on readers than what is actually said.

Richard B. Childs of the *Flint* (Mich.) *Journal* said that his first rule for handling "the drudgery aspects" of "duty" pieces was "to evade." If you are lucky, someone else on the staff will get the job. But if you can't evade, he advised, "relax and enjoy it." Childs said he actually had begun to look forward to Abraham Lincoln's birthday. Each year he tried to find something new to say. He had written about Lincoln's concept of the Constitution, his role as a politician, his faith in people and democracy, his literary abilities, his defense against black writers who sought to picture him a racist and his continuing image as a national hero despite changing national moods.[5] James E. Jacobson of the *Birmingham* (Ala.) *News* said that writing an editorial is easy when someone swipes a Navy ship on the high seas or a scandal erupts at the state capital since everyone has an opinion. "But just . . . try to find something stirring to say about Fire Prevention Week. That's where creativity surfaces," he said.[6]

The "local pride" editorial, which can be a type of duty piece, has the potential of helping a community appreciate the good things it has going for it. James Bartelt of the *Green Bay* (Wis.) *Press-Gazette* acknowledged that his paper had plugged the Green Bay Packers since the team was formed in 1919 in an office of the *Press-Gazette*. He thought that the newspaper's promotion of the team had contributed substantially to a feeling of solidarity in the community.[7]

Many editors try to resist writing editorials that simply promote causes. The *Cincinnati* (Ohio) *Post* announced in 1975 that praiseworthy causes belonged in the news columns and not the editorial columns. Francis P. Locke of the *Riverside* (Calif.) *Press-Enterprise* said that his paper generally refused to write duty editorials but that it had a hard time avoiding civic campaigns, especially when the publisher was involved. He acknowledged that "once in a while we do blow our cool and, with tongue moderately in cheek, join the hysteria over a state championship for a basketball team or even a world championship for the Los Angeles Dodgers." Duty editorials, he felt, offered the opportunity for "honest-to-goodness high-flown flights of literary imagination."[8]

If a newspaper does publish editorials endorsing causes, it should know what it is backing. Lauren K. Soth of the *Des Moines Register and Tribune* said that, when readers see an editorial supporting a drive for contributions, they ought to be able to assume that the editors have studied the cause and found it to have merit.[9] Without that examination, a free plug for a drive can do the community a disservice. Tom Inman of the *Raleigh* (N.C.) *News and Observer* warned that indiscriminate support of charities and causes can result in backing "relatively enormous appropriations chiefly to subsidize diversion for children of the well-to-do" or other activities that ought to be able to stand on their own financial feet.[10]

When you have to write a duty editorial (notice the "when"), one approach that stands a chance of catching readers' attention is to explain the cause in terms to which they can relate personally. In "Looking for a Santa Claus," the writer starts by asking "you"—the reader—some questions and then proceeds to suggest what the reader should do. The local angle is stressed. Perhaps an appeal by the agencies in the news column would have served just as well, but the editorial offered an opportunity to address readers more informally and to try to describe the plight of the needy in more appealing terms.

Looking for a Santa Claus

Have you ever celebrated Thanksgiving or Christmas when you did not have enough money to buy a good meal? On the same holidays have you ever lacked the funds to provide your family with a joyous dinner?

Probably you have never faced this frustrating and demeaning situation. But each year thousands of Americans must face the holidays without joy or hope. And there will be many such people this year in Maricopa County.

If you want to play Santa Claus, or just enter into the spirit of the season, there are agencies which need your support. In particular the St. Vincent de Paul Society and the Salvation Army provide meals for individuals and families who have no place else to turn.

Both of these groups need food donations, money and workers for the holidays. But do not go down to work unless you are prepared to see hopelessness, degradation and tragedy. It is quite a shock going from the Scottsdale area affluence to the poverty of a charity dining room.

On Thanksgiving and Christmas days the St. Vincent dining room expects to serve 2,500 free meals to the needy. It and the Salvation Army facility, however, need support from the community so that they will not have to turn anyone away.

Reprinted from
Scottsdale (Ariz.) *Daily Progress*

Two off-beat approaches to duty editorials should serve well to conclude this discussion. In the first, the publisher of a California weekly newspaper was ordered by the court to write three editorials about drunk driving as part of his probation for a drunk driving conviction: one on the harm of driving while drunk, one on the harm imposed on a person's family and one on rehabilitation programs. Those were real *duty* editorials. The other example is "The Utility Editorial," which can be pulled out whenever a duty editorial is assigned. All the writer has to do is fill in the blanks. It was written by Hoke Norris of the *Winston-Salem* (N.C.) *Journal-Sentinel* for publication in *The Masthead*.[11]

The Utility Editorial

_____ is an issue which is a challenge to us all. Every right-thinking person in _____ will (view with

(state, nation, world, universe)

alarm) (point with pride) (be puzzled by) (be gratified by) (be alarmed by) this latest development, which comes at a time when _____ faces the

(state, nation, world, universe)

darkest days in its history.

All men of good will should band themselves together to (see that it doesn't happen again) (perpetuate it) (encourage it) (discourage it) (deplore it) (praise it). Only in this way can we assure continued (prog-ress and prosperity) (justice and freedom) (peace and joy) in a _____

(state, nation, world, uni-

____ fraught with crisis as never before.

verse)

We must all (get behind) (oppose) this latest development in the ever-changing rhythm of time, in order that the _____ may continue to _____. On the other hand, _____. As _____ has so well said, _____. The future of _____

(state, nation,

_____ hangs in the balance. We

world, universe)

must not fail!

Hoke Norris
Winston-Salem (N.C.) _Journal-Sentinel_

THE TYPES THAT GET NEGLECTED

In this category are editorials on the world of nature, those on the everyday lives of people and those that are written in a humorous or satirical manner. No doubt others could be included.

The World of Nature

Editorial writers who would never hesitate to tread where angels fear to go will turn and flee when asked to venture where the wood nymphs dance. They would rather tackle religion or sports.

Al Southwick, who found himself the house nature writer on the _Worcester_ (Mass.) _Evening Gazette,_ suspected that much of the trouble was psychological. In addition, Southwick wrote, "many newspaper writers shrink from using 'flowery' language," since "it seems to suggest looseness of form and insincerity of purpose." But he saw writing about a setting sun or the delights of picking blueberries as offering him more freedom to use imagination and picturesque phrases than did writing about election returns. It gave him a chance to loosen up metaphors, to let himself go and "to return to the long valley of remembrance." He wrote: "A quiet millpond at dusk, shingled with flat lily pads, may prod your senses into creation. . . . A field of corn wilting in the broiling August sun may recall to memory long hours you spent as a boy weeding and hoeing."

Southwick suggested that a writer who has trouble getting into the mood should go out in the backyard and gaze about, or on a sunny afternoon take the family on a picnic to a secluded spot. He urged the writer to lie back on the grass, look at the sky, the puffs of sailing clouds, the hazy, distant hills. "This is the fabric from which you can weave beautiful things at your typewriter," he wrote. "It is all a matter of seeing and hearing what nature has to offer. Once you catch that, the words will come easily." He was convinced that the same talent that writes an editorial on a school bond issue can describe a babbling brook. "And the chances are that more readers will read about the brook than about the bonds. Furthermore, if they do read about the brook, they may just tarry long enough to dip into the bond disquisition."[12]

Southwick's nature writings proved so popular that 10 seasonal pieces were published in a booklet entitled "New England Around the Year." "Cider—the Nectar of October," one of these pieces, may appeal more to old than to young readers and probably more to residents of New England because of the time period and setting it reflects. But its strong feelings of nostalgia should appeal to a broad readership. One of the strengths of the editorial is the specificity of its images: cider presses; apple-laden wagons pulled by patient, plodding horses; square dances in the old barn. You don't have to have been there to picture the scene.

Cider—the Nectar of October

Cider and October go together like Santa Claus and Christmas. There are few experiences in this life to equal the first glass of dark amber cider in the fall.

Cider is a blend of apple varieties, October air, fond memories and stout, wooden casks. A sip of cider will bring a man back to his boyhood, when the height of childhood enjoyment was centered around the old cider press and its squeezings. It recalls apple picking, and slow, apple-laden wagons pulled by patient, plodding horses, and golden autumn sunsets. It recalls October evenings by the fireplace, when the chestnut logs snapped and crackled and tossed their sparks on the hearth, throwing a flickering light on the contented people gathered around, each with a glass of cold cider in his hand.

Cider brings back the memory of gloomy, dusty cellars, with kegs of ripening apple juice in one corner. It recalls doughnuts, and square dances in the old barn, and fall nights lighted up by the ghostly radiance of the moon.

Cider is more than a beverage; it is an institution—a tradition redolent with significance. When a man takes his first drink of cider in the fall, he is renewing a ritual that was old when the country was born.

Worcester (Mass.) *Evening Gazette*
Reprinted from *The Masthead.*

One of the best known writers of nature editorials was Hal Borland, who for many years contributed the last item in the editorial columns of the Sunday *New York Times.* His writings were collected in several volumes, including *An American Year.*[13] When I was on the *Columbian* in Vancouver, Wash., I could count on exquisitely done pieces—both short and long—on the outdoor world from Erwin Rieger, managing editor of the paper. His steady supply spared me the frightening task of having to switch from bonds to brooks. His "Romance of Clouds Invites Mountaineer," as printed here, is a condensed version of a selection from *Up Is the Mountain,* a collection of Rieger's writings.[14] This particular selection has been described as worthy of a Pulitzer Prize. Part of the success of this piece stems from its highly personal writing. The readers know that the writer is a person who is sharing his own feelings and appreciation of the experience. It isn't only because I have known "Mr. Rieger" (as we always have called him) for a quarter of a century that I feel the personality of the writer shining through in the first few paragraphs; throughout the piece, he seems a friendly guide to places most readers have never been to.

Romance of Clouds Invites Mountaineer

Mountain climbing has had many facets for me. I must feel that one of the more delightful has been my encounters with, and my feeling of intimacy with, the clouds.

I say that despite occasional harsh, often disagreeable, sometimes dangerous experience with clouds.

Most of us look up to see the clouds. Mountaineers may look down on clouds. At other times they meet them face to face and at arm's length. . . .

Volatile indeed is the mountain environment. For mountains are stand-up land, and they thrust their immovable and often-serrated bulk up to interfere with the air currents where live so many of our clouds. Not only that, but some of them can and often do make their own weather. . . .

I am afraid I am a romantic about the clouds in my beloved highlands, even though as a climber I have endured their malevolences many a time and would have cursed them in seven languages had I been able.

I have loved to watch cloudlets a-borning, and even dying. One cannot do that intimately at my home. But on a mountain, or on a mountain top, one can be glancing idly through clear air when for no reason at all, puff! there is a baby cloud; a little tossing handkerchief of visible moisture drifting by. It may grow bigger; it may join with other little puffs as turbulence spawns the right conditions; or—pfft! it may be gone without trace.

Occasionally it is a signal to the climber to be long gone from there. The cloud formation may grow and spin and flatten to a streaming compressed mass of dense vapor, an evil vortex of wind and storm inhabited by seven devils.

I have perhaps never seen a more beautiful birth of the cloudlets than on the lovely day we were relaxing in cloudless sunlight on the summit of Mt. Olympus.

Olympus is scarcely a single mountain in the sense of how we usually think of a mountain like Hood. Its broad sub-top culminates in a series of relatively short, sharp peaks arranged not unlike the upturned fingers of an open hand. West Peak, the summit, is only slightly higher than its brothers or sisters.

And as I looked that day down into the scenic snow-filled "palm of the hand" with the sun already above and behind me, puff! a cloudlet appeared. Over there another. Yonder a third—it went on without end. And the wind began to rise; and the cloudlets closed ranks and gathered mass; and they reached to take hold of the lesser tips of the "fingers." It was time to descend.

I have loved to be in the scenic alplands as the morning sun burned off the condensed water vapor and turned it invisible again. It does that at home too. But in the alplands the weakening wisps will cling stubbornly and beautifully to the pointed spires of the alpine firs, and the gradual parting will open vistas of unguessed slopes and crags above and just ahead; and of the clear sky so blue up there. It is a world apart. . . .

I have loved to toil, maybe for hours, up through a cloud blanket to emerge finally topside into brilliant sunshine as far as the eye can see. Riding airplanes, I have come topside also, the easy way. I suppose because I like to climb I have never felt in an airplane the sweetness of the accomplishment nor felt the sense of "other world" insulated from mundane care beneath the all-stretching silvery sea.

I have loved to be above the cloud sea even at night when there has been a full moon. No place I have ever been has been lovelier than the summit of Pinnacle Peak in the Rainier country, where valleys radiate from the spire in several directions.

It has been my fortune to be on that summit under full moon not once but eight or nine times—most of them with the silver cloud sea filling all the valleys three or four thousand feet below me, and the awesome bulk of Rainier across the way somehow gentled and softened. It has been quiet up there on the pinnacle. The spirit of benediction was upon the peak like a spell.

Yes, I have loved the clouds of the mountains and the high country. Even as I have cursed them in concert with fellow climbers. Even as they have wet me to the bone with their penetrating wind-driven fingers. Even as they have iced me with sleet or stung me with ice pellets driven like needles.

Even as they have pervaded all in the incredible density of the whiteout, where one has difficulty keeping his balance and where travel is tolerable only by compass. . . .

Of all my memories none is more distinctive than one I carry from that hoary giant, Rainier. Forty-six years ago one summer I was pushing up alone from Paradise Valley before daylight, headed for Camp Muir at 10,000 feet. The cloud sea was all-enveloping. But as has so often happened, I came out on top of it at about 8,000 feet—only to realize that a second cloud layer, of which I was seeing the bottom, enveloped the mountain top perhaps 5,000 feet higher. It was a quiescent version of the Mt. Rainier cloud cap I have mentioned earlier. I was "sandwiched" in a most unusual formation.

An hour later and a thousand feet higher, the sun rose—to such a spectacle as I had never seen before. Deep rose color suffused the ceiling above me—and reflected for a few moments on the surface of the sea below me. And not only did the visible portion of the great mountain glow softly pink, but a rainbow-like band of light, parallel to the sunward profile of the mountain, framed the profile. That I have never seen again.

Columbian (Vancouver, Wash.)
Reprinted from *Up Is the Mountain* by
Erwin Rieger.

Lives of People

Editorial writers tend to forget that most readers are more interested in their personal lives than they are in public affairs. Except for letters to the editor, they are not likely to find anything on most editorial pages that speaks to them about their daily lives. The editorial that may have received more favorable response than any other I have written was one I hastily typed for use after a Labor Day weekend. My second daughter was to enter kindergarten the following Tuesday. The result was "To a Barefoot Girl," written in the form of a letter to her. At a session of NCEW later that year, other editorial writers questioned whether or not it was an editorial, since it was written in the first person and did not comment on an issue. But readers of the *Columbian,* especially mothers of small children, didn't care whether it met the requirements of an editorial. One woman, several years later, told me she still carried a copy of it in her purse.

To a Barefoot Girl

Letter to a daughter who went to school for the first time today:

By the time I get home from work tonight, you will have experienced your first day of kindergarten. You'll be bubbling over with stories about the excitement of school—that is, if you aren't already worn out answering questions from your mother, your big sister and the girls next door.

If I know you, you weren't even a little bit scared today. An article in the paper the other evening said parents should expect their five-year-olds to be a little scared the first day, scared of spending two or three hours away from home in a new place. But that's nothing new to you. You've been gone from home longer than that this summer—without telling your mother where you were going. She was the one who was scared.

If your teacher let you paint or color today, I hope she kept a close eye on you. You can do a good job of staying within the lines when you want to. But your mother tells me that everytime she turns her back there's a new mark on the living room carpet or your pillow case. How your teacher is going to keep track of you and 29 other children is beyond me. I wish her luck.

I also wish her luck in getting you to stay on your rug when it's rest time. If she has to stand over you the way your mother and I have to when it's nap time at home, 29 other children are going to be up and around and doing whatever they want to.

I hope you came home wearing your shoes, or at least carrying them. You are a big school girl now, and it's time to start learning to keep track of your shoes. It's all right sometimes to take them off, but you've got to stop forgetting where you left them. The tennis shoes you lost this summer didn't cost too much, but those big saddle shoes we bought you for school cost a lot of dollars, a whole lot more than the six cents you charged me yesterday for lemonade. Maybe it would help if you wrote your name on the inside of your shoes.

I hope you're not going to be disappointed with kindergarten. You have been looking forward to school ever since you knew where your big sister went to school. You always thought she was so smart. She could read and write and do numbers. I've heard you tell people that as soon as you went to school you'd be able to read and write and do numbers, too. It will take you quite a while to learn enough so that you can read a book, or the funny papers, or this letter. Kindergarteners these days don't get much chance to learn to read. Maybe it's just as well. Maybe kindergarten should be a time only for enjoying your new friends, playing games and painting pictures.

The most important thing about school is being able to enjoy it. A lot of big boys and girls are scared of school—boys and girls who are bigger than your sister. Most of them aren't doing very well in school either. They aren't learning what they should be. Maybe they started out being scared from the first day. But maybe what happened was that somewhere along the line they forgot that school ought to be fun. Maybe they had some cranky teachers. Or maybe their parents put too much pressure on them.

I'm not sure you know what I'm talking about by this time. But I guess what I'm saying is that I hope that, even though you are now a big school girl, you will still be that smiling, laughing little kid who has a mind of her own and who is interested in more important things than keeping track of a pair of shoes. We can always buy another pair of shoes or clean the pillow case. But it's not so easy to repair the damage if you let the big people in the world who have forgotten how to smile and laugh keep you from smiling and laughing.

I hope you have fun in school—even if you come home barefoot.

Columbian (Vancouver, Wash.)

Writing about living in a house with the thermostat turned down might not seem like a standard editorial topic, although it might be timely when energy is short and costs are high. "Cold and Togetherness" from the *Raleigh* (N.C.) *Times,* while mentioning fuel prices in passing, is primarily concerned with what it's like wearing itchy long-johns, splitting wood and dressing in a cold bedroom. The scene with the family crowded together, almost too close to tolerate, clearly depicts a scene from everyday life.

Cold and Togetherness

Learning to live in chilly houses is one of those privileges that, if we all had our druthers, we druther forego—and turn up the thermostat and hang the expense.

Since conscience and the fuel bill make unwilling Eskimos of us all, we grin and outwardly bear it. But 'neath each flannel-shielded and sweater-swathed breast burns a secret, passionate hate for some aspect of the thing.

For some it's splitting wood. For others paying for it, and the pang of watching every decrease in the woodpile.

For many "credit-worthy" fuel customers, it's listening for the furnace to come on and cringing dollarsigns when it does—and getting up to check the thermostat for the fourth time because that blower seems to shoosh on so extravagantly often.

Some hate the clumsy bother of getting "dressed for it." Especially in a cold bedroom. One Raleighite demands at least the right to get dressed in warmth no matter what, even if everyone's got to leave the living room so she can change in front of last night's fireplace coals.

Others can't stand the itch of the long-johns. The uncouthness of polar boots as everyday house-slippers. The afghans lying all about where people tossed them when they went to answer the phone. The endless clutter from too many people, owning too many things, bunched into too little space.

Heating only the family room or den or living room—names that on chill evenings mean what they say—brings a kind of intimacy most families had forgotten existed except at Christmas.

For some, it's too much togetherness to tolerate. Child abuse, divorce, suicide seem to lurk just beyond one more hassle over whether to have the TV or the radio or the stereo on, and on which channels—one more display of pique over who gets to lie on the couch or whether Buster cheated at backgammon—one more grim announcement that supper will be in there where it's warm by golly, even if the kids do have to move their homework off the table.

But things do even out. All this indoor population pressure in cold weather and cold times at least forces us outdoors to discover the pleasure of a beautiful snow or a crystalline night in the 20s.

Raleigh (N.C.) *Times*

Included in this group of editorials would be pieces about the weather, Christmas shopping, summer vacations, new hair styles or clothing trends, the computer game rage and what to do with a stack of old newspapers. These editorials may not contribute to the solution of any of the world's problems, but they might help solve some of an editorial writer's problems in getting more people to turn to the editorial page.

Humor and Satire

If used properly, humor and satire can be extremely effective in making a point. They attract readers, who like the chance to be amused, and they lower their defenses, making readers more receptive to the editorial writer's point. But you won't find many humorous or satirical pieces on American editorial pages. Press critic Ben Bagdikian discovered this when he studied pages of editorial writers attending a convention of NCEW. "Where [humor] was conscious it was not very good," he said. "Funny" people are hard to find, he said. "Perhaps it isn't a funny world."[15]

Humor, when used, can put across almost any point. Sevellon Brown III of the *Providence* (R.I.) *Journal-Bulletin* said his paper had used humor to expose the fallacies of Soviet communism, attack anti-black prejudice, criticize the Supreme Court, promote conservation, attack government extravagance, radio giveaways and red tape, "and even to take the curse off a fake story the news editor swallowed and spit up on page one."[16] "Whale Ride" is the result of Brown's last example. In this piece you are not sure what is going on until well into the last paragraph. Evidence that the writer was having fun is provided by reference to "a playful whale" and "a young man of the highest veracity." By sharing this "whale story" the writer asks readers join in the enjoyment of the joke.

Whale Ride

That was a first-rate whale ride that Frank Cabral took. We believe every word of it, and we hope Frank doesn't change it. There he and his pa were, each in his own boat off Cape Race hauling lobster pots. There was the 70—well—60-foot whale surfacing and making a bee line for the elder Cabral. Suddenly there it was under Frank's boat, knocking both Frank and the boat galley west, knocking a hole in the boat, leaving a sample of its own flesh as a rebuke to doubters.

Finally there was Frank landing astride the whale's hump and riding into the blinding spray for the open sea, where he might be this minute if the whale hadn't sounded, Frank hadn't dived, and Frank's pa hadn't picked the likely lad up and brought him back to Provincetown. A first-rate whale story.

If Provincetown were in need of a sea monster to stimulate summer trade, we might be inclined to doubt it. If Frank were given to riding whales we'd be inclined to doubt it. But both suppositions are contrary to fact. Provincetown is doing nicely and Frank's reputation for veracity extends as far as Orleans. So there it is: a playful whale and a young man of the highest veracity riding it in the season's most exhilarating adventure, so far.

Reprinted with permission.
Providence (R.I.) *Journal*

Often a humor piece depends on the clever use of, and a play on, words, exemplified here in "A Shaggy-Fish Story" (p. 220). The writer tries to toss in as many disagreeable-sounding words as possible, shifting from fish to other foods to alcoholic drinks. The almost imperceptible change sets the reader up for the final gagline, which probably provided the motivation for the writing of the editorial.

A Shaggy-Fish Story

Many very edible fish have very unappetizing names, among them the gagfish, the ratfish, the dogfish, the rattail and the grunt.

This worries the National Marine Fisheries Service to the point where it is considering a new system for labeling such fish in the supermarkets and on restaurant menus. The lowly gagfish, for example, has much the same texture and taste as the popular red snapper, and the new labeling would point that out.

We think the National Marine Fisheries Service is wasting its time. A nation that stuffs itself on hog maw, scrapple, pigs feet, grits, souse, gumbo, head cheese, tripe, gruel, blood wurst, mush, hangtown fries and rutabagas is not likely to reject a mess of ratfish.

To the contrary, we probably would celebrate our discovery of this new epicurean delight by throwing down a couple of extra wallbangers, bloody marys, grasshoppers, slings, screwdrivers, fizzes, rusty nails, boilermakers or the hair of the dogfish that bit us.

Los Angeles Times

One of the risks in writing humorously is that readers might take what you write seriously—and not get the point. That risk is even greater with satire. Professor John Murray of Michigan State University has suggested that one reason satire is rare in editorial columns is that it tends to take more space than other types of writing. He also suspected that writers know their efforts will not stand a comparison with the national columnists, such as Art Buchwald and Art Hoppe.[17] One of the better known regional satirists, who has a limited distribution in the Pacific Northwest, is Henry Gay of the *Mason County Journal* in Shelton, Wash. "It Can't Be True" is an example of his satire. The device that he uses here is an imaginary conversation between a man and woman. He manages to work in a lot of detailed information, including a string of figures on national deficits, providing lengthy, though easy, reading.

It Can't Be True

Harold?

Yes, Mildred?

How come the government spends more money when a Republican President is in office than when a Democrat is?

It doesn't, Mildred. You've read all those editorials and listened to all that campaign talk over the years that told you a Republican President brings fiscal responsibility to the office. Remember how Dwight Eisenhower cut down the cost of government when he replaced that spendthrift, Harry Truman?

He didn't, Harold. It got worse while he was in office.

The hell it did! The nation returned to normal with Ike at the helm.

Maybe it did, Harold, but during his eight-year administration, budget deficits grew by $15.8 billion while Harry Truman had a surplus of $16.6 billion during his seven years.

You're crazy. Where are you getting those figures?

They're right here in the almanac, Harold. It's got all the federal budgets since 1789.

Well, forget about Truman and Eisenhower. That was a long time ago. Let's see the figures on those spending fools, Kennedy and Johnson, and compare their eight years with the eight years of conservative leadership given a grateful nation by Nixon and Ford.

It's even worse, Harold.

It can't be. Kennedy and Johnson set out to spend the country into bankruptcy and if Nixon hadn't come along, we'd be out of business.

Kennedy and Johnson had budget deficits totalling $53.8 billion for their eight years. Nixon and Ford presided over budget deficits amounting to $167.5 billion during their eight years.

That boggles the mind. That's three times as much under the conservatives. You sure you've got the right figures, Mildred?

They're right here in the book, Harold. When you add them all up you find that, beginning with Harry Truman, the Democrats have been in office 15 years and spent $37.2 billion more than the government took in, while the Republicans have been in the White House 16 years and put the country $183.3 billion into the hole.

That's not the way it's supposed to go, Mildred. Democratic presidents are supposed to spend money and Republican presidents are supposed to save it. Why did you have to bring up this subject? I think I'm going to get a stomach ache.

I'm sorry, Harold. I thought it was interesting that conservative presidents have put us in debt at the rate of $11.4 billion a year while liberal presidents spent only $2.4 billion a year more than they collected.

Aha! My stomach ache is going away, Mildred. I have the answer. It's the Congress. The Republican Presidents had a Democratic Congress.

The Democratic Presidents had a Democratic Congress, too, Harold. Except for two sessions—one under Truman and one during Eisenhower's tenure—the Democrats have been in control of Congress during the entire period.

Now we're getting somewhere. Look and see how much money Eisenhower saved when he had a Republican Congress.

Here it is, Harold. Let's see—when Eisenhower had a Republican Congress there was a budget deficit. And down here it shows that when Truman had a Republican Congress there was a budget surplus.

I'm confused, Mildred, really confused. This doesn't make sense. Conservative leaders spend liberally and liberal leaders spend conservatively. I sense one of my cherished notions going down the drain.

Let it go, Harold. You'll feel better. Your stomach ache will probably go away.

As usual, Mildred, you're right. In my heart I know you're right.

Mason County Journal (Shelton, Wash.)
by Henry Gay

CONCLUSION

The purpose of this chapter has been to suggest a few of the ways in which editorial writers can offer a heartier, more varied diet of comment to their readers.

They can tackle tough subjects, such as economics and religion, that they might prefer to avoid. They can do a more imaginative job on editorials, such as duty and obituary pieces, that they can't avoid. And they can try their hands at other types of editorials, on nature and everyday happenings, that most of them have been successfully avoiding.

QUESTIONS AND EXERCISES

1. Find an editorial written on an economic topic. Compare the writing and approach to the suggestions offered in this chapter. Does the editorial follow these suggestions, especially concerning the use of figures and the personalizing of the writer's points? If not, how could it be improved?

2. Analyze an editorial that talks about taxes, property taxes if possible. Is it easy to understand? Could it be simplified? Should some points be spelled out?

3. Find an editorial that relies excessively on legal terms. Rewrite it using more common language.

4. Can you find an editorial that formerly would have been called an "Afghanistanism"? Does the editorial seem to have absolutely nothing to do with the interests of the readers who are most likely to read this editorial? Could the subject have been made more pertinent to local readers?

5. Find an editorial on an international topic that stands a good chance of catching the reader's attention—one that is not on a current hot topic. What is it about the editorial that makes it readable?

6. Compare several editorials on cultural subjects. Which seem to have been written simply to get promoters of causes off the backs of the editorial writer? Which are most likely to attract readers? Could the run-of-the-mill editorials have been made more interesting or pertinent?

7. Clip several "easy shot" editorials. What makes them fall into this category? What could save them from this category?

8. Find several "duty" editorials. Would you have published them? If not, what could you have written on the same subjects that you would have felt comfortable writing? What angles could the writers have taken that they missed?

9. Find an obituary editorial that is mostly factual and another that goes beyond the facts. What is the difference in the effect of the editorials? What makes the difference?

10. Examine an editorial that expresses pride in the community or some aspect of community life. Is the editorial sheer puffery, or has the writer made an effort to put the event in perspective?

11. Find an editorial dealing with nature and ask yourself if it has genuine editorial value or value only to bird-watchers or professional naturalists. What is it about the worthy editorial that will appeal to readers in general?

12. Find a humorous or satirical editorial. Is the humor or satire likely to be misunderstood? Is the use of humor or satire appropriate in this editorial?

13. Find several editorials dealing with everyday life. Does the writer succeed in making the commonplace seem interesting? Might the space have been better used for comment on some public issue?

'DEATH RAY, FIDDLESTICKS! WHY IT DOESN'T EVEN SLOW THEM UP.'

—Cartoon by Draper Hill for *The Masthead*

Editorials on Elections

CHAPTER 7

Is there a conscientious editorial writer who doesn't dislike, if not loathe, writing election endorsements? . . . Certainly it is one of the more onerous tasks for me.
—Calvin Mayne
Rochester *(N.Y.)* Times-Union[1]

As chairman of the board it's a relief no longer to participate in the most thankless task in all of Christendom.
—Nelson Poynter
St. Petersburg *(Fla.)* Times[2]

Making endorsement decisions and writing endorsement editorials are among the toughest jobs editorial writers face. As elections approach, conscientious writers think of the hours they will need to devote to interviewing candidates with dread. Some decisions will be difficult—for example, detecting the difference between two good or two mediocre candidates. In addition, members of an editorial page staff may find it difficult to agree among themselves or with the editor or publisher on whom to endorse.

Writers may be concerned that their editorials will have more effect than deserved on uninformed and unthinking voters, that there may be some truth to charges that newspapers control elections. Writers may also be afraid of making mistakes. It is always possible that writers do not know as much as they think they do about a political race and that they could end up making an endorsement they would later regret. Before an election is over, writers may begin to wonder whether newspapers ought to be in the business of endorsing candidates at all. In the event of extreme disagreement with editors or publishers, some writers may even feel that they should quit their jobs and seek employment on more congenial newspapers.

During election time, then, the usually congenial editorial writer, even one who wields the sweetest pen in the world, may come home after a long day to yell at the children, growl at the spouse and kick the dog. The thankless hell that editorial writers go through in making endorsements is probably one of the reasons why some newspapers—although still a small minority—forbear from endorsing candidates in some or all races.

HOW PREVALENT IS ENDORSING?

A survey following the 1980 election found that 29 percent of daily newspapers that responded did not endorse a presidential candidate. The percentage was somewhat larger than in the previous presidential election, when 26 percent abstained. Those who conducted the 1980 survey concluded, however, that the fall-off in endorsements did not reflect a greater unwillingness of papers to endorse candidates in general. "In fact, dozens of editors remained uncommitted in 1980 only because of their dissatisfaction with all the presidential candidates."[3] An examination that I made of endorsements at state and national levels by California newspapers between 1970 and 1980 showed a drop-off in candidate endorsements from 1970 to 1972 but a gradual return to more consistent endorsing beginning in the mid-1970s. In 1972, as in 1980, some editors had not been eager to endorse either presidential candidate, Richard Nixon or George McGovern.

The 1980 survey found that smaller papers were less inclined to endorse than larger papers. Those who conducted the survey speculated that small staffs had less specialized editorial writers, who hesitated to venture into presidential politics; several writers on smaller staffs expressed a desire to avoid becoming "embroiled in controversial issues." The survey also found that independently owned papers were less inclined to endorse presidential candidates than were papers owned by groups—63 percent compared to 75 percent. The independent papers were slightly more inclined to endorse Republican Ronald Reagan and less likely to endorse independent John Anderson; among those that made endorsements, 72.5 percent supported Reagan, 21.6 supported Carter and 5.5 supported Anderson. Among the group papers that endorsed, Reagan had 69.7 percent, Carter had 21.6 and Anderson had 7.9. The survey showed that "few chains required all their properties to endorse the same candidate" but most that did make endorsements endorsed Reagan.[4]

Although the overall percentage of newspapers making endorsements has not changed substantially, some individual newspapers, after wrestling with the question of whether or not to endorse, have altered their policies in recent years—some one way, some the other. In 1972, *Newsday* broke a 30-year tradition of endorsing and announced to its readers that it would no longer make recommendations on voting. (Later in this chapter we will note some of the reasons cited for the change.) Nine years later, under a new publisher and a new editor, *Newsday* went back to endorsing. In 1973, the *Los Angeles Times,* owned by the same company as *Newsday,* told readers that it would no longer "routinely endorse candidates for president, for governor or for senator" but would continue to make endorsements in other races and on issues. Through the primary election of 1982 the *Times* had not endorsed for any of the three major races. This forbearance represented a sharp break with the past; for more than half a century the *Times* had regarded itself as the state's political king maker, and breaker, especially among Republicans. The *Times* actually began moderating its strong partisan stance about 1962, when Richard Nixon, who had been one of the *Times'* favorites, was running for governor of California. The *Times'* support that year was lukewarm, and, according to David Halberstam, its news columns played the campaign straight. Nixon was unaccustomed to that kind of coverage by the large California papers, which was one of the reasons for his "You won't have Nixon to kick around any more" blast at the press following his defeat.[5]

The policy of the *Washington Post* has changed several times, depending on the circumstances of the presidential election. The *Post* endorsed Dwight D. Eisenhower in 1952, partly to help preserve the two-party system, but in 1956, and again in 1968, after assessing both major candidates, it declined to make a strong endorsement. Philip Geyelin, editorial page editor of the *Post,* said that in 1972 the paper carried several editorials that the editors "rather plainly" thought indicated an anti-Nixon stance, but "somewhere along the line it [the message] was lost." In 1976, when a similar statement was made, this one favoring Carter, "it was read as a plain endorsement."[6] In 1980 the *Post* offered a clear endorsement of Carter over Reagan.

WHY ENDORSE?

Both non-newspaper and newspaper people argue about the question of whether or not newspapers should endorse candidates and ballot propositions. Among readers, probably the most frequently heard argument against endorsing is that a paper has no right to use its position of influence to impose its views on the voters. Typifying this attitude, a reader accused the editor-owner of the *Longview* (Wash.) *Daily News* of inflicting on a community "a slanted and one-sided opinion or recommendation" that "could affect the lives of many people." The letter writer feared that people would "take that recommendation as an easy way out for the solution of their undecided vote." The writer thought that, if the editor-owner wanted to express his views, he should take out a political advertisement and label it as such, just like anyone else.[7] A letter writer charged the *Eugene* (Ore.) *Register-Guard* with "meddling into the political affairs of the people of Lane County, dictating to Republicans and Democrats alike." The selecting of candidates "belongs to the people. . . . It's their vote," the writer said.[8]

One of the assumptions apparently held by these critics is that endorsements carry a lot of weight with voters. We will discuss the apparent effect of endorsements later in this chapter, but it might be said that, in general, most newspapers in most elections do not have the overwhelming power that these critics fear. One response to these concerns, then, is that the press does not affect the ultimate outcome of many elections.

A second response to these fears is that elections are just one aspect of public affairs and should not be treated any differently. In answer to the letter writer in Eugene, an editorial in the *Register-Guard,* noting the paper's practice of commenting on public matters throughout the years, contended that for the paper "to comment on issues between elections and then to duck the tough choices would be irresponsible." When *Newsday* resumed endorsing in 1981, the editors said that "a substantial amount of remarkably articulate and persuasive mail chiding us for failing to endorse" had helped convince them that the paper had a responsibility to its readers to make a clear statement of where it stood on certain political races."[9] Nelson Poynter of the *St. Petersburg* (Fla.) *Times* noted that readers want opinions from several sections of the paper, including sports, Ann Landers, food editors and bridge writers. They are even more interested in, and excited by, endorsements. He thought that by not endorsing an editor "risks taking a lot of fun away" from readers. "They want to kill the editor, whereas a punch in the nose of an unfriendly sports writer is usually enough vengeance for honest disagreement."[10]

Among newspaper people the concerns expressed about electoral power by readers are couched in slightly different terms. One argument—the first reason cited by *Newsday* in 1972 when it temporarily stopped endorsing[11]—is that the newspaper's responsibility is to give readers information to help them vote, not to tell them how to vote. In an editorial that has been republished prior to several elections, the *Wall Street Journal* has given as one reason for its policy of never endorsing: "The short answer is simplicity itself. We don't think our business is telling people how to vote."[12] On another occasion a *Journal* editorial writer said that the editorial page staff was more concerned with "politics, principles and philosophies" than with individuals and, by not allying the paper with any one candidate, the *Journal* retained "greater freedom to comment on the good and bad ideas of any candidate . . . [and] to criticize or commend the ideas and actions of an individual after the election."[13] *Newsday*'s editors thought that refraining from endorsing gave the paper a better chance to maintain independence in "criticizing, investigating and disclosing abuses of the public trust," or at least that is what the editors in 1972 thought. As noted, by 1981 new executives had concluded that arguments on the other side outweighed this consideration.

Another argument against endorsing is that readers will think that, if a paper supports a candidate in its editorial columns, it will be biased in that candidate's favor in its news columns. That reason was cited by the *Los Angeles Times* when it announced its partial shift away from endorsing. *Times* editors said they hoped to allay suspicions among readers that "editorial page endorsements really affect the news columns," especially in races that arouse the sharpest political passions.[14] This reason was also mentioned by *Newsday* editors in 1972, but in returning to endorsing in 1981, the new executives concluded that "perceptions of bias had dissipated through our eight years of nonendorsement and that . . . readers recognized our commitment to fair coverage regardless of our editorial stance." In response to the argument about the appearance of bias in the news columns, Clarke Thomas of the *Pittsburgh* (Pa.) *Post-Gazette* asked: "If you say that your news columns are tainted by your editorial policy [on endorsements], then you really open yourself to criticism because doesn't that mean that your editorials on any subject will also taint your news columns on that subject?"[15]

In support of endorsements, we have already noted the argument that newspapers have a responsibility, as part of participating in public affairs, to comment on elections and to make their recommendations known. This responsibility stems partly from the unique position in which most newspapers find themselves in their communities. No other institution, aside from government and political parties, devotes as much attention to political affairs as a local newspaper. Aside from professional politicians, political reporters and editorial writers probably know more about the qualifications of candidates and the merits of ballot propositions than anyone else in the community. They have the added advantage of being less partisan and hence better able to evaluate candidates and issues with some measure of detachment. Even in deciding not to endorse in major candidate races, editors of the *Los Angeles Times* recognized their responsibility to "stand and be counted on important issues" after thoroughly examining the merits of the issues.

The editorial columns of a newspaper are among the few places in a community where the pros and cons of the issues can be discussed at length and in a logical, factual manner. An editorial in *Editor & Publisher* referred to the ability of an endorsement editorial to "sift the campaign propaganda, clarify issues, challenge lies and otherwise stimulate decision-making and debate."[16] Some editors, while not expecting to change voters' minds, see a responsibility to help undecided voters to make up their minds. Some see editorials as helping create increased interest in elections and thereby encouraging more people to vote.

In the years in which I was engaged in writing editorials, the papers on which I worked consistently endorsed candidates and ballot propositions. I was not unsympathetic, however, to the concerns of those who contended that the *Columbian* was trying to impose its candidates on the community. After all, over the years a large majority of the candidates that the paper endorsed were elected. Some critics argued that, since the *Columbian* was the sole source of political reporting in the community, the editors should keep their editorial preferences to themselves. But my publishers and I thought that, precisely because we were the only consistent source of political information, we had a responsibility to dig deeply into the backgrounds of candidates, present the arguments for and against propositions and tell our readers what we found and what we had concluded.

WHAT EFFECTS?

Whether endorsement editorials do in fact influence voters has been a matter of speculation and argument for a long time, especially since Democrat Franklin D. Roosevelt began winning elections in spite of overwhelming opposition from the writers of editorials on predominantly Republican newspapers. By 1952 journalism historian Frank Luther Mott, in his article "Has the Press Lost Its Punch?" concluded: "There seems to be no correlation, positive or negative, between support of a majority of newspapers during a campaign and victory in a presidential canvass."[17] Following the 1952 election, Professor Nathaniel B. Blumberg noted in a study called *One-Party Press?* that "in the 37 presidential campaigns preceding the 1952 election, the winner had the editorial support of a majority of newspapers 18 times and did not have it 19 times."[18] In the eight elections in the period between 1952 and 1980 the press accumulated a slightly better record, with a majority of newspapers supporting the winning candidate for six, for an improved record of 24 wins and 21 losses. Of course, a tally of the presidential endorsements may not be the best test of the effectiveness of newspaper editorial support. The presidential race is only one of thousands of contests that take place in the country on a regular basis—and the presidential vote may be the one least influenced by editorials.

As we noted in the introductory chapter, in spite of the popularity of television news, the public tends to look to the print media for guidance in setting the public agenda. Studies show that voters look in particular to newspapers for information about elections at the state and local levels.[19] One nationwide study of how much voters knew about the qualifications of candidates for the U.S. Senate found newspapers superior to television "as agents of information to help people identify assets and liabilities of important political contenders." The authors concluded: "If reasoning about political choices depends at all on the features of an area's media system, those characteristics will be found in the newspapers that circulate there, not in television coverage."[20] These studies suggest that voters do look, and in fact must look, to newspapers for help in judging candidates. Where can they find a more succinct, better informed account of the assets and liabilities of the candidates than in the editorial columns? Editorials at least offer the potential for such help to voters.

Most editorial writers seem to think that their influence in elections increases as the political arena becomes more local. In addition, the general assumption has been that editorials have more effect on the outcome of ballot issues than on candidate races. But studies have shown some exceptions to these assumptions. One scholar, John P. Robinson of the Survey Research Center at the University of Michigan, noted that "classic research" on voting behavior in national elections showed little evidence of influence by editorial endorsements. His studies, however, showed a notable influence in the five presidential elections between 1956 and 1972: Democratic candidates got between 14 and 24 percent more votes in areas in which newspapers endorsed the Democrats than in areas in which newspapers endorsed the Republicans. In close elections (1960 and 1968) Robinson found that endorsements seemed to influence only voters who claimed to be independents; he saw little influence in the votes of registered Democrats and Republicans. In landslide elections (1956, 1964 and 1972) endorsements seemed to influence members of the losing party as well as independents; members of the winning party remained unaffected.[21]

I found a similar pattern in California in 1980. In circulation areas in which editorials endorsed Carter, votes for him ran an average of almost 7 percent ahead of his statewide average. In circulation areas in which editorials endorsed Anderson the average was 8.5 percent ahead of his statewide average. In circulation areas in which editorials endorsed Reagan the average was actually 4 percent behind his statewide average.[22]

These findings suggest that endorsement editorials do little for voters who already know for whom they are going to vote and have reason to think that their candidate will do well. But endorsements apparently can influence the wavering, undecided voters and strengthen the inclination of voters to stick with a faltering candidate of their own party. If these findings are valid, it would seem logical to conclude that an editorial stands the best chance to be persuasive if it does not try to change voters' mind but instead tries to reinforce underlying political preferences.

The assumption that endorsements influence local elections more than state elections has also been questioned. Studies have found that editorials can affect state elections, especially ballot issues, when voters have little information other than the newspaper on which to base their votes. But the same studies have found that editorials can also have influence at the state level, and presumably at other levels, if voters have been deluged with information that is contradictory. Readers apparently look to newspapers for guidance when they do not have information or when they are confused by contradictory information. Editorials may have the strongest effect on ballot issues that are the least publicized and on those that are the most controversial.[23] In California in 1966, the issue most affected by endorsements was an anti-obscenity measure, which was the most controversial and widely discussed issue on the ballot.[24] A study I did of the 1978 election found that a measure strengthening the death penalty was one of those most affected by endorsements. It, too, was the most controversial and most publicized ballot issue that year. The percentages in the circulation areas of the newspapers that were studied exceeded statewide percentages by about 3 percent.[25]

Overall, however, the influence of 34 California newspapers in that 1978 election was less than this figure indicates. When eight ballot propositions and six candidate races were added together, the total vote affected by endorsements was about 1 percent. For the ballot propositions alone the effect was slightly more than 1 percent; for the candidates it was slightly less than 1 percent.[26] In 1980, 47 papers I studied seemed to have had an overall effect of about 2 percent on two candidate races and 11 propositions, with the impact on the candidates slightly higher than that on the propositions.[27] Averages varied among the propositions and races in the two elections, with the difference ranging from a minus 2.5 percent below the statewide average in a 1978 candidate race to a plus 4.3 percent in a 1980 parks bond issue. When "yes" and "no" votes and Republican and Democratic votes are studied separately, the margins over the statewide average ranged as high as 8 percent (the vote for Carter that was previously mentioned).

In a study of state and local elections, researchers concluded that the *Toledo* (Ohio) *Blade* had influenced between 4 and 12 percent of the voters in a governor's race and between only 2 and 4 percent in a state senate race. Those who conducted the study speculated that the party label was regarded as sufficient reason for deciding how to vote in the more obscure local race. But in the governor's race, in which voters had more interest, readers were open to considering other factors, including the recommendations of newspaper editorials.[28] These findings may seem to contradict the presumption that endorsements have more influence at the local level. But perhaps all that any of these studies show is that newspapers, under some circumstances, can affect the voting outcome, but to what degree depends heavily on the circumstances. Neither the prediction nor the analysis of the effects of editorial endorsements has become a science.

WHOSE VIEWS?

If an editorial should ever represent more than the views of the specific person who wrote it, that time should be at election time. But whether the editorial should be the voice of the owner (publisher) or a broader consensus of staff members is an issue being fought out in newspapers across the country. In most instances the publisher has the power to win in any dispute. But each year an increasing number of newspapers seem to be allowing staff members to influence endorsements.

Conducters of a 1980 survey of endorsements found some evidence disputing the "critical stereotypes [that] show authoritarian editors and publishers, often on the basis of their own prejudices and in opposition to the wishes of their staffs." Rather, the study reported that 21 of the editors surveyed attributed their papers' endorsements to the editorial boards, that various other editors had based endorsements on polls of their entire staffs and that in only seven cases had endorsements resulted from the decision of the editor or publisher.[29] Nevertheless, publishers probably still exercise their final editorial prerogative more strongly and more often on endorsements than on any other type of editorial page decision.

John Zakarian of the *St. Louis Post-Dispatch* described what he called "the publishers' four-year itch" and the "editorial writers' agony." For 47 months many papers carry moderate-to-liberal editorial policies but "on the 48th month of reckoning turn conservative." He described presidential elections as "sacred cows of the highest order." He added: "They are our society's emotional and political hot flashes, occurring (mercifully) every four years and exacting from the publishers' establishment an atavistic impulse to go Republican."[30]

What happens when a publisher wants an editorial endorsing a candidate that members of the editorial staff feel they cannot support? Sig Gissler of the *Waukegan* (Ill.) *News-Sun* recalled that his paper decided early to support Barry Goldwater for president in 1964. He was spared the duty of having to write the editorial; a semi-retired editor was called in to write it. He wondered, however, what he would have done if the publisher had insisted that he write the editorial. Gissler said that he would have respectfully declined, confident that his publisher would have respected that decision since they had an agreement that Gissler would never have to write anything offensive to his conscience. He added, however: "Of course, if irreconcilable differences of opinion continually occur between editorial writer and publisher, the only honest answer is reassignment or resignation."[31] I had a similar experience in the 1972 election (as previously related in Chapter 6) dealing with relations with publishers. As in the Waukegan case, a semi-retired editor was available to write the editorial endorsing Richard Nixon when regular members of the editorial page staff said they could not do so in good conscience. Fortunately, as with Gissler, my publishers would not have demanded that I write something I could not believe in.

Nevertheless, election time can be hazardous for editorial writers. The heightened emotion of a political campaign, plus the black-and-white nature of endorsement decisions, can produce crises and magnify differences of opinion between writers and publishers that might be easily reconcilable at other times. Perhaps these periodic crises serve a purpose in forcing publishers and writers to re-evaluate whether or not they still see eye to eye on major issues. Perhaps such crises keep writers from being lulled into writing whatever they know will get by their publishers and will not infringe too deeply on their consciences. But in these tense situations both publishers and writers can overreact and later regret that they acted precipitously.

Some editors are comfortable with unequivocal decisions coming from the publisher's office. David Brinegar of the (Tucson) *Arizona Daily Star* said he knew of no better way to avoid endorsement crises than "to have one man of wide education, great national and world interests, and long-proven sound judgment do the deciding." Brinegar said he was temperamentally opposed to deciding things in committee.[32] But most editorial writers undoubtedly would like to have a voice, if not an equal voice, in deciding on endorsements.

On papers on which one person does not singlehandedly decide on endorsements, procedures for picking candidates come in an almost infinite variety. The publisher can retain the prerogative of deciding but ask political reporters, editorial writers and other members of the staff to contribute information and ideas, a pattern that Harold F. Grumhaus described when he was publisher of the *Chicago Tribune*.[33] In contrast, the publisher may participate as just one of the members of an editorial board, leaving the decision to consensus. On the *Minneapolis Star and Tribune,* a council consisting of the president, the publisher and several editors considered the opinions of all members in an effort to reach consensus. If the council remained divided, the editor made the final decision.[34]

On occasion a publisher will be willing to allow differences of opinion to appear in the editorial columns, or at least on the editorial page. In 1972 the editorial board of the Du Pont-owned papers in Wilmington, Del., decided not to endorse Nixon or McGovern and said so editorially. Shortly thereafter the owners called for a statement on the editorial page saying that, unlike their editorial board, they favored Nixon.[35] In that same election publisher William Block of the *Pittsburgh Post-Gazette* announced that the paper would support Nixon. When staff writers expressed disappointment, Block suggested that they compose a dissent from the official editorial. After the writers had had a chance to see the endorsement editorial, they wrote a piece making a case for McGovern. The dissent ran in the right-hand column of the editorial page on the same day that the endorsement appeared. "The obvious fairness of the procedure should enhance the paper's credibility, as the conflicting views must have added to the interest of the editorial page," *The Nation* said.[36]

But an out-and-out dissent is not likely to be looked on favorably by many publishers or editors. Publishing a dissent "would only signify a breach between the publisher and his editors," said Barry Bingham Jr., editor and publisher of the *Louisville Courier-Journal.* "While it might be temporarily refreshing, it would have the long term effect of undermining the confidence of the editorial page reader."[37]

John B. Oakes, who had run the *New York Times* editorial page much as he had wanted to, found himself asking for a chance to write a dissent when, in the September 1976 New York state primary, publisher Arthur Ochs (Punch) Sulzberger directed, over Oakes' objections, that the *Times* endorse Daniel P. Moynihan for U.S. senator. Oakes first submitted a 700-word dissenting letter to the editor. The publisher vetoed it. Oakes then wrote a one-sentence dissent, which was published, expressing disagreement with the endorsement in the editorial that appeared on the same day.[38]

Whoever participates in the decision making for endorsements—whether the publisher alone or the entire editorial board—must be thoroughly informed on the candidates and ballot propositions being considered. Not every editor is convinced that interviews with all of the candidates serve a worthy purpose. John Ankenbruck of the *Fort Wayne* (Ind.) *News-Sentinel,* for example, said that he would rather base endorsements "on a candidate's record than a candidate's B.S. during an interview."[39] But, to the extent that they have time, most editorial writers probably prefer to bring candidates into the office, to gain insights into their personalities as well as to hear their views on the issues. A common practice is to mail questionnaires to the candidates before the interviews, asking them to provide biographical information and their statement of platform and principles. Sometimes newspapers will publish the full responses of the candidates so that readers can share the same information the paper has. In extremely important races an editorial staff might tape interviews with candidates and publish a condensed version, perhaps in a special election supplement.

Interviewing candidates consumes so many working hours that talking to even two or three candidates a day can make performing regular editorial page duties almost impossible. Those are the days when the writer may go home to kick the cat. But the editorial writer's only legitimate reason for speaking out is that he or she has devoted enough time and effort to know more about the candidates, the issues and the political situation than do most of the readers. If writers do know more, they have not only a right but an obligation to share their knowledge and insights. That, at least, is how I see it.

WHAT APPROACH?

Writers generally employ one of two basic approaches to endorsement writing. A form that goes back to the early days of the Republic involves making the strongest possible case for your chosen candidate and either ignoring or criticizing the opposition. The second approach presents the good and the bad points of all candidates and then, on the basis of the points made, concludes that one of the candidates is the best. On occasion an editorial will conclude that one candidate is not significantly better than the others.

In its pure form, the first approach is not found as often in U.S. newspapers as it was in the past. Papers are not so partisan as they used to be, and editors recognize that readers who do not agree wholly with an editorial are likely to resent having an endorsement rammed down their throats. Yet Professor Peter Clarke of the University of Michigan reported that a study of congressional endorsements in 1978 found "that in half of the editorial endorsements, it was possible for the editorial writer to come out in support of the incumbent without even mentioning the challenger's name." Clarke concluded that many of these editorials were "crafted, it would seem, by an extremely adolescent mind." Most of the contents of these editorials, Clarke found, discussed the campaign as an event: "The competence of the campaign that the candidate was waging, the adequacy of funds he or she had raised or how good were the TV spots—if they were using TV spots—or billboards, or what have you?" The major portions of editorials endorsing incumbents described the incumbents' experience, while that of editorials endorsing challengers described the candidates' personal characteristics. Only a rare editorial referred to issues.

Editors interviewed by Clarke's researchers acknowledged that the candidates tried to emphasize issues, but these editors said they didn't think that voters were interested in issues or that the issues would affect the outcome of the election. "And that," said Clarke, "spells, in my mind, a giant self-fulfilling prophecy. If *you* believe this stuff doesn't make any difference, and you don't write about it, what is the very likely outcome? It ain't gonna make any difference! People are not going to know about it."[40]

Clarke's team uncovered another embarrassing fact: Many of the congressional members reported that they were never interviewed by editorial writers before being endorsed. Presumably their challengers were not interviewed either. Clarke found that, of the 70 percent of the newspapers that endorsed candidates for Congress, 90 percent backed the incumbent. All this suggests that editorial writers are not doing a responsible job of being watchdogs of members of Congress for their papers or their readership.

These failings are not limited to congressional races. In studying seven major California daily newspapers during the early presidential primaries of 1980, I found almost no editorial comment on the issues. For the most part papers were content to comment on the results of a just concluded primary and to speculate on the outcome of the next one. With a few exceptions, the papers seemed to have no political policies of their own against which to measure the candidates.[41]

Most of the editorials that I have selected to illustrate different types of endorsements show a greater concentration on the issues. The first set of editorials that follows is from the 1978 race between Edmund G. Brown Jr. and Evelle Younger for governor of California. The second set involves a ballot proposition, No. 7, which strengthened the death penalty.

CANDIDATE ENDORSEMENTS

In this section we will look at six types of candidate endorsements. In decreasing order of firmness of endorsement they are: our candidate only, mostly our candidate, mostly the other candidate, both candidates, "given the choices" and no recommendation.

Our Candidate Only

Talking about only one candidate in an editorial is probably not as prevalent a practice as it was when newspapers attempted primarily to satisfy a highly partisan readership. With the subscribers of most newspapers now inclined toward a wide spectrum of political views, most endorsement writers recognize that they should at least acknowledge all of the candidates for the position that is being discussed. But there may be occasions in which this one-sided editorial is appropriate—perhaps when one candidate stands far above any of the others, perhaps when one of the candidates is the main issue of the campaign. For some newspapers in the 1978 California race for governor, the latter seems to have been the case. Papers that supported the incumbent, Brown, and those that opposed him considered his personality and his term in office as their principal concerns.

"Our Support for Gov. Brown," from the *Ventura Star-Free Press,* provides an example of this type of editorial. The editorial opens with the statement that Brown seems to be ahead and that the writer agrees with the inclinations of the voters. Then begins a section, praising Brown's record, that accounts for two-thirds of the editorial. Only in the last third does the writer acknowledge, in five short paragraphs, that Brown had some weaknesses. Finally, the writer concludes with a restatement of firm support. Brown's opponent is never mentioned. The writer may have ignored Younger because, in addition to seeing Brown as the main issue, he or she knew that Brown was running far ahead of his opponent. When the election came, Younger received only 37 percent of the vote. He did, however, have supporters and a record of public service, so even the firmest Brown supporters must have wondered why editorial attention was

Our Support for Gov. Brown

AS THE RACE for governor comes down to the wire, the polls indicate that California voters are strongly leaning toward returning Jerry Brown to office for another four years. We think that choice will be the right one.

Four years ago we were so unenthusiastic about the Brown candidacy that we endorsed his Republican opponent, Houston Flournoy. But Gov. Brown's term in office has been sufficiently satisfactory, and his course for the immediate future of California appears so sound, that the Star-Free Press now urges his re-election without reservation.

Gov. Brown is a politician of a different stripe. And also, as almost everyone agrees, he is an intelligent, perceptive, articulate and fair-minded man who has the people's welfare uppermost in mind.

And his crystal ball is a reliable one: it seldom fails him.

When he took office in 1975, he told Californians that he was about to establish an "era of limits" in which they would be expected to provide more for themselves while the state was providing less.

He has veered from that course at times, but not greatly.

Apparent public backing for the course he mandated the state to follow almost four years ago was demonstrated this year when California voters overwhelmingly approved the Prop. 13 property tax cutback measure.

It's true that Gov. Brown was a vigorous opponent of Prop. 13 prior to its passage. But since it became law, he has done a masterful—and seemingly enthusiastic—job of making it work without completely disrupting local government in California.

Gov. Brown has been an aggressive governor in his quest for the solutions to many of California's long-standing major problems. Not all of his efforts have met with universal acclaim, but he certainly must be given a great big "E" for effort.

In agriculture, in ecology, in the state's economic development and job opportunities, and in warring against fiscal irresponsibility, Gov. Brown has set a most commendable pace. Whenever he has approached a big issue, the governor has done so with personal dedication and vigor—and the results have been generally good.

Weaknesses? Of course, Gov. Brown has them, but what major officeholder doesn't who works at his job the way he should?

A good number of Gov. Brown's appointments have been questionable, and he has not moved promptly to replace them.

He was slow to establish proper rapport with the legislature—but that failing has now been overcome.

He let too many minor but nevertheless important chores of office, such as judicial appointments, dangle for too long without acting on them.

And his apparent desire to become president of the U.S. raises wonder whether he'll devote his primary attention prior to the 1980 national election to Sacramento or Washington.

But by and large, Jerry Brown has been a good governor and his first-term experience gives promise that his second-term performance as the state's chief executive can be even better in terms of fulfillment of the state's long-term goals and aspirations. On the record and on the promise, we firmly support his re-election Nov. 7.

Ventura County (Calif.) *Star-Free Press*

limited to one candidate. Most readers, if they give the matter much thought, probably expect editorials at least to mention all the candidates.

Mostly Our Candidate

Not too far removed from the single-candidate editorial is one that concentrates on the favored candidate but acknowledges the presence of opponents, at least the major ones. The three McClatchy newspapers, the *Bee*s of Sacramento, Modesto and Fresno, published an identical, lengthy editorial talking mostly about Brown. Positive for the most part, it begins with the opening sentence that flatly declares: "We endorse Jerry Brown. . . ." The editorial deals extensively with issues and the Brown personality. Younger is mentioned once in the opening paragraph, and further reference to him is relegated only to a single long paragraph just before a strong conclusion for Brown. Even that paragraph is used to strengthen the case for Brown by disparaging Younger's record and campaign. "For Governor: Edmund G. Brown Jr." is reprinted here.

For Governor: Edmund G. Brown Jr.

We endorse Jerry Brown for re-election for the best of reasons: He has been a good governor. While he has been slow to act on certain pressing problems during his first term in office, he has distinguished himself as an innovative, sometimes unconventional, but consistently industrious chief executive. What makes the choice particularly easy in this election is the inadequate alternative represented by his Republican opponent, Attorney General Evelle Younger.

If one looks at the record in the broadest terms, it's clear that Brown has endowed state government with a rare freshness and vitality. He has imbued it with that sense of the common good which should be basic in every public official. Behind the buzz words he likes to use—"Small Is Beautiful," "Era of Limits," and all the rest—there is an impressive record of getting things done in a restless political period dominated by the impact of Proposition 13.

More specifically:

In his first year, the young governor—he's now 40—presided over marathon negotiations which finally produced the landmark law creating the state Agricultural Labor Relations Board and the first machinery of its kind to deal with collective bargaining for farm workers. The law broke new ground in attempting to bring order out of strife between unions and employers in the state's multibillion-dollar agricultural industry. The board had serious difficulties at the outset and not everyone has accepted its existence. But the important fact today is that the law is working.

Equally important, Brown succeeded in two other politically hazardous areas amidst the most bitter of controversies. One was enactment of some of the strictest environmental controls in the country, crowned by the legislation to protect the state's coastal zone from overdevelopment. The other was the building of an energy program that, with its de-emphasis of nuclear power and its emphasis on alternative sources of energy, has become a national model. As part of that search for new sources, Brown proposed and last year signed a bill giving California the largest tax incentive anywhere in America for home solar installations.

The governor has come under frequent attack by some business leaders who complain his policies on energy and other matters have polluted the business climate in California. Yet the Wall Street Journal recently reported the state's economy has flourished. Both employment gains and corporation profits have exceeded the national average. The Journal also cited Brown's fiscal conservatism which prompted him to veto $1.7 billion in proposed spending during his first three years.

Brown silenced his detractors in another field when he signed bills increasing prison sentences for 40 crimes of violence, including rape, and requiring persons convicted of multiple violent crimes to be incarcerated for longer terms. If he has been "soft on crime," it has escaped the California Peace Officers Research Association which hailed his support of anti-crime legislation in endorsing his re-election.

Brown's record has not been perfect. He was derelict in his failure to act promptly to improve conditions in the state's mental hospitals early in his administration and in tolerating conditions approaching turmoil in the state Health and Welfare Agency. Although he did move eventually to augment the hospital budget and to reorganize the health department, his support of the mental health program continues to be parsimonious and inadequate.

On the positive side, Brown can be credited with working out an acceptable formula to equalize tax support of public schools, eliminating discriminatory lending practices by financial institutions in redlining certain neighborhoods, pushing so-called lifeline utility rates to help people of modest means, improving the court system and hiring people who normally are left out of the governmental process. He has appointed more members of minority groups and more women to high government jobs than any previous governor.

Although Brown opposed Proposition 13, he set out to make it work and to assist local government over the rough spots with funds from the state's multibillion-dollar surplus. The voters, he says, made it abundantly clear they wanted profound changes in the way state and local governments operate. As governor, he responded by trying to implement the initiative measure as effectively as possible.

Brown does not hesitate to acknowledge, as he has in television commercials, that he makes mistakes and changes his mind when necessary. The worst thing, he says, is to "get stuck in a position and just blindly keep banging your head against the wall."

Viewed against the performance and platform of his opponent, Attorney General Evelle Younger, Brown's record becomes even more compelling. Younger has shown himself to be a man of serious liabilities, a person of shifting convictions and insecure positions whose performance in two terms as the state's chief law enforcement officer cannot be termed auspicious. After six weeks of campaigning, moreover, Younger's position and convictions are even more uncertain than they were before the campaign started. He advocates the construction of 50 nuclear power plants, but doesn't say where he would put them or how he would deal with the unresolved problems of waste disposal. He issues irresponsible charges against the state Supreme Court, then acknowledges that he doesn't have the facts to support them. He claims credit as an effective state law enforcement officer but fails either to investigate or explain how his own office withheld information from a grand jury investigating a political friend.

Jerry Brown once told a political rally that he offers no glib promises, no instant solutions. "I'm not a Santa Claus with a bag of tricks," he said. "I don't want to give you the idea it's just a lot of cotton candy—elect me and all your problems will be over." But on the basis of what he stands for and what he knows he is capable of doing, he is without question the superior candidate.

Sacramento Bee
(Also *Modesto Bee* and *Fresno Bee*)

This type of editorial may be appropriate when, as in this case, one candidate has dominated the election, as Brown did. If the opposing candidate is generally regarded as being out of the race, perhaps an argument can be made for bringing that candidate in only at the end of the editorial and then only to make further points for the preferred office seeker. If this imbalance is perceived by voters as accurately reflecting the election campaign, the mostly-our-candidate editorial will probably be viewed as fair. If, however, it is seen as unfair and as a put-down of the other candidate, the editorial may lose its effectiveness in persuading voters who may be undecided about their voting preferences. In any case, both of these first two editorials are likely to be most effective in reinforcing the opinions of voters who are already inclined toward the favored candidate. In a race in which that candidate is running ahead, encouraging supporters is probably the best strategy. These editorials might make less political sense if the race were close or many voters were undecided.

Mostly the Other Candidate

Brown was so much the issue in that election that even editorials supporting Younger dealt mostly with Brown. In "Younger for Governor," the *Desert Sun* of Palm Springs declared its support for Younger in the third paragraph, then analyzed Brown's record until the final four short paragraphs. This editorial may be appropriate when the candidate you oppose is running for re-election and has accumulated a controversial record. Most of the votes are apt to be cast on the basis of being for or against the incumbent. If you think he or she should not be elected, then the best strategy is to make a case in opposition. This type of editorial may not sway voters who are committed to the front-runner, but it may speak effectively to those who are undecided and it may encourage weak supporters of your candidate not to backslide.

Younger for Governor

As California voters prepare to mark their ballot choices in the Nov. 7 gubernatorial election, many will no doubt react to the soaring rhetoric, the assorted hyperbole and the torrent of claims and disclaims typical of the closing days of a major campaign.

Some, however, will take a closer look at the record and make up their minds without undue emotion or misguided prejudice.

And that record clearly shows Atty. Gen. Evelle Younger should replace Jerry Brown as governor of California.

From the earliest days of his administration, Brown has emphasized symbolism instead of action on key issues while taking what we believe to be the wrong position on several important questions directly affecting the citizens of California.

In a sweeping attempt to erode and diminish a lifestyle enjoyed or aspired to by most Californians, he urged us to "lower our expectations." There is little hard evidence that Brown has abandoned such a self-denying philosophy. We suspect, in fact, that such negative exhortations have only been muted until after the election results are in.

In specific actions, the governor has:

—Pushed through a farm labor law that virtually all farmers find distasteful because of its built-in prejudices against them.

—Established an anti-business attitude in his administration that led to the Dow Chemical Co. decision not to build a major plant in the state.

—Taken a strong stand against building nuclear power plants, including a major facility in Riverside County, despite factual showings that no alternate sources of energy will be available when needed.

—Vetoed a capital punishment measure despite the fact that some two-thirds of California's voters endorsed this effort to control crime.

—Confused the public about the size of the state surplus, with the result that statewide anti-Proposition 13 efforts were based on false and misleading assumptions.

And once Prop. 13 was passed, he turned 180 degrees to imply he had endorsed it all along. This was despite recorded pre-primary election statements that Prop. 13 was a "tax trap" and should be defeated.

Finally, the governor has demonstrated precious little administrative ability. Many vacancies still exist on boards and commissions, and those who have been appointed in many cases have proved incapable of effective management or simply incompetent. For example, he allowed the state Health Department to drift with poor leadership for several years in the face of increasing allegation of scandals in mental hospitals and prepaid health programs.

On the other hand, Evelle Younger has consistently shown himself as a skilled manager of a major state department while continually demonstrating a clear awareness of the economic, social and political needs of the state.

His office has developed effective legal programs in environmental protection, in consumer protection and in combating organized crime.

He didn't wait until after the election to voice support for Proposition 13, and he has consistently offered a program of effective tax relief to California taxpayers.

Simply on their respective records, and ignoring the emotion, the symbolism and the media hype conjured by the governor, we urge the election of Evelle Younger as governor of California.

Desert Sun (Palm Springs, Calif.)

Both Candidates

In the 1978 California election editorials that extensively discussed both major candidates tended to be pro-Younger endorsements. In "The Governor's Race" (p. 242–243) the *San Diego Union* acknowledged that Younger's campaign was not going well, but the paper approved of some of Younger's concerns about Brown and evaluated the incumbent's record. After looking at the anti-Brown side, the editorial returned to Younger to make some reasonably strong points in his favor.

This editorial might be regarded as close to the standard endorsement, in which the writer looks at both candidates, examining the pros and cons (not necessarily with the same weight) and concluding for the favored person. This type of editorial should help reinforce voters inclined toward the unendorsed candidate and should stand at least a chance of influencing voters who are undecided or not well informed. These voters may be especially responsive to an editorial that seems to be balanced in its judgment of the candidates. An editorial that treats the candidates fairly, yet reaches a firm conclusion, may be persuasive with the undecided and uninformed. Of course, these readers are usually among those least likely to vote.

The Governor's Race

The striking feature of the California election campaign this year is the emergence of Gov. Edmund Brown, Jr., as the political sorcerer of our generation. If the polls are correct, he has led a majority of voters into one of the pitfalls of democracy—into equating political style with policy substance; into believing the best campaigner would be the best fitted to govern. This, of course, is fallacious. Historically, some of our best office-holders have been ineffective campaigners.

By contrast, Evelle Younger's lackluster campaign has helped create a widespread illusion that Gov. Brown is an effective governor. The steady, sensible qualities, which have unfailingly won the overwhelming endorsement of voters in Mr. Younger's previous elections as district attorney of Los Angeles County and Attorney General of California, appear to have deserted him. His campaign is clumsy and pedestrian against the fancy footwork of the fastest political operator, bar none, in California history.

[The net result thus far is an obscuring of the fact that Gov. Brown himself is the principal issue.

[The governor's record in office, which he often skillfully obfuscates, is what this campaign should be about and what Californians should be voting on.]

Unfortunately, the campaign has degenerated at times into criticisms of Gov. Brown's lifestyle and denunciations of Mr. Younger's pensions and the bathroom in the attorney general's office.

Where Mr. Younger draws some blood is with his description of Jerry Brown as the worst governor of California in modern times. [However, this slash may not be as bad as it appears to be considering the high caliber of California governors from Earl Warren on.]

But Mr. Younger has a point; the overall impact of the Brown administration appears to be essentially negative. [The governor's failure of leadership was a major factor in the loss of a $500 million Dow Chemical plant that would have employed 1,000 persons and fattened the state's tax revenues.

[Dow's bitter experience and Gov. Brown's apathy toward new industry created a damaging anti-business image. A Dun and Bradstreet survey found California's business climate to be the worst in the West and 47th of the 48 contiguous states.

[Sobered by this loss and the public outcry it generated, and sensitive to the need for more payrolls to offset California's soaring unemployment rate, Mr. Brown, to his credit, set out to woo businessmen and create a more favorable economic environment. And California's dynamism has reversed earlier adverse trends; today the economy is healthy.]

Meanwhile, the governor substituted an anti-energy crusade for his abandoned anti-business posture. [Mr. Brown almost single-handedly thwarted the $2.5 billion Sundesert nuclear power project after a consortium of utility companies, including San Diego Gas & Electric, had invested more than $80 million in planning and groping through the red tape of various governmental agencies.

[While extinguishing a power source that would have yielded untold millions in taxes and provided for Southern California's expanding energy requirements during the 1980s, Gov. Brown and his appointees suddenly lowered their environmental concerns and pushed for smoke-polluting coal plants. Along with solar and geothermal power development, the Sacramento vision foresaw electricity from windmills on the hills, burning wood chips, and importing energy from Mexico.

["I like to rattle the cage," the governor said. Just so.]

While he was mobilizing his forces against nuclear energy, Gov. Brown ignored the tax revolution brewing all across the state and thus confirmed his unflattering description as a leader who can deal with only one issue at a time.

Finally, the governor sought to defuse the mounting property tax protest by offering a few crumbs from the multi-billion dollar surplus piling up in the state treasury, the extent of which was concealed from the taxpayers.

[In the end, Mr. Brown called for a mere $480 million in homeowner and renter relief at a time when the $7 billion Jarvis-Gann steamroller was already moving. But the Brown tax proposal was so complicated and so tilted against middle and higher incomes that even the Democratic-dominated Legislature refused in September, 1977, to pass it.

[What followed, as they say, is history. The passage of Proposition 13 was a convulsive fiscal revolution in California with many negative side effects which are still not fully appreciated.]

Gov. Brown was to the California tax revolution what King George III was to the American Revolution; his failure of leadership was primarily responsible for it. [Instead of leading the state in tax relief and reform, as Gov. Reagan attempted to do with Proposition 1 some years ago,] Gov. Brown came on the tax scene too late with too little.

Nevertheless, consummate politician that he is, the governor accepted the mandate of the electorate and moved decisively to implement Proposition 13's far-reaching provisions, displaying surprising leadership in the bargain. His amazing success at seizing this issue and gulling so many Californians into believing he is responsible for their property tax relief is sorcery indeed.

So much for Mr. Brown's record as governor of this state. It is reason enough why Californians should not vote for him to be their governor for the next four years.

Fortunately, there is another good reason, and that's Evelle Younger, [who offers four full years in the governor's office without the distractions of higher political ambition.] He offers the same steady competence which Californians have come to appreciate in their attorney general for almost a decade. That is precisely what is needed at the helm in Sacramento—a steady hand, not one that will be forever rattling the cages.

[Those who trouble to go beyond Mr. Younger's staid statements will find reassurance that the surplus tax revenues still piling up in the state's treasury as fast as ever would be cut back and shared more forthrightly with the taxpayers. They will find reassurance about meeting energy needs, including the use of nuclear power, about creating more jobs and housing for California's growing population. It's all there.]

We repeat, Mr. Younger is far superior to his packaging; beyond the dust of his dreary campaign, we can see him as a good governor.

We urge our readers to mark their ballots next Tuesday for Evelle Younger and his running mate, Mike Curb.

San Diego Union

How the tone of an editorial can be changed through the addition or omission of material is dramatically illustrated in a condensed version of the *Union* editorial that appeared in the *Daily Breeze* of Torrance. (Both are Copley papers.) The *Union* editorial is reproduced here, with brackets indicating the sections omitted in the *Daily Breeze*. The omissions convert a fairly analytical editorial into a much stronger assault on Brown and a less detailed case for Younger. The same words are used, but the overall tone of the shorter version is much more strident and partisan. It probably proved to be less persuasive with the undecided than the editorial in the *Union*.

Given the Choices

Sometimes a writer, after looking at opposing candidates, will conclude that none of them is a clear standout but that under the circumstances, and given the choices, one is better than the others. That is the conclusion in "The Race for Governor," reprinted here in an abbreviated version. (The original was about twice this length. The omitted portions expressed much the same lack of enthusiasm for both candidates as does the editorial reprinted here.) This type of editorial could strengthen the resolve of similarly unenthused voters to stick to the endorsed candidate if they are already inclined to do so. The editorial might appeal to the undecided, who also have trouble making up their minds. It might not prove as effective with the uninformed, since the weak stand is unlikely to spur their interest to any great degree in the contest at hand. Such an editorial certainly will not make much difference in the preferences of staunch supporters of the unendorsed candidate.

The Race for Governor

The race for governor is one of the most difficult decisions facing the voters of California on the candidate portion of the state ballot in the Nov. 7 election. Pitting Democratic incumbent Gov. Jerry Brown against Republican challenger Evelle Younger, the contest is one which finds the voters of neither party very well satisfied with their nominee.

For example, Gov. Brown has met with a great deal of static from Democratic power groups during his term, partly because he has declined to pay political homage to party tradition and bigwigs but more so because he has seen fit to take tough fiscal stands, such as freezing bureaucratic and educational salaries, reducing the state payroll and so forth.

Younger has found himself out of favor with many conservative GOP voters because of his multiple generous personal pensions, because of the growth of his attorney general's office while other state agencies were cutting back, because of his lethargic response to Prop. 13's message and popularity, and so forth.

The Enterprise-Record has kept a careful watch on Brown and Younger, over their years in public service and especially during this election year. And, somewhat to our surprise, we feel compelled to endorse the re-election candidacy of Gov. Brown. . . .

. . . perhaps it was Gov. Brown's unhesitating and full-speed response to Prop. 13 that made him stand out. While most other public officials—even on the local level and especially in the Legislature—were holding back, Brown frankly admitted that he had misjudged Prop. 13 and then energetically took over the key leadership role in trying to make it work as the voters had demanded. Younger, meanwhile, maintained a "finger in the wind" posture on Prop. 13 all the way and permitted Brown to completely steal the issue from him. Younger has never seemed to have any special feeling for or insight into the needs and well-being of the people. During most of his long public career, he has been a man isolated in officialdom and insulated against real contact with and interest in the citizenry. He is more a governmental agent than a public service leader.

In other words, we believe the voters face a strange and difficult choice in this year's gubernatorial contest. Many have reasons why they would vote against Gov. Brown if they had an alternative choice with an inspiring record and a good potential for growth. But Evelle Younger does not stand as such an alternative choice.

Under such circumstances—and based on the hope and prayer that Gov. Brown will continue to develop more along the lines of imaginative conservatism and prompt response to the public will—we endorse the re-election candidacy of Gov. Brown.

Chico (Calif.) *Enterprise-Record*

No Recommendation

Once in a while an editorial will examine two candidates and conclude that it doesn't make much difference who wins. It may be that both candidates are acceptable or that neither is. After not finding much substance to either candidate, the Long Beach *Independent Press-Telegram* concluded: "The choice between Brown and Younger is not one in which we feel comfortable making a recommendation, and we make none. But the prospect for California, no matter who is elected, is not dreary. The state will prosper, and government will function. But the leadership we all desire will have to wait until the 1982 gubernatorial election." In an editorial entitled "Year of the Follower," reprinted here, the *Santa Barbara News-Press* considered each candidate at length and then tried to summarize the characteristics of the two candidates by quoting a supporter of each: Younger attempts to reflect the will of the people; Brown seeks to give voice to citizen unrest. In telling readers to "take your pick," the editorial was suggesting in effect that voters decide which type of individual they prefer for governor.

Year of the Follower

The contest for governor of California has a characteristic so dominating that it will be remembered well in political history: It is a race not between two leaders, but two followers. It will be up to the voters to decide on Nov. 7 whether Gov. Jerry Brown or Evelle Younger will be the better follower of majority political and economic thought.

It is not a reflection on either candidate, in this context, to call him a follower. Both men are proven experts at politics. Both can sense when the time is ripe for leading and when it is ripe for being led. Both have shrewdly calculated that this is the time to be led.

They are being led, of course, by the overwhelming expression of Californians that whoever sits in the capitol does so with a mandate to preside over the reduction of government. It would be hard to recall a time in modern history when the people themselves have taken over the direction of government with such unified force.

Which man, then, is better able to carry out the orders? Each has spent a portion of the campaign time, though not nearly

enough of it, talking about specifics. Neither has been completely convincing. Each apparently has hoped to keep plenty of flexibility for himself. Our policy is to make editorial endorsements in races where the choice is clear, but in this race the choice is not sufficiently clear-cut. We have two experienced men who seem to put somewhat equal value on majority aims. Each voter can, in good conscience, make his selection based on his private political feelings.

What we can do here is reflect on the backgrounds and careers of Jerry Brown and Evelle Younger in the hope of adding some perspective to a campaign that has jumped, back and forth, between the frivolous and the serious.

Younger is more the traditional successful political figure. Brown has made a success of being unconventional. Paradoxically, Brown comes from a political background and Younger does not. Younger, in a long career in public office, has earned a reputation as a good administrator, but not a good innovator. Brown is noted for being an innovator, but not a good administrator.

Younger has always been a low-profile politician, not given to public performances and pronouncements. Brown has been a high-profile politician, highly articulate with his ideas and views.

Most of Younger's experience has been in law, especially in prosecution. He started his career as city attorney for Pasadena in 1950, served as district attorney for Los Angeles County at the time of the Watts riots, and has been state attorney general for eight years. He has earned a reputation for being tough on crime.

Brown's personal history is well-known, his Jesuit days, his interest in philosophy, his experience as secretary of state, his four years as governor, his entrance in the national political arena.

Brown has shown attention to the racial and cultural minorities notably by appointing many from these groups to state offices. Younger as attorney general has been less attentive to this factor, though he has a record of choosing able assistants.

In performance, Brown likes to surprise people with fresh thoughts. An aide described his maxim this way: "The first rule of politics is to be different." Younger is far more cautious and private with his thoughts. A former associate called him "a virtuoso at walking between raindrops."

But which of the two, in this year when the candidates are practicing followship, is the more sensitive to the people's hopes?

Mike Curb, the Republican candidate for lieutenant governor, said of Younger: "Evelle wants to give the people exactly what they want. He's a reflection of what he understands to be their will."

John Pincus, who resigned from Brown's state Board of Education, said of Brown: "His greatest political strength is as a critical interpreter, who perceives and gives voice to citizens' unrest."

Take your pick.

Santa Barbara (Calif.) *News-Press*

It is difficult to speculate on the effect of such an editorial, as it depends on the circumstances. If a newspaper's past endorsement pattern suggests that it could be expected to back one of the candidates, a no-recommendation editorial is more likely to hurt that candidate than the one whose endorsement had not been expected. Study of election results suggests that endorsements that deviate from a newspaper's traditional position are perceived as having more effect on voters than endorsements that are anticipated. A non-endorsement that does not stand in contrast with past policy may have little or no effect on an election, though it may add to existing confusion and perhaps to voter apathy and a bigger stay-at-home bloc.

No doubt some of these editorials convinced some readers to follow the editors' advice—or at least encouraged readers to vote their inclinations. But, when overall local election percentages in the circulation areas of 30 California daily papers, including those cited here, were compared with statewide election percentages for Brown and Younger, I could find no significant differences. You might anticipate that circulation areas in which Brown was endorsed might, overall, show at least a few extra percentage points for Brown over the statewide average and a similar extra margin for Younger in areas in which he was endorsed. This was not the case. How did this race differ from the 1966 election, in which endorsements apparently made a difference when Ronald Reagan defeated incumbent Edmund G. Brown Sr. (Jerry Brown's father)? One factor might be that the earlier race was a close and controversial one, and voters were looking for advice on making a hard choice. The 1978 election, on the other hand, was lackluster and the outcome never in doubt. Voters may have made up their minds well before newspapers began endorsing the candidates.

Ballot Issues

Newspapers probably perform a greater service to readers in helping them decide on a ballot issue than in facilitating their choice of a candidate. Voters can pick candidates on the basis of image, party label or public record, and they can get at least a partial impression of a candidate on television. But ballot measures are complex, often too complex for television analysis. In addition, ballot measures are usually not exciting, and they often involve obscure issues that voters have not thought much about before. On the other hand, these measures may involve thoroughly and widely debated issues that force voters to wade through a morass of conflicting arguments from different sides. The proposition about which I provide sample editorials—No. 7, concerning the strengthening of the death penalty—is such a proposition. Newspaper editorials apparently had more effect on the vote on this proposition than on any state race or issue in California in 1978—a little more than 3 percent. Editorials had slightly more effect on the losing "no" side of the issue than on the "yes" side. The measure carried with 70 percent approval. As in the case of Carter and Anderson in 1980, editorials opposing Proposition 7 may have served to encourage voters to hold to their inclinations to vote "no" in spite of being inundated by political waters flowing in the other direction.

APPEAL TO EMOTION In spite of the potentially emotional nature of Proposition 7, none of the editorials reprinted here can be said to have appealed substantially to the emotions of readers. However, a Copley group editorial, "Yes on Proposition 7" (p. 248), published in the *San Diego Union* and the *Daily Breeze* of Torrance, tossed in the name of Charles Manson, convicted mass killer in the Sharon Tate case, a reference that was no doubt intended to conjure up the horrors of the murders. But most of the rest of the editorial is free from emotion-inciting words. An editorial in similar vein, not reproduced here, attempted to stir readers with the statement that a person convicted of second-degree murder could become eligible for parole after four years. This editorial, from the *San Bernardino Sun,* then devotes an entire paragraph to a list of specific crimes that would require the death penalty or life imprisonment under Proposition 7.

Yes on Proposition 7

The 2–1 vote for a death penalty initiative in 1972 still stands as the clearest evidence that a majority of Californians favor capital punishment. The initiative now before voters as Proposition 7 does not raise that fundamental issue again. It simply refines and strengthens the death penalty statute which the Legislature passed over Gov. Brown's veto last year.

Why is it necessary? The Legislature, faced with high emotion and divergence of opinion within its own ranks, passed a bill limiting capital punishment to a relatively narrow list of types of murder. A Charles Manson, for instance, would not face the death penalty under the legislative statute even though he masterminded an especially brutal series of killings.

Proposition 7's primary effect is to expand from 11 to 26 the specific circumstances of first-degree murder in which capital punishment or life imprisonment without possibility of parole can be exacted.

The proposition represents a well-reasoned attempt to make the death penalty a credible threat of punishment for the full range of offenses which traditionally have been considered capital crimes. In this it does no more than carry out the implicit intention of the 1972 capital punishment initiative.

Some critics of Proposition 7 say the Legislature's statute was drafted carefully to comply with Supreme Court decisions on the death penalty, and that the new language in the initiative might be more vulnerable to a constitutional challenge.

Lawyers experienced in capital punishment appeals tell us they see no obvious constitutional flaws in Proposition 7, and point out that a severability clause would protect the statute as a whole if one part of it were declared unconstitutional.

Society needs to erect the best defense it can against crimes of cold-blooded murder. We recommend a Yes vote on Proposition 7.

San Diego (Calif.) *Union*
(also *Daily Breeze,* Torrance)
Reprinted by permission, the *San Diego Union*

While the editorials themselves are relatively free from appeals to emotion, they appeared in a campaign in which a large number of voters were distressed over rising crime rates and increasing threats to their own safety. So even a calmly written, largely factual editorial may have the effect, perhaps unintended, of stirring the fears of readers and confirming their desire to do something, anything, to express their frustrations. This type of issue poses a severe problem for writers who, while perhaps sympathetic with the purposes of the proposal, see it as an ineffective, unwise or even dangerous measure. How do you get readers to set aside their emotions long enough to listen to rational arguments, or at least arguments the editorial writer thinks are rational?

CONFUSING PROPOSAL A common and often effective argument with such an issue is to discuss the ballot measure's confusing or technically deficient nature. The actual merits of the issue may not be addressed. This approach may be appropriate if the writer knows that an issue, such as the death penalty, is popular with the public and that the only chance of winning votes against it is to convince readers that it would not accomplish its intended purpose. The *Oakland*

Tribune, in its editorial "We Oppose Proposition 7," used this approach to argue that the proposal was poorly written, that it might be worse than current law in standing up to court challenges and that the public deserved a better law on the subject.

We Oppose Proposition 7

The experts tell us the public is too stupid to understand Prop. 7, the expanded death penalty measure. We don't believe that.

The measure is complicated—so complicated that if you want a death penalty, you should vote against Prop. 7.

That's because in attempting to give the death penalty to almost anyone convicted of first-degree murder, Prop. 7 raises more legal questions than it answers.

There's no doubt that Californians want a strict death penalty law. Every poll and survey shows that. The Tribune favors a stricter death penalty, too. But Prop. 7 is not the way to get one.

For one thing, the state already has a death penalty law. That law was carefully drafted so it would stand up to a court test.

But Prop. 7 would throw all that hard work out the window. It's picked up all the odds and ends left out of the present law in trying to appear "tougher." Instead, it would just be more confusing.

Legal authorities doubt its validity.

William O'Malley, district attorney for Contra Costa County, says he supports the expanded death penalty in principle. "But the court has said laws must be interpreted strictly. Prop. 7 is too broad to stand a court test. It tries to cover all the bases and that's where the trouble is."

Lowell Jensen, Alameda County's district attorney, had a similar response: "Prop. 7 is just not as good as the 1977 death penalty law because it's more vulnerable to legal attack."

Even so, Jensen says he would like to see Prop. 7 pass because it would prove to the Legislature that the public wants a tougher death penalty law.

But the public already has made it clear that it wants a strict death penalty law. People don't have to vote for a bad law to get their message across.

Prop. 7 is so poorly written that if the courts throw out some parts, such as changes in jury procedure, some legal experts say the entire law would then be invalid. California could be left with no death penalty at all.

The public has a right to be heard on an expanded death penalty, but it deserves a law that's more coherent and carefully worded than Prop. 7.

The current law, which is still considered one of the toughest in the country, has a much better chance of passing a court test.

The Tribune recommends voting against Prop. 7.

With an issue as important as the death penalty, the public shouldn't say yes to any law that comes along.

Oakland (Calif.) *Tribune*

SOUND CONCEPT, BUT . . . Sometimes a newspaper will take the tack that the general idea of a proposal is a good one but that the specific proposal is less than adequate. In "Murder Law Tough Enough Now" (p. 250) the *Palo Alto Times* points out that it has supported the death penalty in the past and does so now. It then argues that the effect of the proposal would not be felt in the area in which the need is the greatest—administering the death penalty quickly and uniformly.

Murder Law Tough Enough Now

The state's death penalty law always is an emotional and controversial issue, so Proposition 7 on the Nov. 7 ballot, which would toughen the murder penalties, should be studied with care and voted on with thought.

The Times recommends a "No" vote.

This newspaper has supported the death penalty in the past and still does. However, California already has one of the toughest death penalties in the nation—one carefully drafted by the State Legislature in 1977 with an eye to satisfying all the tests of constitutionality. The problem is not that the law is weak, but that its deterrent effect is weakened because the death penalty is not administered quickly or uniformly.

Its application is unpredictable, but it can work with determined judges and strong law enforcement. If a person knew beyond doubt that he would be put to death for committing a murder in any of the six presently specified categories of special circumstances, which cover vast areas, he might change his mind about killing. As it is, chances of delay in courts, a lifetime on death row, or even the possibility of parole, outweigh the specter of death.

Proposition 7 would add more special circumstances categories to the list of those calling for the death penalty, and extend the potential penalties to persons involved in the crime other than the actual murderer. It would change and lengthen the minimum sentence for first-degree murder and increase the penalty for second-degree murder.

The ballot argument in favor of Proposition 7, which is an initiative statute being pushed by State Sen. John V. Briggs of Fullerton, is a sensationalized piece of drivel. It toys with the emotions and prevents a voter from making an educated, rational decision. However, the substance and not the rhetoric is the key issue, and it deserves serious consideration.

One major problem with Proposition 7 is that it could leave juries quite confused. It brings in complicated new provisions about aggravating and mitigating factors and when they do and do not apply. It also has at least one ill-defined special circumstance—"lying in wait."

Conceivably the passage of Proposition 7 could make it even more difficult for a jury to render a decision of guilty in a first-degree murder case than it is now. Assuredly it would expose a broader surface of the law to attack and possible overthrow in the appellate courts.

The problem is not that of creating a more stringent death penalty law, but of making the existing law effective. Bolstering the adequate existing law can best be done, we believe, by voting "No" on Proposition 7.

Palo Alto (Calif.) *Times*

TOTAL OPPOSITION Most of the editorials against Proposition 7 emphasized confusion or the inadequacy of the proposal, probably because editors realized that, with a strong public current running in favor of tougher law enforcement, a head-on attack on the proposal would likely convince only the already convinced minority of voters. But a few newspapers took the occasion to declare opposition to capital punishment on principle. The *Los Angeles Times* took this approach in its editorial "Death Penalty: No on 7." While the editorial also states that the death penalty has been neither swift nor certain, this pragmatic argument is mostly overshadowed by the strong moral tone of the editorial. Such an editorial, in terms of immediate effect, is likely only to strengthen those voters who already are inclined to oppose the proposition. Over a longer period, perhaps years, such a persistent stand on an issue might help create a community atmosphere in which a change in public opinion could occur.

Death Penalty: No on 7

We opposed the existing death-penalty law in California, and we oppose Proposition 7, which would nearly double the categories of first-degree murder for which death, or life imprisonment without parole, could be imposed.

Proposition 7 on the November ballot may be constitutionally infirm, and almost certainly will be attacked in the courts if it passes, but our opposition goes deeper than that. It is based on our conception of what a civilized society ought to be.

A civilized society should not use death as an instrument of punishment, but should, by example, try to reduce the savagery prevalent in this world.

We turn for guidance to the philosophers, not to the lawmakers.

Albert Camus, a resistance fighter against Hitler in the French underground, knew violence and experienced the cruelty that can be inflicted by man against man. He said of the death penalty, ''Justice of this kind is obviously no less shocking than the crime itself, and the new 'official' murder, far from offering redress for the offense committed against society, adds instead a second defilement to the first.''

We turn to history to support our view that the death penalty under present law or under the proposed revision would be carried out at random, as capital punishment has been imposed in the past, and that under these conditions justice becomes little more than the spin of a roulette wheel.

But what of the innocent, and their pleas to be protected from the predators? This can best be achieved by incarceration. Yet our society apparently feels a need for a death-penalty law on the books, but indicates a reluctance to inflict death on a broad scale. The National Crime Commission a few years ago reported, ''The most salient characteristic of capital punishment is that it is infrequently applied.'' Even if it is conceded that the death penalty is a deterrent (and the evidence is not conclusive either way), justice will be neither swift nor certain in capital cases. Our legal processes and society's ambivalence will guarantee that result.

This reality again persuades us that the death penalty is neither an effective deterrent to violence nor consistent with justice and the goals of a humane nation. We hope the day will come when death is not proposed as an answer to death.

Los Angeles Times

UNENDORSEMENTS Once in a while a newspaper will make an endorsement, then discover new information and rescind the endorsement before election day. Such a case was that of the *Rochester* (N.Y.) *Times-Union*. In 1969 this paper endorsed a 34-year-old Republican lawyer for city council, along with two other Republicans and two Democrats. Then, six days before the election, the lawyer began making charges of favoritism in city assessment of buildings owned by a prominent Democrat and one of the city's most influential business leaders. The two Rochester papers published a story investigating the charges three days before the election. An editorial on the same day concluded that the charges were groundless and called on the candidate to withdraw them. Instead, Calvin Mayne of the *Times-Union* reported, the candidate and his supporters ''counterattacked with accusations against the newspapers that attempted to show [the candidate] as a brave lone crusader fighting a big press monopoly.'' On Monday an editorial withdrew the paper's earlier endorsement. In the election, four of the five Republicans won. The lawyer was the one who lost. Mayne concluded that the unendorsement of the candidate should ''guarantee that no candidate of either party will ever try such a tactic so blatantly again.''[42]

On Oct. 26, 1978, the Long Beach, Calif., paper endorsed Republican Mike Curb for lieutenant governor over the incumbent, Mervyn Dymally. Then, two days before the election, in an editorial entitled "Second Thoughts About Curb," the paper noted that Curb had cited newspaper articles as a source for his charges that Dymally was a "criminal" who would be indicted for "criminal wrongdoings." The editorial said: "No newspaper articles do any such things, nor could they. Curb's competence and good sense are clouded at best. The wholesomeness sweepstakes are now a dead heat." On the day before the election the paper's summary of endorsements showed "no recommendation" for lieutenant governor. This type of withdrawal of prior support cannot help but impress readers. At the very least it should help build a newspaper's credibility.

CONCLUSION

Following an election editors are likely to find themselves in as untenable a situation as before the election. If most of the candidates they have endorsed win, the editors and their newspapers are accused of controlling the election and influencing the election of the candidates of their choice. If more than a few of the endorsed candidates lose, the newspapers are perceived to have lost credibility. I have often had voters say to me on election night that the newspaper was, or was not, right in its *predictions*. Somehow these voters seem to think that a newspaper is calling a horse race—waiting to tie its endorsement to winners. While my paper might not seriously have considered endorsing a third-party candidate we knew could not come close to winning, I know that we did not hesitate to endorse obvious underdogs.

Credibility is the only thing a newspaper has to offer in its editorial endorsements. If a staff thinks that it can fairly and knowledgeably endorse one candidate over another, it should be able to do so in a credible manner. If, on the other hand, the staff does not know enough about the candidates or does not see one candidate as better than another or lacks the fortitude to risk the wrath of unhappy readers, it should not endorse. A major task of the editorial page is to comment on public issues. Under the American political system public issues come most directly before the voters in elections. The newspaper that sits out elections sits out a big part of the political process.

QUESTIONS AND EXERCISES

1. What do you think should be the role of the editorial page in an election? Should a newspaper endorse candidates?

2. Evaluate the reasons cited by *Newsday* when it established its non-endorsement policy. Then evaluate the reasons *Newsday* used to explain its return to endorsing. Which reasons are the most persuasive to you?

3. Evaluate the reason cited by the *Los Angeles Times* for endorsing candidates for lesser positions but not for president, senator or governor.

4. Do you think a presidential nominee has legitimate grounds for complaint when newspaper endorsements are lined up four or five to one against him? Why or why not?

5. Could you work on an editorial page that had "publishers' four-year itch"—a congenial editorial policy for three and a half years and then for six months a policy with which you did not agree?

6. Ask editors of newspapers in your area or state how editorial endorsements are determined on their papers. Who is involved in the decision making? Who has the last say if there is disagreement?

7. Ask editors to evaluate the comparative impact they think their editorials have on ballot issues vs. candidate races and on local vs. state and national races.

8. Have any of the papers in your area allowed dissenting editorial staff members to disagree in print with the papers' endorsements? If so, how were the dissents presented? How did the paper explain the presence of more than one opinion? Did publication of the dissent draw comment from readers in the letters column?

9. Find two or more editorials from different newspapers on the same ballot issue or candidate race. If possible, find one that makes comparisons before concluding and one that takes a purely one-sided approach. What type of reader is most likely to be influenced by each approach? For the particular race or issue involved, which editorial do you regard as more appropriate or more likely to influence readers. Why?

10. Rewrite an editorial that compares before concluding in a one-sided style. Then rewrite an editorial of the latter type in the style of the former. Which is easier to write?

—Douglass Marlette
Charlotte (N.C.) *Observer* for *The Masthead*

Letters to the Editor

If tails ever wag dogs, the letters column of a daily newspaper is a likely candidate for the job.
—*Peter G. Fradley*
Providence *(R.I.)* Journal-Bulletin[1]

Letters are about the only part of the editorial page that comes free. But in terms of time, effort and headaches, a good letters column is probably the most expensive part. It's quicker and easier for an editorial page person to knock out a couple of paragraphs of his or her own prose than to prepare a letter to the editor for print.

"Letters give life to an editorial page," Barry Bingham Sr. of the *Louisville (Ky.) Courier-Journal* said. "They also come near to beating the life out of the fellow who has to handle them. Many are illiterate. Others are long, rambling and inchoate. Still others are so abusive in tone that they recall the Turkish proverb, 'Letters written after dinner are read in Hell.' Some of the ones that come to us must be written in the fine frenzy of after-dinner dyspepsia." Then he added: "Letters are worth every bit of trouble they cause, however."[2]

WHY LETTERS?

Editorial page editors put up with—and encourage—letters for one reason: Letters help give readers a better feeling about the newspaper. Letters give readers as citizens one of the few chances they have to speak their minds. They also help create interest in the editorial page and increase readership.

Surveys consistently show that letters are among the best-read parts of the paper. Writing a letter to the newspaper assures the reader "that one small voice in the wilderness can get into print and achieve access to countless thousands of potentates and average citizens alike," Peter G. Fradley, letters editor of the *Providence* (R.I.) *Journal-Bulletin,* said.[3]

Letters give readers a chance to talk about what they want to talk about, especially important in one-newspaper towns with no built-in voice of opposition. Readers are not stuck with the editor's agenda; they have their own agendas. Bingham found, after studying seven papers for a critique session of NCEW, that readers were more likely to talk about state and local affairs and less about national and international than editorial writers were. Numbers and types of letters vary markedly from newspaper to newspaper, but even the largest and best letters column is still only a letters column. "Probably the greatest mistake that can be made about letters to the editor is to assume that they form an accurate barometer of public opinion," Bingham warned.[4] Readers who feel strongly opposed to an issue are more likely to write than are those who approve. Letters in the *Philadelphia Evening Bulletin* on one occasion ran three-to-one against a local proposition, but an opinion poll of the general population showed the same ratio in favor.[5]

Only about one in 10 Americans ever writes a letter to the editor. A study in 1978 of 269 persons who wrote letters to the *Des Moines* (Iowa) *Register and Tribune* found the so-called average American markedly underrepresented. The percentage of male letter writers tended to be higher than that of the overall population, and, in general, people who wrote letters to the editor tended to be older, better educated and better paid. They were more mobile, more likely to be Republican and more active in political affairs. They tended to spend more time reading newspapers and the letters column and relied less on television for their news than the average American. They were two-and-a-half times more likely to write against an editorial stand than to voice support and four times more likely to oppose another letter than to support it.[6]

Some readers, as well as some legal scholars, think that the public should have a right of access to the letters column and the right to express themselves in any way and at any length they wish. Although the U.S. Supreme Court, in *Miami Herald* v. *Tornillo,* held that they have no legal rights of access, readers still react vigorously when their letters are shortened, altered or not printed. Editors and publishers, especially in monopoly situations, have a good deal of self-interest, if not legal interest, in helping readers feel that they do have access to the printed page.

Nearly 30 years ago James A. Clendinen of the *Tampa* (Fla.) *Tribune* urged fellow editorial writers to pamper letter writers as a way of bridging the distance between readers and their newspapers. According to Clendinen, increasing monopolies and group ownership were giving the press the appearance of corporate aloofness. He thought that city newspapers could strengthen their positions by showing that they valued their readers' opinions. He also thought a good letters column could build readership for the editorial page. Readers who may be headed for the sports section or comic page, Clendinen said, may be attracted by good letters and thereby be made curious enough "to look over the editorials to see what all the fuss is about."[7]

Another practical reason for letters is that they give newspaper people the chance to tell readers who complain by phone to write a letter to the editor. "They still won't write a letter, but they'll stop calling on the telephone," said Sylvan Meyer of the *Gainesville* (Ga.) *Daily Times*.[8]

BUILDING A LETTERS COLUMN

Not every newspaper has a strong or large letters section. Some editors say they don't get many letters. Some say most of the letters are dull and repetitious or hold little general interest to the public. Certainly most editors would like more good letters. Over the years editors have tried a number of ways to build letters columns, but basically their efforts have fallen into the following seven areas:

1. Weeding out letters that do not have general interest.
2. Displaying letters in a more dramatic manner.
3. Inviting specific people to write letters.
4. Making it easier for people to submit letters, for example, over the telephone.
5. Suggesting topics for letter writers to write about.
6. Rewarding readers for good letters.
7. Enlivening the other portions of the editorial page.

Later in this chapter we will talk about what types of letters editors think they should and should not run. For now let us note that one way to attract good letters is to run only good letters. Readers who have serious comments to make about matters of public interest are not likely to want their names to appear in a column with letters of low quality. When Reed Sarratt took over the editorial page of the *Winston-Salem* (N.C.) *Journal,* he found that the paper was running many letters, but most of them "just weren't worth printing." Many writers discussed every question in terms of the Bible. He recalled that one heated controversy raged for weeks over the question, "Is there an everlasting, burning Hell?" Sarratt gradually reduced the number of letters citing the Bible that did not relate to public issues. After driving out the bad letters, he set out to attract better ones.[9] We will examine shortly exactly what he did.

One way to show readers that their letters are considered important is to display them prominently. Clendinen said the Tampa paper had been treating letters like "an unwanted shrub given to [it] by an insistent friend." Letters had been planted in the bottom right-hand corner of the page, filling whatever space was left over from syndicated columnists. Headlines were one point larger than body type. To give letters a new life, he elevated them to the top of the right-hand side of the page, put larger headlines on them and devoted half of a second editorial page to letters on Sunday. In two years the number of letters published nearly doubled.

As early as the 1950s the *Tampa Tribune* occasionally reproduced the actual letters on its editorial page, a technique that enlivened the page. It also helped show something else about the writers, Clendinen said. One time the paper reproduced "a vitriolic postcard from a Florida Ku Klux Klan boss, so our readers could see for themselves the ignorance betrayed by the misspelled words and mangled grammar." Showing the letter in its actual form can expose an illiterate writer, and it can also add drama or poignancy to a letter, especially one from a child or a handicapped or an elderly person.

Other typographical devices are possible also. When Norman Bradley set out to bring a new editorial page identity to the *Chattanooga* (Tenn.) *Post,* he gave what some editors might consider sensational treatment to certain letters. For example, an elderly resident wrote a nostalgic account of her home of 40 years or more, which was in the path of an urban renewal project. Bradley had a picture taken of the house and ran it with the letter under a feature head. The letter-picture combination was emphasized by enclosing it in a box. When a resident of a deteriorating neighborhood complained about neglected streets and sidewalks, the *Post* gave a letter on that subject the same treatment.[10]

One way to emphasize letters typographically is to publish a full page of letters on one or more days each week. Robert Lucas recalled that editorial writers on the *Denver* (Colo.) *Post* hit on the idea of a page of letters as a means of escaping from writing editorials for the Saturday page, but they soon found that the page proved popular with readers as well.[11] A year and a half after establishing a Friday letters page, editors on the *Peoria* (Ill.) *Journal Star* found that the number of letters they were receiving had increased 100 percent.[12] The *Philadelphia Evening Bulletin* established a Youth Forum on the Saturday editorial page and sent letters to hundreds of college and high school students urging them to write on current topics. The editors were disappointed with the low response.[13] They were more successful in creating a special place for readers to comment on syndicated columns and columns written by the editorial staff. The heading of this section was "Pro and Con the Columnists."[14]

One of the problems of grouping letters one day a week is that they tend to lose their timeliness. Delayed publication also slows down and probably reduces exchanges between letter writers.

Another technique on which editors do not agree is the actual solicitation of letters from readers. One of the methods that Sarratt found productive in getting better letters involved directly inviting interested and informed people to comment on his paper's editorials. The *St. Petersburg* (Fla.) *Independent* put reporters on the phone to call residents at random for opinions on controversial topics. When an editorial of particular interest was scheduled, the editors sent letters a day ahead to a sampling of subscribers asking them to read the editorials and write their views.[15] But solicited letters do not receive universal acclaim. The letters column is supposed to consist of the spontaneous expressions of readers. As an anonymous editorial page editor has suggested, soliciting letters "has an aspect of deliberate 'planning,' almost of professional stage managing for an otherwise amateur performance."[16]

Making it easier for readers to put their thoughts to paper has been another idea tried by some editors. One way is to accept letters over the telephone. When a tape-recorder answering machine was installed, the *Miami* (Fla.) *News* not only benefited from the call-in letters but also experienced an increase in mailed letters.[17] But this device too has critics. Hap Cawood of the *Dayton* (Ohio) *Daily News* thought that, with phoned-in letters, the paper tuned into people on a different thought level. "When a person sits down to write, he or she usually gets involved in a 'thinking out' process," he said; "that process is skipped on call-ins." Still, he acknowledged that many people talk better than they write, and for these perhaps phoned letters could be justified. But he thought they ought to be limited.[18]

More controversial is suggesting topics for readers to write about. The *Roanoke* (Va.) *World-News* reported some success in suggesting, during a little-noticed recovery of the local economy, that readers write about how they would plan Roanoke's future, attract new business and industry and "instill confidence in your fellow citizens."[19] When we look at the op-ed (opposite editorial) page in Chapter 16, we will note other ways to get readers to express their views on topics suggested by editors.

Various ideas have been advanced for rewarding letter writers. One is to call attention to letters that editors think are particularly noteworthy. The *San Bernardino* (Calif.) *Sun* places stars next to the signatures on letters of unusual quality. Some papers pay a few dollars for the best letters. Sig Gissler on the *Waukegan* (Ill.) *News-Sun* rewarded some of his writers with personal publicity. He ran an editorial page article with photographs giving the background and views of some of the most frequent contributors.[20] The idea of rewarding the best letter writers with an annual banquet was apparently originated by Sillman Evans Sr., publisher of the *Nashville Tennessean,* in 1939. The paper provided its guests entertainment, good food, a speaker and then a chance to stand up themselves in a town hall meeting. "The result of all this has not only been an unending stream of letters, but a feeling on the part of thousands of readers that they are somehow a part of the *Tennessean* family," Lloyd Armour reported.[21]

Some editors remain unconvinced that editors should have to go to these extra lengths to promote their letters columns. Theodore Long of the *Salt Lake* (Utah) *Tribune* thought that "the stimulus of cash prizes, certificates or year-end prizes" could "turn the daily 'town meeting' into a meaningless contest."[22] Many editors, and I am one of those, argue that what is needed most to ensure the flow of good letters is a lively editorial page. Some special efforts may be needed, if a letters column has been long neglected, to get readers to start looking at the column and to make it worth their while to do so. But if editors also offer them stimulating editorials and other editorial page features, the column should soon begin sustaining itself. James Dix of the *Moline* (Ill.) *Dispatch* said his formula for keeping the letters column fired up was to create "a crossfire of disagreement between us and a column, or between us and a letter."[23] The incoming mail took care of itself.

POLICIES CONCERNING LETTERS

How readers view a newspaper's letters column and how they in turn respond to it can depend on how the editors of that newspaper handle the letters they receive. Both the quality of the column and the readers' perceptions of it can be affected by the policies of the paper. Just as editors disagree over whether rewards should be offered to letter writers, they also argue over which policies are most appropriate for the letters column. These policies fall into six general areas: use of names and addresses, verification of names, subject matter, length and frequency, editing and editor's notes.

Names and Addresses

Whether or not publication of writers' names should be required has been debated among editorial page editors for a long time. The trend seems to be toward publishing more names. Of 130 NCEW members who were polled in 1970, 94 said they almost invariably published the writer's name and address. Nineteen others published the name with the city but without a street address, and 17 used the writer's name only. Sixty editors said they would on occasion use pseudonyms or initials, but most of the 60 limited this practice to special cases. Every editor required a name and address for the files.[24]

The case for a strict rule requiring the use of names and addresses rests on the belief that the quality of the letters improves when writers know that they will be publicly associated with what they write. Such a rule, the argument goes, helps bring responsibility to the letters column. A secondary argument is that an opinion is no more valid than its source. Putting a name on a letter may help convince readers that the writer knows what he or she is talking about or, conversely, that he or she represents a special interest in the subject matter of the letter. For newspapers flooded with letters (they should be so fortunate!) the requirement of names can be an initial screening device.

But some editors contend that requiring names on all letters can act as a severe deterrent to readers who have something significant to say but, for one reason or another, do not want their names in print. Letters with names for publication took precedence on the *Green Bay* (Wis.) *Press-Gazette*, but names were not required because editors judged that such a requirement would have resulted in a "sharp drop in volume" of letter writing. The *Fort Lauderdale* (Fla.) *News and Sun-Sentinel* would allow a pseudonym on request in the belief that an unsigned letter from time to time would bring out views that otherwise would not be expressed. One reason for this belief, according to Harvey Call of that paper, was evidence that "some of our retirees are inclined to make it rough on anyone who disagrees with their views."

Sometimes the circumstances behind a letter are so sensitive or controversial that the editor faces the choice of either running it anonymously or not running it at all. Neil S. Raymond of the *Waukegan* (Ill.) *News-Sun* faced this problem when he received a letter from a mother who had discovered that her son was using drugs. The letter had particular value because she explained what she had done about it. Raymond ran the letter without the name. Editors of the *Tucson* (Ariz.) *Daily Citizen* speculated that they might withhold a name if a school teacher were criticizing the school system or a policeman's wife were criticizing the chief of police. Editors on the *Ogden* (Utah) *Standard-Examiner* thought they might withhold a name of a student who was critical of a teacher for valid reasons, but would append an editor's note explaining reasons for deletion. James J. Kilpatrick of the *Richmond* (Va.) *News Leader* thought that exceptions to signed letters should be made only in cases involving personal embarrassment or professional ethics, such as a doctor or lawyer criticizing some professional practice.

There are a couple of ways to handle letters that would embarrass the writers, in addition to printing them without names. The *Cleveland* (Ohio) *Press* used information given in a letter as the basis for a newspaper story without identifying the person who furnished the facts. The *Palo Alto* (Calif.) *Times* sometimes used "no name please" material in a column by the editor or another writer or in a separate place on the editorial page under a heading of its own. An editor's note would explain the circumstances.

Some editors stoutly defend initials and pseudonyms. James Clemon of the *Omaha* (Neb.) *World-Herald* said he did not think that "concerned citizen" names bothered anyone except other editors: "In my memory," he said, "no reader has ever questioned our liberal policy on sigs—probably because the reader's more interested in what's said than in who said it."[25]

Some papers, especially in larger communities, will withhold addresses but print names. On the *St. Louis* (Mo.) *Post-Dispatch* no addresses were used for local letters, but city and state were used on letters from out of town. Readers' requests for the address of a letter writer were forwarded to the writer. The *Hackensack* (N.J.) *Record* eliminated addresses of writers because of cases of harassment. "I told you they take our letters seriously!" Mark Stuart of the *Record* said.[26] But John R. Markham of the *Cleveland Press* thought that the halfway measure of omitting the address was "worse than the old 'Disgusted Reader' signature." The Cleveland phone book listed 23 men named Joseph Kovach. Not using addresses meant that 22 Joseph Kovaches might be thought by their acquaintances to have written a letter that they did not write.[27]

Newspapers that begin requiring names and addresses seem not to return to unsigned letters. The experience that most editors report is that, perhaps after a slight drop-off in volume, the flow returns with the quality improved. The *Calgary* (Alberta) *Herald,* with trepidation, took the step toward signed letters to encourage better letters. Three years later Lawrie Joslin of the *Herald* reported that the quantity of letters received soon returned to previous levels and that "experience suggests that identification in print has resulted in an improvement in general quality."[28] I have never worked on a newspaper that did not require names and addresses. Of course I have no way of knowing how many potential letter writers chose not to write for my letters column. While I sometimes would have liked more and better letters, I thought the letters column gained more in credibility with names than it might have gained in volume without names.

Verification of Names

One of the chores involved in handling letters is determining whether they are actually from the people whose names appear on them. One way, of course, is to try to reach the writers on the telephone or through the mails to verify signatures. But using the mails has at least three disadvantages. First, it is time-consuming. Handling letters takes time, even without the chore of verification. Second, checking out the letter writers, especially by an exchange of correspondence in the mail, results in delayed publication. The possibilities for timely exchanges between letter writers are diminished. Finally, if writers are asked to make a second effort to get their letters into print, such as responding with a return card, some of them will forget to reply and some may decide that they aren't as worked up as they were when they wrote initially and will decide against having their letters used. Phone checks may also be of decreasing usefulness. When both husband and wife work during regular office hours, contacting a home may be difficult, and an increasing number of families have unlisted phone numbers.

Consequently, most editors rely on experience and intuition in determining which letters need specific verification. A poll of NCEW members in 1970 found that 56 newspapers out of 130 verified all letters to some degree. The other 74 indicated that they verified only controversial or suspicious ones. Barney Waters of the *Yonkers* (N.Y.) *Herald Statesman,* who conducted the survey, said he was surprised to find such a large number who verified, but of course verifying to some extent could have included only checking a phone book or a city directory to see if such a person at such an address existed.[29] The check, however, could be quite elaborate. According to Cliff Carpenter, the system used in Rochester was foolproof; it had not only kept out the phonies but doubled "as a friendship-cementer." First, a secretary tried to reach writers by phone. If they were reached, they were thanked for writing and told that their letters would be printed. They were never bluntly asked whether they had written the letters, since people might find this insulting. Carpenter thought that this positive approach was "solid elementary psychology"; it made people feel that they had made a contribution. Those not reached by phone were sent tracer cards phrased in such a way that the recipients would feel complimented by the newspaper's effort to protect them from a malicious use of signatures.[30]

Editors who do not phone or write tend to develop a special sense about whether or not a letter is authentic. Some keep a file card on letter writers, containing addresses, dates that previous letters were published and sometimes samples of signatures. A check of signatures can provide quick evidence of the authenticity of former writers. Many times the contents of letters are such that no one would appear to have any reason to sign someone else's name. But once in a while an editor will be burned. The *Cleveland* (Ohio) *Press* once printed a seemingly harmless letter about a street car accident. After the first edition appeared on the street, a woman called to say that the professed family name signed to the letter was "an obscene Hungarian word," too nasty to repeat.[31]

Kilpatrick told how a Mr. Stuart Little of New York City seduced space from the *Richmond News Leader* with his request for help in finding authentic stories about old crows. His hobby was old crows, he said, the older the better. Many people responded to his requests, including one who sent a package "containing a bottle of an old-time beverage." Another volunteered to send "an elderly female relative by marriage." Kilpatrick reported: "Smiling fondly at the quirks of the amateur ornithologist, we published Mr. Little's letter." Then came a second letter. "But we are not running any more of Mr. Little's crow: We are eating it," Kilpatrick told readers. "For right in the second sentence and in the fourth paragraph was another reference to that 'Kentucky beverage,' and down in the last sentence was still a third mention of this estimable product, and the whole business had about it the faint but unmistakable aroma of the gag, the gimmick, the phonus bolonus." Little turned out to work for a public relations firm that had the account for Old Crow bourbon whiskey. Fifty newspapers had apparently run the first letter.[32]

Subject Matter

Once you decide that a letter is legitimate, you must determine whether the subject matter is appropriate. Most newspapers have rules, stated or unstated, concerning what they will run. Most will not run poetry. "Print a bit of amateur verse and the next day's mail brings deluge because everyone is a poet at heart if not in pen," M. Carl Andrews of the *Roanoke* (Va.) *World-News* warned. Most papers refuse religious pitches or arguments over the meaning of biblical verses. But some will allow Bible references if they relate to public issues. Most will not publish a letter unless it pertains to an issue of some public interest. Many try to avoid thank-you letters, especially those thanking an individual. Some will weed out publicity seekers who try to get their names in print by praising editorials lavishly; some are tough on politicians who try to find excuses for getting their names in the letters column. Many editors will not publish letters from outside their general circulation areas unless they pertain to a local issue or something that appeared in the paper.

Editors need to be aware of the possibility of an inspired letter-writing campaign. Sometimes they can tell that several letters have been written on the same typewriter or have the same wording. Some writers make a hobby of sending the same letter to scores or hundreds of papers. Editors can also be trapped by letter-writing assignments in the schools. A letter from a young person may show up one day and get printed. The next day a letter on the same or a different subject may arrive and be put into the column. Then, perhaps on the third day, 20 letters arrive; the other members of the class had been a little slower than their two classmates. If the editor had known that all those letters were coming, he or she would have waited until they all arrived and selected the two or three best. The two printed first may not have been as good as some of the later arrivals. To keep the column from being inundated from this one source, a majority of the letters, including some of the best, may have to be rejected.

Closely related to this problem is deciding when to call a halt to a long series of letters run on the same topic. At some point editors find that they simply must call a halt to letters on this subject unless something new is said. Letters relating to morals, especially sex and nudity, tend to fall into this category. Charles J. Dunsire said that in three years on the editorial page of the *Seattle* (Wash.) *Post-Intelligencer* the topic that generated the most mail in a fixed period was not Vietnam, taxes or racial turmoil but a city council ordinance regulating topless go-go girls in the city's cabarets.[33] Franklin S. Smith of the *Burlington* (Vt.) *Free Press* recalled, "with considerable grief," the avalanche of mail on a snowmobile controversy.

What should be done about letters that don't make perfectly good sense to the editor who reads them? Hap Cawood of the *Dayton* (Ohio) *Daily News* raised the question in terms of "what to do with madmen who learned to write but, unlike us, do not get to make a living out of that combination." Many letters may be crazy, he said, but they keep the column interesting. He said he had tried writing on all kinds of significant subjects in an attempt to get readers to write letters. "Then a letter was published saying one-eyed drivers should not be licensed," he said. "The flood gates opened. We heard from every one-eyed driver in metropolitan Dayton." I was blessed with a persistent letter writer on the *Columbian* who could start writing on almost any subject but within a couple of handwritten pages would wend her way to talking about sublimating sex in order to delay marriage, births and population crisis. She would write several times a week for a while, then not write for several months. She had been writing to the paper for several years when I took over the editorial page. She was still writing 12 years later when I left. One of her letters was 125 six-by-nine-inch pages in length; many others were long but not that long. I could sometimes use the first few paragraphs before she headed off into sublimation.

Length and Frequency

Some papers have firm, stated policies on the maximum length of letters and the frequency of publishing a single writer. The 1970 survey of editorial writers found that the maximum number of words allowed ranged from about 200 to

500, with 250 to 300 an average for most of the papers. Limiting length encourages readers to write succinctly and saves the editor some work. If the editor sets a firm limit, however, exceptions may have to be made for especially good, but longer letters. And if some writers see letters from other writers that exceed the paper's stated limits, they may wonder why they may not write longer letters. My own experience has convinced me that the advantages of not setting a limit outweigh the disadvantages. Editors may save themselves work by insisting that letter writers do their own editing, though most writers are not good editors of their own work. If the newspaper has made clear to readers that there are no prescribed lengths, either minimum or maximum, editors retain their freedom to use letters of any length. Their only commitment is to preserve what the letter writer intended to say.

On the subject of limiting frequency, Frank Grimes of the *Abilene* (Kan.) *Reporter-News* wrote: "As for the perennial bleeding hearts who write incessantly on everything—they are the bane of the letters columns. They scare off other people by making a joke of the column."[34] Rules vary among newspapers for limiting access to these perennial writers. Once a month is a fairly common limit. Some editors will ease their rules for answers or rebuttals or for a repeater whose letter is particularly newsworthy.

Editing of Letters

Editors disagree sharply among themselves on what is desirable or permissible in editing the letters they decide to run. Of those surveyed in 1970, 66 of 130 editors who responded said they edited letters "sparingly." Thirty-four said they edited liberally, smoothing out sentences and tightening up paragraphs. Another 19 said they would rewrite letters or portions of them in the interests of brevity, clarity and readability.[35]

One person who felt strongly that letters should be run the way they were written argued that the editor should respect the person who takes the trouble to write to the paper. If a letter is illiterate, then parts of it should be marked "stet" or "sic," if it otherwise merits publication, he suggested. "The illiteracy of such a person as revealed in the letter so modifies his opinion that editing should not reveal him as a wholly different person than he is," he wrote. "The important point is that when the letter appears it should be the writer's own, not what the editor thought the writer would accept as being his own." But Grimes disagreed. "Many people of limited education have fine minds; words are merely tools and they have no skills in putting words together, but their ideas may be extremely wise," he said. "They should be edited like any other copy so long as the idea is kept intact."[36]

I found that most letters could be made presentable for print by correcting misspelling, grammar and punctuation and trimming excessive words and redundant sentences and paragraphs. Some editors use ellipses to indicate where words, phrases or sentences have been omitted, but I usually did not use them because I thought they might suggest that the editor had substantially altered the letter when in fact only superfluous detail had been trimmed. I agree with Grimes: The validity of the writer's ideas should not be detracted from by allowing simple writing errors—spelling, etc.—to appear in print.

Editor's Notes

Editor's notes at the end of letters used to be more popular than they now are. A clever note that sets a writer straight may be fun to write. Charles Towne of the *Hartford* (Conn.) *Courant* said he suspected that "some editors, too many if there are any, publish caustic rebuttals out of a feeling of superiority—of being so far above such savage assaults as to be immune." For a time at least the *Houston* (Texas) *Post* ran a large number of editor's notes. On one occasion a Cuban-born letter writer accused the *Post* of ignoring Cuba in its coverage of the Nicaraguan revolution. The editor's note said: "The *Post* knows about Cuba, and it did not ignore Cuba in its reporting and commentary on Nicaragua. But the *Post* is not obsessed with Cuba. The people of Nicaragua knew about Cuba. They also knew about 43 years of the Somozas. They knew that any revolution has its dangers. They chose the dangers in preference to more of Anastasio Somoza, just as Cuba chose the dangers in preference to more of Fulgencio Batista." That note certainly was a case of overkill.

Letters columns are meant for exchanges of opinion among readers. If writers have the feeling that the editor is going to have the last word, they are likely to stop writing. If a statement in a letter is clearly wrong in its facts, perhaps a note is justified if the letter is judged important enough to run. But often the truth of a statement is not easy to determine—one person's perception of truth is another person's misperception—and the editor is best advised to print it and let other readers try to set the writer straight. Instead of one letter, which the editor might put into perspective with a note, the paper may end up getting several more in response.

THE LETTERS EDITOR

The job of handling letters is not one for the novice—or for an impatient, careless or uncaring editor. Cliff Carpenter saw some newspapers handling letters lovingly, but he saw others handling them ineptly and casually and with fear or disdain. "Some pages handle letters as if they were ashamed of them," he said. "And by handling them that way, they get only mediocrity to use as letters—and a vicious circle is created."[37] A person who handled letters on the *Kansas City* (Mo.) *Star* was said to have done it "with a certain amount of tender loving care, a bit of prayer and some tearing of hair." Handling letters can take about as much time as an editor can find to work on them, if a paper receives a strong flow of mail. Carpenter reported that the *Rochester* (N.Y.) *Democrat and Chronicle* used two full-time assistants and a secretary. Murray Moler of the *Ogden* (Utah) *Standard-Examiner* said that on his one-person staff he spent as much time with letters as with editorial writing and he thought the time was well spent.

The letters editor needs a thick skin—literally, at times. Palmer Hoyt of the *Denver* (Colo.) *Post* told of one letter that began: "Dear Palmer Hoyt: We want you to know that we are going to boil you in oil." A week later Hoyt got a letter that said: "Dear Palmer Hoyt: We want you to know that we are not going to boil you in oil after all. We got bigger turkeys than you to boil."[38] A woman brought to the office of the *Burlington Free Press* a three-page letter, typewritten, single-spaced, with a pen name. Franklin Smith tried to explain that the letter was too long for publication and pen names were not permitted. "Finally, after a long, long pause, she looked at me," Smith said, "and said plaintively, 'You don't like me, do you?'"

Letters editors, faceless as they may be to the public, can build special relationships with readers. M. Carl Andrews of Roanoke said that some of his best friends were regular letter writers who had never met him. Three of his most delightful contributors over the years, he said, had been "dear old ladies who always found something good to say about people or things." He reported that two of them had died within the last year. One of them had requested that he be one of her pallbearers.[39]

CONCLUSION

A good letters column can be a lot of work for an editor. Deciding what letters to print and what should be done to get them ready for print requires skill and judgment. Dealing with letter writers requires tact. The editing of letters requires sensitivity, a sense of fairness and a heavy editing pencil. But efforts put into the letters column are usually worthwhile in terms of the readability and credibility of the editorial page. Letters bring readers to the page; they also help readers think that they have a voice in their newspaper. Perhaps the clearest sign of a good editorial page is a good letters column, especially one in which readers respond to the editorials, the columnists and other letters that appear on the page. Such a page is truly a community forum.

QUESTIONS AND EXERCISES

1. Examine the letters columns of the newspapers in your area to determine their policies on the use of names and addresses, condensation and the frequency of publication. Are these policies spelled out for readers?

2. Compare the letters columns of these papers for quantity and quality of letters published. Which papers seem to have the best letters columns? Is there evidence available to explain the success of these papers?

3. Examine the letters specifically for references to previously published editorials or letters. Such references often indicate that the letters column is providing a lively community forum for ideas.

4. Can you find letters that sound as though they were produced by a letters mill that sends the same letter to many newspapers?

5. Do the editor's notes seem fully justified? Do you think an editor might have been wiser not to have written one or more of the notes? Why?

6. Do any of the papers request letters on specific topics, perhaps for a weekly round-up or in answer to a question? If so, what kind of responses do the papers get?

7. Write a letter to one of the papers. See if any effort is made to verify your name and address. If it is printed, see what changes are made. If you think the changes altered the meaning of the letter, call and inform the editorial page editor. If it was not published, call to ask why.

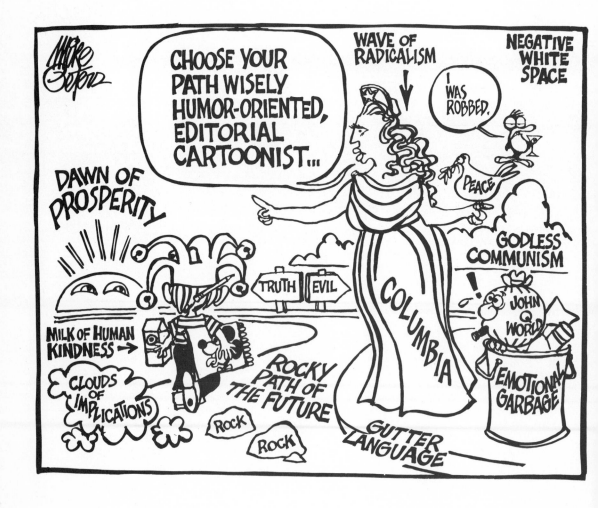

—Mike Peters
Dayton (Ohio) *Daily News* for *The Masthead*

Columns and Cartoons

CHAPTER
15

If the good Lord had not created syndicated columnists, editors would have had to invent them.
—*William W. Baker*
Kansas City *(Mo.)* Star[1]

. . . the syndicate hacks . . . violate the columns of our newspapers and rob them of credulity with bias and distortion.
—*Donald P. Keith*
Easton *(Pa.)* Express[2]

Most newspapers devote more space and less attention to syndicated columns and cartoons than to any other elements on the editorial page. These features are relatively inexpensive, undemanding of editorial attention and extremely useful for plugging editorial holes of any size and number. Some editors have streamlined their editing to the point that every day they slap a regular liberal columnist in one position on the page, a regular conservative columnist in another spot and maybe an interpretive columnist in a third spot. A cartoon by the same artist sits atop the page every day.

The editorial writer on a one-person staff may be thankful that syndicated features are available. With these features, the bulk of the editorial page can be filled with a few minutes' work, and the writer can move on to do what most editorial writers prefer to do—write editorials. But even the writer who has little time for handling columnists serves readers poorly if he or she does not give careful attention to which columnists are selected for print. Deciding which columnists to subscribe to and which to run on any single day can make a difference in how the page is perceived by readers. In this chapter we will talk about the role that columns and cartoons play on the editorial page, how editors decide which ones to use and how they handle the syndicated material. We also will look at efforts to make syndicated writers more credible with editors and readers.

WHY SYNDICATED COLUMNISTS?

Syndicated columnists date back only to the early 1930s. One reason cited for their rise then is that, with the coming of the New Deal, editorial page editors were eager to publish interpretive writers who, because of their inside sources, would be able to tell readers what was going on in Washington, D.C. Underlying was the realization that most editorial page writers were not only unaware of what was going on in the federal government but they were also out of touch with the new trends in policy. The syndicated columnists moved in, Robert H. Estabrook of the *Washington Post* said, because newspapers were not doing a "good enough job providing background and interpretation in their news columns . . . and not doing a good enough job of providing informed comment in their editorial columns."[3] Readers wanted to know what was going on, and the columnists fulfilled this function.

Many of the early columnists, more in sympathy with the New Deal than most editors, provided contrasting opinions to the editorials with which they shared pages. Noting that most newspapers were editorially against President Franklin D. Roosevelt, Mark Ethridge of *Newsday* on Long Island wrote: "Rather than rouse the natives, or maybe to silence their protests, publishers thought it the better part of wisdom to let the columnists fight it out on their editorial page."[4] The columnists who appeared about that time included Raymond Clapper, Tom Stokes, Drew Pearson, the Alsop brothers, Robert Allen, Marquis Childs, Dorothy Thompson and Frank Kent.

Although not the earliest columnist, David Lawrence followed a career that typified what Ethridge called "both the rise—and . . . fall—of the columnists." Lawrence had been a favorite of Woodrow Wilson, Grover Cleveland and Bernard Baruch. "He had the ears and confidence of the mighty, besides the energy to dig," Ethridge recalled. Columnist Walter Lippmann too had been a confidant of Woodrow Wilson and in fact was to pride himself on his close ties with public leaders through more than half a century of editorial and column writing. Robert Allen and Drew Pearson, with their "Washington Merry-Go-Round," provided readers with inside stories, many of them little more than personal gossip. Westbrook Pegler, sometimes published on the editorial page, became known for "reporting" demeaning things about public figures.

Eventually the popularity of these columns declined. The David Lawrence columns I edited for the *Des Moines* (Iowa) *Tribune* in the early 1960s were mostly a rehash of the daily news with a little conservative interpretation thrown in. The news from Washington was well reported in the news columns, and the syndicated columnists knew little more inside information than most reporters. At the same time the editorial policies of newspapers had become more moderate. Editorial writers were more informed about and more sympathetic with what was going on in Washington. Readers also were more informed about the federal government and not satisfied with what Ethridge called the "pontificating, . . . griping, . . . off-the-cuff reflections" that came from the traditional columnists.

But columnists have persisted; on most newspapers they account for about as much editorial page space now as they did when they first became popular. One reason is that a new generation of columnists has emerged. Columnists today serve as more than opinion and information pipelines for individual public officials and provide more than knee-jerk reactions to the day's news. For only a few dollars, an editor can subscribe to syndicated writers who express a number of points of view responsibly and literately. They offer a wide variety of opinions and subject matter, probably more than ever before. These columnists give editors the opportunity to bring readers ideas, insights and opinions that should stimulate even the most informed followers of public events.

One practical reason for using syndicated features is that most editorial staffs do not have the resources needed to fill the pages themselves. "Most newspapers, even large papers, have neither the imagination nor the budget needed to fill an editorial page, let alone an op-ed page, with locally produced copy," William W. Baker of a large paper, the *Kansas City* (Mo.) *Star,* admitted.[5] The *Milwaukee Journal* was forced to give up its practice of filling the page with only local copy, though such papers as the *New York Times,* the *Wall Street Journal* and the *Christian Science Monitor* are still able to maintain a staff of writers sufficient to make syndicated columns unnecessary. The *Times* and the *Monitor* even offer their own columnists for sale to other papers.

In a 1970 poll of 61 editorial writers, Professor Donald Carson of the University of Arizona found that most respondents "believed the syndicated public affairs columnist makes a significant contribution to the thought process they hope their page provokes among readers." The columnist "can raise issues with a bluntness and boldness that we sometimes find difficult to master," said Sig Gissler of the *Milwaukee* (Wis.) *Journal,* a newspaper that until a few years ago ran no syndicated columns. "Then, too, I think readers like the personalized journalism of the columnist," he said.[6]

SELECTING COLUMNISTS

How does an editor go about deciding which columnists to subscribe to? Editors must first decide whether to offer readers a variety of points of view or a fairly consistent point of view, or whether to select the columnists on another basis. Nearly all the writers in Carson's 1970 survey said they tried to balance liberals with conservatives. A survey five years later found that only 60 percent of the editorial people who responded sought to balance columnists. Of these, 12 percent said they selected columnists with philosophies similar to the newspaper's, while 27 percent said they picked columnists for their ability to draw readers, regardless of their philosophies. Most of the pages continued to rely heavily on political writers, most of them out of Washington, though 63 percent said they used humor columns, 33 percent used business columns, 20 percent used religious columns, 34 percent used guest columnists and 5 percent used media critics. This variety seems to represent, to me, a welcome branching out from the traditional column from Capitol Hill.

But diversification has its limits. While I have nothing against using the various other types of columns, including health and medicine,[7] reported by 28 percent of the respondents, I think these columns have their place in a living section, not on the editorial page. Editorial readers should expect to find public affairs discussed on the editorial page most of the time. I tried repeatedly to convince a publisher in Washington state to move "Dear Abby" from his editorial page. His response was that the column attracted readers who would otherwise not read the page. He may have been right, but I suspect they quickly moved on to other pages to find fare more in tune with Abby rather than remaining to read the rest of the editorial page.

My opinion is that columnists should be selected because, first, they write interesting, challenging, even surprising things. Writers are not as predictable politically as they used to be, and a group of writers, even of the same general persuasion, is likely to offer ample diversity if their writing is of high quality. A second important factor in selecting columnists is the necessity for balance.

So who are the most popular columnists with editors today? Robert Schulman of the *Louisville* (Ky.) *Times,* using responses from syndicates plus some guessing in cases of no response, estimated that in 1980 the most widely syndicated columnists were Jack Anderson (approximately 960 papers), Art Buchwald (800), James J. Kilpatrick (400), William F. Buckley Jr. (350), George F. Will (314), Joseph Kraft (300), Jim Bishop (300), David Broder (253), Ellen Goodman (220) and Mary McGrory (200).[8] A survey in 1975 asked editors to identify their favorite columnists by political inclination. Anderson, Kraft, James Reston and Nicholas von Hoffman headed the liberal list; Kilpatrick, Buckley and Will the conservative list. Anderson, the team of Rowland Evans and Robert Novak, and David Broder were rated the best reporters, and Buchwald was rated the best humor columnist.[9]

Some of these names, plus others, appeared in a poll in 1978 of 100 members of the Washington press corps conducted by the American University School of Communications. Broder was acclaimed as the "most respected." Reston was described as an "aggressive competitor, fair reporter, with great sources, literate style and Calvinist integrity" but "overrated." Others who were rated highly were Richard L. Strout, whose column entitled "TRB" in the *New Republic* is syndicated; Carl Rowan and William Raspberry, both blacks; two women, Helen Thomas of the United Press International and McGrory; Will (the most scholarly and graceful of the conservative writers); Kraft (also described as "most pretentious") and William Safire.

Not all columnists are available to every editor. Some metropolitan papers purchase the right to the exclusive use of syndicated features within what they regard as their circulation areas. Sig Gissler complained of this practice in 1967 when he was with the *Waukegan* (Ill.) *News-Sun,* in the shadow of the Chicago papers. "The smaller paper can wail about a 'monopoly of thought' and sometimes pry concessions from the big ones," he said, "but this charity is composed largely of columnar has-beens whose prose is as appetizing as the floor of a parakeet's cage and whose message is as common as a telephone pole. Who needs 'em?"[10]

A partial victory for newspapers in the shadow of larger papers came in 1975, when, in response to threatened action by the Justice Department, the *Boston Globe* gave up its rights to the exclusive use of all syndicated columns in Maine, Vermont and New Hampshire, as well as in eastern Massachusetts, claiming instead only a 12-city Massachusetts area. While 50 daily newspapers were the immediate beneficiaries, the agreement had the long-range effect of putting pressure on other metropolitan papers to restrict some of their exclusivity practices. Schulman found that territorial exclusivity continues to exist but that territories are being opened up as the result of pressure from editors of smaller papers.[11] Papers that are now suffering the most are those in the suburbs, which lie well within the major circulation areas of metropolitan newspapers.

About the time of Schulman's study, Frank Wetzel of the *Daily Journal-American* in Bellevue, Wash., a paper published across Lake Washington from two Seattle papers, reported that the *Journal-American* had trouble obtaining syndicated materials when it went to a daily schedule. He was particularly upset when a larger paper bought the exclusive rights to a column and then ran it only infrequently. Referring to his Seattle competitors, he asked: "How can the editors of those papers argue for a free flow of information when they are selfishly impeding it?"[12]

My paper, the *Columbian* in Vancouver, Wash., across the Columbia River from two Portland dailies, has had the same problem. The only solution we found—a partial one, at that—was to decide immediately to buy a new feature, if it seemed to be a reasonably good one, before the editors on the bigger papers reached their decisions.

EDITING COLUMNS

For the editor who does not use the same column, in the same position, in the form in which it arrives, every day, a number of decisions need to be made. In particular, the editor must decide which columns should be used, to what extent they should be edited, if at all, and how they should be identified on the editorial page.

Columnists, of course, would like their writing to be run every day that they produce a column. Buckley has said that his principal complaint about how editors handle his columns concerns erratic scheduling. "I believe," Buckley said, "that a columnist tends to communicate with his audience in virtue of his more or less continued presence on the scene."[13] It probably is true that, if a columnist is to build a following, his or her columns need to appear on a regular basis. Columnists typically write three columns a week, but some write four or even five. Some of these outpourings, however, are certain to be duds; they may have lost their timeliness or they may be on the same subject that most other columnists also are writing about that day. If quality columns on reasonably fresh topics are to be assured each day, an editorial page editor probably needs to have in hand at least twice as many columns as are necessary to fill the page. If a column appears once or twice a week, that should be sufficient to let readers know that they will find their favorite writer reasonably often.

One way of bringing more opinion onto the page is to publish only key excerpts from several columns and perhaps put them under a standard head of some kind. Care, of course, needs to be taken not to distort the points being made by the writers.

Some editors, and probably most columnists, contend that no heavy editing, let alone extensive chopping, should be done to a column. Columns should be run as the writers wrote them, they argue. "I weep," wrote Buckley, "on seeing here and there columns cut without thoughtful reference to what the excisions do to what is left over." But most editors feel free to cut a column to fit the space available or to fit the space the column merits. Ralph McGill, in recounting what it was like both to run an editorial page, on the *Atlanta* (Ga.) *Constitution,* and to write a syndicated column, said he agreed with editors who insisted on the right to handle, responsibly, the columns as they wished. In his experience on the *Constitution,* he could remember only one syndicated columnist "who made a nuisance of himself by complaining about the cutting of his column or leaving it out." Eventually the columnist asked that his column not be used at all if it were cut or occasionally left out. "When we wrote him we would not use it at all, he was very, very upset," McGill wrote, "and said that he had hoped merely to coerce us into using it uncut." McGill said he continued to trim as he saw fit.[14] While I was on the *Des Moines Register and Tribune,* the writer of a philosophical, non-political column expressed displeasure over our cuts. He said that he had written the column as tightly as possible and asked us not to use it if we would have to cut it. We abided by his wishes for a while, but before long we went back to our old practice, since we had only so much space on the page and we disagreed with him about the supposed impossibility of trimming the column. We didn't hear from him again.

A problem that may be tougher than deciding whether to cut the length of a column arises when an editor thinks that all or part of what a columnist is saying is inaccurate, unfair or biased. Editors of *The Masthead* asked several editors what they would do in such a circumstance. Some argued that the column should be published as the columnist wrote it, that the writer, not the newspaper, was responsible for what was said, and the writer should have his or her opportunity to speak. But other editors contended that they would not want to foist onto their readers material that they thought would mislead or misinform them. They felt as much responsibility for what appeared on the columnists' side of the page as for what appeared on the editorial side. My experience is that columnists can be given much freedom in expressing their views without hurting the credibility of the page, but that columns with obvious misstatements of fact should be discarded without any effort to correct or cut them. If a columnist consistently writes columns that are not usable, for this or any other reason, the editor should drop that column and subscribe to another one.

Another decision for editorial page editors concerns how to identify syndicated columnists. It probably is important that readers know that these writers are not on the local staff and that they are distributed across the country. Perhaps it is even more important for readers to know when a columnist *is* a local writer. One device used by many papers is appending a syndicate credit line at the top or bottom of each column. A more elaborate device is a short note that appears with each column, explaining something about the writer. These notes can be informative if they provide pertinent background information about the writer, but the practice of labeling columnists as "generally liberal," "generally conservative" or "satirical" probably does more harm than good. The political spectrum these days is much more complicated than liberal-conservative labels indicate, since some columnists are liberal on one subject—perhaps fiscal policy—but conservative on another—the environment or civil rights, for example. If readers are told what to expect from a column, their perception of what that column says is likely to be colored. Besides, who knows exactly what liberal and conservative mean today anyway?

KEEPING COLUMNISTS CREDIBLE

Because columnists are distributed on a nationwide basis, far beyond the scrutiny of editors and readers, these writers tend to operate in a vacuum. It is not easy to obtain published replies to syndicated columns; you can't simply write one letter to one editor to set matters straight, as you can with a local editorial. Nor can you know if writers are writing about subjects on which they may have conflicts of interest. An editor can keep an eye on local staff members to see that they avoid such conflicts, but who knows what ties a national columnist may have?

In recent years NCEW and the National News Council have taken steps toward making syndicated columnists more responsible in the areas of reply and conflict of interest. One problem has been, however, that most syndicates will not release the names of subscribing newspapers to a reader who might want to send a reply to the papers that carry a column that he or she objected to. Subscription lists and subscription figures are kept secret by most syndicates, although the sales people who go around the country selling syndicated material know who is subscribing to what. Syndicates have also resisted duplicating letters and sending them to all subscribing papers; fear of a deluge of letters and the high and rising costs of distributing them are strong deterrents. Some of the syndicates leave the decision about distributing letters up to the columnists themselves. An example of this problem was cited by George Beveridge, assistant managing editor and media critic of the *Washington Star*. A man had been criticized in a nationally syndicated column that appeared in the *Star,* among other papers, and he wanted to reply. The *Star* printed his lengthy letter, but the syndicate, the man said, refused either to provide the names of the papers where the column appeared or to duplicate his letter. Beveridge could only tell the man that he was left with no "right of reply" and denounce the situation as "ethically disgraceful."[15]

In early 1974, on the basis of a survey of syndicates conducted for NCEW and the National News Council (NNC), an NCEW committee concluded that "the target of attack in a syndicated column has no assured opportunity to request space for reply from the newspapers that ran the original column."[16] Later that year members of NCEW, at their annual convention, voted overwhelmingly in favor of a resolution that urged syndicates "to provide mailing lists on request and/or distribute replies by targets of syndicated criticism." Columnist Kilpatrick dubbed this resolution the Cranberg Rule, after Gilbert Cranberg of the *Des Moines Register and Tribune,* who had been NCEW's leading advocate of increased responsibility by the syndicates. Kilpatrick liked the rule, commenting: "Its even-handed observance is bound to help our own image of fairness and right conduct."[17] The NCC cited the rule favorably in a 1977 case involving charges against columnist Jack Anderson and United Features Syndicate, which had disregarded the resolution and refused to provide mailing lists.[18]

At first syndicates seemed to resist the efforts of NCEW and other organizations to get them to change their ways. But since then, according to the report made by Schulman, "a dramatic transformation is visible in the industry's attention to affording a day in print to victims of demonstrated unfairness." Schulman concluded that one of the main accomplishments of the Cranberg Rule had been to raise the consciousness of editorial page editors. "Now, the obligations of making up for unfairness in syndicated material are no longer just brushed aside," he said.[19] These obligations, however, are still not being carried out fully, if the handling of a reply to a Buckley column is any indication. A poll of 190 newspapers that had published a column showed that only 72 percent had published a reply that the syndicate had distributed, while 28 percent did not.[20]

At the same time NCEW was working on opportunities for reply, it was also attempting to get the syndicates to adopt conflict-of-interest standards for columnists. The conflict-of-interest issue raised its head during the Watergate hearings in the summer of 1973. Jeb Stuart Magruder, former deputy director of the Committee to Re-elect the President (CRP), told the investigating committee that among cash distributions he had made was $20,000 to a writer named Victor

Lasky. Inquiry by one editor with the North American Newspaper Alliance (NANA), for which Lasky wrote, brought the reply that Lasky had received the money for speeches he had written for Martha Mitchell, a neighbor of Lasky's and also the wife of the head of the Nixon re-election campaign and former attorney general in the Nixon administration. But NANA did not notify any other subscribing newspapers about Lasky's role as both a political columnist and a speech writer paid by CRP.[21] After a subsequent inquiry by NCEW, NANA told subscribers the following February that Lasky had been paid $20,000 "for writing speeches and articles for Republicans." NANA also said that Lasky was a free-lance writer, had always been a supporter of Richard Nixon and had been consistent in his political views over the years.[22] A week later Lasky sent a notice to subscribers, informing them that he was paid to write for Mrs. Mitchell and that the material was non-political.[23]

In April the executive board of NCEW filed charges with NNC, alleging that Lasky had engaged in a conflict of interest and had "abused his position as an editorial page columnist," and also claiming that NANA had failed to accept responsibility to inform its clients of the conflict of interest. The council subsequently upheld the complains and concluded:

> It is our view, first, that a syndicated editorial page columnist is under a responsibility to disclose to the syndicate for which he writes the fact that he benefits financially from an organization active in an area on which he regularly comments and, second, that the syndicate is under a responsibility, once it learns of that relationship, promptly to inform its subscribers. Syndicates are urged to consider establishing guidelines for their columnists on possible conflicts of interest.[24]

When advice columnist Ann Landers traveled to the People's Republic of China in 1974, the American Medical Association and the Chinese Medical Society paid for the trip. NCEW questioned whether she had adequately revealed to readers the financial arrangements of the trip. Landers and Publishers-Hall Syndicate thought she had. An NNC decision in another case noted the complaint concerning Landers but NNC was never officially asked to rule in this case. That same year, when it was discovered that Nelson Rockefeller had given a great deal of money to friends, including Henry Kissinger, columnist Tom Braden wrote a column defending Rockefeller. When it was subsequently reported that in 1954 Rockefeller had lent Braden $100,000 to purchase a newspaper, NCEW expressed "concern over your failure to disclose a prior financial relationship" that was related to a subject of his column. Braden responded by saying that he thought disclosure was not necessary, since a loan repaid at interest was not "a financial benefit."[25] In 1975 the chairman of NCEW's professional standards committee wrote to Buckley concerning a column about oil policies that "raises questions about whether some of the policies advocated by you would benefit you personally." NCEW, the letter said, "believes that editors and readers are entitled to know when writers have interests that could pose a conflict when they write about a particular subject.'' Buckley declined to provide information (''to satisfy a curiosity that is at best pointless, at worse, intimidating'').[26]

It is not easy to reach conclusions concerning these cases, since no clear guidelines have been drawn for syndicated writers. What appears to one person as a possible conflict of interest does not appear so to another. The 1974 resolution by NCEW concerning right of reply also contained provisions calling on syndicates to adopt conflict-of-interest guidelines for columnists. At first most of the syndicates dragged their feet in responding, but Schulman found that, since 1974, all major syndicates have at least announced that they would hold ''their talent to avoidance of undisclosed conflicts of interest in their subject area'' (Schulman's words). But no mention was made of what the guidelines might be.

In cases in which editors suspect that conflicts of interest exist, they have a responsibility to their readers to check those conflicts if possible and express concern to the syndicates, NCEW or NNC if their efforts to obtain information are frustrated. The credibility of their editorial pages, as well as that of the columnists, is involved.

EDITORIAL CARTOONS

Editors on the *Rochester* (N.Y.) *Democrat and Chronicle* decided a couple of decades ago to see how important editorial cartoons were to readers by withdrawing cartoons gradually from the page. No one complained, Clifford E. Carpenter reported. His advice to editors interested in revitalizing their pages was: ''Throw out cartoons. Or at least challenge their appeal carefully and harshly in your community.''[27]

Carpenter's point was that cartoons should not be tossed onto the editorial page merely to break up the type or to give readers a chuckle or even to attract readers to the page. Cartoons need to be selected and worked into the overall editorial product as carefully as columns, letters and editorials.

Purpose and Use of Cartoons

Some newspapers run cartoons that have no connection editorially with anything else on the page, although this practice is probably less common now than it was in the past. An example of running cartoons that reflected exact opposite viewpoints from the newspaper's policies occurred in a Nevada newspaper that supported Richard Nixon for president in 1960 but ran Herblock cartoons on its editorial page every day.[28] Herblock (Herbert Block of the *Washington Post*) had a reputation in that election for drawing an unflattering Nixon, notable in particular for its heavy five o'clock shadow. Before I became editorial page editor of the *Columbian,* cartoons by Herblock, Bill Mauldin and Paul Conrad—regarded then as liberals—all ran on the page. Their liberal political philosophies seemed the antithesis of the paper's policies. When I took over the page, however, these cartoons became more at home.

During the 1950s and 1960s one of the problems faced by newspapers of every political persuasion, especially conservative ones, was the scarcity of good, lively cartoons expressing conservative views. The best cartoonists were liberals, including the three mentioned above. In the late 1960s and 1970s, however, the balance changed. The newest and brightest cartoonists seemed to be conservative. But most recently critics have suggested that cartoonists in general, and particularly the new conservative breed, have lost their punch, a topic we will discuss when we talk about specific cartoonists.

Many cartoons, unfortunately, are run because "an editorial page has to have a cartoon" and because every page "has to have some art work." Cartoons do give life to the page and attract readers. That function is a perfectly legitimate one—and editors should acknowledge it without apology. "The cartoon can be an attention-getter, halting the page-skimming reader midway between the page 1 headline and the sports section," said Laurence Boodry of the *San Diego* (Calif.) *Evening Tribune.* "If compelling enough, it may force a casual reader to scan the words of wisdom with which it shares the opinion page."[29] But the cartoon needs to serve as more than an eye-stopper.

One of the cartoon's roles is to introduce humor onto the page—also a legit- ✔ imate function. Most editorial pages could use a feature that contrasts with their traditional seriousness. Humor can help make unpopular points more acceptable to readers. "Most people will find a harsh truth less offensive if it has a smile on it," cartoonist Kate S. Palmer of the *Greenville* (S.C.) *News* said. But the humor should be a vehicle "for some large or small truth, and it should have arrived there through a logical, natural process," she said.[30] Cartoonist Bill Sanders of the *Milwaukee* (Wis.) *Journal* saw a dividing line between the "political gag cartoonist" and "the situation cartoonist." To qualify as the latter, he said, a cartoonist had to ask three questions: "What is at stake here? Having researched the subject, how do I feel about it? How can I best express my opinion so as to cause the reader to think about the issue and the point I'm about to make in the cartoon?"[31]

When cartoonists were surveyed, 95 percent said that their major role was to ✔ make people think. Other roles mentioned were: to entertain, 75 percent; to express concern, 73 percent; to illustrate problems, 67 percent; and to call for a change, 63 percent. Full-time cartoonists said they tended first to look at national topics for their ideas, while part-time cartoonists tended to look to local topics.[32]

On the question of how much influence cartoonists exert, 32 percent thought they exerted much influence and 42 percent said moderate influence. Forrest M. Landon of the *Roanoke* (Va.) *Times and World-News* once wrote that he regarded a good cartoon as so powerful as to be "unfair competition" to the "turgid prose" of most writing on the editorial page. He noted that a cartoon will use black-and-white lines to depict a 20-sided issue, but "its influence can be equal to 60 column inches by the opinion-writing staff."[33]

Whether or not cartoons actually persuade readers remains an unanswered question, to a greater extent even than the question concerning the effect of editorials. Most cartoons do not offer enough real information to persuade readers on the basis of rational decision making. Their humor may sufficiently soften slightly antagonistic readers on the depicted subjects to make them less antagonistic. But the principal persuasive role of the political cartoon probably is to reinforce prior inclinations of readers who agree with its point of view. A political cartoon also has the power to raise the blood pressure of those who disagree strongly with what it says.

Some studies have indicated that cartoons are more persuasive if they are published in conjunction with editorials expressing the same point of view. But on most daily newspapers that have their own cartoonists, the cartoonists and the editorial writers usually have their own daily agendas of topics, and only by chance might they use the same subject on any given day, even though they may be in agreement on general editorial policies. On papers that must depend on syndicated cartoons, editors must rely on whatever comes in the mail that day. Saving unused—and even used—cartoons can provide a backlog from which to draw when a cartoon is needed to go with an editorial or column. Most cartoons, however, quickly become dated.

A more serious question than whether or not editorials and cartoons should be on the same subject on the same day is whether editorials and cartoons on a page should express the same editorial philosophy. One line of thought among editors is that any cartoon at the top of an editorial page should conform, or at least not conflict, with the policies of the paper. According to this reasoning, the potential impact of a cartoon placed at the top of the page requires that it reinforce the paper's position. "I suspect that even the sophisticated reader assumes that the dominant cartoon speaks for an opinion page," Landon wrote. "If I'm right in that hunch, then logic dictates that we accept what we cannot change—while still allowing the cartoonist some necessary latitude for a freer-swinging style of a signed, personal journalism." But some editors regard cartoons as political columns; they think they should offer readers a variety of opinions and display good cartoons prominently, regardless of the cartoons' editorial points of view.

Most editors who subscribe to syndicated cartoons probably take a middle ground. First, they are not likely to subscribe to cartoons that are completely out of synch with their papers' policies. Second, unless editors subscribe to a large number of cartoons, they must take on a daily basis what they are sent by the syndicates. Finally, the more horizontal layout of editorial pages has encouraged the placing of smaller cartoons within the printed columns. Cartoons are often used as illustrations for columns or op-ed articles, where they can be run without the editor having to wonder whether or not they will be perceived as expressing the paper's policies. In 1972 the editorial cartoons of Paul Conrad were moved from the editorial page to the op-ed page of the *Los Angeles Times*. "I thought it was a good idea," Conrad said. "I think it's a better spot." According to him, one reason for the move was to provide more space for letters to the editor on the editorial page; another reason, he said, was to make clear that only the editorials represented the opinion of the newspaper.[34]

Selecting Cartoons

While surveys show that only about 10 percent of newspapers with circulations of less than 25,000 have cartoonists of their own compared to 80 percent for papers of more than 100,000 circulation, newspapers of all sizes, with only a few exceptions, subscribe to syndicated cartoons. Editors need them when their own cartoonists are on vacation; they need them to illustrate columns and op-ed articles; they need them to brighten the corner of a page; they subscribe to them to give their readers a variety of pictorial editorial comment. And they have a wide variety of cartoons to choose from. Professor Ernest C. Hynds of the University of Georgia counted almost 200 cartoonists listed in *Editor & Publisher Yearbook,* two-thirds of whom devoted full time to political cartoons. Hynds found in surveying the 200 that 23 percent of those who responded said they were syndicated.[35] A glance down the columns of *Editor & Publisher*'s annual syndicate edition shows the many choices that are available. But at any time only a half dozen or so are in great demand.

A survey of editors in 1975 showed that 32 percent thought Pat Oliphant, whose cartoons appeared in the *Washington Star,* was the best cartoonist. In drawing a horizontally shaped rather than a vertically shaped cartoon, Oliphant had earlier set a style that several other cartoonists emulated. The horizontal shape fit in well with the new horizontal makeup of the editorial page. Ranking behind Oliphant were Mauldin, with 16 percent, and Herblock, with 12 percent. When the cartoonists themselves were asked in 1976 who was the best all-around cartoonist, they named Oliphant (18 percent), Jeff MacNelly of the *Richmond News Leader* (14 percent), Herblock (12 percent), Conrad (6 percent), Don Wright of the *Miami News* (6 percent) and Mauldin (4 percent). Herblock (with 33 percent) and Oliphant (25 percent) were rated the most influential. Hynds said he thought these ratings reflected the Washington bases of these two cartoonists. MacNelly was named "best conservative" cartoonist with 36 percent, followed by Don Hesse of the *St. Louis Globe-Democrat* (7 percent), Karl Hubenthal of the *Los Angeles Herald Examiner* (4 percent) and Charles Werner of the *Indianapolis Star* (3 percent). Leading the voting for "best liberal" were Herblock (16 percent), Conrad (14 percent), Oliphant (12 percent), Wright (8 percent) and Mauldin (3 percent). When asked to cite the best woman cartoonist, 89 percent of the cartoonists offered no opinion while 8 of the remaining 11 percent named Etta Hulme of the *Fort Worth Star-Telegram*—which points to how far behind editorial cartooning stands in recognizing women. As far as I know, no racial minority cartoonist is being syndicated.

MacNelly was named by his peers as the "best comer" (16 percent), followed by Tony Auth of the *Philadelphia Inquirer,* Mike Peters of the *Dayton* (Ohio) *Daily News* and Doug Marlette of the *Charlotte* (N.C.) *Observer,* each with 7 percent. MacNelly was so highly regarded by fellow cartoonist Paul Szep of the *Boston Globe* that Szep said MacNelly was the only cartoonist he knew who could be consistently funny and provocative.

MacNelly's style—horizontal in the manner of Oliphant, more whimsical than hard-hitting in editorial comment—spawned a generation of what William A. Henry III, writing in *Washington Journalism Review,* called "MacNelly clones." He mentioned Steve Benson of the *Arizona Republic* of Phoenix, Tim Menees of the *Pittsburgh* (Pa.) *Post-Gazette,* Bob Gorrell of the *Charlotte News,* Kate Palmer of the *Greensboro* (N.C.) *News* and Jack Ohman of the *Columbus* (Ohio) *Dispatch.* Henry contended that none of them draw as well as MacNelly, concentrating on "the outer line rather than the subtler shadowing." He saw them as being "more infatuated with the role of the cartoonist as social chronicler, and with celebrity, than . . . with reporting and reflecting upon the news." Few, he said, seemed driven by moral duty. Concerning cartoonists in general, Henry said they were mostly engaged in throwing a well-aimed cream pie.[36]

Similar criticism was offered by David Shaw, media critic for the *Los Angeles Times.* He reported that, in addition to the term "MacNelly clones," fellow cartoonists were calling these proteges of MacNelly "MacBensons," a phrase coined by Szep. These cartoonists, Shaw said, are accused by peers, editors and syndicate executives "of not using their heads (or their imaginations), of being imitative (rather than original), amusing (rather than provocative)." He quoted cartoonist-playwright Jules Feiffer as saying that perhaps "80 to 90 percent of (today's) cartoonists . . . don't have an idea in their silly little heads."[37]

In 1981 MacNelly decided to drop his editorial page cartoon to devote full time to his daily cartoon strip "Shoe," which drew on the personality of a former boss of his, Don Shoemaker, as the inspiration for one of the characters. But the following year MacNelly returned to editorial cartooning and joined the *Chicago Tribune.*

In addition to the single-panel cartoons, some editors have run Gary Trudeau's "Doonesbury" cartoon strip on the editorial page, claiming that it is more social and political comment than entertainment. Some contended that a cartoon that offers such strong comment should be from time to time in the opinion section. One reason that editors cited for not putting "Doonesbury" on the editorial page was that, as a continuing cartoon strip, it must be run every day, and they wanted to keep their pages more flexible. On occasion, when Trudeau ventured into a highly controversial area, a few editors who used the cartoon in the noneditorial section temporarily suspended publication of the strip. In late 1982 Trudeau temporarily suspended the strip to allow himself time to develop new material.

So these are some of the choices available to editors who are looking for cartoons to brighten their pages and, I hope, to bring visually oriented insights into public affairs. From a practical point of view, editors who lay out editorial pages may have an interest in subscribing to some cartoons that are horizontal and to others that are vertical, since different shapes provide more flexibility in the makeup of the page. Editors may decide to select a range of political views, from conservative to liberal, if indeed they can determine which is which among the cartoonists who are primarily interested in observing rather than commenting. Editors who use two cartoons a day seven days a week will probably need to select and buy at least four cartoonists from the syndicates. Some of these cartoons will be dated by the time they arrive, some will get lost or delayed in the mail, since cartoons are not yet transmitted electronically to any great extent, some will be repetitious, and some will be inane.

Especially blessed are editors who have available to them the talent of a cartoonist on their own staffs. A cartoonist who can draw on a local subject is a jewel to be cherished, though he or she may not get rich. Local topics are hard to depict, since there are no national media to clarify and symbolize such issues. Local cartoons tend also to be more controversial, since cartoonists and editors may encounter the subjects of the cartoons on the street the next day or may have to face them when they storm into the office. But nothing can be more rewarding to a cartoonist than to know that a message has struck a chord—either positive or negative—with readers. A skilled local cartoonist can bring life to an editorial page. But he or she must be more than an artist or a clever gag writer. When asked for ideas on how to get editorial cartoons from a good artist who didn't follow the news, A. Rosen of the *Albany* (N.Y.) *Knickerbocker News,* president of the National Cartoonist Society, advised: "Give up on that person; you'll never make him or her an editorial cartoonist. Instead, seek out a young person who may not draw well but who is interested in public affairs. Hire that person."[38]

CONCLUSION

Rosen's point was that the message is more important than the medium. Editors should not subscribe to and run syndicated columnists and cartoonists only because it is the standard thing to do or because these features spruce up the page or because they bring wandering eyes to the page.

They should use these syndicated features—and their own local columnists and cartoonists—to present their ideas to their readers. They should try to make their readers think—not only entertain them or present them with writers and artists who express opinions and ideas that readers already have. An editorial page should be a place where readers find some familiar faces and names but also some unfamiliar ways of looking at the local community, the state, the nation and the world.

QUESTIONS AND EXERCISES

1. Tabulate the syndicated columns in the newspapers of your area to determine whether they tend to run columnists that agree with their own editorial policies, that disagree or that express a variety of opinions.

2. Do these papers run a few columnists consistently or a variety of columnists infrequently? If they run a few, do these columns have something new and different to say each day? If they run a variety, does any one column appear often enough to build a regular following among readers?

3. How would you judge the overall quality of the columnists published by the various newspapers you have studied? Do some of the papers seem to spend a lot of money on columnists and others only a little?

4. Do any of the newspapers label the columnists they carry, or attempt to describe the columnists' political positions? If so, are the labels accurate and appropriate?

5. Can you find letters to the editor concerning columns that have been distributed by the syndicates?

6. Which cartoonists seem to be most popular?

7. Do any of the newspapers have their own political cartoonists? Where do they appear on the editorial page? Does the local cartoon always agree with the editorial policies of the paper?

8. Ask editorial page editors in your area whether they have had trouble purchasing a column or cartoon because of territorial exclusivity.

9. While you have the editors' attention, ask them how often they receive letters from syndicates in response to columns, and ask them if they always publish those letters.

10. If you still have the editors' attention, ask about their policies on trimming columns.

—Jim Shinn
Columbian, Vancouver, Wash.

Innovations in Makeup and Content

The whole idea of the op-ed page is to bring in ideas we don't necessarily agree with.
—Anthony Day
Los Angeles Times[1]

When editorial page editors sit down to plan the following day's editorial page, and op-ed page if there is one, they must select the editorials, letters, columns, cartoons and other materials that will be used and they must decide on the layout that will best accommodate those features. Some editors, whether by their own choice or someone else's, are stuck with editorial pages that look the same every day and contain the same mix of features. But the trend among daily newspapers seems clearly to be in the direction of varying the editorial page, from one day to the next, in appearance and content. Varied makeup of a page can help attract readers; varied content can provide pleasant and rewarding surprises for readers. The purpose of this chapter is to trace briefly the transformation of the editorial page and the op-ed page from being among the most stodgy-looking pages in the paper to being among the most spritely and most stimulating pages—at least in some newspapers.

EDITORIAL PAGE MAKEUP

For most of the 175 years of the American editorial page's history, editors attempted to gain distinction for their pages through gray respectability. But now, with newspapers fighting for readers' time, editors seek to distinguish their pages through the bold, innovative marketing of their features. Not every editorial page has been drawn into typographical competition with the news columns, but the trend toward more dynamic presentation is unmistakable.

Pages of the Past

Except for William Randolph Hearst, who jazzed up his editorial pages 50 years before nearly everyone else, most editors continued through World War II to make up their pages much as their 19th-century predecessors had. Although the editorial page began to emerge as a separate page, or as a portion of a page, during the first decades of the 19th century, the page was hard to distinguish from other pages. All the type, news and editorial, was set one column in width. News and editorials ran from the bottom of one column to the top of the next column and sometimes from the bottom of one page to the top of the next. Aside from content, about the only distinguishing mark of an editorial, evident as early as 1835 in the *New York Sun,* was a slightly larger type with lines spaced (leaded) a little farther apart. The only headlines were three or four words in italics of the same size and on the same line as the body type. See the second page of the *Sun* for Aug. 11, 1835, reproduced here. This page measured 11 by 15 inches, about the size of the modern-day tabloid, but the type was considerably smaller than the type used in most newspapers today. The size of the *Sun*'s type is hard to measure, but type on the editorial page of the *New York Times* of 1859 was probably 8 points high, compared to 6½ points in the news columns. Most news columns today are set in 9 or 9½ point type, and editorials may be set in 12 point type. It takes 72 points to make an inch, so you can see that reading 19th-century newspapers was more of a strain. Editorial pages were also longer than they are today. The editorial page in Horace Greeley's *New York Tribune* in 1871 had more than 6,000 words on it, while the page of the *Des Moines* (Iowa) *Register* reproduced here (p. 292) contains approximately 3,700 words. A cartoon accounts for a portion of the difference.

Editors were shocked when Hearst and Arthur Brisbane began to set editorials in larger type and wider columns, to run the editorials across several columns (perhaps the original horizontal makeup) and to introduce huge illustrations to the page. Hearst's clouded reputation may even have delayed the brightening of American editorial pages, since "respectable" editors did not want their pages to look like his. An example of the Hearst style, the *New York American* of Oct. 27, 1933, reproduced here (p. 293), uses a (banner) headline the width of the page over the lead editorial. Above the headline is a scripture quotation. Columns are separated by white space and wavy lines, unlike most editorial pages of that day, where the columns were run close together with a thin rule between them. The page is made even more dramatic by a large cartoon.

THE NEW YORK SUN.

TUESDAY MORNING, AUGUST 11, 1835.

Distress in Ireland.—Accounts from Ireland, received by the Sheffield, represent many districts of Ireland as suffering great distress from famine. In one parish, consisting of thirty-four families, in the county of Galway, only three possessed provisions for a week. In another, comprising 322 families, only 37 were provisioned till harvest; and, should they extend relief to their famishing neighbors, the whole stock would not hold out a week. "From an authentic source, we have discovered that upwards of 6,000 persons in the barony of Erris, county Mayo, alone, have, on an average, but six days' provision on hand; and in that number there are 106 persons who can command but half a hundred of potatoes amongst them, and 500 without any, whose sole dependence is on chance shell-fish and sea weed, a sample of which we have seen."

Foreigners, and Foreign Influence.—It cannot have escaped the notice of even the most casual observer of what is passing about him in the moral and political world, that within a very short time past, the patriotism of certain of the presses of this city has become most suddenly and most affectingly sensitive to the appalling dangers which they affect to have discovered overshadowing the liberties and institutions of our republic, by reason of the great influx of emigrants from foreign countries, and the overwhelming influence they are pretended, by these newly fledged patriots, to possess over the judgments and opinions of our native citizens, and the character and destinies of our government.

Caution.—It has been the practice, for some time, for a great mass of well-grown boys, from 14 to 19 years of age, principally the sons and apprentices of respectable mechanics, to assemble, between 7 and 8 o'clock every night, and to continue, frequently, almost all night, at and about engine house No. 40, in Mulberry street, between Grand and Broome, and to insult and annoy the neighbors and persons passing by, as also to indulge in noise, and riotous and disorderly conduct.

The London Courier says the talked of marriage of the Queen of Portugal with the Duke de Nemours is now wholly given up on account of the known aversion of England to such a match.

The Office of the Sun has been removed to the corner of Nassau and Spruce streets, opposite the City Hall.

New York Sun, Aug. 11, 1835

[Reported for the Sun.]

Police Office.—Yesterday.

MORNING RETURNS.

Lawrence Clark, for intemperance and rioting in the street, was fined $1 and costs and committed.

Archibald Madden, for rioting and assaulting Elizabeth Leacroft; was committed.

14A **OPINION** Tues., Apr. 25, 1978

The Des Moines Register
AN INDEPENDENT NEWSPAPER

DAVID KRUIDENIER, *Chairman and Publisher*
MICHAEL GARTNER, *President and Editor*
GILBERT CRANBERG, *Editorial Page Editor*
J. ROBERT HUDSON, *Vice-president/Marketing*
LOUIS H. NORRIS, *Vice-president/Business*
GARY GERLACH, *Vice-president/General Counsel*

THE REGISTER'S EDITORIALS

Progress on SALT

Secretary of State Cyrus Vance's strategic-arms limitation talks with the Russians ended Sunday in Moscow amid warm compliments and sunshine optimism.

Back home, the prospects for prompt or easy Senate ratification of a new SALT treaty with the Kremlin seemed as chilly and cloudy as Iowa's weekend weather.

During his two days of talks, Vance took care not to link the arms issue to other problems that bedevil U.S.-Soviet relations — Russian intervention in Africa, human rights, the neutron bomb. The result, all seemed to agree, was genuine (if modest) progress toward a new arms treaty to replace the one that expired last October.

Jackson

Not everyone in Washington was heartened by the developments. One of the most powerful critics was Senator Henry M. Jackson (Dem., Wash.), chairman of the arms control subcommittee of the Senate Armed Services Committee.

Jackson said Sunday he cannot support the new treaty in the form in which it is being negotiated. He has said privately that he doubts the administration has even half the Senate on its side in support of a new arms treaty, much less the necessary two-thirds.

Jackson is probably right. Many senators, including Iowa's Dick Clark and John Culver, took political risks recently by supporting the unpopular Panama Canal treaties. It may be hard to find 67 senators willing to take another heavy political risk in an election year on behalf of another controversial treaty with another, even more despised, dictatorship.

Before he left on his trip, Vance said any new SALT treaty negotiated by the administration would not sacrifice U.S. military supremacy.

Given the mood of the Senate and the rest of the country, a tough, hard-line agreement is the only kind of agreement that would have a chance of approval.

A failure to reach a new SALT agreement would be a setback for the country. It would spur the costly, suicidal nuclear arms race between the two superpowers and perhaps prompt smaller, poorer countries to enter it. For everyone, it's a no-win race.

To avoid reviving it, Vance and other high officials will have to be as painstaking in their Capitol Hill consultations as they were in their weekend talks in the Kremlin. They probably will discover that, for very different reasons, people like Henry Jackson are as difficult to convince as people like Andrei Gromyko.

Good place to start

Predictably, the nation's postal workers blasted the administration's decision to apply its anti-inflation policy to the postal union's current contract talks. But the average worker covered by the contract negotiations (including mail carriers, clerks and messengers) earns over $15,300 a year in base pay, and almost $18,000 when benefits are included.

Wages and benefits account for about 85 percent of the cost of running the Postal Service. The generous wages given postal workers have been a major factor in the service's continuing string of deficits, and the need to keep raising postal rates. Increases in the cost of mailing a letter or package contribute to inflation.

Under their current three-year contract, which expires in July, postal workers received wage boosts averaging about 8 percent a year. The administration wants the postal workers to settle for less — perhaps around 5.5 percent, which is the wage boost President Carter has proposed for many other federal workers.

Even if such a lid were placed on the negotiated increases, many postal workers would receive more — since postal workers are also eligible for pay increases based on their length of service.

No group of workers wants to be singled out in the fight against inflation. But the fight must start somewhere. The large number of postal workers and the generous wage boosts given them in the past make this a logical place to start.

Curbing the wiretappers

The U.S. Senate has voted with just one dissent to extend the rule of law to all electronic surveillance in this country. The sort of warrantless wiretapping that went on during the Nixon administration for "national security" would be prohibited by the measure, which requires court approval to eavesdrop for foreign intelligence purposes.

Congress insisted that no electronic surveillance be conducted in criminal cases without a warrant when it authorized wiretapping and bugging in 1968. Electronic surveillance in "national security" cases usually involves a search for information rather than for law violations, and this has been left to the discretion of the intelligence agencies and the president.

The discretion was used to bug Dr. Martin Luther King Jr. and to spy on newsmen and others, ostensibly for national security reasons but actually for domestic political purposes. The Senate-passed bill should help prevent similar abuse by making it necessary to convince a judge that the spying is justified.

Unfortunately, judges have been easy to persuade in criminal cases. Rarely have judges rejected police requests to initiate electronic surveillance. The courts almost never turn down requests to extend the original wiretapping or bugging order. The secrecy that will surround requests for court orders in national security cases should make the chances for judicial rubber-stamping even greater in these proceedings than in criminal cases.

Still, the Senate-passed bill is a worthwhile step to protect privacy. The step will need to be combined with effective congressional oversight to realize its full promise.

A question of fraud

Contrary to what Attorney General Richard Turner told Iowa legislators, it does matter whether Laetrile is an effective drug in curing cancer or arresting its spread. A question of fraud can be raised if Laetrile is promoted as a cancer cure but it proved to be worthless.

The possibility of fraud should concern the state's chief legal officer. But Turner argues that using the apricot-pit nostrum is a matter of personal choice, like motorcycle riding, tightrope walking and parachute jumping. Fraud is not a question in those activities.

Risks are involved in many medical treatments, from the surgical removal of a diseased organ to the prolonged use of drugs to control ailments. Those risks are seldom a concern of legislators. But the legal questions that could result from the manufacture and sale of a drug of unproved worth should be.

Polls on Carter are awful; here's why all is not lost

By JACK W. GERMOND and JULES WITCOVER
© 1978, Chicago Tribune/New York News Syndicate

FOR MOST of us, the opinion polls are just a dreadful bore. They take the national temperature daily and quantify the obvious, overwhelming us with trivia. Who cares how left-handed women with red hair between the ages of 35 and 50 feel about the Bakke case. Enough already.

But for Jimmy Carter, they are bordering on disaster. One day the New York Times-CBS survey tells us how poorly he is regarded; the next day it is NBC; and the day after that, The Des Moines Register's Iowa Poll confirms that it is just as bad — maybe even worse — out where he is supposed to have a special rapport with the voters.

The most recent Gallup Poll shows that Carter's popularity dropped 7 points in the first two weeks of April, from 46 percent approval down to 39 percent. The mid-April Harris Poll gave the president only a 33 percent approval rating.

The results are so consistently negative that Carter's entire presidency is being bent out of shape in reaction to them. Does anyone imagine that special Cabinet meeting at Camp David would have been necessary if the polls showed the president with a 60 percent approval rating? Not a chance. Would we be treated to this much-advertised "shake-up" in the White House staff if Carter's standing with the voters were stronger? Never.

But we live in a time when the perception of the public attitude tyrannizes our politicians and public officials even in the White House. And "bad" polls leak a smell of blood that lures the political sharks. On Capitol Hill, insignificant members of the House and Senate shed their crocodile tears about Jimmy Carter's troubles and confide how they don't want him campaigning in their districts this year. They are better on their own, they whisper. Talk about the one-term presidency is all the rage.

There is, of course, a kind of elementary justice in this. The politician who gloats when the news from Gallup is good is obliged to take it like a man when the figures are bad. There is no disputing the polls' value as a barometer of national attitudes; it is at least minimally worthwhile to know what the country thinks about those who are supposed to be running things.

But we are falling into a trap because too often we fail to recognize the limits in opinion research.

In the hand-wringing of the moment we forget, for example, how volatile public opinion can be. Just eight years ago, 15 months into his first term, the story on Richard Nixon was oh, the wonder of it all — imagine, a Republican president proposing such things as an enlightened welfare policy. But 16 months into that term, Nixon treated us to Cambodia. Same old Nixon.

A month into his presidency Gerald Ford was the president we all had been waiting to see. Then came the pardon, and there went good old Jerry Ford.

We forget, too, that opinion surveys of the kind we are reading these days rarely deal with the alternatives. Early in 1972 Nixon was holding only a narrow lead over the then Democratic frontrunner, Edmund S. Muskie, and the polls showed several others, including George McGovern, well within range of Nixon. So, judgments about Jimmy Carter as a one-term president must consider the possibility, for example, that the alternative may be a 69-year-old former movie actor with orange hair.

Beyond that, it is possible that we give too little weight to the changing context in which the opinion surveys are made. One thing that has become increasingly clear in the last few years, for example, is that few public figures wear well with the voters. We sour on yesterday's hero before we identify tomorrow's successor. There is considerable evidence that most voters don't feel very strongly either way about what goes on in Washington.

Finally, there is no question that opinion polls are susceptible to manipulation. If the consensus about Carter within the political community is revised over the next few months, that will be reflected in the press and inevitably in the polls. Such dramatic changes in the conventional wisdom are common. Eugene McCarthy may not be the world's most objective press critic, but few would argue with his contention that political reporters are like blackbirds on a telephone wire — when one flies away, all the others follow.

None of this suggests that the current polls are somehow inaccurate or unfair to the president. The problems of energy, the economy, disarmament, the Mideast, whatever — all are Jimmy Carter's responsibility even if he is not necessarily to blame for them. It goes with the job.

But it does suggest that the politicians and press may be too caught up in the trends of the moment, and it does suggest that the president and his advisers would be making a serious mistake if they allowed their course to be dictated by today's reading of the state of the national mood. There will be another poll coming along tomorrow.

Israel offers 'a process for talks,' not a settlement plan

By JAMES RESTON
© 1978, New York Times News Service

U.S. not very hopeful and still a little irritated by Begin's diplomacy.

WITH Prime Minister Menachem Begin and Foreign Minister Moshe Dayan of Israel coming to Washington in the next few days, the Carter administration is studying carefully Israel's latest formulation of its policy for breaking the diplomatic impasse in the Mideast.

President Carter broke openly with Begin on the meaning of U.N. Security Council Resolution 242 and on how to determine the future of the Palestinian Arabs. The Israeli government now has redefined its position, and while its latest proposals have not been published, it can be stated on the authority of high officials that they are as follows:

- It is Israel's position with regard to Resolution 242 that it is "prepared to negotiate peace treaties in fulfillment of *all the principles* of Security Council Resolution 242." Israel agrees that these principles "will serve as the basis for negotiations between Israel and *all the neighboring states,* i.e. Egypt, Jordan, Syria and Lebanon."
- In enumerating the principles of 242, Israel includes the principle of "withdrawal of Israeli armed forces from territories occupied in the conflict of '67," as well as the principle which calls for "secure and recognized boundaries within which every state in the area will live in peace."
- As far as the question of the Palestinian Arabs in the West Bank and the Gaza District is concerned, Israel holds that they "will have the right to participate in the determination of their future." This right will be exercised in the framework of talks to be held among Egypt, Israel, Jordan, and representatives of these Palestinian Arabs.

This authorized Israeli position does not, of course, meet Egyptian President Anwar Sadat's demands or Carter's expectations, and was not designed to do so, but it is important nonetheless. It is a careful redefinition or tactical move to get the Mideast negotiations going again, and it is important to note what it does *not* say.

It does not commit Israel to withdraw from the West Bank and Gaza in return for recognition of Israel's political independence and territorial integrity. It is not the simple "withdrawal for peace" formulation Washington would like to see Israel negotiate with its neighbors.

In short, it is a process for negotiation and not a policy for settlement. It recognizes that there are different interpretations of Resolution 242, and agrees to negotiate them, but it is very careful to make clear that it will negotiate them "with all neighboring states," which is a polite way of insisting that it will not negotiate with the Palestine Liberation Organization.

On the future of the Palestinian Arabs, the Israeli formulation also avoids any suggestion that it will allow this question to be settled by a vote of the million Palestinian Arabs on the West Bank and Gaza, let alone by the vote of the other 2 million Palestinian Arabs outside these two areas.

The Israeli position now is that Israel accepts the wording of the Carter-Sadat Aswan communique that the Palestinian Arabs "will have the right to participate in the determination of their future," but that "this right will be exercised in the framework of talks to be held among Egypt, Israel, Jordan and the representatives of these Palestinian Arabs" — specifically by negotiation between states rather than by referendum or plebescite, and with the "participation" of the Palestinian Arabs in Gaza and the West Bank and not the scattered Palestinian Arabs

The Carter administration is being very cautious about reacting. It wants to reopen serious negotiations. It recognizes that Resolution 242 did not define "secure and recognized borders"; that it did not call for Israeli withdrawal from "all" Arab territories occupied by Israel after the 1967 war or from "the" territories; that it didn't require Israel to give up "every inch" of territory as demanded by Sadat — or forbid such total withdrawal, either.

All this calculated vagueness was to be left to the parties for discussion, and while the Carter administration is hopeful that the new Israeli formulation will break the stalemate, it is not very hopeful, and is still a little irritated by Begin's diplomacy.

Begin will be coming here for a week to help celebrate the 30th anniversary of Israel's independence. Washington recognizes the significance of the occasion and will certainly take part in it, but a transcontinental tour by Begin, with vast rallies in New York, Chicago and Los Angeles, precisely when all these intricate questions are back on the bargaining table, seems to some high officials a little excessive.

There even has been some discussion among Carter's principal aides about whether the president should receive Begin under such circumstances (he will).

So there will be discussion with Dayan before Begin arrives on what all this means. The administration is relieved that Israel has removed some of the barriers to a renewal of Mideast talks, but it is not yet clear what the new Israeli proposals really mean.

LETTERS

Tuition tax credit

Regarding the letter, "Tuition Tax Credit Opposed" [April 6 Register]: The letter said the Packwood-Moynihan tax credit bill would take $4.5 billion from public revenue. This may be, but has anyone ever figured how much revenue it would take if the private schools were forced to close and public schools had to house all those extra students?

I'm not griping so much about paying taxes for public schools, I'm just asking for a tax break so we can also afford to keep our [private] schools open. — **Chris Kirkman, 6513 S.W. Twenty-eighth Ct., Des Moines.**

Bribes and trades

It is hard for me to understand the difference between Tongsun Park's payoff to U.S. congressmen and President Carter's trade-off with U.S. senators. It seems to me a bribe is a bribe, whether money or in some other form.

It also seems to me that President Carter's method of getting support for his Panama Canal treaties is no better than Tongsun Park's method of getting support for his country. . . . — **Marvin Wahlert, Williams.**

His brother's vote

How interesting to note that Michael Feld did not abandon his IPBN job, according to a grievance committee report [April 7 Register]. And, how surprisingly, his own brother, a member of the committee, voted with the majority in a 2-to-1 decision. I wonder if all state employees may have relatives on the various boards and councils which may process an appeal? — **Arlen Diamond, 800 Second Ave., Iowa City.**

Uncreative music

An April 7 letter to the editor fascinated me. It was written by a 17-year-old who was in basic agreement with Donald Kaul's column of March 29 [which favored] early rock 'n' roll over the pop music of the late 1970s. The former, the letter-writer said, had spirit, while present-day music "has crumbled into a nauseous self-parody."

I fully agree; furthermore, I believe I know the reason why our music has flattened out. In ancient history . . . there were two types of civilizations. One was the mercantilist civilization (Carthage, Philistia, etc.), where gold was the absolute ruler; there was no room for creativity; the arts were borrowed from other civilizations, and almost no artifacts remain for the archaeologists. The other types of civilization, the classical ones (Greek, for example) did not place absolute authority upon gold; creativity flourished, and many of their artifacts remain.

Early rock music was like Greece. Today's music is like Carthage.

Furthermore, I feel that the 1970s will possibly go down in history as "The Decade No One Remembered." — **Doug "Leo" Hanbury, 1521 Sixty-eighth St., Des Moines.**

Libertarians

Every day, our government passes laws which restrict our rights to live as we choose. . . . Over the years, our government has gradually chipped away at [our constitutional] rights.

Fortunately, there is now a movement to reverse the trend. This movement is most closely exemplified by the Libertarian Party. This party is based upon the philosophy that there should be less government interference in our lives and in the economy.

In Iowa, there are two Libertarian candidates who are running for office in November. John Ball is running for governor, and Ben Olson is running for the U.S. Senate. I sincerely applaud the efforts of these two men and of all the other Libertarians in Iowa and in the rest of the country. Perhaps, one day, we may truly know the meaning of "freedom." — **Steven G. Colgrove, 4113 Buchanan Hall, Iowa State University, Ames.**

Disability pay

I read with interest the story in the April 5 Register about members of Congress who receive disability pensions. Of special interest is the fact that Olin Teague of Texas gets $951 per month for the loss of his leg.

My son lost his left leg and the mobility in his right ankle from shrapnel wounds. His disability pension is about half of what Teague receives.

If "a rose is a rose is a rose," it seems to me a leg is a leg is a leg, and they should receive the same amount of disability pay. — **Mrs. C.W Drumm, 929 Eisenhower, Muscatine.**

Guns and garbage

[Regarding the April 10 editorial, "Telltale Trash," concerning a federal court ruling that the government has the right to examine a citizen's garbage.]

I find it very strange that you would write an editorial downgrading invasion of privacy. Your stand on gun control is based on invasion of privacy and repeal of the Second Amendment's right to keep and bear arms. . . . — **Philip M. Thompson, 2301 S.W. Virginia, Des Moines.**

Des Moines Register, April 25, 1978

TRUTH JUSTICE FRIDAY—New York American Editorial Page—OCTOBER 27, 1933 PUBLIC SERVICE

Published Every Day in the Year at 220 South Street, New York City, by the New York American, Inc. President, William R. Hearst, Jr.; Secretary, Austin W. Clark.

Jesus Christ, who hath abolished death, and hath brought life and immortality to light through the gospel.—II Timothy, I, 10.

(The text for today is suggested by Rev. L. D. Woodmancy, D.D., pastor of Grace Methodist Episcopal Church, Manhattan. The next text will be suggested by Rev. Cornelius Greenway, pastor of All Souls Universalist Church, Brooklyn.)

Recognition of Soviet Russia Will Aid World Peace and International Justice

PRESIDENT ROOSEVELT'S effort "to end the present abnormal relations between the 125,000,000 people of the United States and the 160,000,000 people of Russia" ought to commend itself to the thoughtful citizens of both countries. It is a wise act on the President's part and advisable from every point of view.

"It is most regrettable," as Mr. Roosevelt truly says in his cordial message to Mr. Kalinin, president of the All Union Central Executive Committee at Moscow, **"that these great peoples, between whom a happy tradition of friendship existed for more than a century to their mutual advantage, should now be without a practical method of communicating directly with each other."**

To find such a method and to remove the difficulties that have given rise to this anomalous situation are the laudable purpose of the conversations soon to take place in the White House between the President and Mr. Litvinoff, the Russian Commissar for Foreign Affairs.

Mr. Roosevelt does not deny that these difficulties have been serious, but he shares with the American people the hope and the belief that they are no longer "insoluble."

If this free country could continue diplomatic relations with Russia under the government of the old regime, which was opposed to every principle and every ideal on which this nation was founded, we ought to be able to find a way of resuming relations with Russia under the present government, which, although not in accord with our own policies of government, is nevertheless not as diametrically opposed to our ideals as the former despotic autocracy that ruled Russia was.

Nor can we longer question the fact that this form of government is Russia's choice, because it has been firmly established there for fifteen years and there is every indication that it will continue to represent the conceptions of government held by the Russian people.

One of the reasons for this country's refusal to resume diplomatic relations with Russia was the present government's repudiation of pre-war and war-time debts.

This reason seems at present rather ridiculous, as we not only maintain diplomatic relations with France and England, but co-operate in close intimacy with these debt repudiators in regulating the affairs of Europe.

In fact, we have even appeared to be more friendly with these welching nations as they have not paid their just debts and obligations to this country.

* * *

RUSSIA from early days has been the friend of the United States, and a very important friend in past history, and there is every political reason why the two countries should resume this traditional relationship which has proved mutually advantageous in the past and may prove mutually essential in the future.

Japan has of late taken publicly on more than one occasion a very menacing attitude toward the United States.

Some of her less wise but leading statesmen and military commanders have made public utterances which appear to be most menacing in their character.

Furthermore, the moves of Japan, on the diplomatic chessboard, toward absorbing the mandated islands of the Pacific, and her activity in populating the American Territory of Hawaii, and her apparent intention ultimately to take over both the Hawaiian Islands and the Philippine Islands, are developments which would seem to indicate a temptation, if not a disposition, on the part of Japan to disrupt the friendly relations between Japan and this country and to disturb the peace of the Pacific.

Certainly the American people have no desire to see their relations with Japan other than friendly or to be called upon to defend against aggression the peace of the Pacific.

As a great nation and a peace-loving people we cherish nothing but sentiments of friendship for Japan just so long as Japan minds her own business and does not intrude upon American affairs.

But if it be the purpose of Japan, now or later, to dominate the Pacific, violate American rights or menace American territory, insular or continental, America should have an ally or at least a friend in Russia.

Therefore, for the peace of the world and for the establishment of justice among nations of good will, and for the sake of fair dealing and common sense in our international relations, it would seem to be mutually advantageous for the United States and Russia to renew that "happy tradition of friendship" which characterized their relations for more than a century.

We have said little about trade relations because these are, perhaps, the least important consideration. Nevertheless, friendly political relations promote trade relations, and trade relations, when on a basis of fairness, promote friendly political relations, so that the trade aspect of the situation should not be altogether ignored.

* * *

OF THE questions outstanding between Russia and the United States, the most serious is one that can best be removed "by frank, friendly conversations" of the sort that are soon to take place in the White House.

This is the revolutionary activity on American soil against the government and the institutions of the United States, which has been apparently fostered in the past by the government now in power at Moscow.

The American people will share with the President the hope that the Russian Commissar for Foreign Affairs, who is now on his way from Moscow to Washington, will begin his conversations by eliminating, once and for all, this obstacle to the dawn of a new and better day in the relations of these two great nations.

Jobs for Millions

WORK for millions of people would be made possible through a revival of building construction.

It has been estimated that some six million workers are affected by prosperity or lack of prosperity in the building industry. Eighty-five cents out of every building dollar is eventually paid to labor.

Building construction employs thousands of skilled mechanics and laborers. Hundreds of mills and factories employing more thousands of workers must be operated to meet the demand for clay products, woods, metals, cement, paints, textiles, glass, stone and equipment essential to the modern building.

Transportation by rail, air, ship and automobile must be employed to move raw and fabricated materials. Every new building requires new furniture, carpets and rugs, hardware and lighting fixtures. To convert raw material into use for buildings requires tools, machinery and power.

Every building erected means work for architects, engineers, draftsmen and workers in the fields of finance and real estate.

When the amount of direct and indirect employment affected by building is fully realized, the importance of the building industry as an agency for providing jobs for workers is apparent.

* * *

PUTTING men to work is a national and fundamental problem. To quickly accomplish this desirable end it is essential that we concentrate on stimulating those industries which affect the greatest number of workers.

The textile industry excepted, building is responsible for the employment of more persons than any other single industry. Building construction consumes a greater variety of materials produced throughout the United States than any other single industry. Building construction has a greater influence on the trend of general business than any other single industry. The building industry is a barometer that shows the upward and downward movement of all business. Private building construction is the major product of the industry, and therefore is of vast importance in our national economic welfare.

In addition to its Public Works Program the Federal Government should stimulate PRIVATE building construction. The Government should take such steps as may be necessary to remove the obstacles to building, unite forces, and stimulate construction.

To do so will permit employers of labor throughout the United States to put millions of workers back to work.

Keep the Air Clean!

Copyright, 1933, by N. Y. American, Inc.

LIBERTY is not LICENSE. Freedom of the press, which the Constitution guarantees, does not mean that irresponsible or malicious persons may defame others by misuse of the public prints.

Libel laws, which all good publications favor and obey, provide redress when such wrongs are committed.

We also have laws to punish slander (which is unwritten libel), but slander is often difficult or impossible to prove. There remains no written record of a conversation, which would be evidential.

Radio is like the press in its access to the public, and should be like the press in responsibility. But such is not the case, because radio is too often merely disseminated conversation. And slanders sometimes occur with little or no redress.

Out in progressive California they have a law to deal with radio slander. Of that law Governor Rolph has said:

"There should be no difference between a newspaper and a radio station as concerns libel. It makes no difference whether a person is slandered in a newspaper or over a radio; he should have recourse by law in either case."

The Governor proposes to amend the law so as to require every radio station in his State to keep a permanent written record of every radio speech.

Not only California but every other State should have such a law.

Your November Ballot

PERSONALITIES and bossism are not the only issues on which voters of this city are to pass judgment on November 7th.

The ballot will contain, besides its array of nominees for offices, six referenda, consisting of one State-wide proposition, four proposed amendments to the State Constitution, and a charter revision proposal affecting New York City only.

Little has been said of these referenda amid the wild polemics of an excited local campaign. Nonetheless, all are important.

The proposal that will appear on the ballot as "Proposition No. One" represents the public's inevitable duty to destitute families and other victims of the long depression.

It is a proposal to authorize the issuance of State emergency unemployment relief bonds to the sum total of $60,000,000.

Recommended by Governor Lehman and approved by the Republican leaders in the Legislature, there is no opposition to the measure. It MUST be approved. It should be approved UNANIMOUSLY.

Vote YES on Proposition No. One.

* * *

AMENDMENT NO. ONE to the State Constitution will permit a salutary reform in property condemnation procedure in New York City.

Under the amendment a special court will be established, presided over by competent and experienced judges; trials will be expedited, abuses eliminated and "a harmonious body of law and principles of valuation will be developed."

Vote YES on Amendment No. One.

Amendment No. Two proposes to extend "veterans' preferences" in civil service appointments and promotions, preferences now restricted to veterans who were both American citizens and residents of this State when they entered military service.

Without injustice to deserving veterans and their meritorious claims it is doubtful, indeed, if this proposal would do the public service any good and not do it considerable harm. "Veterans' preferences" are a form of class legislation. The civil service should be based upon ability always, and should not be used as an instrument for any kind of extraneous reward, whether political or otherwise.

In the interests of better civil service instead of worse, vote NO on Amendment No. Two.

Amendment No. Three is to permit a highway to be constructed over State lands in the Adirondacks. Inasmuch as the Association for the Protection of the Adirondacks approves, and the State Conservation Department does not oppose, the amendment may properly be carried.

Vote YES on Amendment No. Three.

Amendment No. Four will allow the State to turn over to New York City the West Fifty-third Street State Barge Canal Terminal.

The State has found the site unsuitable for a canal terminal, and the city needs the land for its West Side waterfront developments.

Vote YES on Amendment No. Four.

* * *

NOW we come to the New York City referendum—proposing a commission of seventeen persons to draft a new charter for the municipality.

The city unquestionably should abandon its present obsolete and detrimental "organic law." A modern and useful charter is a basic essential to good local government—but the pending proposal is no way in which to get a new charter.

In the first place, it is a Tammany scheme, railroaded politically through the Legislature, and as such it presupposes the perpetuation of Tammanyized city government. If the proposal is carried at the polls Mayor O'Brien—irrespective of the results of the mayoral election—will appoint this commission. If Mayor O'Brien is defeated he should not make "lame duck" appointments of such consequence. If he should be re-elected a better method of procuring charter reform should be followed.

In the second place, no special legislation is necessary to institute charter reform. Elected officials, UNDER EXISTING LAW, have the power as well as the obligation to do so.

The Tammany scheme should be defeated overwhelmingly.

VOTE NO ON THE CHARTER REVISION PROPOSAL.

A Library in Miniature

CRICKETS.

Questions.

1—To what order of insects do crickets belong?

2—Does a cricket leap or walk?

3—What is a katydid?

4—How does a cricket produce its chirp?

5—Why does a cricket chirp?

6—What is a Mormon cricket?

7—Are crickets destructive?

Answers.

1—Orthoptera, a zoological classification which includes cockroaches, mantids, grasshoppers, locusts and their allies.

2—It leaps. Orthoptera are divided into leaping and walking forms, the former being called "saltatory." The saltatory orthoptera include grasshoppers, both long and short horned, true locusts and crickets.

3—A variety of orthoptera closely allied to the grasshopper. Their name was given in reference to the curious strident sound which they emit and which was thought to resemble "Katy did."

4—By rubbing one forewing across the other. The under side of one wing is equipped with a rough saw-like covering which rasps across the projectir edge of the smooth wing.

5—Only the male chirps and his stridulating is a love song intended to attract the female. Succeeding in that, the cricket lowers his tone considerably. An entomologist has discovered that a cricket makes a full-tone slur downward from the fifth "D" above middle "C" in one-fiftieth of a second.

6—The so-called Mormon cricket is not a cricket at all, but a long-horned grasshopper. In 1848, when the Mormons were attempting to settle Great Salt Lake Valley, a horde of these "black crickets" threatened to devour all the crops, but were stopped by myriads of gulls, which appeared suddenly and devoured the insects. In 1913 a monument commemorating the incident was unveiled in Salt Lake City.

7—Yes. They eat clothes, rugs, furniture, meat, bread, and certain kinds do injury to vineyards and gardens.

Copyright 1933, King Features Syndicate, Inc.

Thwarting Romance by Law? -:- By Winifred Black

MOVIE FANS, don't go to Germany—not if you want to stay movie fans.

Germany is a nice, green, comfortable country, with plenty of rivers and deep, pleasant valleys and nightingales singing in the moonlight and good beer and the best sausages and pretzels in the world.

There is music in Germany, lots of it, all the time.

Everybody plays something.

The postman, if you please, plays the flute.

The grocer plays the drum and the man behind the counter at the drug store plays the piccolo.

And as for the fiddle—every other boy in high school is a violinist of sorts, and on Saturday nights and all day Sunday there is music in the air in Germany.

Good music, too, if you please. And the German moving pictures—have you seen them? They're very good, don't you think?

But Mr. Hitler is mad at the screen stars. He doesn't want any stars in Germany unless their names begin with H and end with r, it is said.

So he's made a brand new law about picture stars.

* * *

THEY aren't stars any more—not in Germany. They're just numbers.

Their names cannot be printed in big type and the name of the play must come first.

Big salaries for stars are out—in Germany. And woe be to anyone who tries to say that one pretty fraulein or one handsome herr is prettier or handsomer than anyone else.

Down with the movie fans—so says Mr. Hitler.

Now, isn't that just too silly of him?

What would you give for a girl who had never fallen in love with an actor, either on the screen or on the stage?

Not a snap of my finger, for my part.

* * *

KYRLE BELLEW, the handsome Englishman, said something to me once about matinee idols. He was a matinee idol himself, mind you.

Why, the girls used to lie in wait for him at the stage door and fairly tear him to pieces when he came out into the street after an afternoon of "The Romance of a Poor Young Man."

"They aren't crazy about me," said Kyrle Bellew. "They're crazy about romance, that's all.

"I'm always a hero in my plays. I'm poor but honest. I'm young but brave. I am humble but brilliant. I offer my life in defense of the lady of my choice. I defy tyrants. In short, I unfasten the wings of romance—they don't even know me, myself, but, ah! the hero of the play, that's different!

"If I had a daughter she'd bore me to death if she didn't have romance enough in her soul to fall in love with a hero once or twice.

"A faraway hero, of course—but a hero nevertheless."

* * *

NOW, Mr. Hitler, are you going to try to crush romance out of the German heart? You'll have to do a good deal of trying, I'm afraid.

The German fraulein hasn't those blue eyes for nothing, let me tell you.

Copyright, 1933, King Features Syndicate, Inc.

New York American, Oct. 27, 1933

A textbook copyrighted in 1936 warned editorial page editors:

> In these days, when the average newspaper reader has less time for reading than formerly—when he does more glimpsing than reading, and confines most of that glimpsing to the headlines and leading news stories or entertaining features—he seems to care little or nothing for newspaper editorials. If his attention is to be captured and held by the editorial page, that page must be unusually attractive physically. It must be even more inviting looking than the general-news pages, and even easier to read.

But editors ignored this advice. Only when the same warning was issued two and three decades later, when television began to compete for audience attention, did editors begin to take heed.

Bolder and Brighter

Traditional editorial page makeup in the 1940s, 1950s and 1960s was usually built around a vertically shaped cartoon at the top of the page. The newspaper's own editorials were assigned to one or two columns to the left of the cartoon. Columns and letters filled the remainder of the page. The *Washington Post* of Jan. 20, 1953, reproduced here, reflects that makeup arrangement, though the use of white space between the columns represents a step away from tradition.

Partly spurred by editorial page critique sessions at the annual meetings of NCEW, editors in the 1960s and 1970s began experimenting with more flexible designs. The coming of "cold type"—which could be pasted anywhere at any angle on a page—opened new possibilities that not even the most skilled printer could have managed with unwieldy hunks of metal type. Contributing to the flexibility was the introduction by a few cartoonists of a cartoon that was wider than it was high. This combination led to pages that, in their boldest form, looked like the Feb. 15, 1979, editorial page of the *Idaho Statesman* of Boise, which is reproduced here (p. 296). One problem with this page is that the long editorial is set in a very wide measure (26 picas, or about 4½ inches). Also, the lines contain more than 60 characters. A rule of thumb suggests that, for optimum newspaper reading, lines should have the equivalent of about one and a half lower case alphabets, or about 39 characters.[3]

Instead of always displaying the cartoon in the most prominent position, editors began experimenting with using cartoons to illustrate written editorial page material. A page from the Aug. 7, 1979, *Houston* (Texas) *Post* provides an example of an article wrapped around a LePelley cartoon (p. 297). Notice, too, how the editorials are indented from the left side of the page. A large amount of white space separates the articles and sets off the headlines. The page also illustrates the preference of some editors to slide the newspaper's masthead (the box that lists the ownership and the executives of the newspaper) to a lower corner of the page. Why, some editors wondered, should the most important spot on the page, the upper left corner, carry the same information every day? The bold labeling of the page as "Commentary" represents another trend among editors: an effort to help readers distinguish between news and opinion.

The Washington Post

EUGENE MEYER, *Chairman of the Board* — PHILIP L. GRAHAM, *President and Publisher*
HERBERT ELLISTON .... *Editor* — CHARLES C. BOYSEN .... *Secretary* — DONALD M. BERNARD, *Advertising Director*
J. R. WIGGINS ...... *Managing Editor* — JOHN W. SWEETERMAN, *Business Manager* — JOHN S. HAYES, *President WTOP Radio-TV*

AN INDEPENDENT NEWSPAPER — TUESDAY, JANUARY 20, 1953 — PAGE 14

Inauguration Day

This is a great day for the American system of government, and a thrilling day for all good citizens of this Republic. Dwight D. Eisenhower will take the oath of office as President of the United States. That means a great change at the White House, not only in occupants, but also in parties. And it is all being done with order and consideration and cooperation, thanks to both the retiring and the incoming Presidents. The transition is something to create pride and awe in the breast of every American.

General Eisenhower will take over the Presidency in the plenitude of the country's power and prosperity. The office is a branch of the American trinity of branches of government. Let us give thanks to our forefathers for the political edifice they outlined. It is refreshing on this day of days to turn back to the *Federalist* to read what the founding fathers had in mind. Madison, Hamilton and Jay were seeking in the *Federalist* to secure ratification of the Constitution. Their basic assumption was that the very definition of tyranny consists of accumulating all powers in the same hands. Whether the hands were hereditary, self-appointed or elected—that made no difference. Thus the founding fathers had already set up a government in three separate and coequal departments in an effort to prevent the rise of tyranny.

The separation of powers upon which our Government rests makes it a tremendously difficult system to operate, because unless there is a considerate relation among the three, the branches could revolve in their respective orbits, and there would be chaos. A balance has somehow to be struck and maintained and be subject, as Dr. Johnson said about friendship, to constant repair in order to insure the functioning of government.

This constant and continuing need for balance calls for a qualification on the part of a successful President, second only to leadership. The qualification is diplomacy. Leadership is obvious enough as a prerequisite, but diplomacy is not often thought about. A President must do his part in getting along with his partners. Harmony between the White House and the judiciary was difficult till there had been general acceptance of a famous dictum of John Marshall, the country's third Chief Justice. "It is emphatically the province and duty of the judicial department," said the great Marshall, "to say what the law is," and when this statement had become axiomatic, the foundation of our constitutional liberties was well and truly laid.

The prime problem of American government as a day-to-day proposition lies in the relation between the President and Congress. Here there is need for a very high degree of diplomacy—of that kind of diplomacy which recognizes the rights under the organic law of both coordinates, yet seeks consciously to respect what in another connection a great jurist called "the law of the unenforceable." The jurist was talking about the behavior of people in a free society—how 95 percent of their actions are governed not by law but by a feeling of right conduct. The same thought could be applied to relations between a President and Congress under the American system. Ideally, one owes to the other a respect for its individuality and authority—that is to say, power at the other's expense is "an encroaching spirit" that gentlemen must resist. "It is one thing," as Alexander Hamilton said, "to be subordinate to the laws and another to be dependent on the legislative body."

It is said, by way of example, that the men on the Hill feel they are professionals in the business of government and must guide the "amateur in the White House." This kind of arrogance is intolerable to the spirit of the Constitution. The new President could respond to any such outcropping with weapons that would be more than salutary, at least in his initial period—the weapons of his vast public support and of his patronage. It is plain he harbors no idea of using a big stick. He is said to be very conscious of his own responsibilities in creating a smooth-working liaison with Congress. The evidence is the report of his purpose to set up a bipartisan council with which to take counsel on foreign affairs. This will show the President's good intent, and the way that the partnership is worked out will depend upon the conduct of the men involved.

If the new President shows this will to cooperate, then he can legitimately expect Congress to respect his constitutional right to the initiative. For the world of free men will depend upon the wise and swift exercise of the initiative in the conduct of American foreign relations. It was not always so. The framers of the Constitution did not envisage a rank for America of high mightiness. They based the organic law upon the feeling that America would be neutralist in a world of big powers. Even as late as the first edition of *The American Commonwealth* Bryce could write that "four fifths of the President's work is the same in kind as that which devolves on the manager of a railway." Now the President's job is Atlas-like.

With power has come responsibility, and the need to be ready for sure and swift action. Congress must realize that the President's initiative must never be allowed to become palsied, that he must show that "vigor of government" within the "perfect security of freedom" which George Washington said was required of the management of the common interests of Americans. May the new President be aided by Almighty Providence in the discharge of the obligations which he will assume today!

Loyalty And Liberty

The country looks with hope to the great American who assumes the Presidency today for a revitalization of its traditional civil liberties. These liberties have sometimes been curtailed—needlessly curtailed—in the name of national security. They are, of course, a vital source of security. They constitute the real roots of American loyalty.

In the championship of civil liberties which he has promised, President Eisenhower can make no better beginning than to establish a Commission on Internal Security and Individual Rights—made up of distinguished citizens, as was the Nimitz Commission which President Truman vainly tried to set in motion—to advise the country and himself as to the effectiveness of its security precautions and the maintenance of its essential freedoms.

Security and freedom are not in conflict; they are, on the contrary, complementary. The American public needs the reassurance which such a commission could afford that disloyalty is being checked without enthroning demagogy. The President needs the counsel of such a commission in maintaining a wise balance between national needs and individual rights.

Conserving Resources

It was characteristic of President Truman to choose the conservation and development of natural resources as the subject of his final message to Congress. The subject is one respecting which he takes tremendous pride—and justly—in the record of his Administration. It is a subject with a long and highly creditable record of bipartisanship—a fitting subject for the final recommendations of a President about to turn over the reins of authority to his successor. And, finally, these natural resources, as the President observed, "are a foundation upon which rest our national security, our ability to maintain a democratic society, and our leadership in the free world."

The conservation movement got its start under President Theodore Roosevelt in 1902 with the enactment of the reclamation laws. These laws have had the support of every President since then, regardless of party; resource development in a variety of forms was given great impetus during the 20 years of the F. D. Roosevelt and Truman Administrations; and, in particular, the accomplishments since 1945 cited by Mr. Truman indicate how much this kind of conservation and development can mean in terms of living standards and general welfare. Some 1300 new soil conservation districts have been formed during the past eight years; about 2,700,000 irrigated acres have been added to the Nation's farm lands; three million acres have been given flood protection; electricity has been brought to one and one-half million farms that didn't have it prior to 1945, making nearly 9 out of 10 American farms electrified.

This is a proud legacy to leave to one's successor. Mr. Truman leaves it with a dual admonition. "We have learned," he says, "that the mark of a well-managed land lies in the care a Nation gives to its rivers." The Tennessee Valley Authority stands as perhaps the greatest domestic achievement of the last two decades—a symbol of what can be done through Federal-State cooperation, imaginative planning and decentralized, local administration. The rest of his warning to the Eisenhower Administration is that "we must make sure that we safeguard the use of these resources for the benefit of all the people. Where the public moneys are invested, the resulting gains must accrue to the public, and not be diverted to the undue benefit of any private group."

Each generation holds the natural resources of the Nation in trust for its posterity. Mr. Truman can relinquish his trusteeship with a clear conscience. He spoke, in this final message to Congress, in behalf of the most vital interests of the American people.

Symbol Of Tradition

For all the revolutionary spirit which General Eisenhower displayed in spurning a top hat and buying a new homburg for his Inauguration, some devotees of reaction or tradition or just high revelry—whatever you like—have defied the new President and appeared, at least on the pre-inaugural scene, in tall silk hats. Perhaps they are Democrats! Whoever they are, their defiance of the example of the hero of the day is pardonable, and, indeed, even deserves our salute. After all, the high hat in different colors is the badge for high occasions, and what occasion in the secular calendar of events could be higher than Inauguration? Even if you simply want something to do something with, after your rejoicing over the day's event (such as kicking your hat into the Potomac), what better object than a topper?

Some of the local stores report they have sold out of homburgs since the general announced his decision on their behalf, while the supply of toppers, in view of Ike's decision, is far from exhausted. But other occasions will come around. And the new President may then relent, for it is our surmise that his ukase was a sudden outburst of independence after acquiescence in ritual over many days, and he simply decided that for a change he would be himself.

The Law And Wilson

We reprint below for the benefit of our readers the statute which Senators have raised in connection with the nomination of Charles E. Wilson to be Secretary of Defense:

> Whoever, being an officer, agent or member of, or directly or indirectly interested in the pecuniary profits or contracts of any corporation, joint-stock company, or association, or of any firm or partnership, or other business entity, is employed or acts as an officer or agent of the United States for the transaction of business with such business entity, shall be fined not more than $2000 or imprisoned not more than two years, or both.

This law was enacted in 1948.

Thanks To Neely

As Senator Case takes over the chairmanship of the Senate District Committee, it is important not to overlook the good work done by the retiring Democratic chairman, Senator Neely. The West Virginia legislator has exercised a conscientious stewardship over District affairs for the last two years. His insistence on punctual meetings of the District Committee was an index to his businesslike approach in getting things done. Particularly to his credit was the manner in which, with Senator Case's cooperation, he fought to see the local crime investigation through against considerable odds. He also was a stalwart champion of home rule for Washington. In extending what we feel confident is the thanks of many Washingtonians, we are glad that Senator Neely intends to continue his progressive interest in District affairs in the new Congress.

"The President Of The United States"

Letters To The Editor

Acheson's Record

It is hard for me to imagine just what cerebral steps led the writer of your editorial of January 15, "Four Years of Dean Acheson," to the analysis that his was a "mind short of conceptions" and that Mr. Acheson had "rated and berated those who wanted to put ideas into foreign policy."

Secretary Acheson was the originator of the Marshall Plan. He worked hard to get it passed by a Congress that found it a very revolutionary concept. He was the prime mover behind the Truman Doctrine. With Mr. Lilienthal he presented the first ideas for the control of atomic energy. Certainly he gave aid and weight to NATO from the start and his presentation of the unifying for peace resolution was the big step forward in the potential strength of the United Nations.

The man who played these roles in such ideas can hardly be said to have left the vision to others. I can only conclude that this editorial reveals to your readers more about the writer than it does about Mr. Acheson. Perhaps your writer has overlooked these points because like most great concepts, once accepted they become taken for granted.

JAMES ROWE, JR.
Washington.

Arlington Buses

Your paper of January 15 carried the good news that we of Arlington may again have the privilege of fighting our way to and from our homes on Mr. Arnold's buses. Hooray! He has agreed to give his men a raise, adding that, of course, this raise will make it necessary for him to apply to the ICC for an "upward adjustment of fares." Several weeks ago he threatened the men that it would be necessary for him to resume bus service with fewer buses "because he would have lost customers during the strike." Just how does Mr. Arnold figure? Where have his customers gone—why will he have lost them?

Before the ICC gives ear to the newest request for a raise in fares, I think it would be very interesting to ask the company what prompted them to cut our bus service beginning last October 27. And they should ask what assurance will he give the people of Arlington that our service will not be similarly botched at the whim of the company, after the raise in fares has gone into effect.

On October 27, the day the company cut at least 10 buses off their schedule, I waited for 55 minutes for a bus going my way. By that time there were so many people waiting with me that I was pushed to the back of the mob and the door was closed in my face. I got home in $1\frac{1}{2}$ hours. It is a 15-minute ride after I get on the bus. And that happened regularly up until the strike.

PATRICIA FLEMING.
Arlington.

Communists In Schools

Your editorials of January 5 and 6 attacking the planned investigations of Communist influences in our colleges are alarming. These views show a frightening lack of understanding of the methods and objectives of the Communist conspiracy.

The May, 1937, issue of the *Communist Magazine* advises Communist teachers to "take advantage of their positions, without exposing themselves . . . Only when teachers have really mastered Marxism-Leninism will they be able skillfully to inject it into their teaching at the least risk of exposure."

Did you ever hear of William Z. Foster's statement that "Our teachers must write new school textbooks and rewrite history from the Marxian viewpoint"? (100 Things You Should Know About Communism — House Committee on Un-American Activities, page 46).

Did you know that 3000 professors have chalked up a total of 26,000 Communist-front affiliations? As expressed in the *Saturday Evening Post* editorial of September 27, 1952, the dismissal of a tiny handful of these shows long-suffering patience rather than a witch hunt.

JULIAN E. WILLIAMS.
Mount Rainier, Md.

One-Man Bolt

The strange spectacle of Senator Wayne Morse first bolting the Republican Party and then setting himself up as a one-man Independent, does not surprise people who had occasion to talk with the Senator several years ago—about political matters.

Back in 1949 I discussed the possibility of the Senator writing some magazine articles under the title "The Bankruptcy of the Republican Party." It was a period when Jenner, Capehart, Bricker and their friends were doing all in their power to sabotage liberal legislation.

Senator Morse was disgusted with these shenanigans and was extremely critical of his own party. I finally asked, "Would you, Senator, be interested in forming a third party?"

Instead of a direct answer, Senator Morse implied that the matter would have to wait until after 1950, since he was standing for reelection in that year.

Today, we have the paradox of a liberal Republican being ostracized from his own party at the same time that other Republicans, who are a disgrace to the country, are lionized and feted.

FRED REINSTEIN.
Washington.

Misusing Fire Boxes

The Washington Post, in glorifying the incident which found a 3-year-old boy pulling a fire-alarm box, is a bit off the beam as far as logical reasoning is concerned. Perpetuation of such left-footed thinking might motivate some cute little cherub to turn in a riot call and await the arrival of police with his trusty machine gun or hand grenade at the ready position for the benefit of enterprising photographers. The malicious sounding of fire-alarm boxes over a period of years has been the direct cause of a number of firemen losing their means of livelihood through injuries sustained in collisions which were an outgrowth of unnecessary responses.

These incidents have ranged in the past from tragic explosions and serious fires to the more routine occurrences which run the gamut from overheated furnaces to unintentional waterless cooking.

The author of this rebuttal was the unwitting victim of grievous injuries in a false-alarm collision between fire apparatus and a carelessly operated commercial carrier (this premise was established in a proper court of law). The fire box, as I recall, was sounded in this instance by a jealous suitor who wished to somehow change the mind of his lady love by creating a furor of sirens and bells. The accident in question cut off the earning power of two men who were using Fire Department paychecks to appease the wolf at the door, and will always affect the physical well-being of the more fortunate firemen who returned to duty.

Firemen and policemen are sworn to do their utmost to aid those citizens in need of their services.

W. G. MOORE,
Editor, The Fire Fighter
Washington.

"End Of Mob Murder"

May I express my appreciation for your excellent editorial of January 4 commenting on the fact that there were no lynchings in the United States during 1952 as presented in the annual report of Tuskegee Institute.

It should be noted, however, that for some years now a truer index of the state of intergroup tensions in the South has been the incidence of violence growing out of racial and religious frictions. Lynchings, heinous as they are, have become so rare in recent years that to say that race relations have improved or deteriorated because there were two lynchings in one year, four the next and none the following year is statistically unsound.

The report from Tuskegee Institute did indicate that during the latter part of 1951 and during 1952 an unprecedented, and largely unpublicized, wave of violence washed through the Nation and particularly the South. The crude, homemade bomb and the dynamite stick became a favored method of expressing hostility toward members of racial and religious minorities.

It is my belief that the interpretation of what this rash of violence means is much more important than the chronicling of the incidents themselves. Interpretation is highly necessary at this time when certain alarmists are warning the United States Supreme Court that a decision by the justices upsetting current segregation patterns in Southern public schools would lead to extreme violence and virtual anarchy, and that the clock of race relations would be set back 50 years.

Some years ago, while speaking in your city before a meeting of the Fellowship of Southern Churchmen, I predicted, and I have since repeated this prediction before a number of other forums, that we might expect considerable violence during this decade. It was, and is, apparent that customs generations old are changing with extreme rapidity. As the walls of segregation begin to crumble, a small minority is attempting to replace the cloak of legality which has heretofore safeguarded this wall, with a cloak of violence.

The incidents of violence we are experiencing now, in my view, represent only a bitter, rear-guard action. The crude bombs and the dynamite sticks may provide stumbling blocks on the road we are traveling toward a more meaningful democracy. They cannot stay for more than a brief moment the forward surge.

This is because the people of the South respect legally constituted authority. They are intensely law-abiding and anarchy is as repugnant to them as communism. There are strong forces in the South — the press, the church, women's groups, the FBI, a growing number of local police authorities—who are determined that the rapid changes in mores be carried out in an orderly fashion. These are the forces that have done away with lynching; that have bested the Klan, the Columbians and similar groups; that have made it possible for an increasing number of Negroes each year to vote and enjoy other attributes of citizenship. These are the same forces which, if the United States Supreme Court rules that segregation in the public schools is illegal, will prevent the chaos and mob violence so direfully being predicted by the prophets of doom.

ALEXANDER F. MILLER,
Director, Southern Office, Anti-Defamation League of B'nai B'rith.
Atlanta, Ga.

Eisenhower Maps Middle Road Course

By Marquis Childs

Childs

AFTER THE LONG drought, the Republican rejoicing is full of a fine fervor. But when the bunting comes down and the paraders go home, this Capital will see the beginning of one of the most interesting experiments in government in many, many years.

The outlines of that experiment are already evident. In essence, it is an effort to apply the management techniques of big industry to big government.

The wisecrack about the Eisenhower Cabinet consisting of eight millionaires and a plumber or, more accurately, a steamfitter, misses the real point. These businessmen now in Government have been handsomely rewarded for their ability. But money reward has been secondary to the fact of the power and the skills they have wielded as the managers of industry financed by thousands of investors large and small.

They will now be managers of the far larger enterprises of Government. Often in the past the complaint about the Government administrators has been that they never met a payroll. The men in the Eisenhower Administration have been responsible for meeting some very large payrolls.

But, with two or three exceptions, they have not met the voters at the polling booth. Republicans in Congress, who feel that through the years they put the political capital into this enterprise, look with skepticism on the experiment of managerial government. The Senate hitch over Charles E. Wilson's confirmation as Defense Secretary because of his General Motors stock indicates the relationship between the managers and the politicians may be difficult.

The new Administration is not, however, without its political managers and very skillful ones, indeed. They come out of the hard-boiled organization built up in New York State by Gov. Thomas E. Dewey. They also have roots in California, where Gov. Earl Warren has demonstrated how to build up a political following transcending the two-party system as we have known it in the past 20 years. Significantly, in this connection, it is in California and New York, the two most populous States in the country, that the decay of the Democratic Party is most conspicuous.

THE AIM IS TO go down the middle of the road with a party having few resemblances to the old Republican Party. Thus a minimum of 10 percent, and perhaps nearer to 15 or 20 percent, of the following that has kept the Democrats in power—farmers, labor, minorities—will be permanently won over. This is the pattern evident behind many of the moves made since November 4, and it promises to become increasingly apparent as the new Administration takes over.

One of the able and successful members of the political team which will work toward the long-term goal is Senator Irving Ives of New York. Ives won reelection last fall by the huge plurality of 1,332,198. He carried New York City, which Eisenhower lost, by a plurality of 2743. In a speech in New York last week, Ives said, in effect, that the Republican Congress was Republican because of the personal popularity of General Eisenhower. The people, he said, were still progressive and there could be "no turning back of the clock of progress." Then Ives spoke of what is the biggest hazard faced by the new Administration:

"With a spirit of mutual helpfulness and cooperation the new Administration can and will succeed. Without it, failure is certain and the Republican Party is doomed to defeat in 1956."

A MEMBER OF the Senate Labor Committee, Ives is hoping to head a subcommittee that will study discrimination in industry and business. The political implications of this are obvious. The Republican majority is expected to agree on a compromise civil rights bill providing for a commission to educate and persuade employers that discrimination is not only unfair, but that it does not pay. This would be labeled as a first step and it would be taken by men like Ives as a trial of what can be achieved by a law without power of Federal punishment.

Thus the pattern will be developed if the able political managers working for the Eisenhower Administration can bring it off. They will have many resources, particularly in the honeymoon phase, and they will be working with some shrewd operators.

One of these is Gen. Lucius D. Clay, now retired, an old Eisenhower comrade with a unique influence although he will hold no office. Clay serves as a kind of bridge between the business community and Eisenhower's familiar military associations. A man of outstanding ability, as he demonstrated in his military career which concluded with his appointment as occupying chief in Germany. Clay is now chairman of the board and chief executive officer of the Continental Can Co. He is also on the board of the General Motors Corp., which gives him a link with top Eisenhower Cabinet officers.

The Washington Post

Registered in U. S. Patent Office

Published every day in the year by The Washington Post Company

The Associated Press is entitled exclusively to use for republication of all news dispatches credited to it or not otherwise credited in this paper and local news of spontaneous origin published herein. Rights of republication of all other matter herein are also reserved.

1515 L Street N.W., Washington 5, D. C.
Telephone NAtional 8-4200

Offices of National Advertising Representatives
Sawyer-Ferguson-Walker Co.—
New York .... 60 East 42nd St., Room 832
Chicago .... 333 North Michigan Avenue
Detroit .... 1530 Guardian Building
Atlanta .... 22 Marietta St.
Philadelphia .... 1400 South Penn Square
Los Angeles .... 612 S. Flower St.
San Francisco .... Russ Building
Miami Beach, Fla.—The Hal Winter Co., 9049 Emerson Ave.
London, England—Joshua B. Powers, Ltd., 14 Cockspur St.

CARRIER DELIVERY—WASHINGTON AREA

Daily and Sunday		Sunday Only		Daily Only	
One week	$ .40	One week	$ .10	One week	[illegible]
One month	1.75	One month	.45	One month	1.30

Elsewhere

Daily and Sunday		Sunday Only		Daily Only	
One week	$ .40	One week	$ .15	One week	$ .30
One month	1.75	One month	.65	One month	1.30

BY MAIL—PAYABLE IN ADVANCE

Daily and Sunday		Sunday Only		Daily Only	
One year	$21.00	One year	$7.80	One year	$15.60
Six months	10.50	Six months	3.90	Six months	7.80
Three months	5.25	Three months	1.95	Three months	3.90
One month	1.75	One month	.65	One month	1.30

Rates outside U. S. A. furnished upon request

Entered at the Postoffice Washington, D. C. as second-class mail matter

Washington Post, Jan. 20, 1953

STATESMAN

Editorials

Robert B. Miller Jr., Publisher
Rod Sandeen, Managing Editor
Jim Dean, Asst. Managing Editor
Jim Boyd, Editor of Editorial Page
Gary F. Sherlock, Advertising Director
Russell W. Ford, Circulation Manager

The comments below represent the opinions of The Idaho Statesman. Columns, commentary, cartoons and letters appearing elsewhere on this page represent the opinions of the authors.

PAGE 6A Thursday, February 15, 1979

"A Part of Life in Idaho"

"...AS MILLIONS TURNED OUT TO GREET AYATOLLAH KHOMEINI UPON HIS RETURN TO IRAN!!
USA

Oil!

Oil! A few years ago you drove to the auto discount store, bought a can of it for 39 cents and poured it in your engine without a second thought. Today it threatens our economy, our security, our lifestyle.

The chaos in Iran serves to give us pause. A government crumbles half a world away, in a country peopled by individuals whose ways we don't understand and whose names we can't pronounce, and we tremble at the prospect of losing the vital link. Admit it. We as a nation are not driven by concern for the well-being of the people of Iran. The drama of recent happenings in that country does, of course, merit our interest. The overriding question, though, is what will happen to Iran's oil.

The Iranian hiatus illuminates the extent of our dependence. We've lost less than 3 percent, and here we are talking of closing service stations on Sunday, waiting lines at the pumps, dollar-a-gallon gasoline, even rationing. The latter is a remote possibility, but if 3 percent is enough to raise the specter of gas-rationing, what fears would stem from a cut of 6 percent? 12 percent?

It would be nice to think we could count on a steady supply of Mideast oil from other exporters. At the moment there appears to be no cause to fear further disruptions. We would be hugely surprised if, say, Saudi Arabia cut its oil shipments. But we were surprised when the Shah of Iran was overthrown. We were surprised again when the Iranian army withdrew its support of the Bakhtiar government. It is foolish to count on anything in the Mideast, because anything can happen there.

Iran underscores the perilousness of relying on other countries for a vital, not to mention dwindling, resource. Washington currently is agog with the lure of Mexican oil, and indeed there appears to be reason for hope. But Mexico's oil, as President Jose Lopez Portillo cautions, should not be viewed as a panacea for America's energy woes.

Mexico, in addition to oil, has a troubled economy, a population explosion, grinding poverty and epidemic unemployment, any one of which could threaten exports. And Mexicans aren't likely to forget overnight the decades of indifference displayed by their rich neighbor to the north. If we look to Mexico for salvation, we're apt to be looking for a good long time.

Mexico, and the Mideast as well, should be viewed only as temporary allies, and tenuous ones at that. If we are to survive and prosper in the long term, we must abandon illusions of salvation at the hands of foreign oil.

We realize the magnitude of what we are saying. A country nurtured and grown to maturity on oil cannot be weaned overnight. But oil, in addition to running the country, has fueled inflation, thrown our trade balance out of kilter, polluted our air and threatened our basic well-being. It is time to begin to look away from oil, foreign and otherwise. It is time to look to ourselves.

We're fond of calling America the most advanced nation on earth, yet we are almost wholly dependent on countries where people ride camels to work and justice amounts to cutting off hands with swords. We do not worship the god of technology, but we cannot believe that it is beyond this nation to become energy independent. If there is salvation, it is in the form of alternative energy sources, and those who scoff should take a closer look.

Solar energy is not some distant, unattainable goal. It is here. People are heating their homes with it — in this city and scores of others. If solar can work, and it does, it can be improved. And if we can heat our homes with the sun's energy, who is to say we can't use it to get from one place to another? Who is to say we can't solve the problems of nuclear power and develop other forms of alternative energy?

The challenges are great, but if this really is the most advanced nation in the world, it's time we started trying to prove it where it counts.

God help the queen

Queen Elizabeth, while visiting the Mideast, is being forced to abstain from wine with meals, wear dresses that cover her from wrist to ankles, and hide her face with scarves. In countries where women are considered insignificant, the queen is being treated as "an honorary man." When you stop and think about it, that's pretty big news. It takes something like this — the queen of England groveling — to make us realize how much the world has changed lately.

CONSTITUTIONAL

"I KNOW NOT WHAT COURSE OTHERS MAY TAKE...."

Legislature needs ethics code

John Corlett

The Lenaghen confirmation squabble brought out the long overdue need for a legislative code of ethics or a conflict-of-interest law. On this subject this column has been a voice crying in the wilderness for many years.

It may be many more years before the people elect a legislature attuned to the moral need for a code of ethics and a conflict-of-interest law, the latter to apply to public officials at all levels of government. The current Legislature is not about to upset a system that is predicated more on political and personal considerations than on the public welfare. This is a legislature that could seriously consider eliminating some of the disclosure provisions of the Sunshine Law, enacted by initiative.

The national Congress has made considerable strides in the disclosure field of elections, lobbying, and the personal financial arrangements and records of its members. The Senate and the House have their own ethics committees, albeit they have moved gingerly in coming down hard on violators, both of the law and of congressional ethics. But a start has been made.

The Sunshine Law of 1974 authorized the disclosure of election financing and activities and expenditures by lobbyists. The law has stood the test of need, although some of the more conservative Republican legislators still oppose it.

As long as Idaho remains a relatively small state and elects purely citizen, as opposed to professional, legislators, it hardly seems necessary for the Legislature to call for financial reports of its members.

As far as the Legislature is concerned, a code of ethics could include a conflict-of-interest provision, and that is vitally needed. The only effort to establish a code of ethics was made about 15 years ago, but it got short shrift, and there has been no effort since. Former Attorney General Tony Park urged the 1974 Legislature to pass a conflict-of-interest law, but it got nowhere.

A conflict of interest arises when a legislator's occupation or financial earnings could influence his vote on a particular law or issue. In other words it could be assumed he was voting for his own private gain, or for benefit of a firm with which he is employed or has a financial arrangement.

In the Lenaghan affair, Senate Majority Leader James Risch was said to have a conflict of interest in his opposition to PUC President Robert Lenaghan because his law firm had collected $17,000 in retainer fees from Idaho Power Company, which has rate increase filings before the Public Utilities Commission.

Under a code of ethics Risch would have been required to disclose his conflict of interest. With the public being given notice of that disclosure, Risch could vote or ask to be excused from voting, whatever his determination. The important point is that a disclosure was made from which the public could decide on the efficacy of any vote.

Without question a poll taken today would show the Legislature at a very low spot on the popularity scale for two reasons. One, it took no action in halting or reducing a 40 percent pay raise, and, two, its members are eating quite high on the hog at dinners at which lobbyists play host, about $20,000 worth in January alone. A friend of mine, disgruntled by the disclosure of the freebies going to the Legislature, said that if the Legislators "are so bad off maybe we better give them food stamps and low-cost housing."

The method used by the Legislature in getting its pay raise was unconscionable. There is a big question about freebies these days. A code of ethics ought to prohibit them, although the disclosure of expenditures by lobbyists at least informs the public about which legislators are accepting the freebies.

In another day, the public probably would have accepted the 40 percent pay raise with a measure of equanimity. But with President Carter calling for others to limit a pay increase to 7 percent, the Legislature could have followed suit.

The Legislature's credibility vanishes now that it is proposing only a 7 percent pay increase for state employees, counting the 5 percent incremental raise authorized by the last Legislature.

Only the Legislature creates the reasons for a code of ethics to inform and protect the public it represents.

(John Corlett is a retired Statesman political editor.)

Letters to the Editor

Government: no friend to NNC

Editor, The Statesman:

In 1941 I completed four years of study at NNC. Employed by the school, I earned my way. I helped build Morrison Hall. For two years I was night police on the campus. Consequently, I am very much interested in what become of Cady as well as the president she attacked in her editorial.

It was not academic leadership that helped me to know what was going on and solve my problems. I believe a man must be honest and blameless before God, create his own atmosphere and live in it. One's spiritual and academic orientation develops from within-out rather than without-in.

NNC was born to give young people Christian education. When it stops doing just that, it has ceased from doing that for which it was born. If the spiritual students of the 1930s were to walk down the road and meet the spiritual students of 1970s, would they know each other? If not, why not?

There is much to be learned from freedom of speech. Everyone will learn that he must walk on criticism or sink. It is futile to sail on praise alone. A person must learn to get power from criticism as well as praise.

Freedom of speech or freedom of the press is not the paramount bug gnawing at NNC's vine. It is the fact that they have accepted government money to run the school. The government is no friend to holiness.

A man was authorized to take a pig to market. On his way he stopped for a cup of coffee. Hanging the sacked pig on a peg with his hat, he ordered his hot coffee. An old maid came by with a pup. She pulled out the pig and placed the pup in the sack.

None the wiser, the man continued his journey. At the market he offers his pig for sale, but to his amazement, out popped a pup. With no sale for the pup, he starts homeward. Again he stops for that cup of coffee. And again the lady comes and changes the pig for the pup. Soon the man goes home with his sack. But what confusion — out wiggles the pig. The point is, don't take time for substitutes. One switch can get you off the track and it is doubtful whether the man with the little mustache ever gets the pig to market and may never even get the pig home. — GLENN STOUT, Boise

Nix negativism

Editor, The Statesman:

The last year or so, The Statesman has shown an interest in the local schools by writing and printing positive articles. I'm very disappointed, however, that Bruce Spence could only see the negative side of the meeting held at South Junior High between parents and school trustees on Jan. 25.

There were 150 people who attended that meeting for the purpose of finding out what we can do to help support funds for Boise schools. A small handful (two or three) voiced concern of "scare tactics." It is unfortunate that parents feel the scare tactics are coming from the schools. I, personally, feel that the parents who are most concerned, talk about it at home and to their friends and the anxiety or enthusiasm goes from parent to child, and from child to child.

We are not using "scare tactics," but if that is what it will take help our schools — fine.

I just hope that everyone will do as suggested at that meeting and write to your legislator and tell them how you feel and that we want our quality education to continue. Our legislators have to know what we want in order to make decisions we elected them to make.

The headlines of Spence's article was not the primary feeling of those attending the meeting, but that is what thousands of Statesmen readers will think because of a handful of negative opinions.

It is unfortunate that the minority seems to be the loudest. — ILAINE TRACY, Boise

Urgent

Editor, The Statesman:

Any TV watcher knows about commercials, but I ponder the sensibility of some of them. Take, for instance the "Mr. Goodwrench" commercial, where a driver, in a GM sedan, looks down at the door, saying "You never had it so good!" as he pats it.

Rather silly, isn't it, or if this is a trend it may bring new ideas in every business. Can't you just imagine a commercial showing a man with his hand on a casket, saying "I'm sure going to feel snuggy in you!" Don't wait, friends. — ANDREW P. DEMBOWSKI, Boise

Kudos for Boise Rhodes Scholars

Editor, The Statesman:

I was pleased to read in The Statesman that Michael Hoffman of Payette (Boise State University), and Thomas A. Smith of Boise (Cornell University), had been successful in the 1978 competition for the American Rhodes Scholarships. I congratulate these young men on their achievement.

As a former Rhodes Scholar, and former secretary for the Idaho Rhodes Scholarships Selection Committee, I now have had an opportunity to look over the complete list of American Rhodes Scholars-elect for 1979. I have thought that friends of the new Idaho Scholars might be interested to know where, from the national standpoint, their election "fits."

According to the regulations of the Rhodes Trust, an American college student may make application for a Scholarship from either the state of his residence, or the state in which his sponsoring school is located. For the purposes of the annual Rhodes competition, the United States has been divided into eight districts: New England, Middle Atlantic, Southern, Great Lakes, Middle West, Gulf, Southwestern and Northwestern.

Only four scholarships may be awarded each year by a district selection committee.

At the Northwestern District interviews this year, Idaho's two candidates competed against young men and women representing Washington, Oregon, Montana, Wyoming, North Dakota and Alaska.

An analysis of the official complete list of Rhodes Scholars-elect indicates that, as in past years, eastern schools seem to exert a disproportionate influence on the competition. This year, 16 of the 32 scholarships made available to the United States went to students at eastern universities: Harvard, six; Yale, four; Princeton, two; Amherst, Cornel, Johns Hopkins and Wellesley, one each.

The current local success is indeed gratifying. I can recall only one previous instance of a double win by Idaho at the Northwestern District test. Boise State University's breakthrough, with the achievement of a Rhodes Scholarship "first," should afford particular satisfaction to the community. — ROBERT S. SMITH, M.D., Sun City, Ariz.

Taxes

Editor, The Statesman:

After reading Guest Opinion by Ken Robison on the editorial page of The Statesman on Dec. 22, it still becomes clearer that our politicians atd bereaucrats still do not want to look the monkey in the face on what the people have told them in the 1 percent in November. So I will take it upon myself to try and get it through their thick, "I am important" skulls.

Most of the Democrats and some of the Republicans, and all of the bureaucrats are liberal spenders, as long as it is some one else's money. Now here is what the people told you in November. Stop big government and reduce the spending. Do it in 1979, not in 1985.

Also they did not say to reduce property tax, then find some other way to tax the people.

Now, here is the way it can be done, if our legislature will put the people ahead of their desires, which is being a big shot, and wanting to be re-elected to something or other.

The first thing to do, is destroy at least half the state or federal bureaucratic agencies that are destroying the people of the United States and the states.

As The Statesman will only publish letters 300 or less long, watch for the second half at a later date if they publish this one, save this so you can continue the next. — DRADGER S. POWELL, Mountain Home

Anti-American

Editor, The Statesman:

Open letter to Sen. Frank Church.

Your speech sharply criticizing Saudi Arabia is the most anti-American we have heard for a long time and certainly the most anti-American we have ever heard come from the American Senate. Why do you seek to antagonize the friends of your country? Who or what influence causes you to make such utterances? Certainly not your conscience to which you attributed your Panama Canal stand.

A copy of this letter is going to the Idaho Statesman because Idaho's leading newspaper must be made aware that you will be challenged on any public utterance you make against the best interests of the United States. — M. E. THOMPSON, New Plymouth

Idaho Statesman, Feb. 15, 1979

2C /The Houston Post/Tues., Aug. 7, 1979

Post/commentary

Woodway's impact

Houston, through the shock of Woodway Square, is once again alert to our need for a better building code. While this awareness lasts, we should press forward briskly but thoroughly. Through mayor and City Council, Houston should follow the best available principles of fire prevention. Our own Fire Department can provide the guidance.

It is the obligation of this city to offer those who live here and those who will move here the protection of adequate building codes. Houston is growing so rapidly that it is essential for high-rise buildings and wide-flung complexes to be built with smoke alarms, sprinkler systems, fire walls and fire-resistant or fire-retardant materials. Given time, anything will burn. The code should enable building inspectors and fire inspectors to insist upon the kind of construction that confines a blaze in a small area or keeps a small fire from becoming a holocaust. Houston fire officials have campaigned steadily for provisions that would strengthen the code. A few gains have been made. But not enough.

In the early 1970s a worldwide rash of high-rise building fires made headlines: two killed, 24 injured in Kushiro, Japan; five killed, 150 injured in the 41-story Avianca Tower in Bogota, Colombia; nine killed in a new old people's home in Atlanta. In 1974 180 people died in the blaze of a 22-story office building in Sao Paulo, Brazil. At the time, Houston was reviewing its building codes.

Fire Marshal Aicus Greer and H. E. Gilmore of the Fire Department's inspection division urged the city to require sprinkler systems in all future high-rise buildings. They also urged fire walls, smoke-alarm systems and retardant materials. Now, Houston does require fire alarms and public address systems in new high-rise buildings. Sprinklers must be installed in new retail sales and exhibit hall areas larger than 12,000 square feet, and in new hospitals and nursing homes. But our code still makes no requirement for sprinkler systems in high-rise buildings.

Many cities require smoke-alarm systems in every house, apartment and building built. They are cheap, easy to install. No house should be without at least one, preferably several. As the smoke alarms have been produced in quantity, they have improved in performance and gone down in price. Cities that have required them report a great reduction in the number of deaths by fire. Certainly our new city code should respect the advice of our Fire Department. In our gratitude that no one died in the Woodway Square holocaust, we should dedicate ourselves to the cause of a new and adequate building code for Houston's future.

No scapegoats

We cannot shout or bully the Organization of Petroleum Exporting Countries into selling us unlimited quantities of oil at pre-1973 prices. And for the United States or Americans to look upon OPEC as either unreasonable or an enemy may annoy them but hurts them not at all. We owe our present plight to our own lack of foresight and self-discipline, not to OPEC.

In 1978 the United States used energy equivalent to 1,842.4 million tons of oil. Japan used 358.5, West Germany 271.3, Britain 212.6 and Canada 206.8. In other words, we used more oil than Japan, West Germany, Britain, Canada, France and Italy combined. After the 1973-74 oil embargo, our allies' consumption stayed about the same or, in Britain, actually dropped. Our use of energy continued to grow. Though American technology and corporate investment helped develop OPEC's oil industry, we have bought the product at cheap prices, used it cheaply, wasted it unnecessarily — much as we did with our domestic oil.

W.W. Rostow, University of Texas professor of economics and history, writes: "We are in the fix we are in because we failed to change course." And, "In a mature democracy like ours, it is unwise to build policy on scapegoats." For us to make an adversary out of OPEC would only hurt the United States, our foreign policy, our economy, our people. Taken individually, many of the OPEC countries are important to us and our allies in our hopes for world stability. Venezuela, one of Latin America's few democracies, is an OPEC country. Its friendship is essential to the stability of Africa. Saudi Arabia, long a friend, is essential to any lasting peace in the Middle East.

OPEC oil will not last. Many of its members expect their supplies to taper off after the 1980s. But they, too, have a growing need for energy as they rush to industrialize. Unless they are to lose all hope of modernization, they, too, must find alternate sources of energy. Instead of calling OPEC names and loudly resenting their refusal to sell us oil at 1973 rates, the United States and our allies should be working with OPEC on what is ultimately a shared problem.

The Houston Post

Written and edited to merit your confidence

Time for no-holds-barred look at Israel

Violations of faith mounting

By Joseph C. Horsch
Christian Science Monitor

Israel again has expressed its disapproval of American behavior. The Israeli government not only has officially rejected an American arrangement for observing the process of peace between Egypt and Israel in Sinai, but it has called the American plan a breach of President Carter's promises at Camp David.

This protest reached Washington along with reports that Israeli air forces were bombing a highway in Lebanon loaded with Sunday evening traffic going home from the beaches. The Israelis were using American planes for the attack in spite of the U.S. position that such American weapons are sold or given to Israel exclusively for the defense of Israel. Women and children were reported to be among the casualties.

There was an American protest about the use of American planes in that raid and a stiff U.S. protest on Israel's rejection of the truce observer force. Secretary of State Cyrus Vance denied the slightest breach of faith. But Israel paid little or no attention to the American protests.

This is not the first time that Israel has scolded the U.S. for doing things which the U.S. regards as being in the interests of the United States. Nor is it the first time Israel has used American weapons for what Washington regards as an aggressive purpose in violation of the terms of the original gift or sale.

The record is dotted with American protests against such use of American weapons. Israel is unimpressed and undeterred. It operates on the assumption that military action it undertakes is "defensive" in character.

I can't help feeling that somewhere, somehow, something is out of scale or proportion in this sort of thing, which has been going on for years. Israel is constantly complaining that Washington is not doing what it ought to be doing to Israel and for Israel. The president of the United States is lectured repeatedly for allegedly being insufficiently considerate

of Israel and Israel's needs.

From the day the State of Israel came into being the United States has been its

protector and its benefactor. American weapons have been its shield in all its wars. American economic aid has sustained its economy.

'Sooner or later we've got to take a stand'

Christian Science Monitor

Before the 1967 war the amount of aid was modest. According to an article in the current issue of Foreign Affairs (by Anne Crittenden of the New York Times) it amounted only to $1.5 billion over the first 18 years. Yet even this, she says, "represented the highest rate of assistance, on a per capita basis, that the United States had ever provided to any nation."

That was trivial compared to what came after the 1967 war when the level went to $500 million per year. Then it jumped again after the 1973-1974 war. That time it went up to an average of $2.5 billion per year.

Now, with the Camp David peace settlement between Egypt and Israel (which I can't help feeling is much to Israel's advantage), the United States is to pay even more. The regular annual aid is now up to $2.8 billion. In addition, the United States is to provide Israel an extra $4.8 billion over three years. This is to compensate Israel for the costs of moving its military installations and civilian settlements out of the Sinai peninsula and back to Israeli home territory.

There is no such thing as gratitude in foreign affairs. Nations act according to what they conceive to be their own best interests at any given time. No one should expect Israel to be grateful to the United States for its continued support at a level above historical precedent. But should it not be considerate of American interests, if only to protect its own standing in Washington?

It is not in the American interest to have American weapons used for killing Arabs with whom the United States has no quarrel.

It is not in the American interest to have Israel continue to plant settlements of Jews in occupied Arab territory in contravention of what the government of the United States considers to be right and conducive to peace. Washington believes they block progress toward an overall peace with the Arab countries.

I can't help feeling that a country which is totally dependent for its survival on U.S. help has been singularly careless of American wishes and interests.

Leadership gap persists

Little America no match for big challenges

By Joseph Kraft

In thinking about the country's leadership problem, the first commandment is not to imagine a heroic past. No doubt there has recently taken place a diffusion of authority in America.

But the United States has never had a national elite. Nor, in peacetime at least, did the country ever need, nearly as much as it does now, a strong capacity to make decisions in one place.

A half-forgotten classic published in 1956 — *The Power Elite* by C. Wright Mills — provides a good guide to the once, present and future leadership of the United States. In that book, Mills advanced the theory that the country was run by a national alliance of corporate executives and labor barons who used as auxiliaries the political bosses and military brass.

Today such a view would evoke hoots of hysterical laughter. It is suggestive that of the more than 18 leaders invited by President Carter to the domestic summit at Camp David, only 10 come from the ranks of industrial corporations and industrial labor. There was only one person from organization politics, and not a

single military man.

The fact is that the part of the country primarily concerned with producing goods — the group I have called Big America — has lost confidence and standing. Their place in the forefront has been taken by persons primarily concerned with improving the quality of life — a group I have called Little America. It is suggestive that 37 of the people invited to Camp David came from academe, the media and the clergy. Of the 10 mayors present, five were blacks.

The change in emphasis from Big America to Little America defines the recent diffusion of authority. The circle of people who can make things happen has grown wider. Connections between leaders and followers are attenuated. Isolated individuals, celebrities, count for more than those who wield the levers of economic power.

But if there has been a softening of the American establishment, it is not as though the system was ever very tight. To be sure, there have been identifiable power structures in many places.

New York City had, and has, an establishment. So do Boston and Philadelphia and Richmond and Charleston and Memphis and Chicago and Detroit and Cleve-

land and Houston and Minneapolis and St. Louis and Denver and San Francisco and Los Angeles.

But the peculiar feature of this country — a quality that sets our national life apart from that of Britain and France and the Soviet Union and Japan — is that nobody ever put it all together here. There is not, and there never has been, a national establishment. There is not, and there never has been, a power elite.

One sign of the difference is that this country has no equivalent of what Oxford and Cambridge do in Britain or the grandes ecoles in France or the Communist Party in Russia or Tokyo University in Japan. The would-be elite on the East Coast of this country may go to the Ivy League schools. But in Michigan and in Texas and in California they go to excellent universities in Ann Arbor or Austin or Berkeley or Palo Alto. There is not, in the United States, even an institution for nationalizing an elite.

This hole in the system didn't matter much for most of our national life. The task of settling a continent and rapidly developing a modern economy was well left to the uncoordinated efforts of different power centers. In times of peril the country was slow to react, but once the

challenge became dramatic — as in World War II — the response was overwhelming.

Now, however, a different kind of challenge confronts the United States. The country's industrial society, with its millions of jobs in major cities, is threatened. Part of the threat comes from excessive demands put upon the system by the environmentalists, consumer advocates and minority groups. Part comes from abroad in the form of deurying rises in the price of oil and increasingly stiff competition in heavy industry from Japan, West Germany and other countries.

Meeting the so-called energy-economic crisis does not merely mean giving up joy-riding on Saturday night. It does not mean saving Chrysler or selling it off to foreigners. It means reindustrializing the country — laying down a new transport system and refurbishing such basic industries as steel and autos.

That task, of course, requires leadership. But it is not the kind of anti-system leadership offered by President Carter and Little America. It is a leadership rooted in Big America — but on a scale and in a detail such as we have never before known in this country.

'Woman of Steel'

Thatcher's program is simple, direct, but politically costly

By Robert Merry
Chicago Tribune

LONDON — Margaret Thatcher has been in power in Britain for more than 2¼ months, and one thing is already clear. She is determined that, whatever the cost in popularity, the British people shall face up to the economic realities that surround them. One is that only through financial prudence and hard work will they get out of the mess they're in.

For any other British politician, such a task might take a lifetime. But Thatcher wants quick results. She has said she has no interest in governing a country that goes downhill all the time.

Each piece of legislation that has come from the Conservative government since the election May 3 has borne the Thatcher stamp. She is running the government just the way she wants.

In the election, it was put around that who better than a "woman of steel" could lead the country out of a sick economy into a land where's a chance for individuals to prosper? With Thatcher's leadership, the Conservatives won their biggest victory since 1935.

If all goes well, Thatcher is in charge for the next five years. Generally, there is an eight- or nine-month "honeymoon" between a new government and the voters. Then the voters tend to become much more critical.

In Thatcher's case, the people agree that she is carrying out her election

pledges. She has cut individual taxes just as she said she would. She is breaking up the bureaucrat-loaded government-owned industries by turning such things as the state airline and the aerospace industries into private companies with stocks offered to investors.

Controls on private industry imposed by the last Labor government are being lifted. British investors can now put more of their money in overseas companies. The only trouble with the tax cuts is that the government, to find the money for them, had to increase a sales tax known here as value added tax. This tax

goes on everything, with the exception of food and other essentials of life.

The effect has been a considerable jump in the cost of living. An inflation rate of 19 percent is expected soon, compared to one of 14 percent at the moment. Rising costs lose votes. Already, opinion polls put the Conservatives 5 percent behind the opposition Laborites. Thatcher's personal rating has also suffered.

But Thatcher is unworried. She understands that the big changes in policies necessary to move from a semi-socialist state to one which goes back to tradition-

al conservative beliefs in free enterprise will be hard for the public to accept. She is prepared to wait.

In a major announcement, the government ordered all aspects of state spending cut by $6 billion.

Thatcher was still not satisfied. She called her ministers together and said government spending must be cut by a further $2 billion. Her arguments convinced her colleagues and they are now setting about trimming their budgets.

It is no secret that Thatcher does not think highly of the trade union leaders. Britain's stagnating economy, she thinks, can be laid at the doorstep of union leaders who refuse to back modernization of industry and yet insist on high wage demands.

So Thatcher has said that the closed shop law will be altered so that workers not desiring union shops can have their wishes met. Government money will be provided so that secret postal ballots can be held before official strikes are called.

There are no restrictions on wage bargaining, but Thatcher points out that if workers demand extravagant pay raises and so put their employers in a bind, the government will not bail the firms out. So modest wage increases mean that jobs will be preserved.

Thatcher believes her policies will help give back to Britons their self-respect. She says it is time to learn the mistakes of the past and to make sure they do not occur again. Margaret Thatcher has the gift of speaking in language that ordinary people understand. The message comes over loud and clear.

The next question editors asked themselves was why each editorial should be set in only the first column or in the first two columns—the traditional position. If the page is to be horizontal, why not spread the editorials into three or more columns? An example of this type of makeup is provided by the April 25, 1978, page of the *Louisville* (Ky.) *Times*. The editorial entitled "Welfare 'Crackdown' Must Not Be Distorted" is dog-legged around the masthead and the lead editorial covers four columns. Another innovation on this page involves the specific labeling of each editorial as opinion. The next step toward flexibility was to display editorials from time to time in the less prominent parts of the page, making them compete with other available material such as letters and columns. An example is the March 15, 1979, page of the *Norfolk* (Va.) *Ledger-Star* (p. 300), which introduced such flexibility when it started the practice of signing editorials, which we noted in Chapter 5. On the page shown here letters are given the most prominence, placed at the top of the page.

A New Traditionalism

The bold, bright look probably still represents the major trend for most American editorial pages. White space, horizontal makeup and sans serif type (letters with plain strokes, without fine lines at the ends of the strokes) constitute the most typical elements. But a number of newspapers, seeking to create distinction for their editorial pages, have hired typography designers who are using more traditional type, column rules and borders. This latest trend may be part of a national mood of nostalgia. The Oct. 19, 1978, page of the *Detroit News,* which is shown here (p. 301), has boxed its editorials within double rules. Boxes surround the masthead and the letters note, and a cut-off rule is placed under the cartoon. The headline type is reminiscent of an old typeface known as Garamond. The other daily in Detroit, the *Detroit Free Press,* has added even more rules, boxing each feature, as can be seen in the page of April 26, 1978, reproduced here as well (p. 302). The typeface is one of the most common serif faces, Bodoni, a more modern face than Garamond but also traditional. The *Free Press* uses a headline on each editorial that contains one word in large type, which identifies the subject of the editorial, and a sentence in smaller type, which makes the point of the editorial. In the April 25, 1978, page from the *Des Moines Register* which we have already noted (p. 292), the designer suggested bold serif type, rules and large initials to provide an old-fashioned feeling. The *Register* also added color: red ink was used for OPINION, LETTERS, the stamp, the boxes around the cartoon and the two pictures, and the plummeting line on the graph.

INNOVATIVE FEATURES

Editorials, columns, cartoons and letters—plus a Bible verse or short prayer and a "back when" column—have traditionally made up the American editorial

Harsh reminder

Study shows much remains to be done to overcome housing bias

While questions about its objectivity are legitimate, a national study by the U.S. Department of Housing and Urban Development still offers powerful evidence of widespread discrimination in the sale and rental of housing.

The discrimination is more subtle than it was, say, 15 years ago, when a black family may have been bluntly told it wasn't wanted.

These days, a house or apartment may suddenly be unavailable when a black inquires about it. A real estate agent may quote a higher price to a prospective black buyer. Or the black may in various sordid ways be "steered" to black areas.

Yet, as the study disclosed, blacks may be treated with such courtesy that they have no reason to suspect they are not getting the same information as their white counterparts. HUD testers found considerable discrimination of this sort in Lexington and somewhat less in Louisville and Indianapolis. The objectivity of the blacks and whites who visited real estate offices separately and asked similar questions about listed properties is the key to the study's validity. If there was a predisposition to find bias, that will color the conclusions.

But the survey appears to have been designed to screen out subjective judgments. The fact that the results were much the same everywhere suggests that the overall findings are valid even if some individual reports were off base.

The findings are not surprising, in any case, at least not to blacks. Anyone who thinks racial antipathies are dead is insulated from reality. Real estate agents and their clients have the same biases as anyone else. Inevitably, sneaky methods have been devised for evading the 1968 Civil Rights Act, which prohibits discrimination in the sale and rental of most housing.

While the law can't extirpate the uglier instincts of human nature, it can, if enforced, at least guarantee that all citizens receive equal treatment when they decide to move to a new home in the suburbs or closer to jobs and schools.

One unavoidable conclusion is that fair housing has not become a reality because there have not been enough systematic and continuous efforts to crack down on those determined to keep it unfair.

There's no sure-fire remedy, particularly for discrimination that is often hard to detect and even more difficult to prove. But the severely unequal treatment for blacks makes it clear that several types of activity are necessary to combat it.

For instance, more frequent monitoring of the type designed by HUD would help provide evidence for court suits against flagrant violators. What's more important, real estate and rental agents would be deterred from discriminatory practices by the knowledge that "auditors" are checking on them.

A bill sponsored by Senator Mathias of Maryland, meanwhile, would strengthen the federal government's ability to enforce the law. HUD must now attempt conciliation between landlord and tenant or a seller and prospective buyer. An individual can go to court if that doesn't work, although the time and cost involved make it difficult for most to do so.

The Mathias bill would allow the Justice Department to file suit on behalf of individuals and would sock the losing party with court costs, including attorney's fees. That, in itself, would tend to discourage real estate agents from politely neglecting to tell a prospective customer about houses for sale in white neighborhoods.

It would be encouraging, too, if leaders in the real estate business would try harder to persuade their colleagues that discrimination is not only illegal, but wrong. The Louisville Board of Realtors, for instance, might do more to publicize Article 10 of its code of ethics, which says that a Realtor "... shall not deny equal professional services" to or discriminate against any person.

There's been a general assumption among whites that the laws passed in the 1960s were the end of the civil rights battle. The pervasive pattern of racial bias shown in this latest report is a harsh reminder that much remains to be done.

ENGELHARDT

Engelhardt in The St. Louis Post-Dispatch
'Now here's something I'll bet would be just perfect for you folks'

Welfare 'crackdown' must not be distorted

When Human Resources Secretary Peter Conn, at the behest of Governor Carroll, sent 20 investigators into Jefferson County a month ago to search for welfare abusers, he was neither acting on a hunch nor going on a wild goose chase. The decision resulted from a year's study by caseworkers who had observed approximately 200 of the 345 abuse situations identified by the investigators and announced yesterday.

In fact, state officials believe the key to the identification was the attention of local workers, since they are closer to the situation than anyone in Frankfort.

Because of its legal arrangement, the welfare system is closely identified with the communities even though the money flows through Washington and Frankfort. Consequently, the best kind of monitoring is done locally, and who better to serve as gatekeeper than the individuals responsible for issuing food stamps and determining eligibility for aid to families with dependent children?

Although the Jefferson County attorney's office will prosecute the bulk of the cases, some of the biggest — involving alleged felonies — will go to the commonwealth's attorney.

In either case, the focus will be on penalizing those who have abused the system. In the past, the emphasis was on obtaining repayments, an often fruitless endeavor.

The human resources department's inspector general, William Burkette, believes that between 20 and 30 new cases may be identified in Jefferson County each month under the system announced yesterday. In addition, a welfare-reporting hotline, which will allow any person who observes a case of suspected fraud to report it, is expected to increase the number of cases for investigation.

The investigators are moving on to other counties now, to continue the work they started in Jefferson. However, they are to be available for return visits when local officials feel the need.

This program is not without merit, but it would be indeed tragic if the emphasis on cracking down on "cheats" turned sour, placing all legitimate welfare recipients under suspicion.

The clear intent at the moment is to assure responsible allocation of public funds. It must not be distorted so that it makes all welfare recipients live under a cloud of suspicion and turns their friends and relatives into stool pigeons.

The Louisville Times

opinion

BARRY BINGHAM JR. VAN A. CAVETT
Editor and Publisher Opinion Page Editor
WARREN BUCKLER KEN LOOMIS
   KEITH RUNYON
   Associate Editors

TUESDAY, APRIL 25, 1978

Add 2 more victims to toll in Cold War

The sketchy accounts of the downing of a Korean airliner in Russia last week raise more questions than they answer. The basic one — how the airliner came to have made a turn of almost 180 degrees and flown almost 1,800 miles off course — may never be explained satisfactorily.

In flight took it into particularly sensitive Soviet territory, so it was natural that Russian aircraft soon appeared alongside. It is in the events that followed that are in dispute.

What cannot be in dispute is that the Russians severely overreacted. There was no need to fire at an unarmed, civilian transport that should have been clearly recognizable as such to any experienced aviator. The equivalent of the old maritime shot across the bow should have been enough to warn the Korean pilot to land the Boeing 707.

Instead, the shots went into the plane, adding two more apparently innocent victims to the Cold War's toll. It was a shameful act.

'We cannot afford to cut off' Mall's 600 block

As the entire length of the River City Mall, including the 600 block, is perceived as part of the downtown, and all planning up to this point seems to exclude it, a comprehensive plan and sense of direction should be initiated for this area. This part of the downtown, including the movie-free area, has many fond memories of the time when it was alive and teeming with people.

With the emphasis primarily towards the river, we cannot afford to cut off from the spine — the 600 block needs to be considered. With its neighbors, the Macauley Theatre and nearby stores, and close proximity to our newspapers, the area is vital in being the anchor of all downtown rejuvenation efforts. If the problems of the 600 block can be corrected, then we will be helping to ensure the success of the proposed Galleria, Performing Arts Center, Commonwealth Convention Center, Hyatt Regency Hotel and all future efforts.

The entire 600 block, including all tenants, property owners and interested parties, must get it together and work together, or nothing but continued decline looms ahead.

Other areas of the downtown must not continue to ignore each other, but must recognize each other and get a little closer, as the success of each depends on the other in these projects. The only competition should be for the success of Louisville as a whole, with the downtown as the nucleus.

The 600 block of the Mall, because of its outstanding theatres, offers an unusual opportunity to provide the Louisville community with a concentrated area to provide artistic and cultural activities, which are now almost totally lacking, while, at the same time, combating severe downtown deterioration. This deterioration of the area is definitely detrimental to the economic health and well-being of the entire downtown and regional area.

The Movie Row Foundation and Up-Downtown promotion have as their goal to give Louisvillians another chance to enjoy our palatial landmarks, while also enjoying fine entertainment, which includes family-type entertainment events. We need to get our people back on their feet again — not afraid to take the bus downtown to conduct their business, living and shopping.

FREDERICK G. BISBEE
2025 Brownsboro Rd., Louisville

Dedicated to religious drama

In light of your March 2 editorial opinion by Keith Runyon, "Troubled 600 can have a future — as a new kind of place to live, play, shop," I would like to inform you and The Louisville Times readers that the key to the survival of the 600 block of River City Mall is the public bending over backwards to utilize the things still there.

The Christian Workshop Community Theatre, a newcomer to the block, is now housed in the old Mary Anderson Theatre, and could attract far more patrons than it does if it received help from interested patrons or grants from arts foundations. Its budget allows it to continue only because of the interest Lincoln Federal Savings has in preserving some dignity in the use of this historic theatre.

On its meager budget, it is, of course, impossible for CWCT to make really noticeable changes to herald its presence. But we are there.

We are the only community theatre in this area dedicated to religious drama, in a town that is steeped in religious tradition. The media have for the most part been very encouraging, but at times we feel as though they skip over us in discussing revitalizing the mall. We feel we have much to offer. Give us the chance!

JAMES OLIVER LYTTLE
Producing-Director
The Christian Workshop
Community Theatre
612 River City Mall, Louisville

Keenland: the best of racing

Since 1935, Keeneland has presented the best of racing with dignity and grace. All the big things and all the little things that are almost inconspicuous in a class operation, have been carefully tended at Keeneland for many years.

There is an entirely different feeling about the horses in the crowds at Keeneland. I suppose that's because to so many of those present, horses are really horses, fine and courageous animals with habits and temperaments of their own, and not just figures in a book or a racing sheet.

ISRAEL GOODMAN
201 York St., Louisville

Against taxes on automobiles

Loomis, "A better way — New laws would make it easier to collect auto tax." Have him check on other automobile taxes — sales tax on new cars, used cars, parts and tires, which go to the state, schools and other taxing bodies.

He failed to mention this revenue, which makes the personal property tax on automobiles look like petty cash. The agencies waste most of it.

He may not know this, but ex-Governor Wetherby had the personal property tax on household furnishings taken off the books. It produced as much revenue as the present car tax, and everything went along fine without it.

ROY E. OHLSON
3874 Darlene Dr., Shively, Ky.

Thanks U of L team

I would like to thank the University of Louisville basketball team and especially Steve Bagg for being so nice to me when I attended my first college game, the U of L-Tulane game. I think they should be ranked No. 1 in basketball and kindness.

JON GADDIS
12298 Brightfield Dr., Louisville

Correction

The April 20 letter by W. David Strait incorrectly gave his address as 1369 S. First St. It is 1396 S. First St. — Editor.

'A funny way for history to be made'

WASHINGTON — The world this afternoon hears the creak of a chair, the thump on a microphone, the shuffle of a piece of paper in this Chamber. Our voices and actions today echo through the streets of Panama City and other capitals of Central and South America.

That, you might agree, is high-flown stuff from Senate Majority Leader Robert C. Byrd, worthy of the last speech before the vote on the second Panama Canal treaty.

Except it was never given. The world didn't hear the creak, the thump and the shuffle. It didn't even hear the speech. The speech was never given.

Sure, it's printed in the Congressional Record for April 18, 1978, and appears just before the vote president intones.

The hour of 6 p.m. having arrived, the Senate will now proceed to vote...

It is a place for those who were in the gallery and for those who were listening on National Public Radio. But what about future historians, those who depend on the printed word in the official record to make great moments live?

Doubtless this bit of fraud will be justified by its perpetrators on the grounds that it was well advertised bert J. Hansell, John Sparkman praising National Public Radio. Strom Thurmond warning of Communist subversion, Jesse Helms quoting from Bankers Magazine, Howard Baker quoting David McCullough, Charles Mathias quoting Macbeth, James McClure quoting from his own never-submitted amendment, Walter Huddleston quoting a 16th century Spanish missionary, Ted Stevens calling himself "a condemned man," Floyd Haskell quoting Dennis DeConcini, Robert Dole quoting the "poor cow, Robert Dole quoting the "poor draftsmanship" of the treaties, Paul Hatfield quoting the Joint Chiefs and, finally, Byrd, with his creak, thump and shuffle, quoting lines from "The Present Crisis" by James Russell Lowell.

"The Present Crisis," however, was in Panama, where the man Jimmy Carter was calling "a loyal ally" made a bombshell announcement that vindicated all the undelivered right-wing diatribes.

Brig Gen. Omar Torrijos, in his moment of triumph, announced that if the Senate had not ratified the treaty, he would have blown up the canal.

Soon thereafter, he submitted to an interview with Barbara Walters.

He repeated his threat. Walters whipped onto the "Baba Wawa" parody of herself familiar to viewers of "Saturday Night Live." The dialogue, which actually happened, deserves a place in the history of inanity.

"And you were going to take me with you last night, if you had done this, so I could watch it," she said in her best "Take that, Walter" tones.

Torrijos replied gallantly. "I thought of taking you along so we have proof that we did it, but I was afraid of the fact that the helicopter might be brought down."

Ms. Walters, who once admonished President Carter to "be kind to us," is always mindful of her role as history's governess. She implored the strong man to mind his manners.

"General, was it wise to say this now, just when the treaty was ratified? Think of the public opinion.

The general was too far gone in macho lunacy to heed. He had unveiled his 10-year-old secret for ideal glimpses to those conservative men that humiliate weak countries like ours."

Senators who had risked their careers to vote for the treaties reeled in horror.

We must not lose sight of Torrijos greater, madder "lesson." He was telling us that nobody would have blown up the canal had been blown up if Barbara Walters had not been there with her camera crew to tell us about it. Unseen on ABC, the destruction of the 50-mile ditch would have been a secret from the world. The first fishing smack to draw up to the first lock — and to find it gone — might after all have had a small radio abaft to butt the Coast Guard "Canal missing."

On both ends, it was a funny way for history to be made in Washington. A false record of what would have been said in Panama a true record of what should have been unsaid. Obviously, we can't do much about Torrijos, but maybe the Senate could straighten up and tell us what really happens in there on what we are beholden to call "an honest occasion."

The Washington Star Syndicate, 1978

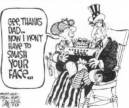

GEE, THANKS DAD... NOW I WON'T HAVE TO SMASH YOUR FACE...

Lynch in The Fort Wayne Journal-Gazette

NCEW EXCHANGE: Frank Callaham, The Ledger-Star, Norfolk, Va.

What gives ex-wives of servicemen a right to benefits?

To the Editor:

After reading a letter in the Open Forum March 6, I decided to express my opinion of the bill presently in Congress, HR 8284, sponsored by 2nd District Rep. G. William Whitehurst. The bill would allow former wives of military men, who were married as long as 20 years though now divorced, to continue to be eligible for military benefits.

THE LEDGER-STAR
OPEN FORUM

Whatever happened to the theory that the wife (not ex-wife) is entitled to these privileges for being the wife of an active duty or retired military person?

I am a government employee, a divorcee from a military man, and a taxpayer. For any ex-wife to retain her privileges after a divorce from a military man is unthinkable. It would seem a settlement is being bestowed upon her by the government and the taxpayers for services rendered. What services?

As a taxpayer, I feel this is a great injustice to the public. A military man performs a service to the public and deserves his privileges, but his ex-wife has earned nothing. The taxpayers shouldn't have to maintain these women in the manner in which they have become accustomed.

SUSAN RIPLEY

Chesapeake

Test-tube conception

To the Editor:

The Department of Health, Education and Welfare will soon decide whether or not test-tube fertilization of human life will be funded with American tax dollars.

We are mistaken if we think that experimentation on human life will not deeply affect us. Laboratory conception of human life will not always and necessarily be implanted and brought to the threshold of conscious human existence. Nor will a beautiful and animated Louise Joy Brown always be the result of in-vitro fertilization.

Many untold numbers of Louise Joy Browns will be fixed on glass slides, frozen in time, and collected, like delicate butterflies pinned to the backs of cards, all of them carefully labeled and studied; all of them mysterious and silent worlds of would-have-beens.

The conception of a human person should always be brought about by an act of human love and responsibility, in human tenderness and human unselfishness.

By comparison, everything else is as nothing.

SCILA HUDSON

Chesapeake

Stay home, Jimmy

To the Editor:

President Carter's frequent and seemingly total preoccupation with the Middle East problem leaves me greatly disturbed. I realize the importance of this attempt to achieve peace. But our economy and well-being are vital to such peace. And I cannot help feeling we Americans elected our president to solve OUR problems and not only those of the world.

No, this is not the view of an isolationist. It is only the concerned opinion of an American who has lived abroad and witnessed the bungled attempts at buying friendship and allegiance that our government has made.

Mr. Carter's aims are admirable but not enforceable. A firm stand by this country should be taken—and then retirement from the center of controversy.

PEGGY S. FERRELL

Chesapeake

THE LEDGER-STAR
Founded 1876
Published by
Landmark Communications, Inc.
Frank Batten, Chairman
Richard F. Barry III, President
Thursday, March 15, 1979

Perry Morgan, Publisher
Robert D. Benson, President
Frank Caperton, Executive Editor
Robert W. Dodson, Managing Editor

Opinion Page
George J. Hebert, Editor
Frank H. Callaham, Associate Editor
William H. Wood, Associate Editor

Browsing the Chrysler

Various forms of sea life are depicted on this 15-inch cameo glass plate by Emile Galle, Nancy, France. The piece, dating to 1900, is on display at Norfolk's Chrysler Museum.

Surry foul-up socks all of us

Some of the facts about the shutdown of five nuclear power plants, including two in Virginia, are a little confusing. We don't know how long it will take to fix them. Or how much it will cost. But one thing is certain:

You and I are going to pay for somebody else's mistake.

We're going to pay in increased costs of electricity. Vepco, which has been getting more than 50 percent of its power from nuclear units, will have to use more coal and oil. Coal- and oil-fired electricity is more expensive than nuclear-powered electricity. Consumers will make up the difference.

We're also going to pay more for gasoline. The shutdown of the five plants means that America will have to import an extra 200,000 barrels of oil each day. That's only a little more than two percent of the oil we're importing now. But, combined with the 900,000 barrels per day we're losing because of the Iranian chaos, it's enough to push up oil prices.

The shutdown of the nuclear plants is in no way analagous to the loss of the Iranian oil. The United States did not have much (if any) control over events in Iran. But the U.S. has control over the nuclear power industry, through the Nuclear Regulatory Commission (NRC).

And the NRC, which is supposed to protect the public interest, blew it.

Here's what happened: A Boston-based nuclear design and construction firm used a computer to figure out specifications for pipe systems at nuclear plants. The pipes had to be able to withstand a certain amount of stress. If they broke, and the water that cools the reactor leaked, nuclear fuel could burn out of the plant—releasing radioactivity.

The firm developed the computer figures. Pipes were designed according to those stress figures. Then the NRC ran

WILLIAM H. WOOD
An Opinion

checks on all safety systems—but never checked to see if the computer formula was accurate.

That formula was used for plants at Surry, and at plants in Pennsylvania, New York and Maine. The people who run those plants apparently never checked on the accuracy of the computer formula, either.

Finally, last December, engineers at the Pennsylvania plant, alarmed by discrepancies in their piping system, found out that the old computer formula was not consistent with current specifications for similar pipes.

And, last week, after further checking, they discovered that the old computer model was, in fact, in error. In devising that formula, the people with the Boston design firm had subtracted horizontal stress calculations from vertical stress figures—when they should have been adding them together! So, in some cases, the pipes were one-sixth as strong as NRC regulations said they should be.

Well, that's pretty stupid. Subtracting instead of adding. And it seems like somebody, either with the NRC or with Vepco, should have checked those figures before the plants were built.

There's a lesson to be learned from this. It's simple: No matter how sophisticated we become in dealing with nuclear power, we can never eliminate the human element. Humans are going to make mistakes, so, in something as potentially dangerous as nuclear power, the government has to set up a fail-safe procedure for checking and re-checking all figures.

If that means that the NRC has to be expanded, at greater cost to the taxpayers, so be it. The costs from this failure—not to mention the disastrous costs if those pipes had failed and the radioactive materials had been released—are far greater.

That's an important lesson to learn. The tragedy is that you and I will have to pay for it.

This may help when you go apply for your gasoline loan

WASHINGTON — As the price of gasoline keeps going up, people may have to resort to buying it on long-term credit.

The scene is the branch of Morgan Chemical Bank of America. Mr. Klingle is ushered toward the loan officer's desk.

"Can I help you, Mr. Klingle?"

"Yes sir, I would like to make a gasoline loan."

Art Buchwald

"Very good. How much gas were you going to buy?"

"A full tank. We want to attend our daughter's graduation."

The loan officer takes out a form.

"We don't usually advance money for a full tank of gasoline without some collateral. What were you planning to put up for the loan?"

"My house. It's in tiptop condition on an acre of land."

"And what else?"

"The house won't be enough?"

"Mr. Klingle, do you know what a full tank of gas costs these days? The bank demands more than just a house for collateral."

"I was afraid of that. What about my house and my 1980 Cadillac?"

"Are we talking about leaded or unleaded gasoline?"

Mr. Klingle said nervously, "Unleaded."

The loan officer looks at his chart. "That won't be sufficient. What else can you give as a guarantee you'll pay back the loan?"

"I have a hundred shares of IBM which is now selling at $340 a share."

"That just might do it. You'll have to leave the stock with us."

"I'll do that. I didn't know the bank demanded so much collateral for a gasoline loan."

"We consider these loans very high-risk ventures," the loan officer said. "When we first started giving them, people would take the money, buy the gas, use it up, and then default. Since there was nothing left in their tanks to recover, we've had to make sure that in the future we could get something else back in exchange. How long do you want to take to pay us back?"

"How much time do I have?"

The loan officer referred to his chart. "You can pay us over a period of 24 months, 36 months or string it out over four years. I am obliged under the 'truth in lending' law to advise you that we are permitted to charge 20 percent interest on gasoline loans. Of course, you can pay the loan back sooner, but there is a penalty."

"I think I'll be able to pay it back in 36 months providing my wife can get a job."

"All right. Here are the papers to fill out and these are for the gas station attendant to sign, attesting to the fact that he filled up your car with a full tank. When you bring in the deeds to your house, automobile, and the IBM stock, we will send the check directly to the gas station."

"Thank you very much, sir. You don't know what this gasoline loan means to me."

"Mr. Klingle, I wouldn't approve it if I didn't have faith in you. Besides, this bank believes people should have the good things in life today and not have to wait until they're old and gray before they can afford to buy a tankful of fuel."

Both men get up and shake hands. The loan officer says, "And don't forget—when you pay us back in 36 months we'll be happy to refinance another tank for you. Have a safe trip."

Not all of our wildlife is vanishing

A lot of earnest people are engaged these days, as for some time past, in efforts to save the wild birds and animals on our continent.

This is all to the good. No reasonable person would have it any other way. The bald eagles, the California condors, the black-footed ferrets and a number of other species which are still losing ground need all the allies they can get.

However, the record isn't all bad, and it would be wrong for Americans to feel under some wholesale indictment. I'm concerned that the angry zeal of some of the very conservationists who have helped improve things may be contributing to an unfair impression.

When I was growing up in Norfolk, a trip to Richmond held a special pleasure—the sight of wild animals gamboling right in the thick of the city's bustle. The gray squirrels living on the Capitol grounds had no parallel in Norfolk, where their habitat had been reduced to the protected acres of City Park.

Today there are squirrels almost everywhere hereabouts, to the point of a pesky surplus—in yards with bird feeders, for instance.

As a kid, the only uncaged opossums I ever saw were dead ones on rural

GEORGE HEBERT
An Opinion

roads. One night not long ago, a good-sized possum stalked nonchalantly through my headlight beam about a block and a half from my house in the built-up northern part of the city.

There are raccoons, too, in a nearby neighborhood, as columnist Guy Friddell has reported, and wild mallards aplenty (a pair came regularly to our door for crackers one summer), and doves and muskrats and herons and bitterns—all within blocks of the monoxide and roar of Hampton Boulevard. I went through early life thinking you had to trek deep into Dismal Swamp or Seashore State Park to see such things.

In those days, too, a bluejay was something you found in a book, or caught a glimpse of, perhaps, between Williamsburg and Richmond. Now, its range has dramatically expandded, and its bright plumage and raucous cries are a familiar part of urban Tidewater.

Almost as familiar are the night-time and early morning rabbits—like the one I saw nibbling grass with great unconcern the other day in the median strip of one of our busiest city roadways.

The occasional, honking wedge of geese of a few decades back is now multiplied many times over. Sightings of Canada geese have been commonplace in the past few months. And within 45 minutes' drive of here, I made, one day this winter, an approximate count of 30,000 snow geese passing over—using the average number of

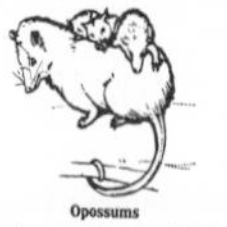

Opossums

birds in an incredible series of big V's flying from farm feeding areas to Currituck Sound. Not to mention, a week or two later in the same area, a flock of about 300 whistling swans.

In this part of the world at least, there is proof we must be doing something right.

Dogged president

Peace: On track

A Carter-orchestrated peace treaty between Israel and Egypt was thought at hand once before—in the euphoria that followed the historic Camp David summit last fall. A comprehensive formula was worked out there; the treaty itself, officials were saying, would be signed before Christmas.

But this didn't happen. Instead the two countries began moving apart. President Carter, doggedly pursuing his role as

FRANK CALLAHAM
An Opinion

peacemaker, initiated further moves in an attempt to bring the two sides back together. These, too, failed to erase the remaining differences.

Finally, Mr. Carter went the extra mile—literally—with his journey to Egypt and Israel. Even this seemed not enough, and the cautious language the leaders used as Mr. Carter prepared to leave Israel added up, in effect, to failure. But the dramatic breakthrough came as Mr. Carter made a final airport stop at Cairo and conferred with Egypt's President Sadat.

Now Egypt has agreed to a pact, the Israeli cabinet has voted yes and Israel's Prime Minister Begin is talking bullishly about winning approval from the parliament.

So a partial Mideast peace is at hand—again. What happened after Camp David invites caution, but this appears to be a genuine accord that is being established between Egypt and Israel.

Even if new obstacles do appear, however, Mr. Carter's performance has been commendable. Beset by troubles at home, some of them of his own making and others not, he has applied great energy and effort and, yes, pressure to bring the two Mideast countries together.

If the Israelis and the Egyptians do not carry through to conclusion the agreement that Mr. Carter put in motion—and kept in motion—then the failure will be the Mideast combatants', not the American peacemaker's.

These firemen turned off their hoses

Landmark News Service

For years the prophets and philosophers have glumly warned us that Americans are losing their moral fiber, their imperative to stand up for right, their sense of caring about their neighbor. We were reminded of this gloomy prediction several days ago by an outrageous incident in Montana.

As fire swept through the rural house of a Montana family the firemen suddenly turned off their hoses in midblaze and refused to extinguish the fire. It seems the firemen checked with their accounting office during the fire and discovered the family had not paid their $25 initiation fee and $15 annual fee for membership in the rural fire association. Given

Rosemary Yardley

this piece of news, the firemen promptly shut off the spigot and allowed the house to burn. The family, who had moved into the house ony hours earlier, claimed they weren't told by the seller about the fees. The fire was a total loss.

On hearing this disturbing story, we recalled how our forebears of an earlier America would have responded to the crisis. The earlier generation, including the frontiersmen who settled Montana, were a special breed that looked out for their neighbor. The first whiff of smoke would have brought wagonloads of friends and neighbors to the blaze where bucket brigades would work wearily into the night to put out the fire.

After the ashes had cooled and the ruins were surveyed, the neighbors would show up several days later, hammer in hand, to raise a new barn or house on the ruins of the other ones. All free of charge, of course.

While it's unfair to let a few rotten apples characterize the entire barrel, it does appear that some Americans have traded their values for a pile of ashes.

(Ms. Yardley is an editorial writer for the Greensboro Daily News.)

Norfolk Ledger-Star, March 15, 1979

Our Opinions

The Battle of West Canfield

The beleaguered residents of historic West Canfield have finally gotten the City of Detroit to pay heed to the problem of prostitution in the nearby Cass Corridor. They have accomplished this not inconsiderable feat by suing in federal court to block construction of a low and moderate income housing project at Third and Cass. By holding this politically important project hostage, they hope to force the city to undertake a vigorous campaign against the prostitutes and pimps in their neighborhood.

Their argument in court is that the federally-backed project has not complied with federal requirements for an environmental impact study. If such a study were conducted, the argument runs, prostitution would be identified as having a "significant and negative impact" on the proposed housing.

The West Canfield residents are not opposed to the housing per se, and have frankly admitted as much. After some initial opposition to a higher-density project, they conceded that this type of housing is badly needed in the area. But they view their lawsuit as a legitimate tactic to force the city's hand on the prostitution issue. The group has spent years waiting for the city and the courts to devise and enforce laws against public solicitation.

A state law passed early this year authorizes the city to close bars which tolerate prostitution, but the city has not yet adopted the enabling liquor control ordinance to do so. The West Canfield people are particularly interested in closing two neighborhood bars that are near-legendary havens for prostitutes.

Enter Detroit Councilman Kenneth Cockrel. Apparently not averse to a little name-calling when it suits his purpose, Cockrel has attacked members of the West Canfield group as "elitist." He went so far as to invite one resident at a recent public hearing on prostitution to "leave town" if dissatisfied with living conditions in Detroit. It is Cockrel's contention that the West Canfield group expects "special treatment" from the city because its members are predominantly white and middle-class. He wants them to withdraw their suit and has asked the city Law Department to research a proposal to remove the historic designation from West Canfield if they continue to block the project. Other, equally "subtle" pressures have been brought to bear on the West Canfield residents by the city, including a threat to block funds for repaving their street and a sudden rash of building inspections.

We would remind Councilman Cockrel that the West Canfield residents he so freely tars are merely using the politics of confrontation that Cockrel himself espouses — when his ox isn't being gored. We would further suggest that all legal obstacles to this needed housing project would quickly vanish if the city made a serious and sustained effort to curb prostitution in the Cass Corridor.

A resident of the area — who returned home late one night to find a couple intimately engaged under his porch — put it rather simply: "whores or housing... they can't have both." This is tough talk but these are tough times, indeed, for West Canfield.

OPEC Demands

Not content with unchallenged possession of the world's most effective price cartel, the Organization of Petroleum Exporting Countries now demands a larger share of the refining and shipping ends of the business.

Pursuing its customary style, OPEC threatens its customers in the industrialized part of the world. The oil nations say if they don't profit more from refining and shipping, they will crank down the valves and either reduce or cut off supplies of crude oil.

The customer nations should not be surprised by the attempt of single-resource nations to wring more economic value out of their one asset. Developing countries are making the same demands everywhere. They want to be processors of their raw materials, not just suppliers. They want the jobs and economic activity from the second stage in the production system.

However, the OPEC nations are distinctively different in one respect. They have the capital to build anything they choose — including elaborate cracking plants. Why have they not done so?

Industrial processing is highly competitive. Efficient companies make money. Inefficient companies fail by pricing themselves out of the market. OPEC nations are not strangers to refining. At present, they process 7 percent of their exports. They therefore have a nucleus around which a vast petrochemical industry could be built. They are making demands for things they have failed to do on their own despite having ample supplies of both raw material and capital.

If the OPEC nations won control over refining and shipping of their petroleum resources, the cartel would be strengthened, and it could work its will on prices in two more areas of the business.

OPEC therefore has given the United States one more strong reason for developing alternative resources that would reduce this country's dependence on foreigners for energy. These resources include nuclear power, synthetic crude from shale rock and coal, the alcohol fuels ethanol and methanol from organic sources, and solar energy.

By greedily pushing for more and more, the OPEC nations encourage the development of the alternatives that may one day be their undoing.

Nursery Beer

Nurses, clergymen and educators in Virginia are chastizing Anheuser-Busch Co. for brewing up and selling a new soft drink that resembles beer but contains less than half of one percent alcohol. They argue that this product "socially conditions" children to the beer drinking habit.

The drink, called "Chelsea," is made up of ginger, lemon and apple flavoring with a malt-flavored base. The product is put up in six-packs and the bottles are topped with foil to resemble a premium beer. When poured, this soft drink forms a creamy beer-like "head."

The brewery spokesmen say Chelsea is intended for the young, suburban adult who

wants a snobbish soft drink. Opponents claim children are buying the stuff in the supermarket where it can be sold because its low alcohol content puts it beyond the pale of either federal or state alcohol agencies.

Virginia became the battleground because Anheuser-Busch is running a "test market" program in Richmond and Staunton, pushing the product through advertising on the cable television system that serves the two cities.

The price for Chelsea is $2 a six-pack. Although that sounds expensive alongside the cost of popular colas, price has not stopped the kids. They are buying it, drinking it, and arguing its merits on grade-school playgrounds.

The brewery claims that a 60-pound child would have to drink a gallon of the beverage in an hour to exhibit "overt behavioral effects." And no child has a stomach large enough for that, they say. But the question of whether a child will get a "buzz" from such a little dab of alcohol is not the paramount issue. The social danger, the well-founded worry, is that from drinking Chelsea children will cultivate a taste that might lead them to stronger stuff at a much earlier age.

Interestingly, the controversy hit the news columns on the same day that the National Institute on Alcohol Abuse and Alcoholism delivered its third report to Congress.

The institute says that 10 million Americans — 7 percent of all adults — are either problem drinkers or alcoholics while 3.3 million teens from 14 to 17 have drinking problems. Alcohol is a factor in 205,000 deaths a year and caused a $43 billion economic loss in 1975 (in lost production, property damage, medical bills). The risk of death from disease, accident, or violence is six times greater for the problem drinker than the population at large.

Joseph Califano Jr., Health, Education and Welfare Secretary, wrote the forward to this report. He notes the seriousness of alcoholism and urges the alcoholic beverage industry to examine its marketing policies. He thinks advertising is pitched too much to youth and that the industry should "lessen the potential ill effects of marketing strategies on youth."

Against the background of the institute's melancholy report, Anheuser-Busch's "near beer" marketing test is at best mistaken and at worst an anti-social act of rare cynicism.

"Must be the National Conference of Editorial Writers . . ."

Jobs for Women: 'Oppose Quotas'

Two articles appeared in the Oct. 11 issue of The News. One was an editorial regarding the Civil Service Commission's proposal to recruit women and minorities for middle and upper-level jobs regardless of merit. The second news article stated that an "estimated 26 million American women lack the basic educational and job skills needed to survive in today's society."

As a woman on the fringe of the "worst-off" group of "displaced homemakers," I would certainly benefit from the Civil Service Commission's proposal.

But I oppose quota systems. This method of hiring is discriminatory. It contributes to the eventual demise of quality education. It contributes to incompetency in every business transaction. It even contributes to stress by placing people in positions they are not equipped to handle.

The opportunity to be equal lies in education. The Civil Service Commission and the National Advisory Council on Women's Education Programs should merge and become the Civil Service Educational Council with the goal of upgrading the scholastic level in this country. It could do this by advocating periodic competency testing for students and faculty, adult education programs, education degree programs geared to part-time students, promotion of part-time employment and tax benefits for businesses that support part-time education and employment programs.

It should also advocate more equitable funding of education instead of property taxes, which make the quality of education in school districts dependent on the assessed values of real estate.

The Tisch proposal and the voucher plan do not offer more equitable funding, only more inflation and decline.

LINDA ROTH
Southfield

Prostitution

On Oct. 10, I attended a public hearing on prostitution in the city of Detroit with our magnificent City Council members.

Approximately 150 people told the council how they have been propositioned, how they and their children have witnessed sex acts on their own property and how their children are bringing home dirty books found on the streets of the city.

Councilman Kenneth Cockrel told one man that if he didn't like prostitution, he could move out of the city. He told another that if he didn't like the way he (Cockrel) was conducting, he could recall him.

I am not going to cross Eight Mile Road just because of Kenneth Cockrel and the prostitutes! Come November of 1981, Cockrel and all other politicians allowing prostitution to flourish will be run out of this city, if not sooner.

JAY E. FLOYD
Detroit

CB System

I agree with your Oct. 11 endorsement of the simple, useful and practical CB rescue system.

The relatively low-cost system makes it possible for use in Michigan and on the major highways of the United States. Let's hope our state government can install this system so that the CB is not used for meaningless babble. It should be used for helping people in distress, not as a toy.

KEN ANGROVE
Southfield

Fall Colors

There are so many people in Michigan now driving north 250 miles or more to enjoy the fall colors. That long drive isn't necessary. Save energy and see just as much right here around Detroit.

One of the best areas is the 22-mile Edward Hines Drive that runs from Ford Road to Northville. The crowds are gone and the trees are waiting. The same thing is true of Belle Isle and many other places.

A tree is a tree wherever it is. Any place up north may equal Detroit's colors but cannot be more beautiful.

HARTINGH W. BABCOCK
Dearborn Heights

LETTERS

The Detroit News welcomes letters from readers. Each letter must include the writer's signature and address, though your name may be withheld for adequate cause. A letter is most likely to be published when it is legible and concise and when it supplies the reasons behind the viewpoint. All letters are subject to editing for space and clarity. Address: Letters, The Detroit News, 615 Lafayette Boulevard, Detroit, Mich., 48231.

No Women?

In an Oct. 3 editorial, you stated that "no woman's face has ever been on an American coin."

I have several coins in my possession. Because of the hairdos and the lack of mustaches and whiskers, I am of the opinion that the faces on these 1923 and 1904 silver dollars are those of women.

JOHN CLARK
Detroit

Private Vices

It was in utter disbelief that I read the Oct. 8 article, "Parents Go to Pot in Front of the Children," referring to parents smoking marijuana in front of their children. The parents' rationale was that they do not hide things from their kids.

Parenting is about the toughest job there is, other than actual delivery. Being responsible for another human being's health, clothing and manners is pretty awesome. You're supposed to be a mature adult with life's experience behind you and one able to guide in decision making.

Child psychologists have proven that children are influenced by parents' behavior. Pot smoking is not exactly an admirable trait to be passed on to another generation. And some adult vices should definitely be kept in the closet. Let's continue to be a little devious in our private vices.

ADRIENNE ZAGACKI
East Detroit

Tasteless Joke

How, after only a few short days, can you make a joke of one of the worst air disasters in our nation's history in the Oct. 6 Draper Hill cartoon?

Even though I personally didn't have any family or friends involved, I still was very upset seeing this cartoon. Please think of people's feelings before anything like that is printed again.

TOM CHOIKE
Fraser

Fatherless

I am replying to Johnnie Oliver's Oct. 11 letter on state aid to pregnant women.

I am an illegitimate kid who thanks God I was not dumped in a garbage can for the next trash pickup.

As for being fatherless, I think men are going to abandon paternal responsibilities either with or without state aid. Don't kill the issue as thousands of women are killing their babies.

CAROL K.
Garden City

Inmate Backed

Yes, prisons are not for prisoners. Although I have never had the opportunity to visit one, I am tickled over the Oct. 6 letter with a prisoner's reaction to his environment.

I agree that it is a bureaucracy of employment, and I believe the inmates should be paid by wages for services rendered, at least the minimum wage.

Our goal is to return money to the system, and rewarding these inmates with a livable income accomplishes that goal. I think it's time our prisons were livable and economical.

MICHAEL AYOTTE
Detrbit

The Detroit News

Published Daily and Sunday by The Evening News Association

PETER B. CLARK, *President and Publisher*

RICHARD M. SPITZLEY, *Senior Vice-President*
RICHARD B. WALLACE, *Treasurer*

ROBERT C. NELSON, *Vice-President and General Manager*

V. LEONARD HANNA, *Vice-President—Finance and Control*
JOHN W. HARMS, *Vice-President and Operations Director*

GENE R. AREHART, *Vice-President and Marketing Director*

•

WILLIAM E. GILES, *Editor and Vice-President*

BURDETT C. STODDARD, *Managing Editor*
EDWIN A. ROBERTS, JR., *Editorial Page Editor*

Assistant Managing Editors
BEN BURNS, LIONEL LINDER, ALFRED W. LOWMAN, CLIFFORD A. RIDLEY

News Editor: NORMAN BORIS *Administrative Editor:* WILLIAM C. TREMBLAY

Thursday, October 19, 1978 Page 26A

Detroit News, Oct. 19, 1978

8A DETROIT FREE PRESS/WEDNESDAY, APRIL 26, 1978

in our opinion

Detroit Free Press
AN INDEPENDENT NEWSPAPER

JOHN S. KNIGHT, Editor Emeritus — LEE HILLS, Publisher
RALPH S. ROTH, President — LEE E. DIRKS, General Manager
KURT LUEDTKE, Executive Editor — JOE H. STROUD, Editor
FRANK ANGELO, Associate Executive Editor

ARMS: A new SALT agreement can work for our interests

SECRETARY of State Vance was being very careful in what he said publicly about his conversations with the Soviet Union out of concern for two parties to these discussions: the Soviet Union itself, and the United States Senate.

On his first arms control mission to Moscow, in the early days after the administration took office, the secretary of state tried to be frank and open with the press. The Soviet Union felt that he was too frank and open, too early in the negotiations, and stiffened its attitudes. So there is some legitimacy to his concern about talking, prematurely, about the bargaining that is going on over a new Strategic Arms Limitation Treaty.

Likewise, there is clearly an overriding need for care in putting together the agreement and presenting it as a package to the U.S. Senate. Even this week, Sen. Henry Jackson was on television, expressing his own very skeptical attitude on the agreement being sought. Even under the best of circumstances, the negotiations with the Senate will be as tough as the negotiations with the Soviet Union.

That is as it should be. On anything as momentous as an arms control agreement, the Senate would be defaulting on its duty if it did not take seriously its responsibility to "advise and consent" with the president. The new SALT agreement should work for the interests of the United States, or it should not be ratified. Indeed, it should not even be signed. The last thing this country needs is mere paper security, without the ceilings and safeguards that ought to be built into arms control arrangements.

Jackson — Vance
A tough, but necessary, bargaining process

But we remain convinced that it is possible to negotiate a treaty that puts effective ceilings on arms development and assures a close enough approximation of equity that it does not leave either side vulnerable. We believe the administration understands this and will act on it.

The United States does not attempt to negotiate such issues with the Soviet Union because we love or trust the Soviet government. There are many ways in which their interests are antithetical to our interests. But on the question of survival in a dangerous world, and on the issue of how to reduce the risk of nuclear war, it is possible to find major areas of mutual interest and to act on them.

The progress reported by Secretary Vance, and such details as are being released or leaked out, do not tell us much. This has been, and ought to be, a painstaking bargaining process. The proof will not be in fragments made public now, but in the agreement as a whole, presented and argued carefully before the United States Senate.

We hope the Senate will keep an open mind and reserve its ultimate judgment until the proposed agreement is put together. This is an effort vital to the security of the United States. It deserves a full hearing and full debate. It also deserves a measure of patience while the negotiators seek to answer all the potential questions they can.

GERALDS: The Legislature shirks its responsibility by delaying his expulsion

WHILE THE state Legislature drags its feet about kicking out convicted felon Monte Geralds, D-Madison Heights, its own credibility is crumbling, the state Constitution being mocked, and the tolerance of voters getting strained to the snapping point.

Rep. Geralds, since his conviction earlier this month of embezzling $24,000 from a law client, has clung tenaciously to his seat, despite a section of the Michigan Constitution declaring ineligible anyone "convicted of a felony involving a breach of public trust. . ." He has refused to resign now and has even announced he will seek re-election.

But his fellow legislators' response to Mr. Gerald's adamancy has been mild, to say the least. First, legislators said nothing would be done until Attorney General Frank Kelley ruled whether Mr. Geralds' crime constituted a breach of the public trust. Mr. Kelley then said it was his legal opinion that it was only a private breach. A vote on expelling Mr. Geralds was expected to follow the Kelley opinion, but, instead, more stalling tactics have ensued.

On Thursday, the House Policy Committee is scheduled to begin hearing testimony on the question of Mr. Geralds' expulsion. And there is no telling what other stumbling blocks to speedy action may be scattered by the Legislature before a vote on Mr. Geralds' worthiness for office finally takes place.

All of this is profoundly disturbing. Despite Mr. Kelley's ruling, it seems beyond dispute that Mr. Geralds, as a lawyer, did indeed violate his public responsibility to serve as an ethical officer of the court—which lawyers are. Moreover, the circumstances of his conviction point to a clear-cut case of the kind of unscrupulous behavior that destroys public trust in elected officials.

The Legislature's slowness in dealing with Mr. Geralds suggests a perhaps understandable reluctance on the part of elected officials to sit in judgment on a peer. But since the Michigan Constitution makes legislators "the sole judge" of their own conduct, only they can expel or reprimand a member. Under these circumstances, legislative inaction becomes intolerable.

Unfortunately, the present impasse gives the impression that no one in the Capitol gives a hoot about voter sensitivity. At the moment, Mr. Geralds is not even functioning as an active member of the House and needs an alternate to vote on pending legislation. If the Legislature doesn't act soon to rid itself of Mr. Geralds, the general cynicism about politicians is going to take over, and incumbents generally can be expected to suffer. This is a case where it is a political crime, at least, to do nothing.

FAIR LANE: The people have a victory in the fight to preserve nature

THE GREEN WEDGE of forest preserved by agreement between the Ford Land Development Corp. and an environmental group may seem small in size; but its 43 acres loom large as a legal precedent and as a symbol of how natural areas can be protected in the midst of rapid urban development.

The area preserved is an L-shaped tract containing an important stand of beech-maple forest and hundreds of varieties of plant life, including several endangered and threatened species. It is home for numbers of birds and small animals such as opossum, raccoons, rabbits, fox and woodchuck.

In years to come, motorists who pass it along busy Ford Road and Evergreen will have a moment's rare pleasure at the sight of the undisturbed woods. So will those who travel its footpaths. And Ford officials have the satisfaction of knowing their company has acted responsibly and generously to preserve one of the last forested remnants of the old Fair Lane estate.

The agreement, reached after the citizens' group sued the Ford Motor Co. subsidiary, leaves the company free to build on an adjoining 163 acres. But naturalists believe the preserved area is large enough to sustain itself in the midst of the surrounding development.

The suit was an important test of the state's Environmental Protection Act of 1970, which gave citizens the right to challenge potentially harmful development. The act has most often been used against possible polluters or projected uses of public lands. This is the first major victory involving a private company seeking to develop private land in a heavily urban area.

By the settlement, both the company and the court have recognized the people's right to influence the use of precious natural areas held in private ownership. That vital understanding should mean a great deal in future battles to save the dwindling green spaces of our region.

Housing is neighborhood's only hope

By BETTY De RAMUS
Free Press Editorial Writer

I USED TO KNOW the neighborhood as well as I know my own name. I knew the small boys who hid behind garbage cans to stone strolling girls with bricks. I knew who had set fire to Mr. Sam's garage, and who had half chopped down a tree.

It was some neighborhood. Mary Hill woke up there one morning seeing spirits streaking across her ceiling and dashed out into the October chill wearing only a fleece sweater and skin. The Kentuckians next door plucked a battered guitar and groaned songs about good-time women, until, finally, the oldest son bashed the guitar over his father's head. The Chicanos edged away from the blacks, afraid people would dump them into the same sooty pot, but it did no good: The Polish kids snubbed them anyway.

DeRamus

Yet people, somehow, raised families there, without any gang fights or sermons from police, so it was ort of sad to read the other day that the neighborhood had never returned to life since urban renewal killed it.

Today only grass grows on the chunk of Fourth Street near Forest where the mountain people and the Chicanos and Mary Hill used to live. And for 10 controversial years, much of the surrounding community has been home only to a few die-hard residents, some missions and churches, bars and parked cars—while bureaucrats and citizen groups and courts have argued about what to do.

Officials and members of the University City "A" Citizens District Council want to build what they call the Calumet Project—102 units of townhouses and garden apartments—in the area bounded by Third, the Lodge Service Drive, Calumet and Prentis.

Vacant lots are no way to bring life back to a decimated neighborhood

BUT SOME area residents, including people who bought and renovated some of the old Victorian townhouses stretching along Canfield between Second and Third, say the community isn't ready to rebuild. It needs to first rid itself of prostitutes or they will move into the new housing and run other residents out. These people, the preservationists, also are concerned with maintaining the area's architectural character, something new buildings could threaten.

I can almost sympathize with the preservationists because there is so little left in Detroit to preserve. Grand old neighborhoods have been sacrificed for freeways, historic homes razed to make space for gas stations. My old flat at 4738 Fourth had been lived in, according to folklore, by Henry Ford: It had ceilings that seemed as distant as the moon and huge cut-glass chandeliers. A perfect place for a college student to fall in love with books. But that didn't save it.

And I can sympathize, too, with the people who say this area should be cleaned up before anything else is built. I can sympathize, but I can't quite agree.

IT IS DEPRESSING walking those old cracked streets. The Midtown Theater where we used to see Saturday matinees is gone, though Greater King Solomon Baptist Church still flashes a sign reading, "Jesus Cares . . . Do You?" on Forest near Fourth.

But the bars are thriving, particularly Anderson's Gardens and the Willis Show Bar, padlocked under the state nuisance law, then unpadlocked by an Appeals Court decision. The Michigan Supreme Court will decide, some day, whether or not they can be closed on the grounds that prostitutes make dates with customers there. Meanwhile, even at midday, people flock inside—most of them young, white and male.

Yet despite all this, there is not much life to these streets. A boarded-up Dairy Foods concession sits, brooding, on the corner of Canfield and Third. King Solomon rules over barren land. Monday afternoon, a couple of elderly ladies chatted at a bus stop about lace-making; a prostitute paraded down the other side of Third in a fringed leather jacket. But they all seemed isolated figures on a mostly empty canvas.

The only thing that can bring this area to life is more housing. The land was cleared for that purpose. Henry Hagood, the developer, promises that the new townhouses and garden apartments will use brick and wrought iron so they blend in with existing structures in the neighborhood. I hope he is right.

Most of the housing projects built in this city—even the middle and upper class ones with fancy names—have had a bleak sameness about them. They have been the kind of places where you couldn't tell the front door from the back or find your own unit after you'd had a few drinks.

BUT MUCH AS I dislike new housing developments, seeing vacant lots where houses should be is a lot worse. Twice, I have been displaced, forced to pull up roots, because someone had other plans for the land. The corner of Farnsworth and John R became a parking lot near the science center; Fourth and Forest is nothing at all.

Prostitution? Yes, it's in the area. In this city, it is everywhere. I've lived here all of my life, and in every neighborhood prostitutes always strutted right around the corner on the main thoroughfare. A cleanup, if it ever comes, will need to take in the whole town. It's a sad but true fact that if people had to wait for prostitution to die before housing could be built, little would ever be constructed in Detroit.

I just hope that when Calumet is finally built—in maybe another 10 years or so—they won't call it a project.

Shabby!

from our readers

Calumet: To build or not to build?

WE GREATLY appreciated Tom Fox's coverage (Free Press, March 26) of the latest attempt of former suburbanites on West Canfield to block housing on the Calumet site, housing for which the community fought for over 10 years and that is desperately needed to give the area new life and hope after the massive destruction of urban renewal in the '60s.

If our courts of law permit West Canfield residents to win their misguided fight, it will be clear that a single block will be able to set aside the wishes of the majority of area people, the unanimous vote of Detroit's City Council and the entire government of the U.S., simply because it is an historic district.

It doesn't matter that Calumet land is outside West Canfield historical boundaries. West Canfield will control it. It doesn't matter that our elected officials designated the land for housing before West Canfield was declared historic, or that when West Canfield sought historical designation, its leader, Beulah Groehn, declared that her association saw no conflict with proposed Calumet housing and actually supported it.

If West Canfield wins, the American principle of equal justice and the self-determination of Detroit will be a nostalgic memory.

RONALD SEIGEL
Chairman and Director
United Community Ombudsman

I LIVE ON PRENTIS between Second and Third and do not want to see the Calumet housing project built for several reasons that were not considered in Tom Fox's article (Free Press, March 26).

The article assumes that prostitution plagues the neighborhood, but its existence there has not been a problem to me.

I don't want to see a housing project whose "focus will be inward, blocking off street traffic" in a neighborhood that has been characterized by openness, tolerance and communication among residents. I don't want to see the cheap, quickly built, quickly deteriorating, unsightly architecture that is characteristic of government projects.

Will the Canfield homes be adversely affected by the Calumet housing project?

I don't want to lose the wild-flower park that now exists. Those fields have an assortment of vegetation, wild flowers, herbs and interesting trees and even birds not usually found in the city. The beauty of these things can be enjoyed through the change of seasons. It's a little bit of country in the city.

LYN ORDON

Speaking too soon

I WAS SHOCKED to read article (Free Press, April 11) by L. Brooks Patterson, prosecuting attorney for Oakland County. I was not so much shocked by the content of his message, as it may well have merit, but by the fact that he has apparently utilized the Free Press for perhaps his own individual political gain at the expense of two individuals who, at this moment, stand presumed innocent of any criminal activity in the tragic homicide on March 20.

In our Anglo-American system of jurisprudence, trial should take place in the courts and not in the press. I would draw your attention and Mr. Patterson's specifically to Disciplinary Rule 7-107 of the Code of Professional Responsibility governing all lawyers, which specifically prohibits pre-trial publicity of this matter.

Subsection (B)1 of that portion of the code prohibits any lawyer associated with the prosecution or defense of a criminal matter, until the commencement of the trial or disposition without trial, from making or participating in making any extra-judicial statements, (that is, a statement not made in court), that a reasonable person would expect to be disseminated by means of public communication that relates to the character, reputation or prior criminal record of the accused. Clearly, an article in the Free Press could be reasonably expected to be disseminated by means of public communication.

Mr. Patterson's rashness in writing this would be inexcusable, and the Free Press' agreeing to publish it at this time was very bad judgment.

WALTER L. HARRISON
Grand Rapids

Intercepted Letters

SEN. EARL NELSON
Lansing
Dear Borrower:

LOANLINESS of the runner.

Pipeline Pete

Detroit Free Press, April 26, 1978

page. Except in letters to the editor, those who wrote and drew for the editorial page essentially talked to one another, mostly about politics and government. It was a page that belonged to professionals. But, as editors began to search for ways to freshen their pages, they discovered a variety of opportunities to bring more diverse views of more people to the page. The growth of the op-ed pages, which we will discuss at length later, provided additional space for experimenting with new features. The innovations have included guest columns and other contributions from knowledgeable persons, in-depth analyses, a question of the week, pro and con arguments on specific issues and critiques of and comments on the press.

One of the first widely noted efforts to bring more non-journalists to an editorial page was a column called "In My Opinion," begun by the *Milwaukee Journal* in 1970. An early participant was Milwaukee's mayor, one of the *Journal's* severest critics. Other participants included a radical student, a welfare worker, a policeman with a gripe about judges and a defense lawyer with a complaint about the police. Columns usually ran between 600 and 700 words and participants were not paid for their contributions. Many columns were good, although there "were . . . some elephant traps—like when you beseech a busy guy to write a column, positive it will be a zinger, and it turns out pretty dull or clumsy of phrase," Sig Gissler reported. "It can be a bit embarrassing to ask him to rewrite." Gissler thought that the column had done a lot to help the *Journal* build an image of journalistic fair play "in an era marked by concern about the misuse of power by the mass media."[4]

After I left the *Columbian,* the editorial page staff invited several literate, informed citizens in the community to serve on a board of contributors. From time to time one of them would write on a timely issue, sometimes local, sometimes state, national or international. On a less formal basis, editors may solicit a manuscript from a person who has knowledge of, and possibly a special interest in, a particular topic. Most of the material used on the op-ed pages of larger papers, such as the *New York Times* and *Los Angeles Times,* is solicited from sources outside the paper.

Extra space also has allowed editors to use their pages for an in-depth look at issues. The *Tucson* (Ariz.) *Daily Citizen* selected a local, national or international topic each day for analysis in depth. Staff writers wrote the stories if they were local, while material for national and international topics came from the wire services, the *Congressional Quarterly* and reprints from other newspapers and other publications. The editors of the *Citizen* said that, while the purpose was to present a wide range of viewpoints, they did not intend that "Perspective," as they called the feature, should provide a forum for attacking their editorial positions.[5] The Pulliam papers in Phoenix and Indianapolis, on the other hand, encouraged the use of the op-ed page for publishing viewpoints opposite to those of the newspapers. The heading for their pages was "As Others See It."[6]

Some papers have used a question of the week for readers to address to make them feel they can have a say. The *Milwaukee Journal* and the *Philadelphia*

Evening Bulletin were among the first to try this feature. On the *Bulletin* a typical page contained 11 or 12 letters from readers, an editorial on the subject addressed and an announcement of the next week's question. The *Journal* gave readers two weeks of lead time. At the *Columbian* some questions would produce a pile of responses; others that we thought would prove popular drew almost no responses. Publishing a coupon on which the reader could write a response seemed to help. Eventually a staff seems to run out of good questions, or at least out of questions that spark enough interest in readers to make them write. Perhaps features such as this should be used for several months, then replaced with something else for several months. More variety may help to keep reader interest.

One attempt to give readers the feeling that they are getting a fair debate of the issues, not just the newspaper's side, is the pro-con package developed in 1971 by editors of the *St. Petersburg* (Fla.) *Times*. They saw the feature as a way to "reduce reader resistance to persuasion" without reducing the newspaper's commitment to its own viewpoint. Robert T. Pittman of the *Times* described the seven elements of the package:

1. A direct, objectively phrased question posing the issue.

2. An introductory statement of the issue and an explanation of how we are dealing with it.

3. The "yes" and "no" arguments, tightly organized and as direct in their rebuttal of each other as possible.

4. Our editorial, briefer and stronger now that the opposing arguments already are on the page.

5. A coupon giving readers a chance to contribute their responses, with a space for comment. These are tabulated and published. The comments appear as brief letters to the editor.

6. Background information when needed.

7. An attractive illustration to draw readers to the package.

Pittman said the response from readers was exceptionally heavy. A local member of Congress was quoted as saying: "The *Times* has never been known to show both sides in the past. Now they are doing it." A state senator with whom the *Times* seldom agreed said: "It doesn't hurt half as much when they blast me when they spell out my side of the story."[7]

The pro-con package has also been favorably received by a number of other editors across the country. Some have prepared their own presentation of opposing sides; others have used a pro-con package offered periodically by the *Congressional Quarterly*. Most write their own editorials on the chosen topic, although Professor Warren Bovee of Marquette University, for one, thinks that adding an editorial provides an unfair imbalance. By coming in on one side or the other, he argues, the newspaper arouses the suspicions of readers that it is not being impartial.[8]

The press itself—whether or not it is being fair, how it does its job—can be a good subject for editorial or op-ed treatment. Newspapers that have media critics frequently publish their critics' articles on an opinion page. Ben Bagdikian, although his experience as a critic on the *Washington Post* was not completely satisfactory, remained convinced that media criticism helps overcome the feeling of powerlessness that most readers have in dealing with the press.[9] Charles Seib, who held a similar position on the same newspaper later, thought that readers are willing to listen to explanations of how things can go wrong and are grateful for those explanations. "But they make it clear that they are interested in performance, not excuses," he said.[10]

Opinion pages offer a place for comment on, as well as criticism of, the press. Editorials and articles that explain news and editorial matters can help readers feel more a part of the newspaper operation. David E. Halvorsen wrote a weekly column for the *Chicago Tribune* called "Reporting the News"; he described himself as a media observer rather than media critic. The *Washington Post* developed a feature called "F.Y.I.," which stands for "For Your Information." It was an editorial that served one of two purposes: either to admit a mistake that was made on the editorial page or to examine the news media as a whole, for either praise or censure. Editorial page editor Philip Geyelin said the idea grew out of a feeling that "it was time . . . to climb down off our high horse and concede a little human frailty, to confess error, and to talk about ourselves and about our problems."[11]

OP-ED PAGES

The first op-ed pages may have been produced by the *New York World* in the late 1920s and early 1930s, when Walter Lippmann was editor. The page sparkled with the names of famous writers: Alexander Woollcott, writing on books; Harry Hanson, on books; Heywood Broun, on whatever he wished; Franklin Pierce Adams, better known as F.P.A. The *World*'s op-ed page was heavily oriented toward the arts and culture. A book on newspaper editing published in 1942 credited the *Louisville Courier-Journal*'s editorial page and "page opposite editorial," or "op ed" page, with setting one of the outstanding examples in design for editorial pages.[12]

Although the idea and the name of the op-ed page have been around for a long time, the *New York Times* is generally credited with setting the example that has led to a substantial number of such pages in recent years. Harrison Salisbury, the first editor of the *Times* op-ed page, said the idea emerged when editors were looking for something to attract readers from the *New York Herald Tribune,* which had just folded. A wider diversity of opinion was the immediate aim. The *Times* was also facing the need to raise subscription and advertising rates; the op-ed page was seen as an opportunity "to give the readers something extra for their extra money," Salisbury said. The *Times* moved its own columnists to the op-ed page, leaving room for more letters on the editorial page, and began to publish a variety of articles on the remainder of the page. Salisbury was given only three-quarters of a page; an advertisement occupied the remainder. He said he accepted the ad partly to anchor the page in the real world but also because he feared he would not have enough material to fill a whole page.[13] The *Times* has been overwhelmed with material ever since. Almost from the beginning it syndicated most of its op-ed features, separately from the syndication of its regular columnists. *Times* material thus began to appear on, and bolster, op-ed pages of other newspapers throughout the country.

Op-ed pages, with variations, were soon being added in many papers. The *Washington Post,* soon after the *Times,* created a page that was more closely integrated with the regular editorial page than was the *Times'.* The *Chicago Tribune*'s page, as described by *Los Angeles Times* press critic David Shaw, was ''part of a continuing trend away from the singlemindedly conservative image the paper had for decades.'' When the *Los Angeles Times* joined the movement, according to Shaw, it deliberately planned a less intellectual page than that of the *New York Times.* Readers got enough reporting on social issues in the news columns and from the columnists. ''I'd especially like us to give our readers a clear feeling of what it's really like to live in Southern California,'' the op-ed page editor was quoted as saying. ''I want personal experience pieces, stories that tell how it feels to drive the freeway and to suffer a death in the family and to be out of work.''[14]

CONCLUSION

The important thing to remember about innovation, whether in layout or in content, is that the primary purpose should be to encourage readers to think more deeply about more subjects. The purpose of page makeup is to get ideas across to readers by attracting them and then holding their attention long enough to stir their thoughts. The makeup of the page itself cannot carry a message to readers, but it can help set the tone of the page. If an editor has a flamboyant editorial style, a flamboyant style of typography will help reinforce the messages. A conservative typography will help reinforce a conservative, reserved editorial style.

Whatever style an editor chooses, page makeup needs to serve two purposes. The first is to distinguish the opinion pages from the news pages. Readers need constantly to be reminded of this distinction. Editorial columns can be wider than news columns. Body type can be larger. Headlines can use different typefaces. Heads can be centered instead of flush left. Sketches instead of photographs can be used. The page can be run in a distinctive and consistent position in the paper.

The second task of typography is to present a page that will attract readers. The makeup needs to say that this is an important page, that the editors have put a great deal of time, effort and thought into it. Thus the page should be deliberately, carefully and attractively laid out. It needs to have enough life to it that it is not always the same day by day, yet it must also have enough consistency in page makeup to suggest that the same editors are producing it each day and that consistency extends to the paper's editorial philosophy. If editors can meet those two criteria, they can design their pages in any manner they wish. In the end, what really counts is what they say on the pages.

The search for new ways to bring more, and more varied, viewpoints to the opinion pages also reflects an effort to keep the pages from becoming routine. Just as readers ought to be surprised from time to time by the appearance of an editorial page, so should they be surprised once in a while by the content. This means that editors must go beyond the traditional staff-written editorials, syndicated columns and cartoons and letters to the editor. The possibilities are limited only by editors' imaginations and their ability to carry out their ideas, possibilities which may include the features discussed in this chapter—op-ed pages, guest columns, solicited contributions, boards of contributors, questions of the week, pro-con packages and reprints from other publications as well as criticism of, and comment on, the press itself.

The purpose of all these efforts, of course, is to promote a greater exchange of ideas among readers and to convince readers that their newspaper is doing a thorough and responsible job of serving them. Even more important is to actually to do a thorough and responsible job.

QUESTIONS AND EXERCISES

1. Examine the makeup of the newspapers in your area. Do you find it easy to distinguish editorial pages from the news pages?

2. Does the liberal or conservative nature of the makeup reflect the liberal or conservative editorial policy of the page? Consider the size of headlines, the style of headline type, the use of white space or rules, the horizontal or vertical nature of the layout.

3. Does the makeup of a specific newspaper change from day to day or remain the same? If it changes, what principles seem to be operating in determining the layout—the relative importance of elements, the readership appeal of the elements or whim? Does the layout change so radically day by day that the page has a disjointed character?

4. What could be done to improve the makeup of the editorial pages in your area?

5. Which newspaper do you judge to have the best makeup? Why?

6. Which newspapers in your area have op-ed pages? How often do they appear?

7. Is there a difference between the material that appears on the editorial page and the material on the op-ed page? What seems to be the policy in determining what goes where?

8. Does the editor of the op-ed page seem to be trying hard to bring contrary and different views onto the page? Does the page contain surprises?

9. What devices does the editor use to try to encourage more participation by more people in the opinion pages? A pro-con package? A question of the week? A guest columnist? An in-depth analysis? Articles by experts?

10. Do any of the newspapers have a media critic? If so, how free does he or she appear to be to criticize the newspaper?

—Herman Auch
Rochester (N.Y.) *Times-Union* for *The Masthead*

The Editorial Page That May, and Must, Be

Truth, crushed to earth, shall rise again;
The eternal years of God are hers
But, Error, wounded, writhes in pain,
And dies among his worshippers.
—William Cullen Bryant[1]

For more than 100 years historians have been prophesying the death of the American editorial page. After the deaths of the great personal-journalism editors of the 19th century, the pages on many newspapers, under the shadow of corporate owners, became bland, anonymous and irrelevant to the interests of many readers. But a principal theme of this book has been that a new era, in which editorial writers have greater opportunities to speak out, has opened. Changes in hiring practices, newspaper ownership and the reading audiences have helped create these new opportunities. The new era is not without dangers, however. Newspapers in metropolitan areas, especially evening papers, are dying. Newspaper circulation is not keeping up with the growth in the number of family units. The time the average reader spends on a newspaper has diminished and a majority of Americans think they get most of their news from television. New electronic systems promise to steal even more reading time and to provide more instantaneous news than even television can provide and more personalized news and information than newspapers can provide. Newspapers, and all other media, are being bought by conglomerates that are only incidentally interested in the media; profits are their greatest, perhaps only, concern.

In spite of these dangers and potential dangers, the immediate future looks bright for newspaper editorial writers, and the more distant future looks bright for journalists who can perform the editorial writing function, in whichever medium it occurs.

TODAY'S CHALLENGES

In recent years the demise of a number of old, prestigious newspapers has given some Americans the impression that newspapers are a dying breed. In the next few decades, newspapers will perhaps be replaced by one or more electronic marvels, but for the immediate future newspapers are likely to continue to play a strong role in providing information and opinion in most communities. Except for problems resulting from the state of the national economy, most newspapers have never been more prosperous. As long as newspapers exist, editorial pages are likely to exist; no newspaper that I know of has ever dropped its editorial page. But if writers and editors are to keep their pages timely, lively and informative, they cannot rest on past performance. Four areas in particular, all of which we have discussed previously in this book, need editorial writers' attention: the editorial page audience, the message of the page, other viewpoints on the page and the messenger.

The Audience

Papers that serve large metropolitan areas may have problems providing efficient delivery service and identifying closely with most of their readers, but newspapers in small and medium-sized communities continue to provide services that readers find essential. In many instances these papers are the principal source of community news, and they may be the only source of editorial comment on community, state, national or international levels. Still, neither news editors nor editorial page editors can count on readers sticking with them if they aren't meeting the needs of those readers.

One of the points that I have made in this book has been that editorial writers need to get out of the office and into the community if they are to know what people are concerned about. They have to talk with business people, neighborhood groups, city officials, political leaders, educators, religious leaders, special interest groups and the unemployed and the handicapped. Writers benefit from getting out in two ways. First, they gain information about the community and can come back to the office knowing what they are talking about. Second, members of the community who see them out and around also come to recognize that these writers know what they are talking about. So writers gain both knowledge and credibility.

The Message

One of the reasons for getting out into the community, of course, is to gain information first-hand. Most editorial writers must rely on more secondary sources than must do reporters, but they must also use primary sources and these sources must be good ones. A major key to editorial writing is to know what information is required for a specific editorial and to be able to put your hands on it in the time available for producing the editorial. You don't have to have all the facts that you need stored in your head, but you do have to have a good idea of what you want and where you can get it—whether through an interview, a phone call, news clippings, an encyclopedia, a current non-fiction best-seller or the merchant down the street. And before you know what to ask or look for, you must know what the problems are. This is one reason that, in Chapter 4, "Preparation of the Editorial Writer," I stress education and continuing education for writers and would-be writers. Writers who would write about modern-day Afghanistan, for example, might be better able to inform their readers if they knew about that country's earlier contacts with Western nations. It might not be especially helpful to know that some vestiges remain from contacts with the Greeks under Alexander the Great, but some lingering resentment from contacts with the British in the 19th century might be pertinent to the more recent contacts with the Soviet Union. In another example, writers who want to write about proposals to pass responsibility for welfare support back to the states and to local communities might benefit from knowledge about how the states and communities handled welfare when they were responsible for it in the past.

Once writers have the information they need to back up what they want to say, they must present facts and ideas in a convincing manner. As we have noted several times in this book, readers today do not want opinions jammed down their throats. They want information and help in forming their own opinions, but they want the feeling that they are discovering truth for themselves. The successful editorial writer is likely to be one who can make a point without antagonizing readers who hold other opinions. Respecting and recognizing the opinions of others does not necessarily mean that the writer must write in a dull, plodding manner. It might be possible to present both sides of an issue in a bold, convincing way before the writer begins an evaluation of which side has the better case. Readers ought to feel that they are wrestling with the issue right alongside the writer.

We have also noted that instant conversions of readers to the writer's point of view are rare. But the impact of an editorial page, and of an editorial policy on a specific topic, can be significant over a period of time. There seems to be no doubt that over months and years the editorial policies of a paper help determine the decision-making climate of a community. A persistent, consistent expression of enlightened concern for a community is almost certain to produce results.

Other Viewpoints

The most effective decision making results when all aspects and all sides of an issue have been considered. For this reason, one of the principal responsibilities of the editorial page editor, especially in a one-newspaper community, is to bring onto the page viewpoints that are as diverse as possible. Relying on the mail to bring letters and syndicated columns and cartoons is not sufficient. Editors have to seek out persons with differing viewpoints. To do this job editors must know what issues need to be talked about and who ought to be asked to say what about them. Not every invited writer needs to be a prominent person. When a special school tax is on the ballot, the comments of a kindergarten teacher might be more interesting to read than the official arguments of the superintendent of schools. After John Hinckley was found innocent by way of insanity in the shooting of President Reagan, the *Los Angeles Times* published an op-ed piece by a local person whose brother, who had not been able to afford an expensive legal defense, had failed in an insanity plea in a sexual assault case.

An editor should try to give readers at least one surprise a day—an unexpected editorial position on a subject, a highly worthy letter to the editor, an outstanding syndicated column or cartoon, a piece by an outsider with something new and different to say, even a different editorial page format, such as a page of photographs that make an editorial point.

The Messenger

One of my main contentions throughout this book has been that, if today's editorial writers are given, or if they can seize, the opportunity, they have the qualifications and abilities to produce editorial pages that will attract, inform and persuade readers. Publishers and general managers, it seems to me, have more to fear from sitting on their editorial writers, and thus producing a boring editorial page, than from giving them room to experiment and speak out, even at the risk of antagonizing some members of the community. Whether or not writers are given this kind of freedom may depend on whether management believes that the principal purpose of an editorial page is to stimulate thinking or to impose a viewpoint. Since today's readers generally resist having opinions thrust upon them, it would seem to make sense to expect editorial writers to use editorials to stimulate, not seek to impose, ideas.

The persons best suited for editorial writing in these circumstances are those who are well educated, well acquainted with people and ideas, skilled in digging out information and skilled in blending into a few hundred words their ideas, facts and conclusions. Aside from having the ability to write editorials, the toughest part of being an editorial writer is keeping up with what is going on in the world. Unless a writer is assigned to a special subject area, almost anything at local, state, national and international levels is a potential topic for an editorial. Consequently the editorial writer must constantly seek ideas, sources and information. This essential requirement can establish a valuable bargaining position for the editorial writer in dealing with publishers, general managers and editorial boards. The informed person stands a better chance of making a case for an editorial position than someone who has a strong opinion but few facts to back it up.

Opportunities for editorial writers and editors to play a strong role in policy making seem to have been enhanced by the growth of group ownership, according to surveys. Major groups contend that editorial policy is set at the local level. In many instances publishers and general managers are more concerned with the business side—profit and loss—than with news and editorial departments. Since groups tend to move their top management from paper to paper, editorial page editors and writers may find that they have been on the paper longer, and have firmer roots in the community, than the publisher or general manager. They therefore should have a better grasp of what is going on in the community and be able to make a strong case for their points of view. On locally owned newspapers as well, the trend seems to be for management to employ professional editorial writers. By that I mean writers who are hired because they possess certain abilities rather than because they agree with management's editorial point of view, if indeed management has a specific editorial point of view.

The trend toward more concentrated ownership of the media does hold potential dangers. Group executives could, if they wished, decide to impose uniform editorial policies on their newspapers. On one such occasion that received national attention, some members of the communities involved and leaders from the newspaper world protested the heavy-handed manner in which the publisher acted; the publisher, however, made his policies stick. Local editors could only quit in protest. A group that is privately owned—that does not sell stock on the open market—may be able to decide for itself how to spend its money and how much financial risk it is willing to run, but a group that sells its stock publicly may try to avoid any risks that might damage the value of that stock. Corporations that own only newspapers usually do so because they want to own and operate newspapers. But investors who buy stock in a company do so not because they are especially fond of the product the company produces; it is not likely to matter whether the product is toilet paper or newsprint. People invest because they want a maximum return on their money—and do not generally look kindly on a corporation that sacrifices profits for community services, especially in a community in which they do not live. Corporations, such as Gannett or Times-Mirror of Los Angeles, that start with newspapers and expand into other areas may keep their original commitment to journalism; income from other properties, in fact, may make them stronger corporations that are better able to publish good newspapers. But the general profitability of newspapers and newspaper groups has made them attractive for acquisition by non-newspaper corporations or conglomerates, which may be primarily interested in maximizing profits and not at all concerned about the editorial product.

Changes in ownership and in ownership patterns are certain to have an effect on editorial policy and the editorial freedom of the newspapers of the future. There is not much editorial staff members can do about these changes, which sometimes come unexpectedly. About all editorial page people can do is try to establish a strong tradition of editorial excellence in their community that stands a chance of persisting through changes in editors, publishers, general managers and perhaps even owners. If readers have become accustomed to a good editorial page, they may also provide a source of support for continued excellence. But, of course, if a company is satisfied with producing a bad newspaper, there is not much that editorial writers or members of a community can do about it. Except for some growing suburban areas, opportunities for starting competing newspapers are rare. Editorial writers can look for jobs elsewhere, but members of a community are stuck with whatever editorial product is sold to them.

One way to strengthen the position of editorial writers, and to improve a paper's relations with its readers, is to give those writers more public recognition. Publicizing individual writers may not appeal to publishers who perceive the editorial voice of a paper as being stronger than the voice of the individuals who produce the editorial product. But any loss in this regard may be more than offset by increased reader interest in the page and greater credibility for the page. Readers are likely to feel closer to the editorial page if they think of the editorial page staff as real people. Newspapers, while not abandoning the traditional anonymous editorials, can use bylined interpretive pieces, or they can publish accounts of travels, since readers seem to have a high interest in well-written first-hand accounts of travel. If editorial writers have the skill, they can write humorous, personal pieces. Op-ed pages can run bylined articles on journalistic subjects, explaining newspaper policies or issues involving the press. From time to time, particularly when a new writer joins the staff, the paper can publish a personality sketch with a photo or drawing of the writer. Names of editorial writers, as well as those of publishers and editors, can be included in the masthead on the editorial page. If a newspaper wants to make its writers known, it can attach signatures to its editorials; there seems to be a modest trend in this direction.

If editorial writers are to be expected to do the best possible job, there must be a sufficient number of them on a staff. Getting readers into the page, getting the editorial writer out of the office and getting the writer to do a bylined piece require time. If a newspaper wants readers to take its editorial page seriously, it needs to budget the personnel needed to make it a serious page. The hope, of course, is that a publisher who realizes the importance of the editorial page will add a second person to a one-person staff and a third person to a two-person staff. Adding another body will not solve all the problems of the editorial page, but additional personnel should improve the product. If a writer has to write only one editorial a day instead of two or three, he or she is almost certain to do a better job. The paper also needs to budget amply for travel and other expenses that editorial writers incur if they are to get out to see what the world is like.

TOMORROW'S CHALLENGES

Newspapers that serve small and medium-sized communities are likely to persist and prosper no matter what happens in the technological revolution now occurring in the mass media. The form in which the paper is delivered may change dramatically; it may, for example, be produced by a printer in the home of the subscriber. As we have noted, you can get more words, and hence more in-depth information, onto a printed page than into a radio or television broadcast. Readers like to have a product that they can pick up and read when they want to, not just when a network producer decides to air the news. Perhaps the printed local paper will persist because readers like to clip out and save news stories—about births, weddings, deaths and major events, such as the shooting of a president, the end of a war or the eruption of a volcano.

Nevertheless, a dramatic revolution is occurring in media technology, and newspapers and journalists can expect to be affected by it. The most dramatic challenges to the printed page are likely to come from multi-channel television, whether through cable or direct broadcast. Local experiments are already under way to provide home viewers with the same kinds of information that they find in their newspapers; newspapers, in fact, are partners in these experiments. Limitations, such as getting in-depth news and getting exactly what you want on the screen, no doubt will be worked out. In theory, this technology potentially can deliver an opinion product that is superior to that of most daily newspapers. For one thing, the product would not be limited to the equivalent of six or 12 columns of type a day. The computer from which the viewer would order written or spoken material could contain many times the number of syndicated columns that editors find space for now. It could contain all the letters to the editor—in their unabbreviated, perhaps even original, unedited forms, maybe even delivered by the writers themselves from their own home consoles. Editorial cartoons could be animated and in full color. Editorials, again unlimited in number, could be written or spoken. An editorial point could be emphasized through the use of sketches, pictures or film footage.

Two-way communication would offer the viewer the opportunity to register instantly his or her reaction to an editorial, letter or cartoon. If moved to write a letter, the viewer could type one directly into the computer without the cost of a stamp or the bother of going to the mail box. The letter could be made instantly accessible to viewers who had pushed the buttons that called up letters to the editor. Letters could also be indexed by subject matter or some other criteria and could thus be viewed in a particular order.

This type of electronic marvel could become a true community forum. It is probably only a matter of time and money until viewers are able to use video display terminals to obtain information on the screen, or in print-out form, of whatever they wish—everything from library materials to grocery orders to opinions.

That day may be a sad one for some publishers and owners of newspaper printing presses. Unless they have diversified into electronics, they may find themselves with an outmoded product. It is no wonder that newspaper companies have been trying to get into cable television, if not in their own communities, at least in someone else's.

That day may be a sad one, too, for editors and editorial writers who love the printed word and the printed page. We would miss the art of page design, headline writing and type arrangement. After all these years of being able to hold a product fresh off the press, we might find it hard to comprehend that we have produced anything. Will string books—the clippings of our prized works—contain only computer printouts or video tapes?

Sad as that prospect may seem to print journalists, they should have far less cause for despair than their associates who own the presses. Opinion, unlike printing, is a function that can be transferred from one medium to another. So can reporting and copy editing. These are functions that will be as much in demand in the telecommunications era as they are now. Skilled opinion writers, reporters and editors who can adapt to a new medium should not lack employment opportunities. The telecommunications era may even provide more jobs for editorial writers than the print era. Most communities are limited to one print source for opinion. With multiple channels and direct access to the computer, editorial voices may proliferate.

Many print journalists shudder when they think about using their skills in television as it exists in most communities. News accounts are brief and superficial. Good film footage is often more important than good reporting and good writing. Many television editorials are thin, emotional harangues with as much complexity as a first-grade reader. But opportunities for serious editorialists should expand in the multi-channel era. While simple-minded editorials will remain for viewers who want them, other channels will provide viewers who are interested with substantive news and opinion.

Some editorial writers may want to practice up on their elocution so that they can deliver their own opinions to viewers. But some editorials will remain in written form, appearing on the screen or as print-outs. Whatever form editorials take, the opinion writers of the future will need all the skills that are necessary today. Writers will need knowledge about the local community and the world, the ability to recognize issues that merit analysis and opinion and the ability to communicate through writing; they will still need compassion, a sense of justice and the ability to reason. In short, their role will remain the same: helping the public to better understand what is going on in the world.

CONCLUSION

If editorial pages are going to provide leadership in the coming years, editorial writers will have to possess some other qualities, more difficult to identify than the skills for obtaining information and putting words on paper. They will need insight, if they are to perceive what is really going on in the world. They will need vision, to help them see what the future can be. They will need optimism, for surely one of the roles of the editorial page is to remind readers that solutions can be found for problems. They will need to retain faith in the "self-righting" process that John Milton wrote about in his defense of press freedom, *Areopagitica*—a conviction that, if all the facts and all the viewpoints are allowed to come forth in the marketplace of ideas, the right decisions will be made and the right actions will be taken. William Cullen Bryant expressed that faith in the poetic credo quoted at the beginning of this chapter.

If this sounds like something out of an earlier, more naive era, let it be so. The editorial as a form had its origins in such an era, when writers such as Sam Adams and Thomas Paine thought that a pen and a little buckshot could free oppressed colonies from a dictator. It would be fitting for an editorial writer of today to possess the dedication to freedom and enlightenment that Milton, John Locke and Thomas Jefferson had. Two and three centuries later, they still look like good company to keep. If Milton could keep the faith when it looked as though the Puritans would never defeat King Charles, and Jefferson could keep the faith when it looked as though the signers of the Declaration of Independence might be signing their own death warrants, surely 20th-century editorial writers can keep the faith in humanity's ability to perceive problems and deal with them. That hope may seem simplistic in an age of complexity and frustration, but life might not seem so complex and frustrating if people today had more of the confidence that editors of earlier days had in our ability to cope with life.

Perhaps the editorial page, with its emphasis on analyzing problems and seeking solutions to them, is an antique left over from the Age of Reason. Perhaps this page is one of the last voices of reason and enlightenment crying out in a dark, irrational world. But if it is, that is all the more reason for holding firm to the pursuit of truth.

References

Introduction

1 William C. Heine, "Many Are Interested," *The Masthead,* 27:26 (Spring 1975).
2 Kenneth McArdle, "The Real Pressure Is to Make Sense," *The Masthead,* 22:8–9 (Spring 1970).
3 Minnie Mae Murray, "What a Wonderful World He Must Live In," *The Masthead,* 19:101–2 (Summer 1967).
4 C.F. Kyle, "Quit Mumbling to Yourselves, Gents," *The Masthead,* 2:11–13 (Spring 1950).
5 Ben H. Bagdikian, "Editorial Pages Change—But Too Slowly," *The Masthead,* 19:96–98 (Summer 1967).
6 Philip L. Geyelin, "Who Listens to Your Bugle Calls?" *The Masthead,* 30:9 (Summer–Fall 1978).

Chapter 1

1 Rollo Ogden, ed., *The Life and Letters of Edwin Lawrence Godkin* (Westport, Conn.: Greenwood Press, 1972), p. 255.
2 James Parton, "Prestige," *North American Review,* 101:375–76 (April 1866), in Frank Luther Mott, *American Journalism* (New York: Macmillan, 1941), p. 385.
3 Isaiah Thomas, *The History of Printing in America* (New York: Weathervane Press, 1970), p. 508. (First appeared in 1810.)
4 Ogden, *Life and Letters.*
5 Allen Nevins, *American Press Opinion: Washington to Coolidge* (Boston: D.C. Heath and Co., 1928), p. 111.
6 Parton, "Prestige."
7 Edward P. Mitchell, *Memoirs of an Editor* (New York: Charles Scribner's Sons, 1924), p. 109.
8 Harrison E. Salisbury, *Without Fear or Favor* (New York: Times Books, 1980), p. 26.
9 Justin Kaplan, *Lincoln Steffens* (New York: Simon and Schuster, 1974), p. 87.
10 Upton Sinclair, *The Brass Check* (Pasadena: The Author, 1920), p. 22.
11 *Ibid.,* p. 14.
12 *Ibid.,* p. 15.
13 Nathaniel B. Blumberg, *One-Party Press?* (Lincoln: University of Nebraska Press, 1954), p. 44.

Chapter 2

[1] Cited in *The Masthead,* 28:29 (Winter 1976).

[2] George P. Crist Jr., "Stimulating Public Awareness, Debate," *The Masthead,* 29:10 (Fall 1977).

[3] Brian Dickinson, "You Win Some, You Lose Some," *The Masthead,* 29:13 (Fall 1977).

[4] Tom Kirwan, "Save Crusades for Important Causes," *The Masthead,* 29:5–6 (Fall 1977).

[5] Jonathan Daniels, "Writer's Everest: Mastery of Words," *The Masthead,* 30:1–13 (Summer–Fall 1978).

[6] Ed Williams, "Do We Shed Light or Generate Heat?" *The Masthead,* 29:8–9 (Fall 1977).

[7] Bob Reid, "Do Newspapers Crusade Too Much?" *The Masthead,* 29:4 (Fall 1977).

[8] Bernard Kilgore, "A Publisher Looks at Editorial Writing," *The Masthead,* 6:47 (Spring 1954).

[9] Paul Greenberg, "Tyerman Sums Up," *The Masthead,* 17:23 (Winter 1965).

[10] Philip Geyelin, "Who Listens to Your Bugle Calls?" *The Masthead,* 30:9 (Summer–Fall 1978).

[11] Elsa Mohn and Maxwell McCombs, "Who Reads Us and Why," The Masthead, 32:24 (Winter 1980–81).

[12] Lenoir Chambers, "Aim for the Mind—and Higher," *The Masthead,* 13:20 (Summer 1961).

[13] James J. Kilpatrick, "Editorials and Editorial Writing," *The Masthead,* 5:7 (Spring 1953).

[14] Symposium, "93 Ways to Improve the Editorial Page," *The Masthead,* 33:19 (Winter 1981).

[15] Neal R. Pierce, "For Best Results, Do Your Homework," *The Masthead* 29:7 (Winter 1977).

[16] Thomas Williams, "New Role Seen for Editorial Page," *The Masthead,* 31:20 (Spring 1979).

[17] Symposium, "93 Ways," p. 14.

[18] Symposium, "93 Ways," pp. 20–21.

[19] R.S. Baker, "The Editorial Writer, The Man in the Piazza," *Montana Journalism Review,* 15:18–19 (1972). (Reprinted by permission of the *Montana Journalism Review.*)

Chapter 3

[1] Robert H. Estabrook, "Why Editorial Applicants Aren't," *The Masthead,* 12:53 (Summer 1962).

[2] G. Cleveland Wilhoit and Dan G. Drew, "Profile of the North American Editorial Writer," *The Masthead,* 31:13 (Winter 1979–80).

[3] Wilbur Elston, "The Editor Goes Status Seeking and Image Hunting," *The Masthead,* 15:1–18 (Fall 1963).

[4] Cleveland Wilhoit and Dan G. Drew, "Profile of the Editorial Writer," *The Masthead,* 23:2–14 (Fall 1971).

[5] Wilhoit, "North American," pp. 8–13.

[6] Elston, "Status Seeking."

[7] William W. Baker, "A Lack of Communication," *The Masthead*, 15:21–22 (Fall 1963).

[8] Elston, "Status Seeking."

[9] Warren H. Pierce, "What Makes a Good Editorial Writer?" *The Masthead*, 10:23–24 (Spring 1958).

[10] David Manning White, "The Editorial Writer and Objectivity," *The Masthead*, 4:31–34 (Fall 1952).

[11] Hoke Norris, "The Inside Dope," *The Masthead*, 8:55–57 (Spring 1956).

[12] Pierce, "What Makes."

[13] Irving Dilliard, "The Editor I Wish I Were," *The Masthead*, 19:51–57 (Summer 1967).

[14] Frederic S. Marquardt, "What Manner of Editor Is This?" *The Masthead*, 19:57–58 (Summer 1967).

[15] Wilhoit, "North American," pp. 10–12.

[16] Samuel L. Adams, "The Almost All-White Editorial Page," *The Masthead*, 31:3 (Summer 1979).

[17] George Neavoll, "Survey Counts Only Eight Blacks," *The Masthead*, 32:33 (Spring 1980).

[18] Wilhoit, "North American," p. 9.

[19] Adams, "Almost All-White."

[20] Symposium, "Miss/Mrs./Ms. Editorial Writer," *The Masthead*, 26:5–29 (Summer 1974).

[21] James H. Howard, "Feedback From Readers Helps Teach," *The Masthead*, 27:12 (Spring 1975).

[22] Donald A. Breed, "Why Publishers Rarely Write Own Editorials," *The Masthead*, 14:21 (Fall 1962).

[23] John H. Cline, "The Quest for 'Good Editorial Thinking,' " *The Masthead*, 18:17–18 (Fall 1966).

[24] Editor in the West, "Not in That Newsroom," *The Masthead*, 18:7–8 (Fall 1966).

[25] Theodore Bingham, "Recruit From City Side—If You Can," *The Masthead*, 18:6–7 (Fall 1966).

[26] Grover C. Hall, "Editorial Writers 'Bypassed by the Interstate,' " *The Masthead*, 18:8–10 (Fall 1966).

[27] William D. Snider, "Try Law, Politics or Campus," *The Masthead*, 18:10–11 (Fall 1966).

[28] Estabrook, "Editorial Applicants."

[29] Ben H. Bagdikian, "Editorial Pages Change—But Too Slowly," *The Masthead*, 17:16 (Winter 1965–66).

[30] Jonathan W. Daniels, "The Docility of the Dignified Press," *The Masthead*, 17:8–14 (Winter 1965–66).

Chapter 4

[1] Lee Smith, "The Poll of Journalism Educators," *The Masthead*, 28:25–29 (Spring 1976).

[2] Robert B. Frazier, "What Do You Read, My Lord?" *The Masthead*, 14:10–16 (Summer 1962).

[3] John Tebbel, "All Is Not Sweetness and Light," *The Masthead*, 16:10–13 (Fall 1964).

[4] Nathaniel B. Blumberg, "What's Happening is *Not* Good," *The Masthead,* 16:17 (Fall 1964).

[5] Norval Neil Luxon, "What's the Matter with Research?" *The Masthead,* 16:14–15 (Fall 1964).

[6] LeRoy E. Smith, "How Colleges and Universities Teach Editorial Writing, 1960–1978," Report of Journalism Education Committee, National Conference of Editorial Writers (1979).

[7] LeRoy E. Smith and Curtis D. MacDougall, "What Should Journalism Majors Know?" *The Masthead,* 27:28–32 (Spring 1975).

[8] Smith, "The Poll of Journalism Educators."

[9] Curtis D. MacDougall, "A Modern Journalism Curriculum," *The Masthead,* 28:30–34 (Spring 1976).

[10] Don Carson, "The Goal: Aiming for Perfection," *The Masthead,* 28:34 (Spring 1976).

[11] Anson H. Smith Jr., "Try an Inspiring Year at Harvard," *The Masthead,* 22:3–5 (Spring 1970).

[12] Sig Gissler, "A Sabbatical: Too Sweet to Be True?" *The Masthead,* 29:30–31 (Spring 1977).

[13] Kenneth Rystrom, "An Editor Returns to Campus," *The Masthead,* 29:12–15 (Winter 1977–78).

[14] Terrence W. Honey, "Our Ivory Tower Syndrome Is Dead," *The Masthead,* 23:26 (Summer 1971).

[15] Frazier, "What Do You Read, My Lord?"

[16] Robert B. Frazier, "The Editorial Elbow," *The Masthead,* 15:5–16 (Summer 1963).

[17] Jack Kilpatrick, "Editorials and Editorial Writing," *The Masthead,* 5:1–3 (Spring 1953).

[18] Irving Dilliard, "The Editorial Writer I Wish I Were," *The Masthead,* 19:52 (Summer 1967).

Chapter 5

[1] J.G. Saxe, *The Masthead,* 21:20 (Summer 1969).

[2] Fred C. Hobson Jr., "A We Problem," *The Masthead,* 18:18 (Spring 1966).

[3] Ernest C. Hynds, "Editorial Pages Remain Vital," *The Masthead,* 27:19 (Fall 1975).

[4] Robert U. Brown, "Shop Talk at Thirty," *The Masthead,* 17:38–39 (Fall 1965).

[5] Floyd A. Bernard, "There Has to Be a Corporate Opinion," *The Masthead,* 23:12 (Spring 1971).

[6] Brown, "Shop Talk at Thirty."

[7] George C. McLeod, "The Paper's Masthead Is Byline Enough," *The Masthead,* 23:13 (Spring 1971).

[8] Charles G. Strattard, "Try to Keep the 'We' at a Minimum," *The Masthead,* 23:23 (Spring 1971).

[9] Ann Lloyd Merriman, "No to Signed Editorials," *The Masthead,* 23:14 (Spring 1971).

[10] Symposium, "Yeah, What About That Monopoly of Opinion?" *The Masthead,* 26:8–30 (Fall 1974).

[11] Calvin Mayne, "Gannett Company," Symposium, "Yeah, What," p. 14.

[12] Reese Cleghorn, "Knight Newspapers," Symposium, "Yeah, What," pp. 18–19.

[13] Merrill Lindsay, "Lindsay-Schaub Newspapers," Symposium, "Yeah, What," pp. 22–23.

[14] Daniel B. Wackman, Donald N. Gillmor, Cecilie Gaziano and Everett E. Dennis, "Chain Newspaper Autonomy as Reflected in Presidential Campaign Endorsements," *Journalism Quarterly*, 52:411–20 (Autumn 1975).

[15] Anonymous, "Editors Say More Leeway on Group-Owned Papers," *Presstime*, 2:36 (May 1980).

[16] Sam Reynolds, "Editorial Transubstantiation," *The Masthead*, 27:2 (Fall 1975).

[17] George J. Hebert, "Going Loose and Lively in Norfolk," *The Masthead*, 28:21–22 (Spring 1976).

[18] Everett Ray Call, "Yes to Initialed Editorials," *The Masthead*, 23:16–17 (Spring 1971).

[19] Warren Bovee, "The Mythology of Editorial Anonymity," *The Masthead*, 24:26–35 (Fall 1972) and 24:54–65 (Winter 1972). (Copyright 1972 by Warren G. Bovee.)

[20] Anonymous, "Report of the 1972 NCEW Continuing Studies Committee," *The Masthead*, 25:37–39 (Spring 1973).

[21] James K. Sunshine, "The Jim Brown Case," *The Masthead*, 19:1–17 (Fall 1967).

[22] David V. Felts, "Roosevelt's 'I' or Victoria's 'We'?" *The Masthead*, 28:20–21 (Fall 1976).

[23] James Partin, *The Life of Horace Greeley* (New York: Publisher Unknown, 1855), p. 78.

Chapter 6

[1] Bernard Kilgore, "A Publisher Looks at Editorial Writing," *The Masthead*, 6:44 (Spring 1954).

[2] Hugh B. Patterson Jr., "When Ownership Abdicates Its Responsibility, Newspaper Suffers," *The Masthead*, 14:16 (Fall 1962).

[3] Kilgore, "A Publisher Looks."

[4] *Ibid.*

[5] Donald L. Breed, "The Publisher and the Editorial Page," *The Masthead*, 3:45 (Winter 1951).

[6] John Lofton, "Can Editorial Writers Afford to Deal With Their Publishers?" *The Masthead*, 3:1–8 (Winter 1951).

[7] G. Cleveland Wilhoit and Dan G. Drew, "Profile of the North American Editorial Writer, 1971–1979," *The Masthead*, 31:10 (Winter 1979–80).

[8] Hoke Norris, "The Inside Dope," *The Masthead*, 8:55 (Spring 1956).

[9] Robert T. Pittman, "How to Free Editorial Writers," *The Masthead*, 22:11 (Spring 1970).

[10] David Halberstam, *The Powers That Be* (New York: Alfred A. Knopf, 1979), p. 573.

[11] Ben H. Bagdikian, "Newspaper Mergers—the Final Phase," *Columbia Journalism Review*, 15:20 (March–April 1977).

[12] Frank W. Taylor, "Relations With the Publisher," *The Masthead*, 2:21 (Winter 1950).

[13] Jon G. Udell, *The Economics of the American Newspaper* (New York: Hastings House, 1978), p. 62.

[14] Donald L. Breed, "Why Publishers Rarely Write Own Editorials: It's a Tough Routine," *The Masthead*, 14:22 (Fall 1962).

[15] Kilgore, "A Publisher Looks."

[16] Patterson, "When Ownership Abdicates."

[17] Taylor, "Relations."

[18] Sevellon Brown III, "Setting Editorial Policy—Editors vs. Publisher," *The Masthead,* 7:22–24 (Summer 1955).

[19] Kilgore, "A Publisher Looks," p. 46.

[20] William H. Heath, "Editorial Policy," *The Masthead,* 19:66 (Summer 1967).

[21] Kenneth McArdle, "The Real Pressure Is to Make Sense," *The Masthead,* 22:8–9 (Spring 1970).

[22] Kilgore, "A Publisher Looks."

[23] Norris, "The Inside Dope."

[24] Taylor, "Relations."

[25] Houstoun Waring, "Fertilizer for the Grass Roots," *The Masthead,* 4:12 (Spring 1952).

[26] Nathaniel Blumberg, "Still Needed: A School for Publishers," *The Masthead,* 22:16 (Spring 1970).

[27] Breed, "The Publisher," p. 47.

[28] Curtis D. MacDougall, "Our Opportunity to Educate or to Sabotage," *The Masthead,* 22:10 (Spring 1970).

[29] Sam Reynolds, "It's Time We Blew the Whistle," *The Masthead,* 29:45 (Winter 1977).

Chapter 7

[1] Clifford E. Carpenter, "When Reporters Speak Up," *The Masthead,* 12:30–32 (Spring 1960).

[2] Edward M. Miller, "Take a Managing Editor to Lunch," *The Masthead,* 22:31–33 (Spring 1970).

[3] Carpenter, "When Reporters Speak Up."

[4] Anonymous, "Policies and Politics," *The Masthead,* 11:43–44 (Summer 1959).

[5] Desmond Stone, "How Does the News Staff Dissent?" *The Masthead,* 23:24–26 (Spring 1971).

[6] Rufus Terral, "In Conference," *The Masthead,* 3:30 (Summer 1951).

[7] David H. Beetle, "Can a Paper Call on a Reporter for Bylined Opinion?" *The Masthead,* 11:69–71 (Summer 1959).

[8] Nathaniel Blumberg, "The Case Against Front-Page Editorials," *The Masthead,* 8:17–20 (Summer 1956).

[9] Jack Kilpatrick, "Why Not Throw Outworn Tradition Away?" *The Masthead,* 6:1–5 (Spring 1954).

[10] James C. MacDonald, " 'News' and 'Opinion' Get All Mixed Up," *The Masthead,* 6:21 (Summer 1954).

[11] Symposium, "The Role of the Ombudsman/Media Critic," *The Masthead,* 28:3–15 (Spring 1976).

Chapter 8

[1] Lawrence H. Paul, "Many Papers Wretchedly Understaffed," *The Masthead,* 24:1 (Spring 1972).

[2] Don Shoemaker, "Mine, by Damn, All Mine," *The Masthead,* 3:10 (Fall 1951).

[3] G. Cleveland Wilhoit and Dan G. Drew, "Profile of the North American Editorial Writer, 1971–1979," *The Masthead,* 31:10 (Winter 1979-80).

[4] Wilbur Elston, "Writers Need Topics, Not Orders," *The Masthead,* 28:10 (Spring 1976).

⁵ Shoemaker, "Mine."

⁶ William H. Heath, "Of Litters, Blondes and the One-Man Page," *The Masthead*, 4:22 (Spring 1952).

⁷ Paul, "Many Papers," pp. 1–3.

⁸ John Sanford, "Interruptions in Reno," *The Masthead*, 19:21–22 (Fall 1967).

⁹ David E. Gillespie, "Hour by Hour in Charlotte," *The Masthead*, 19:22–25 (Fall 1967).

¹⁰ LeRoy E. Smith, "No Superpower in Buffalo," *The Masthead*, 19:33 (Fall 1967).

¹¹ William G. Peeples, "A Definite Pattern in Louisville," *The Masthead*, 19:36 (Fall 1967).

¹² John G. McCullough, "Consulting Some Other Oracles," *The Masthead*, 28:5–6 (Spring 1976).

¹³ Hugh B. Patterson Jr., "When Ownership Abdicates Its Responsibility, News Suffers," *The Masthead*, 14:18 (Fall 1962).

¹⁴ William P. Cheshire, "A Memo to Editorial Boards," *The Masthead*, 19:2 (Summer 1972).

¹⁵ Pat Murphy, "Fie on the Conference," *The Masthead*, 28:8–9 (Summer 1976).

¹⁶ Robert B. Frazier, "You Can't Meet While Working," *The Masthead*, 28:7–8 (Summer 1976).

¹⁷ Gilbert Cranberg, "Skull Sessions Over Lunch," *The Masthead*, 28:10–11 (Summer 1976).

Chapter 9

¹ James J. Kilpatrick, "How the Question Came Up," *The Masthead*, 18:2 (Summer 1966).

² Norman A. Cherniss, "In Defense of Virtue," *The Masthead*, 18:4 (Summer 1966).

³ Symposium, "Proposition No. 1: To Be Involved?" *The Masthead*, 18:1–15 (Summer 1966).

⁴ Robert M. Hitt Jr., "Yes and No," *The Masthead*, 18:12–13 (Summer 1966).

⁵ Kilpatrick, "How the Question Came Up."

⁶ Hal Burton, "The Skiing Is 300 Miles Away," *The Masthead*, 18:15 (Summer 1966).

⁷ Kilpatrick, "How the Question Came Up."

⁸ Jameson G. Campaigne, "Twice Bit, Still Shy," *The Masthead*, 18:11–12 (Summer 1966).

⁹ Worth Bingham, "The Responsible Can't Duck," *The Masthead*, 18:10 (Summer 1966).

¹⁰ E.L. Holland Jr., "16 Years of the PTA," *The Masthead*, 18:7–8 (Summer 1966).

¹¹ Jonathan Marshall, "Rather Be a Newspaperman," *The Masthead*, 18:6 (Summer 1966).

¹² Donald L. Breed, "The Publisher and the Editorial Writer," *The Masthead*, 3:47 (Winter 1950–51).

¹³ Robert T. Pittman, "How to Free Editorial Writers," *The Masthead*, 22:11 (Spring 1970).

¹⁴ Joe Stroud, "The Subtle Blackjack," *The Masthead*, 22:15 (Spring 1970).

¹⁵ Sylvan Meyer, "No Union *and* No Strikes," *The Masthead*, 14:34 (Fall 1962).

¹⁶ Robert Lasch, "If He Can't Be Trusted," *The Masthead*, 14:32 (Fall 1962).

¹⁷ Martin Perry, "Put Up or Shut Up," *The Masthead*, 11:57–65 (Summer 1959).

[18] H. Brandt Ayers, "Does a Plane Ticket Buy Your Soul?" *The Masthead*, 28:3–4 (Winter 1976).

[19] John Causten Currey, "Is It Better to Nurture Ignorance?" *The Masthead*, 28:4–5 (Winter 1976).

[20] Smith Hempstone, "Self-Righteousness Gives Cold Comfort," *The Masthead*, 28:5–6 (Winter 1976).

[21] Richard B. Laney, "Code Gives No Real Guidance," *The Masthead*, 28:6–7 (Winter 1976).

[22] Robert Estabrook, "Those All-Expense Tours," *The Masthead*, 4:39–41 (Fall 1952).

[23] Mark Clutter, "Don't Be Churlish," *The Masthead*, 12:5 (Spring 1960).

[24] Jack Craemer, "One Who Refuses Feels Lonely," *The Masthead*, 12:8 (Spring 1960).

Chapter 10

[1] Vermont Royster, "Parsley and Pot-Boiled Potatoes," *The Masthead*, 8:38 (Fall 1956).

[2] George Comstock, Steven Chaffee, Natan Katzman, Maxwell McCombs and Donald Roberts, *Television and Human Behavior* (New York: Columbia University Press, 1978), pp. 319–28.

[3] Werner J. Severin and James W. Tankard Jr., *Communication Theories* (New York: Hastings House, 1979), p. 248.

[4] Wilbur Schramm and William E. Porter, *Men, Women, Messages and Media*, Second Edition (New York: Harper and Row, 1982), pp. 110–11.

[5] Elsa Mohn and Maxwell McCombs, "Who Reads Us and Why," *The Masthead*, 32:21 (Winter 1980–81).

[6] W. Phillips Davison, James Boylan and Frederick T.C. Yu, *Mass Media*, Second Edition (New York: Holt, Rinehart and Winston, 1982), p. 173.

[7] Alexis S. Tan, *Mass Communication Theories and Research* (Columbus, Ohio: Grid, 1981), p. 103.

[8] Schramm and Porter, "Men, Women," p. 188.

[9] Tan, "Mass Communication," p. 149.

[10] Henry M. Keezing, "Who Are Your Readers?" *The Masthead*, 8:47 (Spring 1956).

[11] James J. Kilpatrick, "Editorials and Editorial Writing," *The Masthead*, 5:6–7 (Spring 1953).

[12] Don R. Pember, *Mass Media Law,* Second Edition (Dubuque: William C. Brown, 1981), and William E. Francois, *Mass Media Law and Regulation*, Third Edition (Columbus, Ohio: Grid, 1982).

[13] Tan, "Mass Communication," p. 140.

[14] Schramm and Porter, "Men, Women," p. 196.

[15] *Ibid.*

[16] Tan, "Mass Communication," p. 139.

[17] Davison, Boylan and Yu, *Mass Media,* p. 190.

Chapter 11

[1] James J. Kilpatrick, "Editorials and Editorial Writing," *The Masthead*, 5:5 (Spring 1953).

[2] Harry Boyd, "They Write by Ear," *The Masthead*, 8:31 (Fall 1956).

3 R. Thomas Berner, "Let's Get Rid of Those Pesky Pronouns," *The Masthead*, 31:32 (Summer 1979).
4 Galen R. Rarick, "The Writing That Writers Write Best—or Should I Say 'Better'?" *The Masthead*, 21:3–5 (Winter 1969–70).
5 Rudolph Flesch, *The Art of Readable Writing* (New York: Harper & Bros., 1949), and *How to Test Readability* (New York: Harper & Bros., 1951).
6 Francis P. Locke, "Too Much Flesch on the Bones?" *The Masthead*, 11:3–6 (Spring 1959).
7 *Wall Street Journal*, "On the Other Hand," *The Masthead*, 7:20 (Fall 1955).
8 Kilpatrick, "Editorials," p. 4.

Chapter 12

1 Creed Black, "Government Is Great, But—," *The Masthead*, 19:23 (Summer 1967).
2 Lauren K. Soth, "How to Write Understandable Editorials About Economics," *The Masthead*, 6:19 (Winter 1954).
3 Francis P. Locke, "A Word for Afghanistanism," *The Masthead*, 19:33 (Summer 1967).
4 John M. Harrison, "The Editorial Page and the Arts," *The Masthead*, 23:37–39 (Spring 1971).
5 Richard B. Childs, "When You Can't Pass the Buck," *The Masthead*, 29:3–4 (Summer 1977).
6 James E. Jacobson, "Keeping the Computer at Bay," *The Masthead*, 20:7 (Spring 1968).
7 James Bartelt, "When the Packers Are a Worthy Cause," *The Masthead*, 20:11 (Spring 1968).
8 Francis P. Locke, "Slaying 'Puff' the Magic Dragon," *The Masthead*, 20:8–9 (Spring 1968).
9 Lauren K. Soth, "From Alpha to Omega," *The Masthead*, 20:3 (Spring 1968).
10 Tom Inman, "When Duty Is a Disservice," *The Masthead*, 20:17–18 (Spring 1968).
11 Hoke Norris, "The Utility Editorial," *The Masthead*, 4:14 (Spring 1952).
12 Albert B. Southwick, "Why Not More Nature Editorials?" *The Masthead*, 9:53–55 (Winter 1957–58).
13 Hal Borland, *An American Year* (New York: Simon and Schuster, 1946).
14 Erwin Rieger, *Up Is the Mountain* (Portland, Ore.: Binfords and Mort, 1973), pp. 17–21.
15 Ben H. Bagdikian, "Editorial Pages Change—But Too Slowly," *The Masthead*, 17:20 (Winter 1965–66).
16 Sevellon Brown III, "Keep Your Wit About You," *The Masthead*, 1:12–15 (Spring 1949).
17 John Murray, "Some Devices Are More Useful," *The Masthead*, 27:17–18 (Spring 1975).

Chapter 13

1 Calvin Mayne, "Speaking of Elections: At Least There's the Issue," *The Masthead*, 25:15 (Spring 1973).

[2] Nelson Poynter, "Speaking of Elections: The Case for Endorsements," *The Masthead,* 25:20 (Spring 1973).

[3] Fred Fedler, Lowndes F. Stephens and Tim Counts, "Endorsement Surprises," *The Masthead,* 33:49 (Spring 1981).

[4] *Ibid.,* pp. 44–45.

[5] David Halberstam, *The Powers That Be* (New York: Alfred A. Knopf, 1979), pp. 95, 117–118, 349–351.

[6] Philip L. Geyelin, "The Editorial Page," *The Editorial Page,* ed. Laura Longley Babb [the Washington Post Writers Group] (Boston: Houghton Mifflin, 1977), pp. 16–17.

[7] "Paid Ads or Endorsements?" [letter to the editor], *Longview* (Wash.) *Daily News* (date unknown).

[8] "Candidate Endorsements—Who, When and Why: A Complaint and a Reply," *The Masthead,* 20:19 (Summer 1968).

[9] Sylvan Fox, "New Day at Newsday," *The Masthead,* 33:41 (Summer 1981).

[10] Poynter, "Speaking of Elections."

[11] "Newsday Ends Its Endorsement of Candidates," *Editor & Publisher,* Sept. 9, 1972, p. 11.

[12] "A Touch of Introspection," *Wall Street Journal,* Sept. 20, 1976.

[13] M. Cowl Rider, "Candidate Endorsements—Who, When and Why: Ideas, Not Individuals," *The Masthead,* 20:16 (Summer 1968).

[14] "Some Changes in the Editorial Page," *Los Angeles Times,* Sept. 23, 1973, Part 6, p. 2.

[15] Clarke Thomas, comment in critique group, national convention of National Conference of Editorial Writers, Hilton Head, N.C., October 1976.

[16] "Endorsement of Candidates," *Editor & Publisher,* Sept. 19, 1972, p. 6.

[17] Frank Luther Mott, "Has the Press Lost Its Punch?" *The Rotarian,* Oct. 1952, p. 13.

[18] Nathaniel B. Blumberg, *One-Party Press?* (Lincoln: University of Nebraska Press, 1954), p. 11.

[19] George Comstock, Steven Chaffee, Natan Katzman, Maxwell McCombs and Donald Roberts, *Television and Human Behavior* (New York: Columbia University Press, 1978), pp. 136, 319–328.

[20] Peter Clarke and Eric Fredin, "Newspapers, Television and Political Reasoning," *Public Opinion Quarterly,* 42:143–160 (Summer 1978).

[21] John Robinson, "The Press as Kingmaker: What Surveys From the Last Five Campaigns Show," *Journalism Quarterly,* 51:587–594, 606 (Winter 1974).

[22] Kenneth Rystrom, "Measuring the Editorial Profiles of California Daily Newspapers and the Apparent Impact of Endorsement Editorials of Those Newspapers in the 1978 and 1980 General Elections," Unpublished Manuscript (1981).

[23] James E. Gregg, "Newspaper Editorial Page Endorsements and California Elections, 1948–62," *Journalism Quarterly,* 42:532–538 (Fall 1965).

[24] *Ibid.*

[25] Kenneth Rystrom, "Rating the Newspapers as Political Persuaders," *California Journal,* 10:287 (August 1979).

[26] *Ibid.*

[27] Kenneth Rystrom, "Voter Response to Newspaper Endorsements," *California Journal,* 12:366–367 (October 1981).

[28] Norman Blume and Schley Lyons, "The Monopoly Newspaper in a Local Election: The Toledo Blade," *Journalism Quarterly,* 45:286–292 (Summer 1968).

[29] Fedler, et al., "Endorsement Surprises," pp. 48–49.

[30] John J. Zakarian, ''Speaking of Elections: Sacred Cows of the Highest Order,'' *The Masthead*, 25:3 (Spring 1973).

[31] Sig Gissler, ''Somebody Else Wrote It,'' *The Masthead*, 17:2 (Spring 1965).

[32] David F. Brinegar, ''One-Man Decision,'' *The Masthead*, 17:10 (Spring 1965).

[33] Harold F. Grumhaus, ''Speaking of Elections: Prerogative of the Publisher,'' *The Masthead*, 25:12 (Spring 1973).

[34] Leonard Inskip, ''Candidate Endorsements—Who, When and Why: Firm Opinions Moderately Stated,'' *The Masthead*, 20:13 (Summer 1968).

[35] Zakarian, ''Speaking of Elections.''

[36] Clarke M. Thomas, ''Speaking of Elections: On the Other Hand,'' *The Masthead*, 25:7–9 (Spring 1973).

[37] Barry Bingham Jr., ''A Thorny and Misunderstood Subject,'' *The Masthead*, 25:2 (Spring 1973).

[38] ''The Editorial 'We,' '' *Newsweek*, Sept. 27, 1976, p. 87.

[39] Dennis Ryerson, ''Endorsements: No Consensus,'' *The Masthead*, 28:42 (Winter 1976).

[40] Peter Clarke, ''Endorsement Editorials,'' *The Masthead*, 33:36–37 (Spring 1981).

[41] Rystrom, ''Voter Response.''

[42] Calvin Mayne, ''The Unendorsement of a Candidate,'' *The Masthead*, 22:21–26 (Spring 1970).

Chapter 14

[1] Peter G. Fradley, ''Inclusiveness Is the Best Policy,'' *The Masthead*, 28:12–13 (Fall 1976).

[2] Barry Bingham Sr. in ''Dear Sir You Cur! A Symposium on Letters to the Editor,'' *The Masthead*, 3:38 (Fall 1951).

[3] Fradley, ''Inclusiveness.''

[4] Barry Bingham Sr., ''How One Paper Operates the Letters Column,'' *The Masthead*, 10:58 (Summer 1958).

[5] *Ibid.*

[6] Steve R. Pasternack, ''Who Writes Letters to the Editor?'' *The Masthead*, 31:24–25 (Spring 1979).

[7] James A. Clendinen in ''Dear Sir You Cur!'' p. 37.

[8] Sylvan Meyer, ''Two Forums Better Than One,'' *The Masthead*, 20:24–25 (Fall 1968).

[9] Reed Sarratt, ''Custom Tailored Letters,'' *The Masthead*, 7:46–48 (Fall 1955).

[10] Norman Bradley, ''When Starting a New Paper,'' *The Masthead*, 20:23 (Fall 1968).

[11] Leveritt A. Chapin, ''Project Saturday Off,'' *The Masthead*, 9:5–7 (Spring 1957).

[12] George Magenheimer, ''Vox Pop Once a Week,'' *The Masthead*, 8:74–75 (Summer 1956).

[13] John G. McCullough, ''A Forum Every Saturday,'' *The Masthead*, 22:34–36 (Summer 1970).

[14] Donald McLean, ''Readers vs. Columnists,'' *The Masthead*, 18:17–18 (Spring 1966).

[15] Charles VanDevander, ''Building a Readers' Forum,'' *The Masthead*, 18:16 (Spring 1966).

[16] Anonymous in ''A Further Forum on Letters to the Editor,'' *The Masthead*, 4:37 (Fall 1952).

[17] Joanna Wragg, "Readers Can Write—or Phone," *The Masthead,* 28:5 (Fall 1976).

[18] Hap Cawood, "Should Madmen, Illiterates Be Heard?" *The Masthead,* 28:6 (Fall 1976).

[19] M. Carl Andrews, "How Letters to the Editor Influenced a Community," *The Masthead,* 13:24–26 (Spring 1961).

[20] Anonymous, "Interview Your Letter Writers," *The Masthead,* 17:31 (Spring 1965).

[21] Lloyd Armour, "A Banquet for the Best," *The Masthead,* 22:16–18 (Fall 1968).

[22] Theodore Long, "Happiness Without Boredom," *The Masthead,* 20:18–19 (Fall 1968).

[23] James Dix, "Customers Love Crossfire," *The Masthead,* 20:22 (Fall 1968).

[24] Barney Waters, "Handling the Daily Mail," *The Masthead,* 22:47 (Fall 1970).

[25] James Clemon, "In Defense of Initials, Pseudonyms," *The Masthead,* 28:16–17 (Fall 1976).

[26] Mark Stuart, "Keeping the Kooky Writers at Bay," *The Masthead,* 28:7–8 (Fall 1976).

[27] John R. Markham, "A Letter Is a Dangerous Thing," *The Masthead,* 5:19 (Fall 1953).

[28] Lawrie Joslin, "Making the Readers Feel Welcome," *The Masthead,* 28:15 (Fall 1976).

[29] Waters, "Handling the Daily Mail," p. 44.

[30] Clifford E. Carpenter, "The Letter Litter, Its Dangers and Potentials," *The Masthead,* 19:80 (Summer 1967).

[31] Markham, "A Letter," pp. 18–19.

[32] *Ibid.,* p. 20.

[33] Charles J. Dunsire, "Topless Dancers and Twitching Pens," *The Masthead,* 20:11 (Fall 1968).

[34] Frank Grimes in "A Further Forum," p. 33.

[35] Waters, "Handling the Daily Mail," p. 45.

[36] Grimes, "A Further Forum."

[37] Carpenter, "The Letter Litter," p. 78.

[38] Palmer Hoyt, "A Publisher Looks at Editorial Writing," *The Masthead,* 6:49 (Spring 1954).

[39] M. Carl Andrews, "Pity the Editor Without Letters," *The Masthead,* 20:49 (Fall 1968).

Chapter 15

[1] W.W. Baker, "Everybody's Happy," *The Masthead,* 19:5 (Spring 1967).

[2] Donald P. Keith, "Champions of Truth or Claques for Extremists," *The Masthead,* 19:60 (Summer 1967).

[3] Robert H. Estabrook, "Their Varied Views Are Important," *The Masthead,* 10:22–24 (Fall 1958).

[4] Mark Ethridge, "The Come-Back of Editorial Pages," *The Masthead,* 18:28–32 (Summer 1966).

[5] Baker, "Everybody's Happy."

[6] Donald W. Carson, "What Editorial Writers Think of the Columnists," *The Masthead,* 23:1–5 (Spring 1971).

[7] Ernest C. Hynds. "Editorial Pages Remain Vital," *The Masthead,* 27:19–22 (Fall 1975).

[8] Robert Schulman, "The Opinion Merchants," *The Masthead,* 32:21 (Spring 1980).

[9] Hynds, "Editorial Pages."

[10] Sig Gissler, "Color Me Peeved," *The Masthead,* 19:5 (Spring 1967).

11 Schulman, "The Opinion Merchants."

12 Frank Wetzel, "Territorial Exclusivity Is Attacked," *The Masthead,* 30:3–4 (Winter 1978).

13 William F. Buckley Jr., "Major Complaint Erratic Scheduling," *The Masthead,* 27:5 (Winter 1975).

14 Ralph McGill, "From Both Sides of the Table," *The Masthead,* 19:18–19 (Spring 1967).

15 George Beveridge, "Talking Back to the Columnists," *The Masthead,* 29:20 (Summer 1979).

16 Gilbert Cranberg, "The Role of Syndicates," *The Masthead,* 26:60 (Fall 1974).

17 James J. Kilpatrick, "Life and Times With Cranberg Rule," *The Masthead,* 27:9–12 (Winter 1975).

18 National News Council, "Nicaragua Government Information Service against Jack Anderson/United Feature Syndicate (1977)," Complaint No. 101, March 22, 1977, p. 11.

19 Schulman, "The Opinion Merchants," p. 22.

20 Gilbert Cranberg, "Right to Reply 'Obligation,' " *The Masthead,* 26:19 (Spring 1974).

21 Lauren Soth, "Conflicts of Interest by Political Writer, Editor," *Des Moines* (Iowa) *Register,* Nov. 29, 1973.

22 North American Newspaper Alliance, Editor's Note No. 281, Feb. 22, 1974.

23 *Ibid,* Editor's Note No. 405, March 1, 1974.

24 National News Council, "Findings of the National News Council," *The Masthead,* 26:53 (Fall 1974).

25 Kenneth Rystrom, "NCEW Wrestles with Its Conscience," Unpublished Manuscript (1978).

26 Gilbert Cranberg, " 'Dear Mr. Buckley—Dear Mr. Cranberg,' " *The Masthead,* 27:54 (Summer 1975).

27 Clifford E. Carpenter, "Get Out of the Ivory Tower," *The Masthead,* 16:30 (Summer 1964).

28 John Sanford, "After All, Who's Editor?" *The Masthead,* 13:9 (Spring 1961).

29 Laurence Boodry, "Conflicting Views Make for Brighter Page," *The Masthead,* 23:5 (Summer 1971).

30 Symposium, "Editorial Page Humor: A Status Report," *The Masthead,* 29:3–11 (Spring 1977).

31 *Ibid.*

32 Earnest C. Hynds, "Survey Profiles Editorial Cartoonists," *The Masthead,* 29:12–14 (Spring 1977).

33 Forrest M. Landon, "Effective Cartoons Clearly a Plus," *The Masthead,* 23:2 (Summer 1971).

34 Paul Conrad, Speech at Editorial Page Session, Western Newspaper Foundation, University of Southern California, May 1978.

35 Hynds, "Survey."

36 William A. Henry III, "The Sit-Down Comics," *Washington Journalism Review,* October 1981, pp. 27–28.

37 David Shaw, "Cartoonists—Picture Is Changing," *Los Angeles Times,* March 17, 1982.

38 A. Rosen, Discussion Session, American Press Institute, Columbia University, May 1972.

Chapter 16

[1] David Shaw, "Newspapers Offer Forum to Outsiders," *Los Angeles Times,* Oct. 13, 1975.

[2] John E. Allen, *Newspaper Makeup* (New York & London: Harper and Bros., 1936), p. 332.

[3] Miles E. Tinker, *Legibility in Print* (Ames, Iowa: Iowa State University Press, 1963), pp. 74–107.

[4] Sig Gissler, "A Better Forum for Our Readers," *The Masthead,* 23:31–32 (Spring 1971).

[5] Tony Tselentis, "Another Page, a Better Understanding," *The Masthead,* 23:33–34 (Spring 1971).

[6] Hillier Krieghbaum, "The 'Op-Ed' Page," *The Masthead,* 23:7–10 (Winter 1971–72).

[7] Robert T. Pittman, "Ten Best Bets for Edit Pages," *The Masthead,* 26:34–38 (Summer 1974).

[8] Warren Bovee, "An Unstacked Forum," *The Masthead,* 26:57–59 (Spring 1974).

[9] Ben H. Bagdikian, "Press Profits From Self-Criticism," *The Masthead,* 28:3–5 (Spring 1976).

[10] Charles Seib, "Who Will Watch the Watchdog?" *The Masthead,* 28:13–15 (Spring 1976).

[11] Philip Geyelin, "F.Y.I.," *The Masthead,* 22:27 (Spring 1970).

[12] Norman J. Radder and John E. Stempel, *Newspaper Editing: Makeup and Headlines,* (New York and London: McGraw-Hill, 1942), pp. 332–33.

[13] Harrison E. Salisbury, "An Extra Dimension in This Complicated World," *The Masthead,* 23:29–31 (Spring 1971).

[14] Shaw, "Newspapers Offer Forum."

Chapter 17

[1] William Cullen Bryant, "The Battle-Field," *Poems* (Philadelphia: Henry Altemus Co., 1895), p. 124.

Bibliography

EDITORIAL WRITING AND EDITORIAL PAGES

Babb, Laura Longley, editor, *The Editorial Page* [of the *Washington Post*]. Boston: Houghton Mifflin (1977).

Hulteng, John L., *The Opinion Function: Editorial and Interpretive Writing for the News Media*. Hayden Lake, Idaho: Ridge House Press (1973).

MacDougall, Curtis, D., *Principles of Editorial Writing*. Dubuque, Iowa: Wm. C. Brown (1973).

Stonecipher, Harry W., *Editorial and Persuasive Writing: Opinion Functions of the News Media*. New York: Hastings House (1979).

Waldrop, A. Gayle, *Editor and Editorial Writer*. Third Edition. Dubuque, Iowa: Wm. C. Brown (1967).

PRESS CRITICISM

Irwin, Will, *The American Newspaper*. Ames, Iowa: The Iowa State University Press (1969). (First appeared in *Colliers,* January–July 1911)

Sinclair, Upton, *The Brass Check: A Study of American Journalism*. Eighth Edition. Pasadena: The Author (1920).

COLUMNISTS

Abell, Tyler, editor, *Drew Pearson Diaries, 1949–1959*. New York: Holt, Rinehart and Winston (1974).

Allen, Robert S., and Pearson, Drew, *More Merry-Go-Round*. New York: Liveright (1932). Published anonymously.

Allen, Robert S., and Pearson, Drew, *Washington Merry-Go-Round*. New York: Liveright (1931). Published anonymously.

Anderson, Jack, and Boyd, James, *Confessions of a Muckraker*. New York: Random House (1979).

Anderson, Jack, *The Anderson Papers*. New York: Random House (1973).

von Hoffman, Nicholas, *Left at the Post*. Chicago: Quadrangle Books (1970).

CARTOONISTS

Block, Herbert, *Herblock's State of the Union*. New York: Simon and Schuster (1972).

Block, Herbert, *The Herblock Gallery*. New York: Simon and Schuster (1968).

Editors of the Foreign Policy Association, *A Cartoon History of United States Foreign Policy, 1776–1976*. New York: William Morrow (1975).

Miller, Frank, *Frank Miller Looks at Life*. No publisher or date listed.

Nelson, Roy Paul, *Cartooning*. Chicago: Henry Regnery (1975).

Salzman, Ed, and Brown, Ann Leigh, *The Cartoon History of California Politics*. Sacramento: California Journal Press (1978).

Trudeau, G.B., *But This War Had Such Promise*. New York: Holt, Rinehart and Winston (1973).

Trudeau, G.B., *The President Is a Lot Smarter Than You Think*. New York: Holt, Rinehart and Winston (1973).

BIOGRAPHY

Brown, Francis, *Raymond of the Times*. New York: W.W. Norton (1951).

Carlson, Oliver, *Brisbane*. Westport, Conn.: Greenwood Press (1937).

Carlson, Oliver, *The Man Who Made News: A Biography of James Gordon Bennett*. New York: Duell, Sloane and Pearce (1942).

Catledge, Turner, *My Life and The Times*. New York: Harper and Row (1971).

Childs, Marquis, and Reston, James, editors, *Walter Lippmann and His Times*. New York: Harcourt, Brace (1959).

Cochran, Negley D., *E.W. Scripps*. Reprint. Westport, Conn.: Greenwood (1972).

Daniels, Jonathan, *They Will Be Heard: America's Crusading Editors*. New York: McGraw-Hill (1965).

Hale, William Harlan, *Horace Greeley: Voice of the People*. New York: Harper and Brothers (1950).

Howey, Walter, editor, *Fighting Editors*. Philadelphia: David McKay (1946).

Johnson, Gerald W., *An Honorable Titan: A Biographical Study of Adolph S. Ochs*. New York: Harper and Brothers (1946).

Johnson, Walter, *William Allen White's America*. New York: Henry Holt (1947).

Kaplan, Justin, *Lincoln Steffens*. New York: Simon and Schuster (1974).

Klurfeld, Herman, *Behind the Lines:* The World of Drew Pearson. Englewood Cliffs, N.J.: Prentice-Hall (1968).

Knight, Oliver, editor, *I Protest: Distinguished Disquisitions of E.W. Scripps*. Madison, Wis.: University of Wisconsin Press (1966).

Luskin, John, *Lippmann, Liberty and the Press*. University, Ala.: University of Alabama Press (1972).

Martin, Harold H., *Ralph McGill, Reporter*. Boston: Little, Brown (1973).

Maverick, Augustus, *Henry J. Raymond and the New York Press*. Reprint. New York: Arno Press (1970).

McKee, John DeWitt, *William Allen White*. Westport, Conn.: Greenwood Press (1975).

Mitchell, Edward, *Memoirs of an Editor*. New York: Charles Scribner's Sons (1924).

Nye, Russel B., *William Lloyd Garrison and the Humanitarian Reformers*. Boston: Little, Brown (1955).

Ogden, Rollo, editor, *The Life and Letters of Edwin Lawrence Godkin*. 2 vols. Reprint. Westport, Conn.: Greenwood Press (1972).

Pilat, Oliver, *Pegler: Angry Man of the Press*. Boston: Beacon Press (1963).

Rosebault, Charles J., *When Dana Was the Sun*. Reprint. Westport, Conn.: Greenwood Press (1971).

Sanders, Marion K., *Dorothy Thompson*. Boston: Houghton Mifflin (1973).

Seitz, Don Carlos, *James Gordon Bennett*. Reprint. New York: Beckman (1974).

Seitz, Don Carlos, *Joseph Pulitzer, His Life and Letters*. New York: Simon and Schuster (1924).

Steel, Ronald, *Walter Lippmann and the American Century*. Boston: Little Brown and Co. (1980).

Steffens, Lincoln, *Autobiography of Lincoln Steffens*. New York: Harcourt Brace (1931).

Storke, Thomas L., *California Editor*. Los Angeles: Westernlore Press (1958).

Swanberg, W.A., *Citizen Hearst*. New York: Charles Scribner's Sons (1961).

Swanberg, W.A., *Pulitzer*. New York: Charles Scribner's Sons (1967).

Tebbel, John, *The Life and Good Times of William Randolph Hearst*. New York: E.P. Dutton (1952).

Wells, Evelyn, *Fremont Older*. New York: Appleton-Century (1936).

White, William Allen, *Autobiography*. New York: Macmillan (1946).

Winchell, Walter, *Winchell Exclusive*. Englewood Cliffs, N.J.: Prentice-Hall (1975).

HISTORY

Andrews, J. Cutler, *Pittsburgh's Post-Gazette*. Reprint. Westport, Conn.: Greenwood Press (1970).

Berger, Meyer, *The Story of The New York Times*. New York: Simon and Schuster (1951).

Canham, Erwin D., *Commitment to Freedom: The Story of the Christian Science Monitor*. Boston: Houghton-Mifflin (1958).

Copley, *The Copley Press*. Aurora, Ill.: Copley Press (1953).

Emery, Edwin, and Emery, Michael, *The Press and America*. Fourth Edition. Englewood Cliffs, N.J.: Prentice-Hall (1978).

Gottlieb, Robert, and Wolf, Irene, *Thinking Big: The Story of the* Los Angeles Times: *Its Publishers and Their Influence on Southern California*. New York: G.P. Putnam's Sons (1977).

Harper, Robert S., *Lincoln and the Press*. New York: McGraw-Hill (1951).

Hart, Jim Allee, *The Developing Views on the News: Editorial Syndrome 1500–1800*. Carbondale, Ill.: Southern Illinois University Press (1970).

Heaton, John L., *The Story of a Page* (The New York World). Reprint. New York: Arno Press (1970).

Hooker, Richard, *The Story of an Independent Newspaper: One Hundred Years of the Springfield Republican*. New York: Macmillan (1924).

Kobre, Sidney, *Development of American Journalism*. Dubuque, Iowa: Wm. C. Brown (1969).

Lyons, Louis M., *Newspaper Story: One Hundred Years of the Boston Globe*. Cambridge, Mass.: Belknap Press (1971).

Nevins, Allan, *The Evening Post: A Century of Journalism*. New York: Boni and Liveright (1922).

O'Brien, Frank M., *The Story of the Sun*. Reprint. Westport, Conn.: Greenwood Press (1968).

Rice, William B., *The Los Angeles Star, 1851–1864*. Berkeley and Los Angeles: University of California Press (1947).

Roberts, Chalmer, The Washington Post: *The First 100 Years*. Boston: Houghton Mifflin (1977).

Salisbury, Harrison E., *Without Fear or Favor: An Uncompromising Look at* The New York Times. New York: Times Books (1980).

Talese, Gay, *The Kingdom and the Power* (The New York Times). New York: World Publishing (1969).

Tebbel, John, *An American Dynasty: The Story of the McCormicks, Medills and Pattersons*. Garden City, N.Y.: Doubleday (1947).

Thomas, Isaiah, *The History of Printing in America*. Reissue. New York: Weathervane (1950). Original publication 1810. Second edition 1874.

MISCELLANEOUS

Osgood, Charles, *Nothing Could Be Finer Than a Crisis That Is Minor in the Morning*. New York: Holt, Rinehart and Winston (1979).

The Times, *Fourth Leaders from The Times*, 1955. London: The Times Publishing Co. (1956).

Index

NEWSPAPERS

NAMES

ABOUT THE AUTHOR

Kenneth Rystrom had 17 years of editorial writing experience in the states of Washington and Iowa before becoming professor of communications at the University of Redlands, in Redlands, California, in 1978. He wrote editorials for the *Des Moines* (Iowa) *Register and Tribune* from 1960 to 1965, then became editorial page editor, and later managing editor, of the *Columbian* in Vancouver, Washington. He has been a visiting professor at the University of Montana and Washington State University. Rystrom was elected president of the National Conference of Editorial Writers in 1974. After receiving a B.A. in journalism from the University of Nebraska at Lincoln in 1954, he obtained an M.A. in political science from the University of California at Berkeley in 1955 and an M.A. in journalism from the University of Southern California in 1981. Now pursuing a Ph.D. in political science at USC, he is working on a dissertation that examines the apparent effects of newspaper endorsement editorials on voting.